DRY CARGO CHARTERING

TutorShip

The Distance Learning Programme
of
The Institute of Chartered Shipbrokers

Witherby Shipping Business
A Division of Witherby Publishing Group Ltd

4 Dunlop Square, Livingston, Edinburgh, EH54 8SB, Scotland, UK

Tel No: +44(0)1506 463 227 - Fax No: +44(0)1506 468 999
Email: info@emailws.com - Web: www.witherbys.com

Published for the Institute of Chartered Shipbrokers

2011/2012 Centenary Edition

ISBN 978 1 85609 455 9

© Institute of Chartered Shipbrokers

British Library Cataloguing in Publication Data
A catalogue record for this book is available from the British Library.

Printed and bound in Great Britain by Bell & Bain Ltd, Glasgow

Published by

Witherby Publishing Group Ltd
4 Dunlop Square, Livingston,
Edinburgh, EH54 8SB,
Scotland, UK

Tel No: +44(0)1506 463 227
Fax No: +44(0)1506 468 999

Email: info@emailws.com
Web: www.witherbys.com

TUTORSHIP COURSE BOOKS

PREFACE

Gain a professional qualification and the knowledge to develop your career in the shipping industry by embarking on a TutorShip course of the Institute of Chartered Shipbrokers (ICS).

The Institute of Chartered Shipbrokers (ICS) is the professional body to commercial shipping worldwide. The ICS syllabus reflects the breadth and complexity of all the shipping sectors. The syllabus aims to be Relevant to and Respected by the shipping industry whilst being a Robust challenge to those candidates embarking on a career in shipping.

The TutorShip series of course books are aimed at preparing students for ICS examinations through a distance learning programme. Each course has a combination of self assessment questions and a tutor marked assignment at the end of each chapter. Additionally students are encouraged to submit a mock examination for marking. On enrolment of a TutorShip programme a student is allocated a tutor – an experienced practitioner in their sector – who will guide a student through the course by marking and providing feedback on the assignments submitted.

Although the TutorShip course books are an invaluable reference to any shipping company library their true value can only be realised by enrolling on a TutorShip distance learning programme supported by the expert knowledge of the approved tutors.

For further details on TutorShip courses please contact **tutorship@ics.org.uk** or visit **www.ics.org.uk**

DRY CARGO CHARTERING SYLLABUS

DRY CARGO CHARTERING

NB. Students will be expected to be able to draw simple plans of main vessel types and identify main characteristics and dimensions

SHIPS

Understand the fundamental differences between dry bulk cargo ships, general purpose ships, liners (container, break bulk and RoRo) and tankers.

Thoroughly understand the differences in the types of ships employed in dry cargo trades including Capesize, Panamax and Handy size bulk carriers, General Purpose (Tramps), Container, Ro/Ro, Ore/Bulk/Oil and Ore/Oil carriers, short sea and coastal traders.

Understand the basic dimensions, design and construction details including decks, holds, hatches, derricks, winches, cranes and specialised cargo handling gear.

Thoroughly understand the terminology of measuring ships including dimensions, actual tonnages – deadweight (dwat & dwcc), displacement (total & light), pseudo tonnages – NT & GT, capacities – bale & grain cubic, TEUs.

Understand what information is contained in Capacity, General Arrangement and Stowage Plans.

Thoroughly understand the central importance of ship classification, the importance of charterers' inspections and questionnaires.

CARGOES AND TRADE ROUTES

This subject should interlink with ships so that students can understand how particular ship types are required for the different cargoes and trade routes.

Thoroughly understand the nature, characteristics, hazards and stowage requirements of the four main dry commodities namely Coal, Ore, Grain and Fertilizers.

Understand the different sub-divisions within these categories and the trade routes that apply.

Understand the nature and characteristics, main places of origin and appropriate trade routes of other important cargoes.

Understand the stowage factors of goods. Be aware of the importance of proper packing, angle of repose, ventilation and prevention of stowage hazards.

Understand the use of alternative routes, the existence of seasonal variations and their impact on markets.

FREIGHT MARKETS

Thoroughly understand the role of the different market practitioners; Charterers, Shipowners, Operators.

Understand the structure of the international dry cargo chartering market and the relative importance of the major market centres.

Thoroughly understand the role of the Broker and its relationship to the Principals as an Agent (Owners Broker, Charterers Agent, exclusive Broker, competitive Broker, intermediate Broker).

Understand the advantages and disadvantages of different methods of communications.

Understand the structure and content of market reports and market indices.

Thoroughly understand the nature and impact of external factors affecting the market including natural catastrophes, environmental, aid programmes, political crises.

Be aware of the effect that merchants' trading terms (INCOTERMS) may have on the shipping contract and the impact of documentary credits especially on documentation.

Understand the rationale of joint ventures and shipping pools and be aware of how these operate.

Thoroughly understand the impact of e-commerce on market practice, its advantages and disadvantages. Be aware of the main alternative electronic solutions available to Brokers.

CONTRACTS

Thoroughly understand the basic format and purpose and content of those main clauses common to all charter party forms.

Thoroughly understand the differences between the structure and purpose of voyage charters and time charters.

Understand the reasons for the use of standard forms of voyage and time charter parties and their suitability to different trades including a working knowledge of the content of commonly used standard forms including: voyage charters - Gencon, Norgrain, Amwelsh and time charters – Baltime, NYPE.

Understand the reason for charter party interpretation rules and be aware of the contents of Voylay Rules 1993 and FONASBA Time Charter Interpretation Code 2000.

Thoroughly understand the importance and proper use of additional clauses and addenda and be able to draft simple specimen clauses.

Understand the individual rights responsibilities and liabilities of owners, charterers and Brokers which arise under the charter party.

Understand the use of consecutive voyage contracts and contracts of affreightment and be aware of the particular terminology required.

BILL OF LADING

Thoroughly understand the role of the Bill of Lading in charter parties and in particular the liabilities of the Shipowner to the Bill of Lading holder. Understand the relationship to Mate's Receipts and potential problems arising from the demand for clean Bills of Lading. Be aware of cargoes that pose particular problems in this context including steel, grain, etc.

Thoroughly understand the requirements regarding delivery of cargo against Bills of Lading. Understand the problems arising from the non-production of originals at discharge ports and practical solutions.

Understand the particular problems for Owners arising from Bills of Lading under time charters and the potential special problems of freight prepaid Bills of Lading.

CHARTERING MARKET PRACTICE

Thoroughly understand the procedure of negotiations including cargo circulars, indications, and firm offers.

Understand all the customary abbreviations used during negotiation.

Understand the process of offer, rejection and new offer (counter offer, accept/except) and acceptance.

Thoroughly understand the details to be included in offers for both voyage and time charters and be able to draft a firm offer.

Understand what "subjects" are, be able to identify some common examples of subjects and explain how they are lifted. Understand at which point the ship and cargo are "fully fixed".

Understand the role of the post fixture department and be able to identify and explain its functions.

Thoroughly understand the legal, tactical and ethical requirements of the market and the avoidance of conflicts between them.

Thoroughly understand the Brokers' responsibility to the Principal and the circumstances under which breach of warranty of authority (with and without negligence) might arise. Be aware of the consequent penalties.

Understand the importance of professional negligence and indemnity insurance for Brokers and be aware of the cover provided.

Be aware of the remedies available to the Broker in the event of the Principal defaulting on its obligations.

FINANCIAL ELEMENTS OF CHARTER PARTIES

Thoroughly understand the various ways in which freight (rates per tonne or lump sum) and hire calculations (rate per day or per dwt/month) are made and the time when payment is due.

Thoroughly understand that reasons for and calculation of additional payments due under charter parties and the appropriate clauses: for Voyage Charters – deadfreight, demurrage/despatch, damages for detention and freight taxes; for Time charters – payment for bunkers, ballast bonuses.

Understand the importance of clauses in time charters relating to late hire payment and the remedies available to the Owner.

Understand the importance in time charters of performance claims and the nature of off-hire events.

Understand the arrangements for and relevant clauses regarding delivery, final voyage and re-delivery.

Thoroughly understand how commissions and brokerage are calculated and who is responsible for payment.

Understand the use of freight market derivates as a hedging tool and be aware of the operation of the derivates market.

LAYTIME

Thoroughly understand the importance of the clarity of notice of readiness clauses and be able to draft a concise clause.

Understand the procedure for tendering a valid NOR and common problems relating to acceptance.

Understand the point at which laytime commences and the circumstances under which laytime may be interrupted; understand what time is excluded from laytime.

Thoroughly understand the principle of "once on demurrage always on demurrage" and the rare exceptions.

Thoroughly understand the extent and nature of the information contained in the Statement of Facts and how the Laytime Statement is prepared. Be able to calculate the laytime used and demurrage/despatch earned from appropriate data.

Understand the application of "Voylay Rules" with particular reference to Berth-v-Port charters and Weather Working days.

CALCULATIONS

Thoroughly understand the essential procedures used to create a voyage estimate and be able to make complete calculations from given data.

Be aware of the main variables including change of loadline zones, fresh water allowances, draft limitations (including draft calculation – tpi/tpcm) also the importance of careful bunker planning.

Understand the techniques used and be able to make the calculations to compare alternative routes, alternative voyages, compare voyage with time charter, compare $/tonne with lump sum rates and $/day with DWT/month.

Understand the reason for and means of calculation of Ballast Bonus in time charters.

GENERAL

Thoroughly understand the charter party clauses for the resolution of disputes including the application of arbitration and jurisdiction clauses. Be aware of the BIMCO Arbitration Clause.

Understand the roles of the commercial courts, arbitration and Alternative Dispute Resolution (ADR) in settling disputes and be aware of the differing procedures.

Understand the importance of Shipowners' P&I Associations and their role in the context of cargo claims, be aware of the other sectors of Owners' P&I cover.

Understand the role of Intermediaries P&I Associations and the classes of cover offered to Brokers and Agents.

Be aware of the importance of keeping full and proper records to assist in dispute resolution.

CONTENTS

7   VOYAGE ESTIMATING   123

8   BILLS OF LADING AND CARGO CLAIMS   137

Chapter 1

DRY CARGO SHIPS

1.1 INTRODUCTION

This Dry Cargo Chartering text sets out to ensure that a conscientious reader will finish up with a thorough basic knowledge of this specialised sector of shipbroking.

It explains in detail the commodities involved, their carriage requirements and the vessels serving this market. The book covers in depth the role of those participating in the market, the Charterers, Shipowners, Operators and Brokers, as well as the freight markets themselves and their documentation, charter parties, bills of lading, letters of credit, etc.

The mechanics of offers and counter-offers are dealt with as well as warnings regarding the dangers of fraud and unethical practices. Close attention is paid to aspects of freights and hires, with extensive explanation of how to perform laytime calculations and voyage estimates.

Finally, world trades and geography affecting the dry cargo market in particular are examined as well as explanations of how dry cargo chartering organisations are operated, their office techniques, computerisation, the settling of disputes by reconciliation, arbitration and by resort to law, and relevant insurance protection.

It is an extensive undertaking in just ten chapters, but this publication has been designed to help readers in a practical fashion, taking them chapter by chapter in a logical manner through the many and varied facets of this fascinating sector of the world's maritime industry.

This first Chapter introduces the reader to dry cargo ships. It does not set out to be an exhaustive study of the subject, but it explains many every day expressions as they are used in connection with the vessels that participate in this market.

The international dry cargo market is immense, served by numerous ships of all sizes, ranging from general cargo and specialised vessels through to commonplace bulk carriers, and from small 'coasters' with a cargo capacity of a hundred or so tonnes up to enormous 'capesize' bulk carriers capable of carrying cargoes in excess of a quarter of a million tonnes of a bulk commodity such as iron ore. There are many elderly ships engaged in this most fascinating of markets, as well as the latest, highly sophisticated, fuel-efficient and 'cargo friendly' modern vessels.

Some ships are highly specialised and able to carry only one particular commodity, others are flexible in design and able to transport a variety of cargoes.

In this Chapter, we will be examining some of the ship types to be found in the dry cargo sector of the international shipping market, their basic design and constructional details and their suitability for certain cargoes and trades.

1.2 SHIP TYPES

Appendix 1 shows the inter-relationship of various dry cargo ship types, and it should be noted that some basic designs are adapted to enable the vessel to become involved in more than one trade. Modern designs of certain multi-deck vessels, originally conceived to carry general cargoes, are also capable of carrying a part or full cargo of containers or, perhaps, a bulk cargo, in addition to or instead of 'break-bulk' parcels of various commodities.

If they are additionally equipped with a high capacity crane or derrick (termed a 'heavy lift') capable of safely lifting from shore to cargo hold and vice versa, an article weighing in excess of 100 tonnes, they have yet another facility of advantage to the vessel's owners/operators. There are some vessels designed specifically with even heavier lifts in mind and these can use two heavy lift cranes in combination to lift loads up to 1,000 tonnes at a time. Thus vessels with this cargo flexibility can intrude upon the specialised markets developed around the marine transportation of containers, bulk commodities and 'heavy lift' items, in addition to the carriage of bagged and baled goods.

Certain bulk carriers, outwardly the simplest design of dry cargo vessels, are adapted by their Owners and/or builders to engage in specialist trades when an opportunity arises; for example, the carriage of lumber in cargo holds and on deck. Or the dimensions, design and fittings of the ship may permit trading to particular geographical regions e.g.: The Great Lakes, or to ice affected areas of the World.

There are even vessels, 'combination carriers', capable of engaging in both 'wet' markets and 'dry'. These vessels (usually of 60,000 tonnes cargo capacity plus) are equipped to carry cargoes of crude-oil or dry-bulk commodities, such as ores, coal or grain.

In all cases, however, the concept behind dry cargo merchant ship design has altered dramatically in the period since World War II. Nowadays, vessels must be *'cargo friendly'* basically designed and equipped to speed cargo handling at load and discharge ports within a minimum of time and with a minimum of shore labour but with the capability of efficiently carrying the maximum amount of freight earning cargo. The soaring cost of oil fuel (referred to as *'bunkers')* since the 1970's has also meant that modern main engines have been designed to consume considerably less during sea passages than was once the case, and this emphasis on *'performance'* has led to hull design innovations, such as the wide-spread introduction of the *'bulbous bow'.*

Developments are still taking place in both engine and hull design, although now the driving force is preventing airborne pollution. Ships are obliged under international conventions to minimise their polluting effect and some states, or in the case of the European Union, groups of states, have expressed their intention of imposing stricter limits still. Reducing pollution from engines can mean a small increase in fuel consumption depending on the technology chosen but experts and ship designers share a belief that changes to hull designs could result in a 10 to 20 per cent cut in fuel consumption within the next ten to fifteen years. Some of the changes proposed (multi hulls and longer narrower vessels) may not meet with operator approval and may also need changes to ways ships are measured for tonnage and charging purposes.

As ports have been enlarged, deepened, developed and, in the richer countries, equipped with relatively sophisticated cargo handling equipment, so merchant ship naval architects have been required to incorporate general port needs into vessel design, and to plan yet larger vessels, capable of maximising earnings potential for their owners and of transporting goods world-wide at the lowest unit prices for the commodities involved. So let us now study the basic dry cargo ship types, broadly divided into the common categories of:

1. General Cargo
2. Bulk Carriers
3. Containerships
4. RO/RO Ships
5. Specialised
6. Short Sea

1.3 GENERAL CARGO

Commonly referred to nowadays as *'multi-purpose'* vessels, general cargo ships are able to adapt to world trades and demands and to carry a variety of cargoes.

These vessels were first mass-produced during World War II, when the famous 10,000 tons deadweight 'Liberty' type ships were built. Later, many of these vessels were sold to surviving and aspiring Shipowners as the basis of modern post-war fleets, and their *'three-island'* design (i.e. forecastle, midships-located bridge accommodation, and stern superstructure) remained in vogue until the 1960s), when new designs, principally the British 'SD14' and the American designed but Japanese produced 'Freedom', as well as the German 'Liberty Replacement' (the GLR), first appeared. There still remain a few elderly vessels at sea with bridge and engines located amidships, most modern ships have aft-superstructure, bridge and engines, and with 'cargo friendly', unobstructed hatchways and holds between these and the forecastle; and without the inconvenience of a *'shaft-tunnel'* covering a lengthy propeller shaft linking the *'midships'* main engine and the vessel's propeller, being exposed to potential damage from poorly-operated 'cargo grabs' when discharging a bulk cargo, or from heavy units of cargo (e.g. scrap metal) being carelessly loaded.

(Those engaging in the chartering of general cargo ships may still encounter Charter Party Clauses placing the onus of damage to a ship's shaft-tunnel on the Shipowner, if that tunnel is not adequately protected).

Moving the accommodation and engine room aft was a sensible option when ships relied on mechanical drive to the propeller, but it does have its drawbacks. On a container vessel for example the height of the deck cargo is restricted because of sight limitations from the bridge, which is why the latest generation of 10,000TEU+ ships may now feature a more central navigation bridge and accommodation, although the engine room usually remains aft. On all vessels there is more vertical movement at the ends of the ship making living there less comfortable than amidships where movement is much smaller. Today, electric drive is becoming more common and actively promoted. The ship's engines (there will be more of them but smaller) can be located at any point onboard and will generate electricity which can be fed to motors in podded propellers outside the ship using cables that can run between frames. The added advantage of this configuration is that a ship is not disabled if one engine breaks down or the ship's structure is damaged in a collision or grounding.

1.3.1   Cargo Liners and Tramps

Multi-purpose vessels operating in the deep sea markets tend to be fairly small by today's standards, most being in the 10/25,000 deadweight size category. Those employed on scheduled routes are normally more sophisticated and sometimes are built to custom serve that operation, being termed, perhaps, *'cargo liners'*, but such vessels are declining in numbers, line operators frequently chartering-in conveniently placed and priced *'tramp vessels'* from the international dry cargo market; vessels which ply the oceans voyage by voyage, their owners/operators seeking cargoes in the vicinity of where their vessels happen to be available.

A Typical Cargo Ship

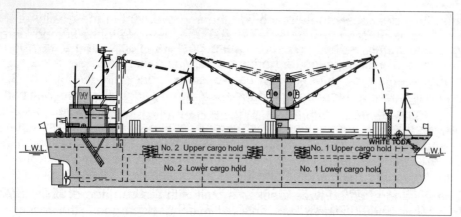
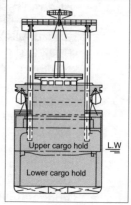

Principal Particulars

Length (o.a.)..110.67 m
Length (b.p.)..102.16 m
Breadth (mid.) ....19.20 m
Depth (mid.) ....8.80m/13.50 m
Draft (mid.) ....9.200 m
Gross tonnage 7,442
Deadweight.. 11,443 MT
Main engine.......................................Makita-Mitsui-MAN B&W 6L35MC (Mark VI)
MCR ....3,900 kW × 210 rpm
NOR ....3,315 kW × 199 rpm
Speed (max. trial) ....15.298 knots
      (service)..13.63 knots
Complement... 20 P
Classification...NK
Handling gear Twin-deck crane ....60 t (30 t × 2) × 24 mR × 1 set
              Derrick boom ....30 t × 1 set
Loading capacity (grain) .... 16,680.85 m³
              (bale) .... 15,760.16 m³
              (others) ....hot coils on tank top with dunnage
Builder.. Nishi Shipbuilding Co., Ltd.

1.3.2   Liquid Cargo

With the introduction of containers and of *'parcel'* tankers, there is nowadays less demand for small quantities of liquid cargoes to be carried in the *'deep tanks'* of cargo liners, but there is increased demand for vessels with holds and decks capable of carrying several tiers of containers. Tank containers have, therefore, mostly removed the need for deep tanks. The internal as well as the external designs of general cargo/multi-purpose vessels have altered in recent years and these changes can perhaps best be explained by studying various aspects applicable and, in some cases, peculiar to these vessels.

1.3.3   Dry Cargo Spaces

Modern general cargo ships are nearly always constructed with two (very occasionally three) decks and can be termed *'tweendeckers'* the upper deck being the *'main'* or *'weather-deck'*, and the lower deck the *'tweendeck'*. Most tweendeckers have just one 'tweendeck' located somewhat closer to the weatherdeck overhead than to the bottom of the cargo hold beneath, about two-thirds up the height of the holds (See note at the end of this sub-section).

The cargo area enclosed between the tweendeck and the weatherdeck is, logically, referred to as the *'tweendeck space'*, and the area beneath the tweendeck down to the bottom of the cargo area, the *'hold space'*. These vessels are ideal for the carriage of bagged, baled and drummed commodities, the support of the tweendeck meaning that a high tier stowage of these goods can be safely accommodated, whereas the same number of tiers in a bulk carrier, for example, might well lead to splitting of lower stowed bags or crumpling of drums due to the sheer weight pressing down from above. It is true to say, however, that this is less of a factor than was previously the case, given the improvement in the quality of the cargo bags and the subsequent tendency to larger sized bags (e.g. one tonne 'jumbo' cargo bags, although these can equally be a problem when they require stowing in the wings or ends of holds).

The relatively large number of individual cargo spaces (the SD14, for example, has eight separate, various sized cargo compartments) is another advantage when faced with several commodities to be carried at the same time, yet kept separate from each other e.g. to avoid 'tainting' by smell, etc. or to enable loading and discharging at several ports during a voyage, without extra handling of cargoes.

Where a modern general cargo tweendecker is built with the carriage of bulk commodities and containers in mind, in addition to conventional 'tweendeck cargoes', the vessel can more accurately be termed a *'multi-purpose'* ship. An example of such a ship, a Freedom Mk II, being equipped with *container fittings* and with *retractable tweendecks* that fold against the sides of the holds to facilitate the loading and discharge of bulk commodities.

NB: The bottom of a cargo hold is not the bottom of a vessel. Between the cargo hold and the ship's bottom will be located various tanks, designed to carry water ballast or bunkers. These are termed *'double bottom'* tanks and the top of these tanks, their *'ceiling'* forms the bottom of the cargo hold located directly above and, consequently, usually referred to as the *'tank tops'.*

1.3.4   Cargo Fittings

In order to carry goods efficiently, general cargo vessels need built-in facilities to handle safely a whole variety of commodities, as well as equipment to load, stow, secure and discharge those goods. Most hold spaces will be provided with fire-smothering equipment e.g.: CO_2 *fittings* used to contain outbreaks of fire, certain commodities being prone to spontaneous combustion (e.g. bagged fishmeal) and/or easily combustible (e.g. baled jute). Some ships will be additionally equipped with *mechanical* or, more likely *electrical ventilation* in their cargo carrying spaces; useful particularly for commodities that 'sweat' heavily (e.g. bagged rice). Older tweendeckers may have 'coamings' around tweendeck hatchways, designed as a safety feature to protect those working in the tweendeck spaces from the danger of falling into the holds below. Since the 1960's, however, with the widespread introduction of fork-lift trucks used to facilitate cargo handling, these tweendeck coamings have been almost universally dispensed with, the tweendeck hatchcovers fitting level with the surrounding tweendeck floor and providing a clear, flat unobstructed area. Such vessels, unobstructed by tweendeck hatch coamings, are termed *'flush' tweendeckers'.*

Other obstructions possible in a tweendecker's cargo compartments are columns or pillars supporting overhead decks. It is essential to check on the location of such obstructions if intending to use a vessel for large, bulky cargo.

Some tweendeck vessels are fitted with *'cargo battens'* (strips of timber fixed at intervals usually horizontally but very occasionally vertically) along the sides of holds and tweendeck spaces, and designed to keep bagged and baled commodities from being damaged by touching the sides of a ship which are invariably wet through condensation and/or slight seepage through microscopic faults in the plating. Cargo battens also increase ventilation and reduce damage from moisture or sweating. However, they are frequently damaged and have to be removed entirely and stored elsewhere when handling a bulk commodity. Since they are expensive to maintain in good condition and it is labour intensive to keep repairing and removing cargo battens, it is nowadays unusual to find tramp general cargo ships fully equipped with this facility. Instead *cargo nets* might be used, but more commonly cargo is protected when necessary by a combination of *kraft paper* and other *dunnage* material fitted sometimes by the crew but more commonly by shore stevedores as loading progresses. Dunnage can be of various material but is usually loose wood of various kinds and sizes laid at the bottom of a cargo hold to keep lower stowed goods clear of bilge water and from obstructing drainage, and also wedged between parts of the cargo to keep the stow secure and safe (e.g. for the carriage of drums). Certain trades traditionally use other, local materials for similar purposes, 'cargo mats' and bamboo, for example, being utilised as dunnage material for the export of bagged rice from South-East Asia.

It may also be necessary to secure some commodities with lashings. In these cases *'pad eyes'* may need to be welded to tank tops and/or hold sides, so as to provide safe anchorages for the lashing material. The cost and time of welding and removing these pad eyes is usually for the account of the Charterer, with Charter Party clauses drafted accordingly, perhaps adding that, if not removed following discharge, the Shipowner is to be reimbursed by payment of a set rate, say US $10.00 per pad eye left *in place.* Naturally, care must be taken with any welding work in the vicinity of oil bunker tanks located beneath tank tops. Such a Charter Party clause may go on to list the lashing materials supplied by the loading Stevedores/ Charterers, stipulating that the Shipowner is to ensure that his Officers take care of these and hand them over to Charterers' representatives in good condition at the end of the voyage.

Since the late 1990s, all vessels are obliged to carry a cargo securing manual which details what fittings are attached to the ship and their loading limits. Additional fittings can still be attached but their loading limits may have to be certified by a surveyor before they can be used. The manual must also include details of lashing materials such as wire ropes, twistlocks (for container ships) and shackles and turnbuckles used for fixing and tightening wire ropes. This equipment list should be updated regularly and provides a useful reference for Charterers involved in disputes over damage to lashing materials.

1.3.5 Bulk Cargoes

With some general cargo ships of certain designs, additional special fittings might be required before a bulk grain cargo can be carried safely to protect against the cargo shifting dangerously when at sea. Most modern tweendeckers and multi-purpose vessels are designed to carry grain without special fittings, some being fitted with permanent *'partial centre-line bulkheads'*, preventing the sideways shift of cargo. Older vessels engaging in this trade might require the construction of temporary wooden centre-line bulkheads before permission would be given to set out to sea.

As we shall see later, true bulk carriers are commonly fitted with 'self-trimming' facilities for high stowing bulk cargoes such as grain. It is not usual for tweendeckers to have this facility although attention to this deficiency has been given by the designers of some modern multi-purpose vessels.

The principle of hinged, hoistable tweendecks has also been utilised in modern multi-purpose vessels, such as the Freedom Mk II.

1.3.6 Containers

With the revolution in cargo handling, the design of general cargo ships has had to adapt and conform to new methods. Consequently, the cargo spaces of modern multi-purpose vessels tend to be as square as is possible, so as to assist the stowage of containers and palletised cargo, whilst on the weatherdecks, modern designs allow for storage of containers, often two or more tiers high, bearing in mind vessel stability, visibility from the bridge, and deck strengths. All purpose-built container ships, and many of the multi-purpose vessels, will have special fittings that secure the containers against movement. A purpose-built container ship may be fitted with cell guides in the holds or else pads into which locking devices attached to the corners of each box will slot. There are also twistlocks which perform the same function, locking each tier of containers to the one below it. Lashing rods fixed at diagonals at the ends of containers link adjacent containers in the tiers. Charter parties for ships capable of carrying containers should detail what container fittings the ship is equipped with.

1.3.7 Ballast and Bilges

Older general cargo vessels were designed to carry quantities of liquids e.g. palm oil and many had small 'deep tanks' fitted with heating coils for this purpose. Occasionally cargo holds, capable of being flooded to provide extra stability when the vessel is in ballast or partly laden condition may be termed 'deep tanks', although it is better to refer to them as 'floodable holds' to distinguish their purpose. An example of a 'floodable hold' in a general cargo vessel can be found by reference to cargo hold No. 3 of the SD14. A very few modern multi-purpose types have been equipped with older style deep tanks, but generally this trade has been taken over almost totally by *parcel tankers'*.

After washing cargo spaces, dirty water is drained away from the hold bottoms into *'bilges'* through *'strum boxes'* which act as filters and prevent solid matter from blocking bilge pipes and damaging pumps. Prior to loading bulk commodities, these bilge openings might be intentionally covered over for the same reasons.

1.3.8 Shelter Decker

A term that might be encountered especially in the short-sea market sector is *'shelter-decker'.* The 'shelter' refers to a design specifically adapted to overcome stringent tonnage regulations, by which vessels could maximise cargo capacity and intake (and thus maximise earnings potential) yet restrict the registered tonnage assessed against the vessels and reduce those expenses and liabilities which are based on the ship's registered tonnage (e.g. port costs and certain liabilities as to crew numbers). The tonnage regulations creating these innovative designs have long been altered and there is now no need for clever naval architecture to overcome this legislation. Nevertheless, the term lingers on in certain market sectors, and where the term 'shelterdecker' is used today it should be taken to mean 'tweendecker'.

1.3.9 Cargo Gear

The most obvious exterior cargo fitting on a general cargo ship is her *'gear',* her *derricks* or *cranes.*

Derricks may be old in design, but they remain important equipment; their use (and dangers) being readily understood throughout the world, relatively simple, as they are, to rig and to maintain, and being reasonably inexpensive. There are basically three parts to a derrick (see **Appendix 2**):

1. A vertical supporting pillar a 'samson post' sunk into the ship's weatherdeck, to the base of which is attached

2. The boom, and

3. rigging (e.g. wire ropes, blocks and tackle).

Derricks are operated by winches, usually electrically or hydraulically driven (see **Appendix 2**).

All parts of the cargo lifting equipment must be rigorously and regularly checked with certificates issued attesting to the 'Safe Working Load', (SWL) of each unit. These inspections can be carried out by Classification Societies or by certain other internationally recognised authorities specialising in this activity. Certainly, it is always best to ensure that a Charter Party contains confirmation by the Shipowner that a vessel's gear certificates are up-to-date and will remain so during the currency of the voyage/timecharter involved. Failure to attend to this aspect could cause shore workers to refuse to handle a vessel or, worse, injury or death resulting from defective or uncertificated gear could render to those involved enormous financial penalties in certain areas of the world.

The basic derrick can be extremely versatile and is capable of adaption for certain trades. *'Union purchase'* is a method of joining derrick booms to a particular rigging method, simple to use and fast in operation, so that loads can be moved speedily from shore to cargo hold, or vice versa. The problem with the system is that once the rigging is set up it has to be altered to adjust the places of lifting and setting down of each load. Cargo has to be moved to an exact position prior to lifting and taken away from another exact position at the end of each movement cycle. It is therefore a labour-intensive method (although this is not a problem in certain areas of the less developed world). Additionally, however, the union of derricks in this way reduces the SWL, so that two 5-tonne swl derricks might have a union purchase capacity of less than half the individual SWL, say 2 tonnes. However, for bagged goods, this may well not be a problem, and the system has its advantages for the discharge of bagged goods in less developed regions.

Where heavy loads are involved, union purchase is obviously not the answer. The winch arrangement of certain vessels enables two parallel derricks to be linked together with two adjacent cargo winches in a system termed *'swinging derricks'* (see **Appendix 2**). Swinging derricks maintain the speed of operation of union purchase, but enable liftings up to the maximum capacity of the smallest derrick or cargo winch involved, using in place of a third cargo winch a *'deadman',* a suspended deadweight on one line (e.g. a mass of old wire) the purpose of which is simply to provide tension. One winch is used to 'swing' the boom from over the hatchway to the quayside, a second winch being used to 'swing' the boom back to its original position.

A variation is the *'self-swinging derrick',* or *'crane derrick'*, a single derrick system that works in the same fashion as a crane, by using only its own immediately associated winches and therefore does not interfere with cargo handling at adjacent hatchways. Such a derrick is normally to be found in isolation at a hatchway and, just like a crane, is capable of extremely fast operation by only one, skilled driver utilising a joystick control. A commercial example of a self-swinging derrick is the 'Velle' type.

Typically cargo derricks lift between 5 and 15 tonnes SWL, but it is not unusual for conventional-type derricks to be adapted for lifts of up to 50 tonnes. Some general cargo ships are equipped with *'Stulcken derricks'* (see **Appendix 2**) which, in some cases, can safely lift weights of up to 450 tonnes, having the added advantage of serving two hatchways immediately fore and aft of the location of its samson posts.

(Naturally, when chartering general cargo, multi-purpose ships, the location, safe working loads and capabilities of the vessel's derricks may be of paramount importance, and the broker acting for a Charterer should ensure that he or she is entirely familiar with the requirements of his principal and can properly evaluate the ships proposed for the business with regard to their cargo gear potential).

In a chartering sense, the term *'double-rigged'* means that two derricks serve each hatchway.

Modern multi-purpose vessels are almost always equipped with *cranes.* These are usually electrically powered, having the advantage over most derricks of being more versatile and capable of accurately placing and picking up cargo from a variety of adjacent positions. Cranes are, however, more sophisticated and expensive to maintain, also requiring more efficient handling than derricks. Fewer cranes are needed than derricks, though, and they are self-contained in their own units, not requiring supporting samson posts, etc. Typical lifting capacities of shipborne cranes range from 5 to 40 tonnes SWL, with most modern vessels tending towards the higher capacities, perhaps having the facility to unite the lifting capacity of two adjacent cranes, thereby substantially increasing the maximum capacity, e.g. 2 x 25 tonnes cranes equating to 1 x 50 tonnes.

To recap, most newbuildings are fitted with cranes of around 25 to 60 tonnes SWL, derricks still being used to provide a heavy-lift facility, where required.

Schippersgracht 18,900-dwt Multi-purpose Cargo Ship

Mitsubishi Heavy Industries, Ltd. delivered the 18,900-dwt multi-purpose cargo ship *Schippersgracht,* to the Dutch Owner Spliethoff's Bevrachtingskantoor B.V. at The MHI Shimonoseki Shipyard and Machinery Works on January 14, 2000. The ship is the first of six sister ships. (Three ships were built by MHI and the other three ships were built by Tsuneishi Shipbuilding Co., Ltd.).

The ship is a multi-purpose cargo ship with wide side loaders which can facilitate the transfer of multi-purpose cargoes such as timber, paper, general cargoes, bulk, containers, hot coils, ore, various plants, dangerous goods, etc.

Features

1. A total of five (5) side shifters (16 t S.W.L. per set) fitted in enclosed structure on the vessel's starboard side can facilitate the transfer of paper cargo between quay and hold spaces in all weather. The elevators housed in 10m high towers on the upper deck are hoisted down to the cargo hold bottom. These arrangements are not affected by the great difference in tidemarks.

2. A total of three (3) deck cranes (Max. 120 S.W.L. at 14 m radius per set) are installed, two (2) at the port side and one (1) at the starboard side, can facilitate the transfer of maximum 240 T capacity of heavy cargoes by tandem operation.

3. The main cargo holds can be accessed through three hatches by hydraulic operation. Removable tweendeck formed of pontoon-type covers will achieve various cargo

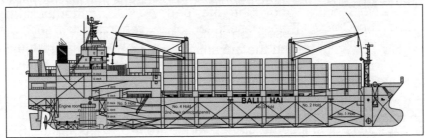

stowage permutations by locking into position at three levels and can also be used as partial transverse bulkheads.

A multi-purpose Cargo Ship

Principal Particulars

Length (o.a.)..160.73 m
Length (b.p.)..151.20 m
Breadth (mid.) ....25.00 m
Depth (mid.) ....12.80 m
Draft (mid.) ....9.20 m
Gross tonnage 17,111
Deadweight...17,913 T
Main engine..6UEC60LA
MCR ....19,625 kW (13,087 PS) $\times$ 124 rpm^{-1}
NOR ....8,663 kW (11,779 PS) $\times$ 120 rpm^{-1}

Speed (max. trial) ....19.43 knots
        (service)..18.0 knots
Complement 25
Classification..NK
Handling gear .... Electro-dydraulic deck crane 40/30 t × 20 m/min × 26/26 mR × 2 sets
Loading capacity (grain)...15,219 m^3
        (bale)..12,481 m^3
        (container).. 20' container: 854 units
        (car/vehicle) .... Standard car: 609 units
Builder.. Shin Kurushima Hiroshima Dockyard Cp. Ltd.

1.3.10 Cargo Hatches

Most vessels are fitted with steel hatchcovers of what is known as *'Macgregor type'* Macgregor's being an organisation which pioneered and patented hatchcover designs in the period following World War II, and which still plays an important role in the design of cargo handling equipment. These hatches open and close with a concertina like action but other types are also commonly encountered. Some will roll either to the end of the hatch or on large bulk carriers to the side where they provide some protection for personnel working on the deck during loading or discharging operations. Some ships have piggy-back hatches where the covers stack on top of one another and for container ships, pontoon hatches, which are lifted on and off using similar fitting as found on the containers, are most commonly used.

Most hatchcovers are opened and closed by electric or hydraulic power and some by winches and chains. They are relatively labour free but, like derricks and cranes, are subject to stringent testing by Classification Societies to ensure that they remain safe and watertight. Cargo damage by moisture may well be found to result from water ingress through hatchcovers and, as with cargo handling equipment, Charter Party clauses usually stipulate that Owners will maintain hatchcovers in efficient, watertight condition.

Depending upon the design of the vessel, tweendecks and cargo holds may be served by one or more hatchways. In the case of the Freedom Cargo Hold/Tweendeck No.1 can be seen to be served by Hatchway No.1, whereas Cargo Hold/Tweendeck No.2 is served by Hatchways 2 and 3, Hatchway No.2 located above the forward part of the cargo hold/tweendeck and Hatchway No.3 located above the after part. A similar pattern will be observed over Holds 3 and 4. The Charter Party description of a Freedom Mk I should therefore contain the expression '4 holds/6 hatches', whereas an SD14 would be described as having '5 holds/5 hatches'.

Some multi-purpose vessels, however, have what are referred to as *'twin-hatches'* – i.e. hatchways located side-by-side rather than fore and aft as in the case of the Freedom Mk I. The object of twin hatches is to provide easy access to the sides of a vessel's holds and tweendeck spaces to facilitate the handling of heavy and bulky articles, such as containers or, perhaps, railway wagons. The main disadvantage of twin hatchways, however, is the need for a supportive centre-line beam running longitudinally between the two hatchway openings, (and sometimes an entire centre-line bulkhead), hampering bulk cargo handling.

In most cases 'tweendeck hatchways' are located more or less exactly beneath weatherdeck hatchways, thereby facilitating cargo handling. They usually also have the same dimensions. However, this may not be the case, especially with older vessels, and it is good practice to check this aspect when chartering tweendeckers.

1.4 BULK CARRIERS

Some of the items covered under general cargo vessels above, items concerning for example, gear and hatchways, can apply equally to bulk carriers and bulk carriers can also, especially since the introduction of stronger synthetic cargo bag material, be found engaged carrying commodities that were once the main preserve of the tween-deck market.

Within the very near future there will be some significant changes to bulk carrier construction brought about by an increasingly poor safety record for type generally. These changes are being pursued by the IMO (the United Nations body responsible for maritime affairs) and IACS (the International Association of Classification Societies).

Almost all existing large bulk carriers have a single hull, meaning that between the cargo and the ocean there are just millimetres of steel. Older bulk carriers tend to suffer from a lack of maintenance which coupled with the corrosive effect of some cargoes has caused loss of side plates in some cases and total loss of the ship in far too many others. In recent years there has been a trend for some bulk carriers to be built with double hulls just as all new tankers are. There will be some benefits from this change, not least a faster discharge because cargo will not "stick" between the frames of the ship's sides and a consequent reduction in mechanical damage caused by the practice of dislodging stuck cargo using cargo grabs as hammers and swinging them at the hull.

Another change has been the re-introduction of the forecastle (the raised area at the very front of the ship). This was dropped in the mid-late 1980s and is blamed for the failure of forward hatchcovers in extreme weather conditions when green water is shipped on deck. The loss of the *Derbyshire* was when this failure was first bought to light.

From the chartering point of view the most far reaching effect of the changes will be for bulk carriers to be classed for light, medium or heavy cargoes. Today a bulk carrier is free to contract for any cargo type but in future only ships suitable constructed and strengthened will be able to carry all types of bulk cargoes. Ships built with medium weight cargoes in mind will be able to carry light cargoes but vessels designed specifically for light bulks will be restricted to those cargoes only. Until these changes are introduced and single skin bulkers phased out, it is justified in looking at the situation that exists today and what features will remain unchanged.

Bulk carriers have distinctive features. They are single deck vessels, those engaged in deepsea markets and up to 50,000 tonnes deadweight size frequently (but not always) equipped with cranes or, occasionally in older designs, with derricks. The majority of bulk carriers over this size, however, (as well as many modern short sea 'bulkers'), are *'gearless'*, having no cargo handling equipment themselves and reliant on shore facilities to be loaded and discharged.

They range in approximate size from coastal craft of around 100 tonnes to vessels of over 250,000 tonnes deadweight and, as their name implies, are intended primarily for the transportation of bulk dry cargo commodities, although they can be adapted for the carriage of other goods, cargoes such as lumber, steel products, containers, and even motor cars.

Larger bulk carriers of between about 60,000 and 80,000 tonnes deadweight are usually constructed with a beam and draft suitable for limitations imposed on the market by the dimensions of the Panama Canal, an important waterway for this type of vessel, giving rise to the term *'panamax'.*

Typical dimensions of a 'panamax bulk carrier' would be:

LOA (length overall): .... 224 metres (735 ft)
Beam (width): .... 31.8 metres (104.5 ft)
Draft: .... 13.35 metres (43.8 ft)
Summer Deadweight: .... 64,500 tonnes
Cubic Capacity of: .... 73,625 cubic metres
Cargo Holds: .... (2,600,000 cubic ft)
Holds: 7
Hatchways: .... 7 (each about 14 metres long by 13.5 metres wide)

The Panama Canal Authority has a project in place to expand the capacity of the canal and some work has already been done in widening and deepening certain sections. In October 2006 the country voted on plans to build new sets of locks and as a result new locks will be constructed. These locks will have chambers 427 m long, by 55 m wide, and 18.3 m deep and have been designed to take the largest vessels projected to be used by trades which could benefit from using the Panama Canal. When built, the shipping world will have to redefine the term Panamax and many established trade patterns will undoubtedly change.

Following the announcement of the planned new locks, some owners have ordered vessels able to pass through them. These vessels are being referred to within the industry as 'New Panamax' types. The first of these vessels – mostly bulk carriers but also some container ships – are now being delivered although until the new locks are built they are confined to routes where passage through the canal is not required.

Bergen Trader 75,933-dwt Panamax Bulk Carrier

The 75,933-dwt Panamax bulk carrier *Bergen Trader* was built at Kanasashi Co. Ltd., and delivered in October 2000.

The vessel is designed for carrying grain in bulk, coal and ore, and is one of a series of 75,500 dwt type Panamax bulk carriers built at the yard.

Cargo space is divided into seven (7) holds and the vessel has topside tanks and double bottom with side hopper. Heavy cargo is to be loaded alternately in Hold Nos. 1, 3, 5 and 7.

No. 4 cargo hold is also used as ballast tank for safe navigation at rough sea.

The vessel has wide hatches of 16.15 m long × 12.80 m wide for No. 1 hold; 18.70 m × 14.00 m wide for Nos. 2-7.

The main engine is low speed, long-stroke diesel engine *Kawasaki-B&W 7S50MC-C.* And a high performance propeller with turbo ring saves fuel oil consumption.

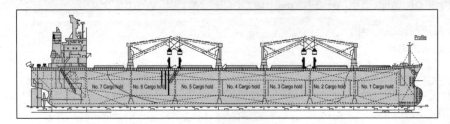

To comply with NK MO classification, a 24-hour unattended machinery space system is provided.

A Panamax Bulk Carrier

Principal Particulars

Length (o.a.)..224.94 m
Length (b.p.)..217.00 m
Breadth (mid.) ....32.26 m

Depth (mid.) ....19.50 m
Draft (mid.) ....14.119 m
Gross tonnage 39,871
Deadweight... 76,302 MT
Main engine.. B&W 6S60MC (Mark-VI)
MCR... 10,320 kW × 89.0 rpm
NOR .... 8,770kW × 84.3rpm
Speed (max. trial)..16.834 knots
　　　(service) ....15.25 knots
Complement 25
Classification...NK
Handling gear.. 30 tons × 4 sets
Loading capacity (grain) .... 90,740.4 m³
Builder... Imabari Shipbuilding Co., Ltd.

Pierre LD 172,561-dwt Capesize Bulk Carier

The 172,561-dwt Capesize bulk carrier *Pierre LD* was delivered in September 1999 to Louis Dreyfus Armateurs (S.N.C.) by Tsuneishi Shipbuilding Co. Ltd./Hashihama Shipbuilding Co. Ltd. This type of Capesize bulk carriers were designed by NKK Corporation.

The vessel has achieved maximum hold capacity and deadweight within the limitation of the Port of Dunkirk.

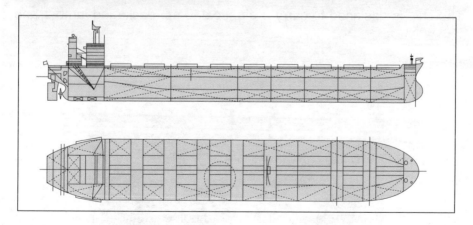

NKK surf-bulb is also fitted.

A Capesize Bulk Carrier

Principal Particulars

Length (o.a.)..289.00 m
Length (b.p.)..279.00 m

Breadth (mid.) ....44.98 m
Depth (mid.) ....24.40 m
Draft (mid.) ....17.95 m
Gross tonnage 87,590
Deadweight .... 171,009 MT
Main engine .... Mitsui B&W 6S70MC
MCR .... 16,857 kW (22,920 PS) × 91.0 rpm
NOR .... 14,327 kW (19,480 PS) × 86.2 rpm
Speed (max. trial)..16.7 knots
          (service) ....14.7 knots
Complement 32
Classification...ABS (ACCU)
Loading capacity (grain).. 190,153 m³
Builder..Sasebo Heavy Industries Co., Ltd.

Vessels too wide to transit the Panama Canal are termed *'capesize'* and usually this term is taken to mean vessels in excess of 100,000 tonnes deadweight, there being few bulk carriers between 80,000 and 100,000 tonnes deadweight size.

Bulk carriers of between, say, 20,000 and 50,000 tonnes deadweight size are frequently loosely termed *'handy sized'* whereas there is a specific class of bulk carrier around 20,000/30,000 tonnes deadweight designed with measurements enabling transit of the St. Lawrence Seaway, and access to the Great Lakes system of North America, these maximum dimensions being:

Length: 730 feet
Beam: 75 ft 6 ins.
Draft: 26 ft freshwater
Height above water level not to exceed 117 ft.

Tonghai 47,100-dwt Bulk Carrier

A 47,100-dwt bulk carrier *Tonghai* was build at Sakaide Works of Kawasaki Heavy Industries, Ltd., and delivered to Cosco Bulk Carrier Co. Ltd. in January 1999.

Features

1. The ship is a flush decker with forecastle and has five cargo holds with steel watertight hatch covers. Four 25 LT deck cranes provided on the center line between hatch covers enable cargo handling at the port without cargo handling facilities.

2. The ship is designed to carry grain, coal, ores, packaged lumber and steel products (hot coil).

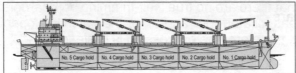

3.	Provision of portable stanchion on the ship's side enables packaged lumber to be loaded up to about 7 m on upper deck (about 4.5 m on hatch covers.)

A Tonghai Bulk Carrier

Principal Particulars

Length (o.a.)..199.96 m
Length (b.p.)...181.00 m
Breadth (mid.) ....32.20 m
Depth (mid.) ....17.30 m
Draft (mid.) ....12.26 m
Gross tonnage 29,407
Deadweight ....52,050 T
Main engine..DU-Sulzer 6RTA48TB diesel × 1
MCR ....8,100 kW × 118.0 rpm
NOR ....6,885 kW × 111.8 rpm
Speed (service)...14.70 knots
Complement 25
Classification ....Nippon Kaiji Kyokai
Handling gear deck crane: ....30 T × 21.0 m/mis × 4 sets
Loading capacity (grain)...65,100 m³
Builder ....IHI Marine United Inc.

### 1.4.1	Handy Size Bulker

Vessels transiting the Panama and Suez Canals and those trading to the Great Lakes require special fittings in addition to being dimensionally suitable, and such requirements will be dealt with in greater detail in Chapter nine.

### 1.4.2	Cargo Spaces

Bulk carriers have a basically simple design, where superstructure, bridge and engines are located aft in nearly every case, leaving relatively unobstructed access to cargo hatchways. To avoid the expensive necessity of employing shore labour to ensure that bulk cargo safely fills extremities of the holds i.e. it is safely *'trimmed'*, most bulk carriers are constructed with *'upper wing tanks'* (see **Appendix 3**), sometimes termed *'topside tanks'*, providing *'self-trimming'* facilities on their underside. These upper wing tanks are used to carry ballast water when the vessel is empty at sea or only partly laden, other areas used for this purpose being tanks located forward and aft ('fore peak' and 'after peak' tanks) and, perhaps, a midships located 'floodable hold', as discussed in the general cargo vessel section.

Because some bulk cargoes are relatively light (e.g. bulk barley) and so a vessel's hold can be filled before she comes down in the water to her permissible loadline marks, some 'handy-sized' bulkers utilise the space in these upper wing tanks for certain commodities (again bulk barley might be an example) that are relatively free-flowing. By loading through openings in the weatherdeck above the upper wing tanks, these spaces can be drained of ballast water at the loading port, washed through, cleaned and dried, the cargo then fed into the vacant spaces, thereby using otherwise wasted deadweight capacity.

At discharging ports, the cargo is 'bled' into the cargo hold immediately beneath through openings which are sealed when all cargo has been discharged and preparation made to take on ballast water. The operation also gives rise to the term *'bleeding wing tanks'*. Although occasionally used, the system is by no means universally employed owing to the difficulties of satisfactorily cleaning and drying out the wing tank spaces, especially in cold or humid conditions and the increasing expense in human labour terms of the entire operation.

Purists will argue that there are no true 'self-trimming bulk carriers', since such a vessel would require sloping areas located fore and aft of the hatchway openings, as well as to port and starboard and that, therefore, the expression is misleading.

In reality you should be fully aware of the limitations of 'self-trimming' vessels although, to be fair, there may be legal problems when utilising this expression, with certain commodities in rare situations giving rise to serious disputes. Some Owners prefer to use the less onerous expression *'easy-trimmer'* when describing their vessels.

In the bottoms of the cargo holds are *'tanktops'* covering *'double bottom tanks',* just as for general cargo ships, and in some cases (see **Appendix 3**), bulk carriers have *'side'* and/or *'lower wing tanks'.* The upper sides of lower wing tanks in the cargo holds give rise to the expression *'hopperedholds',* although some bulk carrier designs have virtually square-bottomed, flat hold floors, particularly specialised *'container bulk carriers'-'con-bulkers'-*designed to perform in both the bulk cargo and container market sectors, and needing this facility for the convenient and safe stowage of containers and, perhaps palletised cargo.

For other bulk carrier types, e.g. colliers, hoppered holds are desirable to assist the safe security of bulk cargo and to minimise its movement at sea.

1.4.3 Cargo Stowage

Bulk cargoes can vary considerably in their stowing properties, e.g. iron ore stows around 12 cubic feet for every tonne, whereas coke may stow as high as 90 cubic feet per tonne. Obviously, in the cases of iron ore, full deadweight will be reached with cargo holds little more than a third full, whilst a cargo of coke will fill cargo holds to capacity and the vessel may theoretically be losing potential revenue earnings because of lack of space in cargo compartments. (Unlike free-flowing bulk barley, coke cannot be loaded in upper wing tanks, because it would not only be extremely difficult and time consuming, if not impossible, to load it through the restricted deck openings to the wing tanks, it would probably continually block the 'bleeding' apertures when it came to discharge).

For heavy cargoes of iron ore, it is important that bulk carriers be loaded so they do not become too 'stiff' and dangerous in their handling at sea. Consequently, cargo is normally loaded in adjacent holds, say Holds 2, 4, 6 and 8 of a 9-hold bulk carrier, the vessel being especially *'hold-strengthened'* during the building process to facilitate the demands of this trade.

The facility of carrying cargo in adjacent holds with others empty is particularly useful for loading or discharging at more than one port when carrying commodities other than heavy ores. Whether this practice has contributed significantly to the poor loss record of bulkers is currently under review along with the changes mentioned earlier.

In 2006 new rules were introduced concerning part loading of bulk carriers and a ban was imposed on sailing with empty holds for some ship and cargo types. The ban is in line with Regulation 14 of SOLAS XII which was adopted in December 2004. Ships affected are those over 150 m in length and carrying bulk cargoes with a density of 1,780 kg/m^3 or above (Stowage factor around 20) and so will relate to ores and concentrates.

The reasoning behind the new regulation concerns hold flooding scenarios and the strength and stability of the vessel. These matters were the subject of a 1997 IMO SOLAS amendment based on work done by IACS on bulk carrier issues and covered in a string of IACS Unified Requirements (URs) – notable S17-S23. Ships built after 1998 will comply with the stiffer IACS requirements and are therefore unaffected by the ban. For other ships, the ban comes into force as soon as a ship reaches 10 years of age. Such ships must show that they comply with the provisions of IACS UR S17 (longitudinal strength of the hull girder), S18 (evaluation of all corrugated transverse watertight bulkheads) and S20 (evaluation of allowable hold loadings based on shear strength of the hold's double bottom). If they do not then the ban will apply.

In practice this means the vessel will not be permitted to put to sea with any hold loaded to less than 10% of that hold's maximum allowable cargo weight when fully loaded. Fully loaded is considered as meaning carrying a cargo equal to or above 90% of the ship's deadweight capacity at the relevant assigned freeboard. The restriction will be noted at the front of the ship's loading manual and so should be flagged up whenever the ship is preparing to load a cargo.

Sailing with empty holds is common when multiport operations are being carried out, but since this would typically involve the ship sailing with around 60-70% of a full cargo after a partial load or discharge, the ban on alternate hold loading will not apply. Operators can of course continue to operate with empty holds if the ship meets the strength requirements of the new rules, but where it does not then a decision will have to be made about strengthening the ship.

1.4.4   Cargo Gear

Some bulk carriers are fitted with *'self-discharging'* facilities. These may be a simple arrangement by which the vessel carries its own cargo grabs which can be fitted to the ship's derricks or cranes and used to discharge or perhaps even to load cargo. Some vessels have a *'gantry'* arrangement, by which a 'travelling' crane moves longitudinally the length of a bulk carrier along a gantry rail and is so able to operate over any particular hatchway.

Other bulk carriers, perhaps designed for a particular trade, may be fitted with sophisticated discharging apparatus that operates on a *conveyor belt* and/or *screw system* (e.g. Siwertell System), loading being left to shore based equipment.

Such machinery is usually tailored for a specific cargo type and trade - e.g. bulk cement and is not normally suitable for a tramp bulk carrier.

With certain bulk carrier sizes, however, ship's gear is a definite disadvantage, trades having developed around sophisticated and speedy shore equipment which needs clear, unhindered access to cargo compartments. Consequently, most panamax and almost all capesize bulk carriers are 'gearless' and close attention must be paid by their operators, charterers and brokers alike, that each vessel 'fixed' for a particular trade can physically fit beneath shore loading and/or discharging apparatus, not only when laden but, prior to commencement of loading and following discharge, in ballast condition. The dimension that determines a vessel's suitability is the distance between the waterline surrounding the vessel and the top of her hatchway coamings, frequently referred to as the vessel's *'air draft',* and not to be confused with that other *'air draft',* being the distance from the waterline to the top of the highest fixed point on a vessel (see the Great Lakes dimensional restrictions earlier in this Chapter).

1.4.5   Cargo Fittings

Unlike general cargo vessels it is unusual for bulk carriers (especially older ones) to be fitted with electric ventilation, but many have fire smothering (e.g. CO_2) facilities serving cargo holds.

Most have steel hatch-covers, opening fore and aft on the majority of handy-sized vessels, whilst the larger vessels, from panamaxes upwards, are frequently fitted with hatch-covers opening sideways when, in the open position they cover the deck between coamings and the ship's rail, supported by a steel framework to allow ship's crew and shore workers to pass underneath when moving about the vessel's decks. This enables a bigger open hatchway space than would otherwise be the case, the better to accommodate large shore-based cargo handling equipment and speedier cargo handling. This hatch cover system is known as *'side-rolling hatchcover'.*

1.4.6   Specialised Bulk Carriers

We have already examined some specialised bulk carriers, for example, those designed to transit the Great Lakes Seaway and the Panama Canal, and also those equipped with self-discharging apparatus and thus able to trade to areas where port equipment may be inadequate. We have also encountered the 'conbulker' equipped to cross the boundaries of the container and the bulk cargo markets.

There are others, however, and a brief description of some would be useful:

Loggers. Usually around 15/35,000 deadweight, these bulk carriers of particularly heavy construction are often fitted with derricks or with cranes in the region of 15/25 tonnes swl, capable of loading and sustaining heavy logs in addition to other, conventional bulk cargoes.

Logs may also be loaded on deck, secured by *'stanchions'* alongside *'bulwarks'* (rails or steel sheeting running alongside the edges of the weatherdeck), and by *heavy chains and securing tackle.* Stanchions may be of the *'permanent'* steel variety, or *'collapsible'* along bulwarks adjacent to cargo hatches so they can be lowered to lie horizontally on the deck and allow clear unhindered access between shore and hatchways, essential when cargo equipment is

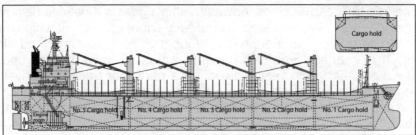

used for loading or discharging. Where a logger is not fitted with steel stanchions, however, temporary wooden stanchions are sometimes used by shaving down suitable logs from the cargo, to enable them to fit into *stanchion sockets* in the edge of the weatherdeck adjacent to the bulwarks.

Ace Century 32,786-dwt Log/Bulk Carrier

Principal Particulars

Length (o.a.)	178.03 m
Length (b.p.)	170.00 m
Breadth (mid.)	28.00 m
Depth (mid.)	15.00 m
Draft (mid.)	10.55 m
Gross tonnage	21,185
Deadweight	35,117 T
Main engine	6UEC52LA
MCR	7,080 kW (9,627 PS) × 133 min^{-1}
NOR	6,018 kW (8,183 PS) × 126 min^{-1}
Speed (max. trial)	16.45 knots
(service)	14.5 knots
Complement	25
Classification	NK
Handling gear	Electro-hydraulic deck crane 30 t × 24 mR × 3 sets
	30/20 t × 24/25 mR × 1 set
Loading capacity (grain)	45,427 m^3
(bale)	43,591 m^3
Builder	Shin Kurushima Dockyard Co., Ltd.

The substantial construction of loggers is also of use when carrying heavy cargoes such as ores, cement or cement clinker.

Lumber Carriers. The aim of the designer of a lumber (or timber) carrier is to create sufficient space in holds and on deck and hatch covers for the maximum amount of this high stowing cargo to be carried. Once again stanchions are essential and the same remarks above under 'loggers' applies to 'lumber carriers'. With the latter vessels, however, the chains and tackle are of a lighter construction so as not to damage the cargo. Shifting of lumber cargoes at sea is a risk that all those engaged on this trade dread, and it is essential that no short cuts are taken when stowing and securing the cargo, which must always be to the Master's absolute satisfaction. Timber carriers have clear, unobstructed and squarish holds and wide/long hatchways, sometimes fitted with longitudinal and/or transverse supports as a constructional safety feature.

Because of the nature of this commodity, when a full cargo of lumber is carried, special regulations regarding loadlines are applied, which means that an alternative *'lumber loadline'* can be used, permitting deeper loading. This is on the basis that with a full and secure lumber deck cargo, vessel buoyancy and inherent safety has increased, and the effective *'freeboard'* (the distance from the waterline to a prominent position on the vessel, usually the top of the weatherdeck, which governs the position of a vessel's loadline) can in fact be adjusted to increase cargo intake of this particular commodity.

Woodchip Carriers. These vessels can be as large as 40/50,000 tonnes deadweight and are specially designed for the carriage of high stowing woodchip products destined for use in pulp mills. They are usually of light construction and unsuitable for the carriage of heavy, dense cargoes such as ores. Nevertheless, where they can be employed on a regular run, e.g. from the West Coast of the United States and Canada to the Far East, they have in the past been adapted for the profitable carriage of motor cars on the otherwise valueless ballast leg (return journey), thus obtaining freight earning ability on both passages.

Ore Carriers. At the other extreme from woodchip carriers, ore carriers have small, compact cargo spaces because the nature of their trade is concerned with heavy dense mineral commodities. In response to a demand by ore terminal operators, ore carriers have grew rapidly from the 1970s onwards. Today there are only a very few specialised ore carriers

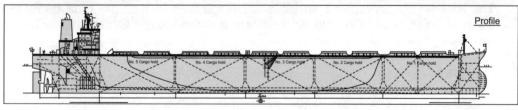

under 100,000 dwt, and most are between 200,000 and 300,000 dwt. The increase in size has given rise to a new descriptive term, 'VLOC', or very large ore carrier. There is no set size where this term begins to apply. Some operators describe 230,000 dwt vessels as VLOCs but for others 300,000 dwt is the threshold. The present order book for new ore carriers includes a considerable number of vessels of 400,000 dwt.

An Ore Carrier

Principal Particulars

Length (o.a.)..316.94 m
Length (b.p.)..307.00 m
Breadth (mid.) ....55.00 m
Depth (mid.) ....24.30 m
Draft (mid.) ....18,100 m
Gross tonnage 118,249
Deadweight...233,694 MT
Main engine...B&W 6S80MC-C
MCR ....23,280 kW × 76.0 rpm
NOR ....19,790 kW × 72.0 rpm
Speed (max. trial) ....17.596 knots
        (service) ....15.4 knots
Complement 30
Classification...NK
Loading capacity (grain) .... 157,390.1 m³
Builder... Imabari Shipbuilding Co., Ltd.

Bulk Cement Carriers. There are a few sophisticated mechanical and pneumatic bulk cement carriers, and even those that act as 'mother' or 'factory ships', off-loading from other vessels and storing or even bagging bulk cement aboard. Often these vessels are converted from suitably dimensioned bulk carriers, and serve a particular trade route or are stationed in a particular area, the better to meet the cement demands of a nearby market. Otherwise, for odd cargoes, ordinary bulk carriers can be readily adapted for the carriage of bulk cement or cement clinker (part manufactured cement without the setting agent, gypsum), by the cutting of small holes in hatch covers to facilitate loading and/or discharge without creating unacceptable dust pollution, these holes being made good to Classification Society satisfaction before the vessel leaves port. This operation is usually covered by an appropriate Charter Party clause, under the terms of which Charterers usually reimburse the Shipowner for the cost of the hole-cutting and rewelding operation, with time so used to count as laytime, if employment on a voyage basis is involved.

1.5 CONTAINER SHIPS

These are ships specially designed for the carriage of containers and are the modern equivalent of the cargo liner of the immediate post war years. These large vessels tend to be employed on scheduled voyages on fixed routes, travelling at high speeds of around 25 knots or more. They normally serve sophisticated container terminals where extensive shore equipment is available and, for this reason, most of them are gearless. Their turn-round time in port is very short, perhaps only a matter of hours rather than days.

Victoria Bridge 3,484-TEU Container Ship

The 3,484-TEU container ship *Victoria Bridge* was built at the Marugame Headquarters of Imabari Shipbuilding Co., Ltd. and delivered to the Owner Cypress Maritime (Panama), S.A. on July 6, 1998.

Features

1. The vessel has eight container holds with 3-row hatches in transverse, seven of the

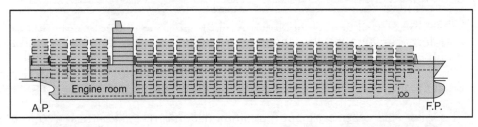

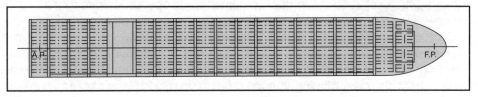

holds are arranged in front of the engine rooom and one back.

2. Containers can be stowed in eight tiers and ten rows in the holds and five tiers and thirteen rows on the hatch covers.

3. 45' containers can be loaded on No. 8 hatch covers and above the aft mooring deck.

4. The vessel can carry a total of 300-FEU refrigerated containers in the holds and on hatch covers.

A Typical Container Ship

Principal Particulars

Length (o.a.)..299.90 m
Length (b.p.)..283.80 m
Breadth (mid.) ....40.00 m
Depth (mid.) ....23.90 m
Draft (mid.) ....14.00 m
Gross tonnage 75,519
Deadweight .... 81,171 T
Main engine ....DU-Sulzer 12RTA96C diesel x 1
MCR .... 61,350kW × 97.7rpm
NOR .... 52,150kW × 92.5rpm
Speed (service)..25.0 knots
Complement ....36 persons
Classification ....Nippon Kaiji Kyokai
Loading capacity (container) 6,492TEUs

Builder ....IHI Marine United Inc.

By their nature container ships are almost exclusively chartered by operators in the liner trades, either enhancing their own fleet or very frequently today by liner companies operating services with entirely time chartered tonnage. The greater part of the daily market activity is in the short sea and middle distance trades, the largest sizes being fixed almost exclusively on longer term time charter with the major liner companies.

Containers are stowed below the weatherdeck in a secure, cellular steel framework ('cell guides'), in heights of eight to ten tiers, with up to three to four tiers on deck. Just as for conventional cargo liners, however, the old stability rule of 'heavy weights at the bottom, light on top', holds good for container ships.

These modern vessels have large hatchway openings of the same width and length as the holds they serve, and the hatch covers are frequently steel slabs ('pontoon hatches') lifted on and off by shore gear.

Usually there is longitudinal framing along the main hold within a double hull; this double 'skin' being required to compensate for the loss of vessel strength owing to large hold areas and open hatchways.

Whilst the size of almost all other merchant ships is normally described in tons (or the metric counterpart - tonnes), the capacity of container ships is usually expressed in terms of the number of containers it is designed to carry. As the standard container sizes are traditionally either 20 feet or 40 feet long, you will encounter the expression TEU meaning 'twenty-foot equivalent units'. Vessel sizes can range from about one hundred TEU to over 8,000.

The latter size vessels exceed Panamax dimensions and are referred to as 'post panamax'. At the beginning of 2008 the largest container ships operating were those of the Emma Maersk class owned by AP Moller-Maersk. The Owner describes the ships as having a capacity of 11,000TEU which is probably correct based on using the conventional 14 tonnes per TEU method but the space available on the vessel would suggest a teu capacity of between 13,500 and 15,000 TEU. Since the launch of the Emma Maersk orders have been placed for even larger vessels and the Korean builder STX has announced a basic design for a 22,000 TEU ship.

A consequence of the increase in size of container ships beyond 10,000 TEU is that the accommodation and superstructure has had to move forward on the ship to allow navigators to see a reasonable distance in front of the ship. The engine room has remained in the aft position to avoid the need for long propeller shafts. The space under the accommodation in such ships cannot be used for cargo (impossible to access) and in most is used for bunker tanks.

In February 2011 AP Moller Maersk announced plans for a series of between 10 and 30 vessels of a new type of 18,000 TEU container carrier called the 'Triple E' type. These ships are wider and less streamlined than traditional container ships and are designed to run at a lower speed of 18.5knots instead of the more usual 24-27 knots for most other container ship designs. The owner has said that consideration is being given to a twin-engine, twin-propeller propulsion system. When announcing the new ship type, the owner referred to the Emma Maersk class as having a 15,500TEU capacity confirming what most in the industry had already suspected.

Table 1 Characteristics of Typical Container Ships

	Short Sea and Feeder	Middle Sea	Medium Deep Sea	Large Deep Sea (Panamax)	Large Deep Sea (Post Panamax)
TEU	500	1,100	2,000	4,000	8,000
loa	120 m	180 m	200 m	290 m	300 m+
beam	20 m	24 m	28 m	32 m	40 m+
draft	7 m	10 m	11 m	13 m	14 m+
deadweight	9,000 mt	20,000 mt	35,000 mt	50,000 mt	65,000 mt
speed	14 kts	18 kts	22 kts	25 kts	25 kts

TEU is used to provide an approximate indication of the vessel's container carrying capacity, each container space being called a slot. However, when trading a vessel will carry a mixture of 20 foot and 40 foot containers, some of the stowage positions may only be suitable for the smaller size, so that a more specific description of the vessel will indicate the number of 20 foot slots available (TEU) as well as the number of 40 foot slots (FEU); because the vessels deadweight cargo capacity is also relevant the maximum average weight of the containers will also be stated.

e.g. 748 TEU overall (350 FEU + 48 TEU at 11.6 tonnes)

The smaller container vessels are used as *'feeder'* ships, feeding the hinterland around major container terminals with loaded containers inbound from abroad, before feeding containers for export back to the container terminal on the return journey. Because these vessels serve less sophisticated container ports they may well be geared, probably with gantry cranes, enabling them to load and to discharge containers with their own shipboard equipment.

Relevant container terms are:

Fully Cellular: A containership fully fitted with cell guides.

Fully Fitted: A containership fully fitted with cargo securing equipment, e.g. twist-locks, lashings, etc. and with strengthened decks.

Hatchless: Some of the latest designs extend the cell guides above the weather deck, so that there are no hatch covers.

Shiptainer: A ship-borne gantry crane.

Over the past few years 45 foot boxes have become popular in certain trades, particularly short sea movements within Europe. These longer boxes are better suited to the maximum sized trailers allowed on roads. Many new types of container ships are being designed to accommodate these boxes and although it may take many years before the 20 and 40 feet boxes become outmoded, there are those who believe that their demise is inevitable.

Certainly the 45-foot box does make economic sense in terms of maximum utilisation of lorry capacity, but as most new container ships have been built around the standard TEU configuration the majority of operators are clearly confident that any major change is at least 20 years away.

1.6 RO-RO VESSELS

The RO/RO (Roll-on/roll-off) vessel can vary from a very simple river ferry design used only in inland waters to some of the most sophisticated vessels afloat today including passenger ferries with leisure facilities approaching those of cruise vessels. For areas of the world possessing only limited port facilities, the RO/RO ship with its 'self-sustaining' ability to load and discharge provides an ideal mode of transport.

Ohyuh Maru 6,490-dwt Ro/Ro Ship

The 6,490-dwt roll-on and roll-off type cargo ship *Ohyuh Maru* was built at Marugame Headquarters of Imabari Shipbuilding Co., Ltd. and delivered to the Owner, Maritime Credit Corporation and Seno Kisen Co., Ltd. and Shikoku Kalhatsu Ferry Co., Ltd. on February 15, 2000.

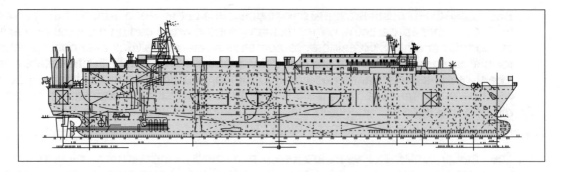

Features

1. This vessel was designed as a high-speed Ro/Ro cargo ship for carrying various kinds of cargoes, trailer chassis, trucks, cars and containers.

2. She has four (4) decks and each vehicle is loaded on "C" deck by passing the rampway located at bow and stern. The vehicles run between "B" – "D" deck on the slope way and are lifted up and down between "C" – "E" deck by a cargo filter.

3. She has a pair of lin stabilizer and each with bow and stern thruster, which are to ensure safe voyage and good manoeuvrability in harbour.

A Roll-on/roll-off Vessel

Principal Particulars

Length (o.a.)	161.84 m
Length (b.p.)	150.00 m
Breadth (mid.)	26.60 m
Depth (mid.)	16.05 m (Registered Depth)
Draft (mid.)	6,800 m
Gross tonnage	912,560
Deadweight	6,500 MT
Main engine	S.E.M.T. 12PC4-2B
MCR	15,900 kW × 428 rpm
NOR	13,515 kW × 405 rpm
Speed (max.trial)	24,003 knots
(service)	abt. 21.00 knots
Complement	22
Classification	NK
Handling gear	
Stern Ramp:	27.2 m (L) × 6 m (B) × 50 t SWL × 1 set
Forward Ramp:	23.0 m (L) × 7 m (B) × 50 t SWL × 1 set
Loading capacity Passenger Cars	200 cars
Chassis (12 m)	151 units
Roll Paper	2,236 units
Builder	Imabari Shipbuilding Co., Ltd.

A typical deepsea RO/RO vessel is usually equipped with its own fork-lift trucks and tractors and, perhaps a crane or two, and is capable of handling from alongside a whole range of wheeled vehicles as well as palletised and containerised goods. Access to the interior of RO/RO vessels is usually via a stern 'ramp' which, in modern ships is capable of sustaining very heavy loads of up to several hundred tonnes, and sometimes of being *slewed'* around and raised or lowered to suit whatever berth access may be available.

Once inside a RO/RO vessel, ramps or lifts lead up or down to various deck levels where a whole variety of goods may be stowed, decks and tank tops being strengthened to take heavy loadings. Every commodity that lends itself to transportation via a RO/RO or a LO/LO ('Lift-On/Lift-Off') system may be carried on this type of vessel, which can sustain all kinds and most sizes of rolling stock and merchandise that can be placed on wheels.

Because RO/RO vessels form an extension to the natural road transportation environment for wheeled vehicles, particularly for articulated lorries which can unhitch and deposit their trailer on board, certain RO/RO ships are sometimes referred to as *'trailer-carriers'*, their capacity for the carriage of these trailers being described in terms of length of available *'lane metres'.* The width of a 'lane' varies according to the construction of an individual ship, though these must be a minimum of just over 2.5 metres (8 feet), to suit standard vehicle and container dimensions. To allow adequate space for lashing and securing cargo, however, the realistic minimum of a lane should be 3 metres (10 feet).

The 'family' of RO/RO vessels can be expanded to include ferries which frequently carry a mixture of passengers as well as wheeled cargo, and vessels such as 'railway' or 'train-ferries', complete with rail track on decks to accommodate railway carriages and trucks, equipped with a sophisticated and sensitive ballasting system to enable the ships' rail tracks to be safely and securely connected to the shore rail system.

Another variety of RO/RO is the Car Carrier, *'Pure Car Carriers'* (or *'PCC'S'* as they are usually known) being specially designed with fixed decks and sophisticated ventilation system for the carriage of motor cars and nothing else. A development from this basic design is the *'Pure Car and Truck Carrier'*, the *'PCTC,* in which the clearances of some decks can be adjusted to accommodate larger vehicles as well as cars. All lend themselves to highly efficient cargo handling, during which an entire cargo of perhaps 6,000-7,000 motor cars can be driven on or off in a matter of hours.

In chartering terms this is another specialised market, the main players being the liner and ferry operators and the automotive industries.

Meridian Ace 5,059-unit Type Pure Car and Truck Carrier

This 5,059-unit type pure car and truck carrier *Meridian Ace* was built at the Marugame Headquarters of Imabari Shipbuilding Co., Ltd. and delivered to the owner, Meridian Shipholding S.A. on June 8, 2000.

Features

1. This vessel is a single screw diesel engine driven "Pure Car and Truck Carrier" (PCTC) with 12 car decks.

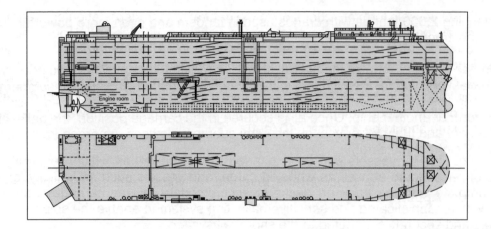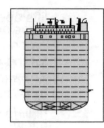

2. She has a big capacity with a stern ramp of S.W.L. 150 tons and two center ramps of S.W.L. 30 tons at both sides near midship. She has also five liftable decks, especially, the two decks over the free board deck are continuous two tiers liftable type for carrying taller or larger vehicles.

3. She has five movable slope ways connecting deck to deck in the hold and the slope way can be moved to suitable positions depending on the kind of cargoes or on the order of loading. In addition, many large cargoes can be loaded, because fixed slope ways are kept as few as possible.

A Type Pure Car and Truck Carrier

Principal Particulars

Length (o.a.)..199.99 m
Length (b.p.)..192.00 m
Breadth (mid.) ....32.26 m
Depth (mid.) ....34.52 m
Draft (mid.) ....9.70 m
Gross tonnage 60,175
Deadweight... 20.144 MT
Main engine .... Mitsubishi UE 7UEC60LS II (P/U)
MCR..14,315 kW $\times$ 105.0 min^{-1}
NOR..12,170 kW $\times$ 99.5 min^{-3}
Speed (service)...20.65 knots
Complement 30
Classification..NK
Handling gear.. F.O. HOSE: 8.8 kN $\times$ 11 m/min. $\times$ 2
.... SUEZ B., PROV. & E/P: 39.2 kN $\times$ 11 m/min. $\times$ 2
Loading capacity (car/vehicle) ....6,354 (RT43 base)
Builder...Mitsubishi Heavy Industries, Ltd.

1.7 SPECIALISED SHIPS

1.7.1 Heavy-Lift Ships

We have already read of general cargo vessels fitted with heavy-lift derricks. But there are certain articles moved by sea that are far too heavy for even heavy-lift derricks capable of sustaining weights of up to 450 tonnes. To meet this demand, there are specialised heavy-lift ships.

There are basically two types of heavy-lift vessel, the smaller capacity unit reliant on lifting cargo on and off with its own gear, and capable of sustaining lifts of around 600 tonnes unit weight. These ships are generally of a conventional appearance and from outside look very much like a multi-purpose ship. Some of the more specialist vessels can now make single lifts approaching 2,000 tonnes with cranes used in tandem and even more powerful vessels are under construction.

The far larger, second type of heavy lift ship is the *'semi-submersible',* equipped with a powerful ballasting system by which tanks are flooded as required, sufficient to submerge the vessel's cargo area, which can be located beneath the object to be transported - e.g. an oil drilling platform or another ship. Once all is secured in the carriage position, the ballast tanks are pumped dry and the mother vessel, the semi-submersible itself, emerges from the water bearing the weight of the cargo.

To discharge the cargo, the procedure is reversed. A typical semi-submersible vessel is illustrated under **Appendix 4**.

1.7.2 Barge Carrying Vessels

Cousins of heavy-lift vessels are barge carrying ships, of which there are several designs. In fact barges can be readily compared with containers, in that they are self-contained units capable of being loaded and discharged at the places of origin and destination of their cargoes, being transported between the two by mother conveyances. However, the capacity of a barge is much greater than that of containers and these larger, floating units lend themselves to the carriage of large unit commodities.

The barge units are 'dumb' (unable to self-propel) but are designed for ease of transport under one of several carrying systems.

LASH ('Lighter Aboard Ship') and SeeBee both employ a system by which lighters are lifted on and off mother vessels, being collected and distributed along waterways by towing craft. BACO (Barge Aboard Catamaran) uses a system of floating barges into the mother ship through large bow doors. The USSR had a particularly extensive LASH and SeeBee system for strategic purposes, with mother ships capable of carrying individual barges of over 1,000 tonnes deadweight. Frequently, a combination of barges and containers can be handled. Despite the obvious attractions of this type of ship for certain trades it has to be said that it has failed to capture popular imagination and is likely to remain an interesting but very niche market.

1.7.3 Livestock Carriers

Livestock carriers can be divided into two categories, those designed to transport sheep, and those for larger animals such as cattle. The obvious design difference is the extra deck height required for the larger animals, but both require fodder storage, extensive water supply, excellent ventilation, suitable methods of animal waste disposal, non-slip decks, carefully designed ramps, and accommodation for those tending the animals.

Most livestock carriers have been converted from existing vessels, notably sheep carriers from oil tankers, but occasionally specialised ships are constructed for the larger animals. Sheep carriers tend to be far larger than cattle carriers, as can be seen from **Appendix 5**.

1.7.4 Refrigerated Vessels

These vessels are specifically designed and built to transport the many goods (meats, fruits, fish and vegetables, for example) which would rapidly deteriorate in ordinary hold conditions. Modern 'reefers' are built with holds and decks providing good access for standard sized pallets and for fork-lift trucks, and are usually fitted with 'side-ports', openings in hull sides permitting immediate access to cargo decks, the floors of which line up with quaysides.

The layout of these vessels also makes them suitable for the carriage of motor cars which fit beneath the restricted deck-heights, as well as for other non-refrigerated and palletised cargo, although many of these vessels trade exclusively in the refrigerated markets on long-term contract employment. Certain reefer trades are losing out to the containership market with the advent of refrigerated containers, but there remains a substantial and lucrative reefer market for those with specialist knowledge and vessels.

Asian Olive 390,000-cft Refrigerated Cargo Ship

The 390,000-cft refrigerated carrier *Asian Olive,* built at Setoda Works of Naikai Zosen Corporation, was delivered to Golden Helm Shipping Co., S.A. on September 30, 1999.

Features

1. The vessel is a flushdecker with a forecastle. The engine room and bridge are arranged aft. This 390,000-cft refrigerated carrier is provided with a bulbous bow and a stern bulb, a fixed pitch propeller and a mariner rudder.

2. The refrigerated cargo space is divided into a total of 15 compartments, with the No. 1 hold being divided into three tiers and the Nos. 2 through 4 holds into four. The temperature in

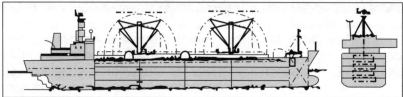

the holds can be controlled within a range of –25°C to +15°C. There is a special device to extend the expiration date of stored food by sealing nitrogen gas in the refrigerated holds during transit.

3. Besides bananas, other fruits and refrigerated items (meats) for which the vessel is mainly intended, a total of 26 40-foot containers can be stowed on the upper deck and hatch covers. Arrangements are also made to accommodate passenger cars on each deck in the holds.

4. Each hold has a hatch with a folding type cover at deck level, and four sets of 5-t burton-system derricks are arranged on the upper deck

A Refrigerated Cargo Ship

Principal Particulars

Length (o.a.)..136.42 m
Length (b.p.)..125.00 m
Breadth (mid.) ....20.00 m
Depth (mid.) ....12.80 m
Draft (mid.)..8.20 m
Gross tonnage 7,355
Deadweight.. 8,753 MT
Main engine ....Alaska-Mitsubishi 6UEC52LA
MCR..9,600 PS × 133 rpm

NOR ....8,640 PS × 128 rpm
Speed (max.trial)..21,623 knots
    (service) ....18.2 knots
Classification..NK
Loading capacity (bale) ....400,602 cft

1.7.5 Combination Carriers

There are basically two types of *'combination carrier'* capable of transferring successfully from the distinctive dry-bulk market to what might be termed the 'wet-bulk trades'. Both tend to be large ships in excess of 60,000 tonnes deadweight, frequently more than 100,000 tonnes deadweight.

The most common (and usually the smaller) type is the 'OBO' ('Ore/Bulk Oiler') which unlike the impression given by its name, has sufficient cubic cargo carrying capacity to enable it to carry economically not only heavy, dense ore, but also lighter stowing commodities such as coal and even grains. The distinctive feature of an OBO is that the same cargo compartment that has been used to carry a dry-bulk commodity can be discharged and then prepared for the carriage of a cargo of crude oil. Those Charterers engaged in the dry and wet trades may prefer in ideal circumstances to employ specialised bulk carriers or tankers, as the case may be, but frequently Owners of an OBO have an in-built freighting advantage over their specialised rivals, in that ballast runs can be reduced because of their vessel's ability to indulge in two markets instead of just one.

Thus, even though the upkeep of these vessels is frequently higher than for a simpler ship specialising in just one market sector, encouraging profits can be achieved from such ships given efficient marketing and voyage planning.

Appendix 6 shows a section through an OBO as well as the midship section of its rival in this specialised market - the *'O/O' ('Ore/Oiler')*. Here the reference to ore is accurate, Ore/ Oilers having separate small cargo compartments specifically designed for the carriage of heavy ores, the crude oil part of their cargo commitments being carried separately in oil tanks. Ore/Oilers can carry dry-bulk commodities other than ores, but they would fill their cargo spaces very quickly and be unable to use their full deadweight. Not only that, but because they are not constructed with self-trimming facilities, extra time and expense would be needed to 'trim' the cargo surface level. Consequently, it is very unusual for Ore/ Oilers to be engaged in the carriage of other than iron ore or crude oil, and they tend to be in excess of 100,000 tonnes deadweight, this size of cargo being particularly attractive to those engaged in the steel making industry. (**NB.** These diagrams do not show the now mandatory outer hull.)

It should not be overlooked that once it was fairly commonplace for oil tankers which would usually be engaged in the transportation of crude oil occasionally to carry cargoes of grain when the market so warranted the expense and time in cleaning tanks. In the late 1980's a United States food aid cargo was carried in an American-flag VLCC (Very Large Crude Carrier) in excess of 250,000 tonnes deadweight, carrying a large grain cargo from the United States West Coast to Pakistan. The cargo was loaded through spouts and discharged by vacuvators (portable suction machines).

1.8   SHORT SEA VESSELS

Short sea vessels are not just smaller versions of deep-sea types, they have modifications peculiar to their trades. The modern dry cargo coaster needs flexibility of intake of cargoes in order to survive in a very competitive business. Because of this they are usually constructed with just one hold served by a large 'open hatch' steel hatch cover, their hold *'box shaped'* (see **Appendix 7**) the better to obtain good intake and safe stowage of containers and palletised cargo.

Modern short sea vessels are built with steel floors to their cargo compartments, facilitating discharge by grab, although older vessels may well have a wooden, concrete or tarmacadam sheathing as protection to the tank tops.

Few older vessels had self-trimming facilities so that free-flowing bulk cargoes, which are liable to shift dangerously at sea, were secured by a combination of bagging and strapping part of the cargo at the top of the stow. For most grains this amounts to around 10% of the cargo, the 90% loaded underneath the bags and strapping being in bulk. With some particularly free-flowing grains, however, (e.g. rape seed), perhaps 20% of the cargo will require to be bagged.

By contrast the modern box shaped single decker in the short sea and middle distance grain traders is usually equipped with at least two moveable bulkheads enabling the vessel to arrange for a completely full compartment comprising 80 to 90% of the ship's capacity and a small compartment where the balance can be slack without the need for bagging and strapping.

Latest European designs allow for river and canal trading by creating a low profile' vessel, by which the superstructure located at the after end of the hull can be hydraulically lowered to enable the ship to pass beneath bridges and other overhead obstructions, with any masts being lowered.

1.9   SELF-ASSESSMENT AND TEST QUESTIONS

Attempt the following and check your answers from the text and/or appendices.

1.   Define and explain the terms:

   1) SWL

   2) Flush tweendeckers

   3) Pad eyes

   4) Centre-line bulkhead

   5) Bilges

   6) Samson post

   7) Union purchase

   8) Double-rigged

   9) Twin hatches

   10) Shaft tunnel

2.   Your Principals are seeking to charter a tweendecker for the carriage of bagged cargo, but none of the candidate vessels are cargo batten fitted. Inform them of alternatives to cargo battens and advise about who, (in your opinion), should 1) supply and 2) fit these alternatives.

3.   Define and explain the terms:

   1) Gearless

   2) Top-side tanks

   3) Hoppered holds

   4) Gantry cranes

   5) Air draft

   6) Stanchions

   7) Side-rolling

8) Self-trimming

9) Capesize

10) Conbulker

4. What ideal SWL capacity and type of gear should be fitted on a vessel to be used extensively in the heavy logs trade, and what deck equipment is essential?

5. Define and explain the following terms:

1) Cell guides

2) Pontoon hatches

3) Slewing ramp

4) PCTC

5) Semi-submersible

6) LASH

7) Side ports

8) Vacuvators

9) Bagging and strapping

10) Low profile

6. As an exporter, you have a regular shipment of around 1,000 tonnes monthly of harmless chemical resin in jumbo bags from the United States East Coast to Italy.

   What are the alternative shipment methods open to you?

7. Sketch a typical Panamax bulk carrier. What physical differences are there between this type of ship, a Handymax and a Capsize vessel?

Having completed Chapter One attempt the following question and submit your essay to your Tutor.

List the standard items which you consider should be included in a period time charter party clause covering the description of the deep-sea multi-purpose vessel "Seagull".

For each item on your list, and referring where necessary to the material in this Chapter, explain fully the reasons for its inclusion in your list.

Chapter 2

DRY CARGO SHIP TONNAGES, LOADLINES, DIMENSIONS AND CARGOES

2.1 INTRODUCTION

Chapter One introduced the reader to various terms and expressions that may be expected to encounter in the dry cargo shipping market.

There are other aspects, however, not necessarily peculiar to just dry cargo ships, of which any practitioner must have a basic understanding.

2.1.1 Tonnages and Loadlines

When describing a ship it is quite common to hear people state that she is 'of so many tons', and leave it at that. In fact, in shipping, the word 'ton' has many different meanings and ship tonnage can be based on either *'weight'* or on *'volume'.*

2.1.2 Ship Tonnage Based on Weight

The actual weight of the ship plus the weight of all it is carrying is termed its *'load displacement tonnage'* or, simply *'displacement tonnage'.* It is used to describe the size of certain ship types not built for cargo carrying (e.g. icebreakers or naval vessels) but has little practical value in the dry cargo market.

The weight of an empty ship, its *'light displacement tonnage'* or *'ldt'* for short, is equally of little value to dry cargo chartering personnel, although it is of particular interest to those engaged in the sale and purchase of ships, for the ship demolition prices are based on this tonnage, which is used to establish a ship's steel weight.

The two tonnage descriptions of particular value to the dry cargo market sector are a ship's *'deadweight'* *('dwt')*, (referred to several times in Chapter One) which not only happens to be the difference between a ship's loaded and light displacement tonnages but, more importantly, represents the total weight a ship can carry. This total weight will include, of course, not only cargo, but bunkers, fresh water, stores, spare parts, etc. Those engaged in chartering activities sometimes describe this tonnage as *'dwat'*, short for *'deadweight all told'*, to distinguish it from *'dwcc'*, short for *'deadweight cargo capacity'*, which is found after deducting the amalgamated weights of bunkers, freshwater, stores, spare parts, etc. from the vessel's 'deadweight all told', dwcc therefore represents the quantity of cargo a vessel should be able to load.

It is usual to base references to deadweight on what can be carried when loaded to *'summer marks'*, a vessel's *'summer deadweight'* (occasionally expressed as *'summer freeboard'*) all of which expressions can be found under the heading of *'Loadlines'*. It is important to understand that when a dwcc is quoted this is usually also based on summer marks and a full quantity of bunkers etc. In practice the dwcc is infinitely variable depending on the weight of bunkers and spares and fresh water onboard. Consideration also has to be given to any waste oil and water the ship is carrying since in most parts of the world these can no longer be dumped at sea with impunity.

Loadlines may be referred to as *'Plimsoll marks'* or *'Plimsoll Lines'*, after the British politician Samuel Plimsoll who, in the late nineteenth century campaigned against Shipowners who loaded their ships to a depth which endangered seamen's lives. Eventually, in 1890, a system of calculating and marking a safe *'freeboard'* (the distance from the water line to the weatherdeck) was devised and adopted in the United Kingdom, although it was not until 1930 that this finally became international law.

A drawing of the actual 'marks' is shown below and it will be seen that there are, in fact, six 'load lines'. This is because account is taken of the world's geography and weather conditions in assessing the hazards of any particular voyage, as well as whether a ship is transiting a salt or, technically safer, fresh water area. The initials on the loadlines represent:

TF-Tropical Fresh
F-Fresh
T-Tropical
S-Summer
W-Winter
WNA-Winter North Atlantic

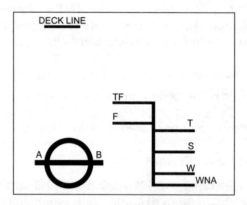

The actual loadline mark (the disc with a line through it) lines up with the summer load line referred to earlier. On this mark you will see the letters 'A' and 'B'. These relate to the Classification Society which surveyed the ship to determine the positioning of her marks and thereafter arranged for them to be 'cut-in' and painted on the side of the hull on behalf of the nation in which a ship is registered. In this case the 'AB' stands for 'American Bureau', but there are many Classification Societies in the world and, from these, common letters that might be seen could be LR (for Lloyd's Register), BV (Bureau Veritas), NV (Det Norske Veritas), GL (Germanischer Lloyd), and so on.

Loadline Certificates are issued based on the surveyor's calculations which must follow the rules laid down in the Loadline Convention and without such a document a ship cannot trade legitimately. Most Shipowners prefer the marks to allow the ship to load as deep as possible but there are occasions when an Owner will opt for a "surplus freeboard" and put the mark slightly lower down on the hull. This might be because the ship will trade to ports where charges are based on summer loadline draughts but the type of cargo envisaged will mean that the ship will never load that deep. Reducing the draught thereby reduces the port costs to be incurred.

(Lumber carriers referred to in Chapter One, are granted a second set of loadlines when carrying a deck load of lumber, 'lumber loadlines', and can sail with reduced freeboard when so laden).

By international agreement, the oceans and waterways of the world are divided into 'loadline zones', either permanent summer, winter or tropical, or seasonal summer, winter or tropical, depending upon the prevailing weather conditions likely to be experienced at different times of the year. These zones are shown on a special Loadline Chart (published in the United Kingdom, for example, by the Hydrographic Office).

A ship passing through a summer loadline zone can load down to but no further than the top of the summer loadline. The same arrangements apply for trading in winter or in tropical zones, but extra allowance can be made when trading in what are assumed to be safer freshwater conditions. Ships with an overall length of 100 metres or less, are further restricted when trading in the North Atlantic Ocean in winter.

Great care must be taken when planning a voyage to think ahead and to avoid transitting a loadline zone when too deeply laden to be able to comply with these international regulations.

2.1.3 Ship Tonnage Based on Volume

IMO International Tonnage Convention: In 1982 a new international system of measurement for ships came into force, under an IMO (The International Maritime Organization, part of the United Nations) resolution. This applied immediately to all newbuildings, and from 1994 all existing vessels had to conform to its provisions.

The resolution defines how a ship's internal volume should be measured in accordance with standard international rules, resulting in *'gross tonnage' (GT)* and *'nett tonnage' (NT)*. GT is roughly the volume of all enclosed spaces, and NT is calculated after certain deductions for non-revenue earning spaces (e.g. allowances for the bridge, engine room, crew accommodation, etc) have been taken from the gross figure.

As a result, GT is a measure of how large in volume a ship really is, and most safety regulations are therefore based on this figure.

NT is more a measure of a ship's cargo spaces, and hence her earning capacity. Harbour and canal dues and similar expenses are usually assessed against one or other of the tonnage figures.

Registered Tonnage: These (also known as 'national tonnages') applied to vessels built before 1982 and remained in use until 1994 when replaced by the new ITC system. This system also referred to gross and nett tonnages commonly abbreviated to GRT and NRT Do be aware that many people still confuse these two measurements with GT and NT and it is important to clarify exactly which figure is being referred to.

Canal Tonnage: Both the Suez and Panama Canal Authorities have their own rules for the measurement of gross and nett tonnage, upon which their fees for canal transits are based. There has been talk of these authorities adopting the IMO tonnage but so far no definite decision has been taken.

Cubic Capacity: As we have already considered in Chapter One, when calculating cargo intake, not only does a voyage estimator or ship's Officer have to consider deadweight and loadline zones, as well as requirements for bunkers, etc. it is necessary to calculate how much cargo the hold spaces will accommodate.

To do this, two measurements will be provided by shipbuilders for dry cargo vessels. These are the *grain* and *bale capacities* which are used for measuring cargo space availability for bulk or for general (non bulk) cargo. The measurements can be expressed in either *cubic feet* or in *cubic metres;* reference books such as ships' registers (e.g. Lloyd's Register) frequently nowadays use the metric system. However, a large proportion of dry cargo market practitioners still utilise cubic feet when describing the stowage properties of cargo, and so it is important for all involved in this aspect of the industry to know that: *1 cubic metre = 35.3158 cubic feet,* as conversion calculations from one measurement system to the other will frequently be required.

Grain Capacity is the capacity of cargo spaces measured laterally to the *outside* of frames, and vertically from the tank tops to the *top* of the under weatherdeck beams, including the area contained within a vessel's hatchway coamings. Grain capacity is therefore an indication of space available for any bulk cargo, not just for bulk grain.

Bale Capacity is the capacity of cargo spaces measured laterally to the inside of frames or of cargo battens (where fitted), and vertically from the tank tops to the underside (or bottom) of the under weatherdeck beams, but again including the area contained within a vessel's hatchway coamings. Bale capacity is therefore an indication of space available for other than a bulk commodity e.g. bagged or baled goods.

The grain capacity will usually be greater than a ship's bale capacity although the short sea vessel described in Chapter One, and built with one, box shaped smooth sided cargo hold, for example, will have one common cubic measurement, identical for grain and for bale capacity.

In trading, dry cargo ships are frequently described in different ways. RO/RO tonnage might be referred to in terms of available 'lane-metres', for example, or a containership by the number of "teu's" or "feu's" it is capable of handling. Depending upon the cargo, however, general cargo ships and bulk carriers might be described in terms of summer deadweight or grain capacity or, more probably in the case of general cargo ships, in terms of bale capacity.

Table 2.1 – Comparison of Tonnage Measurements

Tonnage	General Cargo	Bulk Carrier	Container
Nett	5,000	25,000	8,000
Gross	7,000	36,000	15,600
Deadweight	12,500	54,000	17,000
Load Displacement	18,000	72,000	23,000

2.1.4   Paragraph Ships

Many shipping regulations are based on gross or on deadweight tonnage. Shipowners therefore construct vessels to take advantage of regulations that place differing requirements on vessels above or below certain sizes, hence ships of 499 or of 1599 gross tons, for example, are popular. Such ships are known as 'paragraph ships' because they take advantage of a 'paragraph' of the regulations. The latest example of this is the *Common Structural Rules* developed by IACS and applying to bulk carriers and tankers exceeding 150m in length.

2.1.5   Plans

A merchant ship is likely to be equipped with no less than 200 plans. Usually a full set will be kept onboard, and a further set in the Owner's office. Shipbrokers will need to familiarise themselves with two plans containing much important data, since it may be necessary to obtain data from these particular plans in order to conclude fixtures and/or to prosecute voyages. These plans are known as:

a)   the *General Arrangement Plan*
   AND
b)   the *Capacity Plan* (including *Deadweight Scale*)

The former plan shows the design of the vessel, the layout of her equipment, cargo spaces, etc. and her dimensions. It should show a *profile*, a *plan* and a *midship section* (a view from forward towards the after part of the vessel, illustrating the shape of the cargo spaces - see **Appendix 3** in Chapter One). It should also state the scale to which it has been drawn, and this enables distances between parts of the vessel to be measured and calculated from the plan's data. Most ship plans are drawn on the scale of 1/200 (that is that one centimetre on the plan equates to 200 centimetres on the ship). But this is not always the case. Smaller ships will have plans drawn, perhaps, 1/150, and large, 'capesize' vessels 1/300. It is therefore essential that the scale is always checked prior to performing measurement calculations as an error at this stage can cause serious practical difficulties.

The Capacity Plan provides details of capacities of cargo compartments, bunker and water tanks, etc. The plan will include a Deadweight Scale (see alongside) which enable drafts and displacements to be calculated by relating one to another. Draft* can, therefore, be used as an indication of the weight of cargo, stores, bunkers, etc. that the ship has loaded or discharged. The draft of the ship itself can be established by checking the level of the water against the figures painted on the ship's bows and stern.

(*NB You may encounter the spelling as 'draught')

For some bulk cargoes, this is the method used to quantify or check the amount of cargo loaded. When this is the case, it is usually carried out by an independent surveyor and called a *'draft survey'.*

2.1.6   Dimensions

We have already encountered some important dimensions in this and the previous Chapter. To recap:

LOA (Length Overall): The extreme length of a ship, from fore to aft.

Beam: The width of a ship. It is important to establish the 'extreme' length and breadth of a vessel, to ensure that passages in confined waterways are possible and that it is physically feasible for a vessel to enter certain ports.

Draft: The depth of a ship in the water. (A floating ship will be deeper in freshwater than in salt. The difference is shown on the Deadweight Scale as that vessel's 'freshwater allowance'.

Air Draft: Can mean either:

i)   the distance from a vessel's surrounding waterline to the highest fixed point on the ship. (Obviously this can be substantially adjusted by specialist ships such as 'low profile' vessels – see Chapter One).

OR

ii)   the distance from a vessel's surrounding waterline to the top of her hatch coamings – an indication of whether a particular vessel can manoeuvre under shore cargo handling equipment.

In both cases these measurements can be varied by ballasting or de-ballasting various tanks, but it must not be overlooked that a dry cargo vessel's ballast tonnage capacity will almost certainly be far less than her deadweight capacity. So, a fully ballasted vessel will be higher out of the water than if she was loaded and where height restrictions are severe, calculations should be carried out on the basis of a vessel being fully ballasted, not loaded.

Other important dimensions include:

Hatchways: The length and breadth of hatchways and, for general cargo ships both weatherdeck and tweendeck hatchway sizes. It is occasionally the case, usually with bulk carriers manoeuvering beneath shore cargo handling equipment, that it is necessary to know distances from a ship's rail to the inside edge of her hatch coamings and to the far side of the hatchway, as well as the length overall from forward of the foremost hatchway to aft of the aftermost hatchway.

Tank Tops and Decks: The square floor area/dimensions of a vessel's hold bottoms and decks, also the height of holds and tweendecks. Strength in tonnes per square metre must also be known for any part of the ship where cargo will be loaded.

2.2   PROPULSION

Although a few of the larger and older vessels (e.g. ore/oilers) are equipped with steam turbines,the majority of dry cargo vessels are today powered by either slow speed or medium speed diesel engines. Particular attention is paid in modern ships to the fuel preparation equipment, thereby enabling vessels to burn low cost residual *Intermediate Fuel Oils ('IFO')* efficiently and without harm to the engines. Increasingly engine makers are modifying new engines to burn even heavier oils which are cheaper to buy.

Although a few very modern types (referred to frequently as 'eco-types', 'eco' being short for 'economical') use IFO in both their main and auxiliary engines, many vessels consume *Marine Diesel Oil for their* auxiliary equipment (e.g. generators), and all vessels carry some MDO on board for possible use when a vessel is entering or leaving port and/or whilst navigating in confined waters.

This is because the response of a main engine to a change of throttle position is very slow when burning IFO. As this could affect the safety of the ship when an instantaneous response by the main engine is required, the fuel will be switched to MDO for an almost instantaneous response. With the diesel electric ship becoming more accepted, the configuration of engine types and propulsion systems will undoubtedly change. In the case described a better way of achieving a more instantaneous response will be done by putting more engines on or off line using electric switchgear just as power stations ashore adapt to changes in electricity demand. Most modern vessels will be 'fully automated', which is to say that the main engine can be directly controlled from the navigating bridge.

When negotiating a vessel for timecharter employment, it is usual to describe the daily consumption at sea against each of a particular range of speeds at which the timecharterers may instruct the Master to operate. It is also necessary to include the vessel's port consumption when 'idle' - when the main engine is immobilised and the vessel is using auxiliary engines to provide heat, light and power but cargo gear is not being used. Port consumption 'working' allows for extra consumption needed to power a vessel's cargo equipment e.g. her cranes and it is usual to additionally describe 'working' consumption against, say, every '8 hours working' or 'per 24 hours, all gear working'.

Fuel oils are graded according to quality. Heavy fuel oil is usually described around 380 c/s (centistokes) but many modern ships are capable of burning 500-700 c/s fuels. Many Panamax and small vessels burn IFO (Intermediate Fuel Oil) 180 c/s in their main engine or even better quality, say, IFO 150 c/s. Certain operators also opt for higher quality gas oil rather than diesel oil in auxiliaries, and with smaller, short sea craft, it is common to run both main and auxiliary plant on marine diesel or gas oil.

Finally, it is frequently the case that timecharterers need to know the capacity of a vessel's bunker tanks, so they can accurately estimate maximum times between replenishment of bunkers and plan voyage strategy.

Because of the likelihood of damage to a main engine caused by burning the wrong fuel type, most charter parties will stipulate a grade in accordance with the internationally accepted standard for marine fuels ISO 8217. Some Owners may go beyond this demand and require any fuel to be tested free of contaminants. This is the result of unscrupulous bunker suppliers using marine fuels as a method of disposing of waste chemicals. In 2001 Singapore suffered a spate of incidents caused by suppliers adding dry-cleaning chemicals to fuel resulting in several cases of severe engine damage as oil seals in the engine disintegrated.

Environmental considerations have led to a major debate over the polluting effect of ship operations and in particular emissions from ships burning fuels high in sulphur. There is an internationally agreed limit laid down in MARPOL and international recognition of Emission Control Areas (ECAs) in the same regulations but despite this some nations and groups of nations (the EU for example) have introduced their own more restrictive regulations. As a result some ships will have to carry different grades of fuel oil to be able to comply with the regulations and this in turn can affect operating costs, charter rates and even charter parties.

2.3   CARGOES

The variety of commodities carried at sea is greater now than it has ever been and the list is continually increasing. The volume of the various seaborne commodities alters year by year, of course, but dry cargo goods can nevertheless be classified into the following categories:

> Grains and agricultural products
> Coals and cokes
> Ferrous ores
> Minerals
> Timber
> Metals
> Cements
> Chemicals
> Refrigerated goods
> Unitised goods
> Wheeled and heavy units
> Livestock and animal products

Those concerned with dry cargo chartering should aim to have a complete knowledge of the physical characteristics, carriage requirements and trade routes of those commodities with which they are closely involved, as well as a good, working acquaintance with other dry goods.

It is important too, to keep up-to-date with events in the real world. As countries try to make more of their natural resources some trade patterns may well change. As an example, rather than transporting coal and iron ore to Europe for steel manufacture and exporting the finished product around the world there is a valid political and economic argument for transferring steel production nearer to the sources of coal and iron ore and only transporting what steel is required for European consumption long distances.

Cargo Measurement: This is an all important area as much of the structure of commercial ship trading depends on the amount of cargo a vessel can carry, and the 'freight' a carrier will receive or a shipper pay for the transportation of that cargo.

Gradually the international shipping market has moved away from traditional methods of cargo measurement based heavily on 'imperial' or 'local' units, towards the all-embracing metric system. Thus nowadays it is more usual to encounter 'metric tonnes' rather than 'long tons' or 'short tons' to describe the weight of a bulk commodity, or measurement in 'metres' rather than in 'feet'.

The one exception to this drift towards metrication is that of 'stowage factors', which is **the amount of space occupied by a given quantity of any dry commodity** whatever its mode of carriage, whether it be 'loose' (e.g. 'in bulk') or 'contained' (e.g. in bags or on pallets). It is usual nowadays to describe the stowage factor of a commodity as 'per metric tonne' rather than as 'per long ton', but the stowage factor itself is usually described in terms of 'cubic feet per tonne' instead of 'cubic metres per tonne', mainly because it is so much easier for practitioners to remember stowage factors of particular commodities in terms of cubic feet rather than in terms of cubic metres.

Consequently, it remains essential to be able to readily and fluently convert imperial into metric units and *vice versa,* particularly so for the following:

> Long tons to metric tonnes
> Feet to metres
> Cubic feet to cubic metres
> Inches to centimetres

Some cargoes (like iron ore) stow heavily and others (like coke) stow lightly. In fact, reference to the CD 'Cargoes of Importance' will reveal that iron ore will stow around 13 cubic feet per tonne, whilst coke requires around 80 cubic feet per tonne. That means that a given space can contain around six times more tonnes of iron ore than of coke. In terms of ships, imagine you are operating a bulk carrier of 55,000 tonnes deadweight cargo capacity (dwcc), with a cubic capacity in her cargo holds of two million cubic feet. If asked to estimate approximate intake of either coke or of iron ore, you would calculate as follows:

2,000,000 ÷ 13 = 153,846 tonnes iron ore

AND

2,000,000 ÷ 80 = 25,000 tonnes coke

It should be immediately obvious that the ship is limited by her deadweight to a maximum cargo of iron ore of 55,000 tonnes, which will fill only approximately a third of available hold space, whereas all hold spaces will be full if loading coke, but only about half of the available deadweight will have been used. This is a fairly extreme example to illustrate the relationship of cargo stowage factor versus ship cubic capacity and deadweight that a dry cargo chartering person must constantly bear in mind. Nevertheless, the freight rate per tonne for 25,000 tonnes of coke must be around double that for 55,000 tonnes iron ore to provide the same approximate return to the Shipowner.

With certain ship types, the amount of bulk cargo that can be loaded will be greater or lesser than for a different ship type with an equivalent cubic capacity. For example, tweendeckers might suffer from a restricted tonnage intake compared with a self trimming bulk carrier, because the 'overhang' created by fixed tweendecks will interfere with the stowing of cargo in the lower holds, creating unusable, wasted space.

But not all cargo, of course, is carried in bulk. Much cargo is carried in 'packages' of one kind or another, from traditional bags through to modern pallets. Whereas many bulk commodities will 'flow' into the sides and corners of a ship's cargo compartments, bagged or palletised goods must be stowed and often cannot fit between hold frames and, indeed, may be intentionally kept clear of hold sides by devices such as 'cargo-battens', in order to encourage cargo ventilation. As explained earlier dry cargo ships have two cubic capacities, 'grain' (for measurement of bulk commodities), and 'bale' for 'non-bulk' goods.

Finally, it should be emphasized that while stowage reference books will provide comprehensive guidance there are several ways in which the stowage factors of some cargoes can change significantly. For example, roundwood floated down river and therefore very wet, the density of pressed bales etc. It is always worth investigating the experience of others in a trade when new cargoes/commodities or sources are being worked.

2.3.1   General Cargo

Before containerisation the conventional ('break-bulk') method of moving general cargo in ships around the world's oceans and waterways was by means of a variety of packages, in bags, bales, chests, barrels, casks, baskets, or simply by lashing goods together. Given today's widespread usage of the ubiquitous 'box', much of the skill (time and tedium) of loading general cargo vessels has been transferred to packing ('stuffing') containers at container terminals, factories and such like.

It is now rare for a general cargo vessel to be employed for the carriage of such a variety of general cargo, most of today's 'liner' trades that are not totally 'containerised' depend on 'parcels'. These will usually comprise larger lots of cargo, (parcels) that are not suitable for containerisation, and in particular cargo for infrastructure projects such as new power stations or chemical plants where much structural steel or indivisible large pieces are included. Basic steel movements of beams, billets, tinplate coils, etc often provide the regular base cargo for such parcel liner services.

However, it is still likely for a general cargo vessel to carry a full cargo of bagged goods, e.g. bagged rice or bagged fertilisers, which require knowledge of the importance of ventilation, and methods of securing, manifesting and tallying bagged cargo.

2.3.2   Bulk Cargoes

Most modern bulk carriers are described by their owners as 'self-trimmers'. However, this expression must not be taken too literally as meaning that no extra trimming of bulk cargo by shore appliances is required. Firstly, not all bulk cargo flows easily. For example, bulk scrap metal will need careful stowage and, because of handling difficulty, it is important to divide a vessel's bale cubic capacity by the stowage factor of scrap metal in order to arrive at a more realistic estimate of cargo intake quantity for this commodity.

Secondly, the expression 'self-trimming' applies normally only to lateral trimming across a ship's cargo compartments, and rarely to self-trimming in either end, fore and aft, of a cargo compartment. The expression applies also to full holds. It follows that for a commodity which only partly fills a cargo hold beneath the angled, self-trimming upper hold sides, that shore trimming might still be essential to spread the cargo across the compartment to render it safe for seaborne transportation. The expression must not be taken literally, although it is reasonable to assume that a fully laden bulk carrier described as a 'self-trimmer' should be capable of loading a cargo without shore trimming assistance.

Nevertheless, if the term 'self-trimmer' is used too freely for all commodities and without bearing in mind the full particulars of loading methods, it is possible to create an expensive dispute. As a result, some operators of bulk carriers prefer to use the term 'easy-trimmer', which it is considered conveys a more realistic appraisal of a bulk carrier's capacity when loading bulk commodities.

2.3.3   Dangerous Goods

Most Shipowners are naturally eager to exclude the carriage of dangerous goods and the 'cargo exclusions clause' can form one of the most contentious parts of a negotiation leading to a dry cargo timecharter fixture. The Shipowner will seek as many exclusions as possible, whilst the Charterer will aim to have as few restrictions on vessel employment as it is possible to negotiate.

There are, of course, specialised vessels and Shipowners willing to carry (at a premium rate!) most commodities, dangerous or not, but analysis of cargoes commonly excluded by most Shipowners will usually reveal four categories of 'dangerous' goods:

1.   Those likely to imperil a ship - e.g: explosives,

2.   Those likely to harm it in some other way - e.g: sulphur,

3.   Those of danger to a vessel's crew or stevedores - e.g: ferro-silicon,

      and

4.   Those goods liable to damage others - e.g: copra.

A 'new' commodity, toxic waste, should be added to the list of undesirables, not only of danger to those coming into contact with it, but a cargo likely to be rejected by the country of destination, thereby creating enormous problems for Shipowners forced to carry it from port to port seeking a means of removal.

Certain Shipowners/operators are extremely strict on what cargoes can or cannot be carried in their vessel(s), the list expanding item by item on the basis of experience. By comparison, other Shipowners specialise in handling dangerous cargo in compliance with the IMO rules.

However, the intention of a timecharterer expressed in a time charter party to carry a particular commodity does not remove the risk or the need to include a comprehensive list of excluded cargoes in the contract. An 'intention' may be changed to a choice of a 'dangerous', unexcluded cargo.

Also, following arbitral precedent in New York, the exclusion of 'petroleum and/or its products' does not exclude 'petroleum coke' nor, it is believed, would the exclusion of 'cement' naturally exclude 'cement clinker'.

International rules for the packing, labelling and carriage of dangerous cargo are set out in the IMO Dangerous Goods Code.

2.4 SHIPS' DOCUMENTS AND CLASSIFICATION

There are a number of documents that a ship is obliged to carry if it is to trade legitimately. The documents are issued by a number of bodies often on behalf of the ship's Flag State.

Each time the ship calls to a port it will be necessary for the Master, via the ship's Agent, to show the documents to appropriate authorities and if any of them are not in order the ship may be prevented from working.

Documents issued by or on behalf of the Flag State include the following:

Ships' Certificate of Registry – confirming that the ship is entitled to fly under the flag of the State which issued it. Usually a ship can only have one Flag State but some nations allow ships on bareboat charters to be put on a bareboat registry for the period of the charter.

Loadline Certificate – this certificate and its purpose have already been covered.

Safety Construction Certificate – confirms that the ship has been constructed in accordance with the relevant sections of the SOLAS conventions.

Safety Equipment Certificate – confirms that the ship's safety equipment (which includes navigational charts and publications) are in accordance with SOLAS requirements

Safety Radio Certificate – again a SOLAS certificate confirming that the ship's communications equipment is in accordance with relevant conventions. This certificate may well be of interest to potential charterers since it shows if the ship is allowed to sail world-wide or is restricted to certain areas because of the limitations of its communications equipment.

There are four categories of equipment A1, A2, A3 and A4. A1 would allow the ship to trade only in certain coastal waters, A4 is world-wide and A3 world-wide except arctic waters. A2 covers all other areas. If a ship has to voyage through a higher rated area than stated on its certificate to reach its destination, then it may not be suitable for the contract under consideration. Sometimes though the Flag State will allow the voyage providing it receives sufficient notice.

Safety Management Certificate (SMC) – this certificate is issued to ships when they have proved compliance with the International Safety Management (ISM) code. It should be noted that this certificate is issued to the operating company rather than the ship and if the ship has changed hands or management it immediately becomes void. However, all ships must have valid SMC onboard or they will not be permitted to work by Port State control authorities.

ISPS Certification – the ISPS code, or to give it its full name, the International Ship and Port Facilities Security Code, is a part of the SOLAS convention devised by the IMO as a response to concerns over security and terrorism.

The ISPS code came through the committee process very quickly as a result of the terrorist attacks on New York in September 2001 but it does include elements of two other problems, piracy and stowaways that have been of concern for many years.

As the full name suggests the ISPS code works on two levels, ships (but only those over 500GT) and ports. Governments and maritime administrations must appoint **Recognised Security Organisations (RSOs)** to certify the security arrangements that have been made in ports, on ships and in the shore offices of shipping companies. Exactly what sort of organisation can become an RSO is entirely at the discretion of national Governments. Within the UK, only the Maritime and Coastguard Agency (MCA) has the power to vet ships but many Flag States have delegated the work to Classification Societies.

To comply with the code, ships and ports have to be subjected to a risk assessment after which a security plan is drawn up. The plan is then reviewed by the RSO and after a successful inspection and audit of the port or ship, a certificate is issued. Port States are able to deny entry to any ship which does not have a certificate, as well as ships coming from ports which have not been certified as complying with the code.

What happens in practice varies so much, but the US has fully implemented every aspect of the code from the coming into force date, a threat that the Owners of ships trading to the US on a regular basis have taken seriously.

On a practical level both ports and ships operate on a three stage security alert with the precautions taken dependant on the security threat assessed. This means that, for the most part both operate at the lowest level until some intelligence received makes a higher level desirable.

A ship that does not have a certificate will be limited in the number of states and ports it can operate to and so the presence of a certificate needs to be established early on in charter negotiations.

Because of the attitude taken by some states to ships which have visited ports with no approved security system, Shipowners may be wise to insist on a clause in any charter party affecting the ship, excluding calls to such ports.

Oil Pollution Prevention Certificate – either an International or domestic certificate (depending on ship's trading areas) issued to ships over 400 GT and confirming compliance with MARPOL convention 73/78 relating to pollution prevention measures.

Minimum Safe Manning Certificate – details the minimum number of crew and their ranks which the ship must carry.

Most of the certificates are issued for a period of four to five years subject to an annual inspection. If any of these are invalid the ship will be considered as not fulfilling the requirements of charter parties in relation to seaworthiness and could result in a timechartered vessel being considered off hire.

2.5 CLASSIFICATION

Classification is not a legal requirement for ships in every country, although it can affect the Owners' ability to arrange insurance or even attract cargoes.

The earliest Classification Society was Lloyd's Register founded in 1760. Its original purpose was to provide details of ships' condition which would allow insurers and cargo interests to consider the likely risk of shipping goods on any particular ship.

From initially providing an assessment of condition, Lloyd's Register went on to overseeing construction of ships from the earliest stages. The result is a class notation which is assigned to the ship and which requires regular re-inspection to be retained. Each five years a ship has to undergo a Special Survey which requires the vessel to be dry-docked (something which is always mentioned and allowed for in timecharter parties).

Lloyd's Register's example was adopted in many countries and there are now many classification societies, most are good but a few have dubious reputations. The largest have formed The International Association of Classification Societies (IACS), details of which can be found at www.iacs.org.uk

It is normal for all charter parties to include details of a ship's classification society and its class notation. Attention should be paid to notations because they are becoming very complicated. From an initial simple grading of overall condition, the notation has come to include much more information about machinery type, degrees of automation, specialist ratings, ice class and acceptable light loaded conditions. The Classification Societies will answer any questions about their notations and it is good practice to clarify any uncertainty before concluding a fixture since important information can often be overlooked.

2.6 SELF-ASSESSMENT AND TEST QUESTIONS

Attempt the following and check your answers from the text and/or other sources available to you.

1. Define and explain the following terms:-

    1) DWAT   6) Grain capacity

    2) DWCC   7) Bale capacity

    3) Summer marks   8) Paragraph ship

    4) Gross tonnage   9) Air-draft

    5) Nett tonnage   10) Centistoke

2. Draw a plan, profile and midship section of a bulk carrier. Provide a description including deadweight, draft, grain and bale cubic capacity, loa, beam and air drafts.

3. Define and explain the following terms:

    1) Stowage factor   6) Break-bulk

    2) Cargo battens   7) Tallying

    3) Angle of repose   8) Hydroscopic

    4) Self-trimmer   9) Cargo manifest

    5) Easy-trimmer   10) Stowage plan

4. Give the stowage factor, method of packing (if any), and any special precautions required during loading and carriage for:

    1) Jute   6) Cement

    2) Petroleum coke   7) Manganese ore

    3) Barley   8) Wet hides

    4) Woodchips   9) Salt

    5) Sulphur   10) Drummed asphalt

Having completed Chapter Two attempt the following and submit your essay to your Tutor.

Under your control is *"Gannet"* a multi-purpose vessel of 20,000 mt dwcc, with folding tweendecks and a capacity of 1,000,000 cubic feet grain and 950,000 bale. Allowance has been made for draft, bunkers and constant weights.

For each of the following commodities, advise what special fittings the vessel might require, what precautions might be necessary, and estimate the quantity of cargo the vessel could be expected to lift, commenting where appropriate on the reason for the cargo quantity:

1)	Bagged fishmeal	4)	Packaged lumber
2)	Bulk wheat	5)	Bulk foundry coke
3)	Steel products	6)	Ferro-silicon

Chapter 3

FREIGHT MARKETS AND MARKET PRACTICE

3.1 INTRODUCTION

The Dry Cargo Chartering Market cannot be rigidly divided into separate segments, but it is possible to identify local and world-wide business 'arenas' in which chartering activity takes place. Nevertheless, the all-embracing world-wide international dry cargo market has its rough divisions, according to ship type and size, and according also to particular commodities, whilst geographical markets exist that concentrate on regional trades, often specialising in smaller, coastal or 'short-sea' as opposed to 'deep-sea' tonnage.

One example of a highly sophisticated international chartering arena is that developed around specialist *'heavy-lift'* business, although from time to time ships may be employed in this sector that would more commonly be found in another market. Alternatively, for example, there is a 'reefer' market, comprising refrigerated ships and cargoes only.

There is no single geographic centre, since this 'market-place' is truly international, business being conducted by word of mouth, on the telephone, facsimile, electronic mail (E-Mail) either through the Internet or specialist providers, while telex is still important to some areas where the telephone is less reliable. All you need to participate in this 'market' is the responsibility for some goods, e.g. a ship or a cargo, the appropriate communication equipment, and a lot of courage.

Even so there was a time when such wonders of modern communication equipment were not available and freight markets therefore developed around 'traditional' shipping centres. Many of these historical centres remain active in dry cargo shipping today, and participants are likely to maintain offices in places such as London, Oslo, Hamburg, Piraeus, New York, Singapore, Hong Kong and Tokyo. There are also regional centres, such as Paris, Sydney (Australia), Bangkok, Montreal, Rio de Janeiro, Stockholm and Seoul, from which those specialising in locally controlled tonnage and cargoes negotiate locally or 'plug-in' to the international market to cover their requirements.

3.2 THE BALTIC EXCHANGE

The only physical market place in the world specialising in the chartering of dry cargo ships and commodities is the Baltic Exchange, in London, although with the advent of modern communications fewer and fewer fixtures are being made every year. Nevertheless, members of the Exchange, both corporations and individuals are engaged in numerous other spheres, ranging from the sale and purchase of ships and aircraft through to commodity trading and futures markets.

The motto of the Exchange, "Our Word Our Bond", is the same as that of the Institute of Chartered Shipbrokers, and symbolises the importance of ethics in trading, the principal of treating others as you would wish to be treated yourself, and it remains possible to walk on to the Exchange in a Broker member's capacity and to leave an hour later having verbally committed your Principal to employ a ship or to provide transportation for a cargo.

3.2.1 Market Practitioners

It can be seen that the persons populating the international dry cargo shipping 'market' have nationalities, knowledge and backgrounds as varied as the range of commodities and ship types and sizes that are to be found. But the people at least can be sub-divided a little more certainly into the following categories.

3.2.2 Charterers

Those who 'charter' ships to carry commodities. There are many kinds of Charterers, from individuals operating small corporations and concerned only with the carriage of a particular commodity, through to major international trading houses whose involvement in the international dry cargo market (significant as that may be to that market) represents a very small part of their overall corporate activities. Consequently, some Charterers are involved as **Traders**' in the world-wide purchase, sale and transportation of a range of goods, e.g. grains, fertilisers, minerals, etc., others, perhaps Manufacturers, Mine-Owners, Farmers, Shippers or Receivers, for a single commodity or from a particular geographic area.

Still other Charterers may be state operations e.g: the President of India (in other words the Indian Government), Government employees being given the task of securing suitable ships for the state needs. It is a worthwhile exercise for those learning about this subject to make a point of studying as regularly as possible lists of reported dry cargo fixtures, and to try to categorise Charterers into one or more appropriate headings.

To help you get started, sample pages from Fairplay International Weekly Shipping Magazine will be found in **Appendix 8** listing representative fixtures for particular weeks a month apart, and not only will this type of data supplement what should already have been learned about ships and cargoes in Chapters One and Two of this book, but trades, types of Charterers and markets can be identified.

3.2.3 Shipowners

Just as for Charterers, there is a wide variety of Shipowners. Some Owners are of a single ship; others of larger fleets. Some concentrate on ships of a particular type (e.g. tweendeckers) or size (e.g. panamax bulk carriers). Others operate a varied collection of vessels. Some are state-controlled, or run their ships under the flag of the country in which they reside, whilst others operate **'offshore'** under a **'convenient'** flag, from which derives the term 'flag of convenience'.

The term 'Flag Of Convenience' (FOC) is applied to vessel registries of nations offering registration facilities to any Shipowner who meets their local requirements irrespective of the Shipowner's nationality or place of business. An FOC country may provide all or any of the following:

1) Anonymity for a Shipowner, who may operate his vessel(s) from behind a 'faceless' corporation registered in the same nation as the flag flown by the vessel(s).

2) Freedom for the vessel to be manned by a crew in whatever numbers or nationality the Shipowner selects, at whatever wage scale the crew/Owner negotiates.

3) Levies a very low tax against the vessel Ownership and little or no taxation against the earnings of the vessel. Some are more concerned about the quality of the vessel management and condition than others, but it is fair to say that some of the best maintained ships in the world fly a Flag of Convenience, as well as some of the worst.

Flags of Convenience are subjected to a great deal of criticism from many organisations inside and outside the shipping industry. In some cases the criticism is justified but for every substandard vessel trading under a Flag of Convenience there is another just as bad flying a national flag. One of the most common accusations levied against FOC countries is that they allow their ships to flout international regulations. Perhaps it is worth reflecting upon the fact that every IMO resolution and convention requires the support of a certain number of nations representing a certain percentage of the world fleet for that convention to become internationally binding. Without the support of Panama, Liberia, Cyprus and Malta, all FOC countries, none of those conventions would ever become law, such is the percentage of the world fleet that is flagged out.

A number of traditional maritime nations have created second registers as a means of 'competing' with FOC countries, e.g: Norway, while in other cases the Owners have found a national route that offers similar advantages, e.g. Isle of Man. In such cases the advantage to the Owner is related to taxation or crew nationality, wages and social security costs and not to any relaxation of safety standards or crew size.

Many Shipowners operate from one or more of the traditional or regional centres that maintain an important presence in the international dry cargo market. Others operate their enterprises from these or from locations in their own country, although (in order to avoid taxes levied against ship earnings) often under an *'agency agreement'* with the 'offshore' owning corporation officially located, perhaps, in a more exotic and 'convenient' part of the world.

3.2.4   Operators

This is a term used to describe an organisation or individual experienced in the market and in its mechanisms, setting out to create income from 'trading' in ships and cargoes. Some Operators specialise in securing ships on charter from Shipowners, thereafter hoping to re-employ the ship(s) to other Charterers at a higher freight/hire rate, thereby securing a profit. Other Operators concentrate on securing contracts for the carriage of cargoes and, by fixing-in outside ships at lower freight rates, thereby cover their commitment to the original Charterers and, at the same time, make themselves a profit.

Certain Operators trade in both ships and cargoes and, at any one time, have a mix of short, medium and long-term commitments to Charterers and/or Shipowners, needing great skill and a reasonable level of good fortune to maximise potential returns.

Of course trading as an Operator is a high-risk business, and losses can be sustained as well as profits gained. Consequently, although many Operators perform their undertakings perfectly well, it must be appreciated that inevitably a few Operators will become bankrupt, being unable to discharge their commitments satisfactorily. This is a risk that Operators and those trading with them have to consider and, ultimately, may have to bear. Nonetheless, Operators nowadays form a vital element of the international dry cargo market and are a prominent feature of international trading.

Indeed some well known container liner companies are actually Operators as they run their liner services entirely with container tonnage chartered in for the service.

Operators who employ a ship and then 're-employ' (or 're-let') that vessel for further business, charter her out in a new role, are described as **'Disponent'** or **'Timecharter Owners'**. A disponent Owner is a party deemed to be the Shipowner having control of the vessel by timecharter. Some Operators, having secured a vessel for a period, only to find to their good fortune that freight rates increase substantially in their favour, are liable to 're-let' the vessel to a Charterer or to another Operator, thereby locking-in a profit for the remainder of their commitment to the original Shipowner.

We have seen that from time-to-time the party acting as the "Owner" may, in fact be the "disponent Owner" such as the party who has the ship on timecharter. Occasionally there may be more than one link in the chain between the actual Owner and the disponent Owner involved in the immediate fixture.

In the case of charterers it is probably more the rule than the exception for more than one entity to be involved; three different parties would not be at all unusual. A typical situation might be that the actual charter being arranged with a merchant who could have bought the cargo FOB from the producer who will then be the shipper; the merchant could then have sold the cargo to the consignees who would be the third element. One should also remember that the producers and the consignees could well have to employ terminal operating companies to do the physical loading and discharging of the material. The term Operator is used in a wider sense to include true Shipowners, managers and disponent Owners.

3.2.5 Shipbrokers

The individuals or corporations who, acting as Brokers in the middle of this market-place of Charterers, Shipowners and Operators of all corporate sizes and of many nationalities, identify supply and demand for ships and cargoes and thereby help the main players to secure cargoes for their ships and ships for their cargoes. In other words, Shipbrokers provide the lubrication that enables the market mechanisms to function.

A Shipbroker's income is in the form of the reward of **'commission'** (known also as **'Brokerage'**) paid for a successful introduction and negotiation between Shipowner and Charterer, leading to a **'fixture'**. Even after much hard work and expense, a negotiation that does not lead to a fixture will normally result in no payment of any kind to the Shipbroker in the middle. Thus, Shipbrokers are naturally keen on 'fixing'. Near misses, however exciting, are not only profitless but a drain on resources, time and energy. (More information about commissions will be found in Chapter Five, under the heading "Financial Elements of Charter Parties").

Some Shipbrokers are specifically hired as employees by Shipowners or by Charterers to 'work' their tonnage or cargoes. Most, though, are separate individuals or corporations acting for principals in an **'exclusive'** or **'semi-exclusive'** capacity or fixing as an opportunity presents itself, as **'competitive'** Brokers.

The term 'Shipbroker' is, however, wide-ranging. Other functions than that of a dry cargo Shipbroker abound. Activities, for example, covering Port Agency work; the Sale and Purchase of ships, the employment of specialist vessels such as tankers of 'offshore' craft; Liner Agency and Ship Management. All are roles in which Shipbrokers will be found.

A Shipbroker specialising in acting for merchants seeking ships to carry cargoes may be known as a **'chartering Broker'** or as a **'chartering agent'** and, as noted above, such a Broker may be either the employee of the merchants, dealing solely with that merchant's business, or the Broker may be retained on an exclusive basis, i.e.: the merchant's business is his or his company's to handle exclusively. This exclusivity may be limited to a chartering centre, e.g: 'exclusive in London', or it may be world-wide. Certain merchants prefer to employ a chain of 'semi-exclusive' Brokers to cover several shipping centres, perhaps feeling that this will enable a more thorough coverage of the 'market' for suitable ships, and the Brokers concerned may possibly describe themselves as **'direct brokers'** for the merchants concerned.

A Shipbroker in one centre may have **'correspondent brokers'** that will be used co-operatively to seek suitable tonnage or cargoes in another centre. Most Brokers will act 'competitively' if they find a suitable 'non-exclusive' ship for a 'non-exclusive' cargo during their forays around the international marketplace, and a few merchants will not employ Brokers in an exclusive role but prefer to treat all Brokers as competitors with one another, releasing details of their requirements onto the freight market as widely as possible and negotiating thereafter with the Owners of any suitable ship that is proposed to them through whichever broking channel the Owner selects.

Shipbrokers are naturally keen to secure 'exclusive' accounts, not only does the Brokerage these create provide valuable financial underpinning to their company, but working for an 'exclusive' principal enables the Broker to exercise his or her full professional potential in terms of providing a continuous flow of market information and expert advice. Principals operating competitively sometimes tend to push their Brokers into a purely 'dealer' role. Few can afford to rely totally on 'exclusive' accounts, however, and most Brokers compete against others for additional income.

It is therefore important for Shipbrokers to circulate details of new business – **'orders'** – as soon as possible, and to maintain good and close contact not only with those principals providing business, but also with 'correspondent' Brokers and with those representing Shipowners, whose vessels they may need to fix. Even when there is no particular order to quote, it is advisable to maintain chartering and shipowning relations current and good-tempered, in order to foster relationships and, hopefully, to make it easier to conclude future business.

Certain Shipbrokers specialise in finding and fixing cargoes for the ships of exclusive and semiexclusive client Shipowners, maintaining a list of 'open' tonnage expected to become available in the weeks ahead and, just as other Shipbrokers circulate details of available cargoes, so they circulate this 'tonnage list' to Chartering Brokers and their principals, in their quest to locate suitable cargoes. The larger Shipbroking companies will probably have broking staff representing both Chartering and Shipowning clients, as well as those acting in a competitive capacity.

But securing a 'fixture' is only part of a Shipbroker's responsibility. Following his function as the sole or one of several Brokers involved in negotiations leading to a 'fixture' the Charterers' Shipbroker then has the task of:

a)   drawing up the charter party faithfully recording all that has been agreed,

b)   dealing with any subsequently amendments and/or additions to the negotiations,

c)   handling communications between the parties, and,

d)   dealing with financial exchanges, e.g: payments of freights, voyage balances and hires.

Although it is normal practice for a Charterer's Shipbroker actually to draw up charter parties, the Shipowner's Broker must check the draft version of that document, and attend to the other activities details above on behalf of his own principal.

Consequently, most medium-sized and large shipbroking companies maintain a '**post-fixture'** department, the duties of which are to handle efficiently the operations of a concluded fixture, leaving the 'front-line Broker to concentrate on the fixing of further business. With smaller companies, or individuals, however, the Broker will handle the entire operation from original negotiations through to the final financial transaction.

A typical deep-sea dry cargo fixture will involve at least two Shipbrokers, one representing the Shipowner, the other the Charterer, sometimes there will be more Brokers in the 'chain'. Whereas it is comparatively unusual for just one Shipbroker to be employed on a deep-sea dry cargo fixture, for short-sea and some specialised trades occasionally only one Shipbroker will be engaged between two principals. Therefore more than ever, if acting as a sole Shipbroker, that Broker must act in a scrupulously professional manner, using all his endeavours to promote harmony in the negotiations and in post-fixture activities.

3.2.6   E-Commerce

Because of its international nature, chartering might seem an ideal subject for carrying out over the Internet directly between Charterer and Owner. And yet despite several attempts, no solid Internet-based chartering platform has been successful. Without doubt, many Charterers and Owners who were first introduced by Brokers, continue to work together but dispense with the unfortunate intermediaries. In some ways this is a compliment to the Brokers because the principals are obviously satisfied with the calibre of partner they have been introduced to.

Direct contact through the Internet is not yet trusted because very often the principals have no way of establishing the other party's credentials in the way Brokers do. Moreover the meat of negotiations varies with every fixture, and what one Owner is quite happy to concede, another may resolutely refuse to give way on. Points needing clarification are unlikely to be the same in every case, and so a constant stream of questions back and forth is inevitable.

The Internet has been adopted successfully by some liner companies but there the cargo is invariably containerised, the itinerary published and well known in advance and freight rates non-negotiable except for a very few favoured clients. The difference between liner trades and chartering could be likened to the difference in buying an "off the peg" suit or an individually tailored one.

Conceivably, there will come a time when Internet chartering will become accepted but, in the opinion of many, only some specialist trades with standard terms and conditions, tankers for example will prove to be suited to this form of negotiating.

3.2.7 Trading

The dry cargo shipping market is closely identified with letters of credit and these documents frequently influence charter party terms and conditions and the manner in which **'bills of lading'** are worded and released, and in which freight is paid. It is therefore vital that those engaged in this part of the international shipping industry have a good basic knowledge of all aspects of international trade.

Freights will be dealt with in Chapter Five, and trading documents, such as Bills of Lading, in Chapter Eight. Nevertheless, a brief acquaintanceship with trading practices will assist in understanding this and the following Chapter Four.

The International Chamber of Commerce (ICC) publishes a standard set of terms for the international sale of goods. These terms are updated on a regular basis with the 2010 version becoming effective in January 2011. As from 1 January 2011 some sales contracts will be done using the new Incoterms 2010 definitions whilst others will continue to use the older version. The parties to a sales contract are free to choose which rules apply but they should make clear exactly which set of rules are in operation.

The new Rules have been revised to take into account developments in international trade over the past ten years as the volume and complexity of global sales has increased, to address security issues arising in recent times and to provide for the ongoing changes in electronic communication. The new Rules also recognise the growth of customs-free areas.

With the introduction of the new rules, there are some entirely new terms that might be used.

Four terms (DAF, DES, DEQ and DDU) from the previous version have been replaced by just two new terms; Delivered At Place (DAP) which should be used in place of DAF, DES and DDU; and Delivered At Terminal (DAT) which replaces DEQ. These terms may be used irrespective of the mode of transport.

The starting point is that the merchant sells his goods where they are at his place of business, that is `ex works' (Incoterm EXW)** and the Buyer will have to make arrangements for storage of the goods, transportation to the carrying vessel and eventual loading. More commonly **Free Onboard (FOB)** terms are used under which the Seller will arrange delivery to the port and loading the cargo onboard. Note that the actual point at which responsibility for the cost of handling and transport moves from the Seller to the Buyer is at the ships rail. The Buyer is responsible for any stowage, lashing and securing costs. However, in most places there is a 'custom of the port' by which the separation of the costs is made. The Buyer also has to arrange the chartering of a vessel, payment of freight, insurance of the goods and delivery at the port of discharge. Variations may be **'FCA' ('Free Carrier')** and **'FAS' (Free Alongside Ship),** under both of which terms a Seller undertakes to deliver goods to the loading place, leaving loading procedures and costs to be arranged by the Buyer.

Where a Seller arranges a sale **'CFR' (Cost and Freight),** goods are sold on the basis that the Seller himself arranges carriage and delivery to the Buyer **'CIF' (Cost, Insurance and Freight)** stipulating that in addition the Shipper arranges and pays for insurance.

No two contracts are necessarily identical, and it is important to all concerned to follow carefully basic safeguards and to avoid documentary shortcuts.

It is also important not to confuse these *Incoterms* (FOB etc) which relate to the contract between the Seller and Buyer of goods, with the shipping terms FIO, Free In etc which describe the division of responsibility and costs between a Charterer and a Shipowner.

A Seller will not wish to release his property until he is assured that the correct payment will be safely received by the time of this release. Equally, a Buyer will be reluctant to pay for goods which have not been safely received and/or have not been confirmed as being in the condition described in the contract. Furthermore, the transaction will perhaps be complicated by Seller and Buyer being located thousands of miles away from each other, with the goods perhaps being located far away from either party.

The transfer of goods and money must obviously take place at a time and in a manner which ensures that both parties are satisfied their contract has been properly honoured.

There are various ways of achieving this objective, depending on market forces (i.e. on the pressure or otherwise for a Seller or a Buyer to trade) and on degrees of trust between the parties concerned.

The simplest means of all, is for a Buyer to pay in advance for goods, e.g: cash with order.

The opposite case is where goods and their documents are despatched, the Seller awaiting payment against his invoice.

Where either Seller or Buyer are then exposed, however, they suffer loss of cash flow in that funds are tied up awaiting finalisation of trading arrangements. For this reason alone, these payment methods are unpopular, quite apart from the risks involved.

A satisfactory alternative and one widely utilised is for the Buyer to draw up and to issue a **'Documentary Letter of Credit'** through a bank of good repute, satisfactory to the Seller. A documentary letter of credit may be **'revocable'** or **'irrevocable'**, although the former, being open to cancellation or amendment by a Buyer provides little security for a Seller and is therefore rarely utilised. Irrevocable Letters of Credit instead are commonly used and under the terms of such a document, the bank involved will undertake to pay the Sellers without fail (i.e. irrevocably) but only when appropriate pre-conditions have been met within the time stipulated, these pre-conditions and times being clearly specified in the letter and usually being scrupulously adhered to by the bank.

Major preconditions specified in a **'Letter of Credit'** naturally include some safeguard in respect of the condition of the goods received and, since it is impracticable for a bank to examine the goods themselves, bankers will often rely solely upon the description of the condition of the goods as provided in a **'Bill of Lading'** (see Chapter Eight).

If a Shipowner (or a Ship's Master) confirms that cargo received aboard is in good condition at the port of loading, bills of lading will be issued containing no adverse remarks about the condition of the cargo, in other words **'unqualified'** or **'clean'** bills will be issued, and these are frequently a pre-requisite before a Letter of Credit can be honoured. Having issued **'clean'** bills at a loading port, the Shipowner assumes responsibility for the carriage of the cargo and for its safe delivery into the custody of the eventual holder of the bill(s) of lading at the port of discharge, when the cargo should be in substantially the same condition as received onboard.

Other than bills of lading, documents commonly required as pre-requisites to release funds under a letter of credit are:

1) Insurance papers (either a policy of certificate) in accordance with the sale agreement.

2) Invoices covering the goods,

and,

3) Certificates of origin of the goods.

A further method of transacting international payments is by 'bill of exchange', a traditional and versatile document which can be used either as the vehicle of payment under a documentary letter of credit, or in place of the letter of credit.

3.2.8 Market Reporting

As with many professions, it is of little use learning a large amount of information and expertise if you are unable to communicate this knowledge to a third party. The whole basis of a Shipbroker's working life is based on the giving of information and advice and, whilst a certain amount can be done verbally, a great deal of communication is in writing.

Consequently, all those engaged in shipping, and Shipbrokers in particular, must gain experience and ability in the preparation of written reports to their principals and seniors. Some will concentrate on a relatively small market sector perhaps designed to provide data on the shipment of a particular commodity, ship type or size, or geographic region, reporting fixtures, available cargoes, trading deals, market gossip, etc.

Other reports will be of a general nature, intending to illustrate in overall terms the state of the freight market. Examples are those produced by broking houses such as Galbraiths and Clarksons. In **Appendix 9** the dry cargo Panamax, Capesize and handysize markets are reported upon briefly together with relevant reported fixtures, the weekly report designed for mailing to various clients, not one in particular.

One of the fascinations of the international dry cargo freight market is that one can see in day-to-day trading activities the effects of far-off political and climatic events affecting the demand for ships and for cargo space and, consequently, freight rates. A world-wide depression in trade will ultimately have its effect on the shipping market and ships will lay-up for want of profitable employment. On the other hand, a buoyant freight market will result from active trading and there might be too few ships to satisfy demand, leading in turn to high freight income for those Shipowners/Operators fortunate enough to be in particular trading areas at particular times.

Read your national newspaper with a view to transposing the events recorded in the general news, political and business pages into what you believe will be the effect on the dry cargo shipping markets, whether local or international. Will the bankruptcy of a grain dealer seriously affect freight rates for that particular market sector and whether for better or for worse? And what about a serious famine and subsequent aid relief cargoes destined for a beleaguered community in the Third World? What effect will they have on immediate, medium and long term trade in, for example, grain?

So your source of information in producing reports for your principals should be obtained not only from market sources but relative also, every now and then, with reference to the probable effect of 'outside' events. After all, your particular freight market does not exist in isolation from the others or from the effects of world trades, events and politics.

3.3   METHODS OF SHIP EMPLOYMENT

These can conveniently be divided into the following main elements:

1) Voyage Chartering
2) Consecutive Voyages
3) Time Chartering
4) Bareboat Chartering
5) Contracts of Affreightment
6) Joint Ventures
7) Shipping Pools
8) Parcelling
9) Project Cargoes
10) Slot Charters

3.3.1   Voyage Chartering

Voyage Chartering occurs when a vessel is employed for a single trip, loading cargo from one or more ports for discharge at one or more ports. (Those fixtures listed under the headings Grain, Coal and Iron Ore in **Appendix 8**, for example, are all voyage fixtures). In return for the carriage of the cargo and, perhaps for the expenses of loading and/or discharging the cargo, the Shipowner will receive monetary reward termed 'freight'. This freight can either be in the form of a lump sum payment or, more commonly, it will be payable *pro rata* in respect of the quantity of cargo carried, usually so much per tonne.

It is normal to specify the amount of time a Charterer is allowed for loading and discharging the vessel the **'laytime'** and should this time be exceeded, then liquidated damages, termed **'demurrage'** will become payable.

The dates between which the vessel is required to be presented at the loading port, the **'laydays'**, will also be recorded, as well as the cargo type and size that is to be carried.

3.3.2 Consecutive Voyages

Sometimes the parties to a voyage charter are content to co-operate on pre-agreed repeat business. They will then sign an agreement which commits the ship to performing a number of voyages, either a predetermined number, or occasionally for as many as can be accommodated within a fixed period of time. All the voyages are covered by the same basic terms and conditions although it may be agreed that the freight rate fluctuates over the period of the contract.

Each of the voyages is treated as a separate contract for purposes of demurrage and despatch.

Should the ship be lost for any reason, then the contract comes to an end and the Owner is relieved of any further commitment to the contract. In this the Consecutive Voyage Contract differs materially from the apparently similar Contract of Affreightment.

3.3.3 Time Chartering

Where vessels are hired for a specific period, e.g: for 12 months (15 days more or less) the responsibilities of the parties differ substantially from those involved in voyage chartering. A Timecharterer assumes control of the operational (let us call it, the 'commercial') destiny of a vessel including, for example, the appointment and payment of port agents, purchase of bunkers, etc. leaving the Shipowner responsible for the management of the ship, with particular regard to maintenance, crewing, insurance, etc.

The Shipowner is rewarded by the payment of regular amounts of hire money, normally paid monthly or semi-monthly in advance. However, should the vessel fail to perform properly or suffer such interruptions to the smooth performance as mechanical breakdowns, she may be considered **'off-hire'**, during which period the Owner will not be entitled to remuneration.

Many Charterers find it expedient to employ vessels on a timecharter basis for single or round-trip voyages (refer, for example, to the tweendeck fixtures reported in **Appendix 8**) and this practice has given rise to the term **'trip-chartering'**. A trip-charter is similar to voyage chartering with regard both to the duration of the venture and to the fact that the intention of the parties is to employ the vessel for, say, one or two voyages, but there the similarity ends, and the roles of Charterer and Owner are identical to those assumed for time charters of longer periods.

Division of Time Charter responsibilities:

Shipowner	Charterer
Crewing	Employment
Repairs	Bunkering
Maintenance and Spares	Port Expenses
Classification	Canal Tolls
Surveys	Stevedoring
Lubricating Oils	Cargo Handling
Freshwater	Insurance of Cargo
Insurance of Vessel	Insurance of Bunkers
Stores and Provisions	
Heating and Cooking	

Under Voyage Chartering arrangements, most of the above responsibilities will become those of the Shipowner, with the exception that usually (but not always) the Charterer retains responsibility for Stevedoring, Cargo Handling and the Insurance of Cargo.

Quite often a time chartered vessel is employed on a liner service operated by the time charterer. Some vessels are taken on very long charters for this purpose, while others may be taken for short periods to cover dry-docking, repairs or seasonal fluctuations in cargo levels.

Charterers usually negotiate the right to temporarily rename the vessel if it is to be employed on a liner service so that its new name can be more easily connected with the route or line it is trading on. Occasionally the parties may even agree to a change of flag as well.

3.3.4 Bareboat Chartering

Sometimes termed **'demise'** chartering, Bareboat chartering arises on those occasions where Shipowners hire out their vessel to a Charterer, who virtually runs the ship as if he were the Shipowner, assuming both the Time Charterer's responsibilities (as defined above) and most, if not all, of the responsibilities of the Shipowner. In return, the Shipowner receives a lower hire payment, commensurate with reduced responsibilities and risks.

Strictly defined, 'demise' chartering differs from 'bareboat' chartering in that it may be agreed between the parties that the Shipowner provides a Master and/or officers and/or crew and, perhaps, organises the vessel's insurance.

Demise and Bareboating are in reality finance tools, designed to enable Investors to purchase ships, leaving the operation and management of the ships to Charterers with more expertise in those areas. The Charterers may, in fact, be Shipowners without the financial resources to fund such a purchase directly.

3.3.5 Contracts of Affreightment

These occur when a carrier, either a Shipowner or an Operator, contracts to carry a given quantity of cargo between named ports on agreed voyage chartering terms over several voyages. The carrier may thereafter employ his own vessel(s) or charter-in outside ships in order to fulfil contractual obligations. Unlike a consecutive voyage contract, the governing detail is the cargo and, in the unfortunate event of the Owner's intended ship sinking or being effectively eliminated from carrying, the Owner is obliged to make other alternative arrangements to complete the contract.

The advantage of such a contract to a Shipowner is that security of employment is obtained for his vessel(s) for the duration of the Contract of Affreightment, especially valuable if the Shipowner considers that freight rates are about to fall. For Operators in a similar freight market situation, the advantage is in the profits they hope to realise by taking advantage of being able to fix-in tonnage at lower freight rates than those they will receive from the Charterers.

But the Charterers may also be able to obtain financial advantage in the event that market freight rates rise once they have committed Owner or Operator 'locked-in' to the Contract, always assuming that the Owner/Operator will keep their end of the deal and perform. But even if the market stays in 'neutral' or moves against the Charterer by freight rates falling, at the very least the Charterer has exchanged the unreliability of the daily market place, for freight rate stability, thereby enabling emphasis to be placed in the development and marketing of the commodities involved.

Under a Contract of Affreightment, the covering document is basically a modified voyage charter party form, with each voyage ship being nominated in a booking form detailing dates and cargo quantity.

3.3.6 Joint Ventures

Where those controlling cargoes negotiate and come to terms under a 'joint venture' arrangement with those controlling ships. Normally profits and losses will be shared, not only perhaps on the seaborne freight element, but also on production and/or purchase and/or sale costs of the goods involved. These ventures can be fairly simple and of a short duration, perhaps for a single, occasional cargo, or they can be of major importance, involving the mutual exploitation of a nation's mineral deposits, the building and administration of ports, marketing of products, as well as the training of personnel for each section of the entire structure. An example of this degree of joint venture was the liaison between the Norwegian Klaveness Group and the Guinean Government in the bauxite production, transportation and marketing of the joint venture concern 'Guinomar'.

3.3.7   Shipping Pools

Where a group of Shipowners band together to 'pool' their tonnage and collectively market their combined fleet. They may well become involved in extensive contracts of affreightment and joint ventures with outside groups, and this type of operation is often used where a specialised commodity or trade is involved (e.g. reefers where numerous Charterers may become involved in contracts with the pool).

Pool income is collected together and once pool running costs have been deducted, remaining income is distributed amongst members by means of a **'weighting system'** by which each entered vessel's individual characteristics are taken into account and measured against a 'pool model average', debits and credits being applied accordingly.

Freight market risks are somewhat alleviated for an individual Shipowner, perhaps with little or no previous shipping experience, gaining admission to a well run pool. Furthermore, management overheads will be considerably reduced by collectively managed chartering, commercial and financial operations.

3.3.8   Parcelling

Generally in dry cargo shipping, the smaller the quantity of a commodity, the more expensive it is to ship. Recognising this, some Operators specialise in transporting smaller parcels of a commodity by grouping them together in a vessel sailing from one or more ports in a particular region to one or more ports in another area. This trade is prominent, for example, in commodities exported from Australia to destinations in the Far East and in the Atlantic Basin. Specialist Operators in the area contract to move parcels of commodities, thereafter grouping these together with other parcels in one 'bottom', probably contracted in on a trip-timecharter basis. (Even today you will encounter the old fashioned expression 'bottom' as an alternative to the word 'ship' or 'vessel' tradition dies hard in the shipping industry).

Consequently, in addition to negotiating the highest possible freight rate and best terms for each, individual parcel, the Operators seek the widest possible date speed during which to load the parcel and a wide cargo quantity margin, so as to give themselves maximum flexibility to fit the individual hold compartments of whatever ship they contract, thus easing their chartering restrictions for suitable tonnage.

Having identified the most suitable vessel, the Operators then rely on their shipping expertise to time charter the ship at a cost which is, overall, less than the freight they expect to earn from the collection of various parcels the ship will carry the difference, less their overheads, creating the profit element they seek.

3.3.9   Project Cargoes

A specialised form of joint venture/contract of affreightment is terms a **'project cargo'** or a **'turnkey project'**, a term commonplace in the heavy-lift market, whereby a marine specialist undertakes complete responsibility for the seaborne movement of both small and large prefabricated structures, constructional equipment, and raw materials (e.g. cement) together with all the paraphernalia of major projects (e.g. site huts and machinery) to the project's eventual location. An example would be the movement of material and equipment necessary to construct a de-salinisation plant or cement factory in a developing nation.

3.3.10   Slot Charters

We have seen how a liner operator may have an interest in timechartering a vessel for his liner service.

There is another form of chartering space prevalent in liner (particularly containerized) trades.

As liner ships have increased in size the Owners have sometimes found themselves having difficulty in filling their ships. Some freight forwarders and even former Operators of smaller liner ships that have lost out to the bigger competitors have found themselves in a position whereby they were controlling large quantities of cargo. Rather than merely contracting with the liner Operator as a Shipper they have contracted to take a set amount of space or slots on each voyage the ship makes. They then sell this space on to their customers as if they were in fact the line Operators. People who do this are known as NVOCCs (Non Vessel Owning Common Carriers).

The NVOCC pays the head Owner freight based on a fixed rate for each TEU slot he has contracted for possibly with a premium for hazardous cargoes. It is usual for the Owner to agree a reduced rate for any cargo supplied in excess of the contracted amount.

The contract, usually on the standard SLOTHIRE form, allows them to issue their own bills of lading, set their own freight rates and generally act as if they were the vessel Operator. Of course they have obligations too and should only contract to carry on terms similar to the true Operator, furthermore they will be responsible for settling their clients' cargo claims and if the vessel is making a call at a port solely for their convenience, to cover the port costs incurred.

The head Owner can make any number of slot agreements with different NVOCCs so the same ship may appear to be running on several different lines at the same time.

3.4   CHARTERING NEGOTIATIONS

Having found a potential ship to carry a Principal's cargo, or what appears to be a suitable cargo for a ship, the Shipbrokers concerned usually converse to exchange additional facts, so as to ensure the business is mutually interesting and workable with a fair chance of success, all this normally prior to discussion with the Principals. One or other Broker will then seek and receive his Principal's authority to make an offer for the business. Although this may, at first sight, seem a simple procedure, serious problems can arise if a basic code of conduct and practice is not followed in the tendering and receipt of such offers.

First, negotiations need to be conducted with care and attention to detail, as there must be complete agreement between the two Principals for an enforceable contract to come into being.

A day-book or log, or some kind of firm offer check-list which can be amended as negotiations proceed, should be carefully kept and re-confirmatory facsimile or telex messages summarising the final agreement, should always be sent to both parties. Some Shipbrokers, in fact, feel it is advisable, in the interests of certainty, to confirm each offer and counter-offer in that manner. Shipping is, after all, an international business and, although most chartering negotiations are conducted between parties fluent in the use of the English language, honest errors do occur and are best identified at an early stage.

The advent of e-mail and internet-based chartering platforms will mean that in the modern world a lot of negotiations will be carried out using methods not available in the past. While it is likely that these forms of communication will come to be universally accepted in time, it should be noted that many legal systems do not yet recognize such methods as being legally binding. It would therefore be sensible for the finalized document also to be transmitted using one of the methods that are legally enforceable.

Verbal communication both during negotiations and outside (e.g. passing on instructions to the Masters of ships) should always be re-confirmed back to the instructing Principal.

Initially, the elements of a standard opening offer for dry cargo voyage business can be itemised as follows:

(N.B. A number of abbreviations are used which are explained in Chapter Four.)

Essential details of a Firm Offer for Voyage Business

Reply by: (place and time limit)

For account of: (name and perhaps background Charterers)

Name of Ship: (including description, e.g. flag; year of build; loa; beam; deadweight; draft; cubic capacity; single/tween; number of holds and hatches; gear)

Position and estimated readiness of vessel:

Cargo Description and Quantity: (more or less %)

Load Port(s)/berths: (always afloat/naabsa)

Discharge Port(s)/berths: (always afloat/naabsa)

Laydays/Cancelling:

Loading Rate: (per ww day/shinc/shex)

Discharging Rate: (per ww day.shinc/shex)

Freight Rate: (where, when and how paid)

Demurrage Rate: (half despatch)

Loading/Discharging Costs: (fio)

Address Commission:

Brokerage:

Charter Party Form:

Subjects: (detail/stem/shippers' – receivers' approval)

The procedure concerning offers and counter offers in timechartering is similar to voyage chartering, except that such offers will be tailored for the major elements of a time charter, e.g.;

Essential details of a Firm Offer for Time Chartering:

Reply by: (place and time limit)

For account of: (name and perhaps background of Charterers)

Name of Ship: (description as for voyage chartering plus speed and consumption)

Position and estimated readiness of vessel

Redelivery: (When/where ready; aps; dop; passing 'x')

Laydays/Cancelling:

Duration (Trip):

Delivery: (When/where ready; dop; passing 'x')

Trading Area: (e.g. world-wide; Atlantic Basin)

Intended Trade: (e.g. grain trading, trip with coal)

Cargo Exclusions:

Hire Rate: (daily; per deadweight tonne per month)
(? including overtime) (where, when and how paid)

Ballast Bonus: (gross or nett)

Bunkers: (prices and quantities both ends)

Address Commission:

Brokerages:

Charter Party Form:

Subjects: (details)

NB Ballast Bonus is a sum that the Charterer agrees to pay to the Owner for sending the vessel in ballast to the point of delivery. It is particularly common for bulk carriers because trade in many cargoes is usually in one direction only and the Owner has no possibility to contract a voyage charter to put the ship in a position acceptable to the Charterer. When ships are scarce a Charterer is often willing to contribute to the Owner's costs by paying for a ship he particularly wants, to run in ballast to the delivery point. Conversely when there is a plentiful supply of ships the Owner may not be able to negotiate a ballast bonus and must absorb the costs himself.

There are tactical reasons to consider when discussing ballast bonuses. Firstly, a bonus is only payable once the ship is delivered into the time charter, so if for any reason the ship fails to make the cancelling date, the Charterer does not have to accept the ship and therefore is relieved of the liability to pay the ballast bonus.

Secondly, it could be argued that a higher daily rate and no ballast bonus might be agreed. There are points against this from both views: The Owner may send the ship on a long ballast run but may not be able to recover all his costs from a higher daily rate if the charter is for a short period, or if the vessel is redelivered very early for any reason. A Charterer on the other hand may wish to keep the daily rate low because he does not wish to signal to the market that he is willing to pay premium daily rates for ships.

3.5   OFFERING AND COUNTERING

The art of offering and counter-offering is governed both by legal dictates as well as by a code of professional conduct, the two not necessarily coinciding. Legally, for example, having made an offer, you are free to withdraw it any time prior to its acceptance by the other party or before any time limitation on the validity of the offer expires. Professionally, however, you are expected to maintain the offer, unaltered, until it is either countered or accepted, or until its time limitation has expired.

Again, legally, while negotiations continue, one can alter what has already been 'agreed'. Professionally, this is frowned upon, although it may be that such **'back-broking'** is acceptable if terms subsequently revealed during negotiations substantially affect what has previously been settled and which one party ought to have disclosed to the other at an earlier stage.

Incidentally, you will often hear the expression 'counter-offer' and when actual negotiations are proceeding (especially near the closing stages) you will even come across the words 'Accept-except' which obviously means that the party saying it is prepared to accept the other's offer with only a few (although they could be vital) alterations. However, let us be very clear on one point, when a counter offer is made it is in fact saying 'I decline your offer and I now make you the following firm offer'. Consequently until both parties have agreed on **all and every** detail, there is no contract and the one last in receipt of an offer (or counter offer) from the other is free, at any time, to 'walk away' from the negotiations. Just because the parties have started to negotiate this in no way binds them to continue, although to break off capriciously and without warning whilst it may be legally permissible, it would not be counted as ethically good practice.

There is an exception to the 'each and every detail' having to be agreed, in the USA. This is dealt with towards the end of this Chapter.

Remember also there are two rules of paramount importance in chartering negotiations, and which you must remember and apply throughout your chartering career. These are:

1) **Always to act within your authority**

2) **Do not offer the same ship or cargo to more than one party at the same time.**

3.5.1 Warranty of Authority

A Shipbroker is deemed to enjoy the full authority of his Principal, and should never act without that full authority. In fact, it is incumbent upon the Broker to ensure that he has full authority for all offers and counter-offers made on the Principal's behalf. If for some reason, a Broker does not have authority for an offer made, he may be legally liable in an action brought by an injured party receiving and accepting an unauthorised offer. Such an action would be on the basis of **'breach of warranty of authority'**, either **'with'** or **'without negligence'**. (The Broker 'warrants' i.e. guarantees that he or she has the authority to make the contract).

In the case of a breach **'with negligence'** a Broker mistakenly or intentionally makes an erroneous offer. Where a Broker merely passes on an incorrect offer, this is a breach **'without negligence'** but still a breach for which the Broker is responsible.

In either case, a Broker will be legally liable but, for a breach **'without negligence'** the Broker is entitled to legal recourse against the party passing him the mistaken or erroneous offer. In practice such an action may not succeed, especially in such an international market place involving many different codes of law. Even if legally successful under one or more codes, the chances of full financial recompense may be limited.

The difference between these breaches can be illustrated diagrammatically as follows:

SHIPOWNER ←→ BROKER A

BROKER B ←→ CHARTERER

Let us assume that the Shipowner offers his ship to Broker A at US$ 25 per tonne, Broker A passes the offer correctly to Broker B, who mistakenly passes the offer to the Charterer at US$ 24 per tonne. The Charterer accepts.

There is no contract between the Shipowner and the Charterer, but Broker B could be liable for an action for breach of warranty **with negligence**.

Alternatively, let us assume that the Shipowner offers his ship to Broker A at US$ 25 per tonne, but on this occasion Broker A mistakenly passes on the offer to Broker B at US$ 24 per tonne, who in turn passes the offer at US$ 24 to the Charterer. Again the Charterer accepts.

There is still no contract between the Shipowner and the Charterer, and Broker B is still liable for breach of warranty of authority, but this time **without negligence**.

Broker B may have the right to proceed legally against Broker A for passing an erroneous offer, but may face problems in gaining appropriate recompense for the reasons detailed above.

The two principals could insist on the contract being fulfilled in which case the Broker's liability would be for the difference between the authority given by the Owner and the acceptance given by the Charterer.

The breach of warranty could be on an item far less easily apparent than a dollar difference in the rate and may, therefore, not come to light until the ship's voyage is well advanced. The Principle, however, remains the same in that the Broker from whom the injured party received the erroneous offer is responsible for the damages the principal suffers.

This may seem very harsh in the case of 'without negligence' as the Broker being held responsible will have acted at all times in good faith and meticulously passed on such offers as he or she received from the errant Broker. How very much more unfair, however, it would be to the injured party if action against the nearest Broker was not the accepted legal route particularly as the Broker who initiated the breach may be in another country. The injured Principal was completely innocent and what the law is really saying is that a Broker has to satisfy himself of the *bona fides* of those with whom he or she is dealing.

Prudent Brokers usually insure themselves against both sorts of breach of warranty of authority. Fortunately cases which prove intractable to an amicable solution are rare but when the worst happens it can be spectacular. A few years ago there was a case where there was a fraudster in the 'chain' of Brokers. He is now languishing in an American prison but the funds were never recovered and the London Brokers had to make a three million dollar claim against their insurers.

3.5.2 Firm Offers

The second rule of paramount importance involves firm offers. It must be remembered that a ship cannot be under firm offer for two or more cargoes at the same time (other than for part cargoes or unless the intended voyage dates were such as to allow both voyages to take place as contracted) as, if both offers were accepted, the vessel could not carry both at the same time. Similarly, a Charterer cannot offer the same cargo to more than one ship at the same time. Even where a Broker is confident his Principal's firm offer will not be accepted by the other party, **only one firm offer at a time can be made**.

When broking pressure is intense, and when perhaps more than one opportunity presents itself, it may become very difficult to negotiate so as to select the best alternative for a Principal, because it may be that by concentrating upon one order or upon one ship, a second, better alternative slips away. But negotiations cannot be performed by means of offering to more than one party at a time. An original offer must have expired (or been withdrawn) before a second offer is made to the alternative candidate or, at least, a counter-offer received and declined. Naturally a Broker may have to exercise much skill and tact to perform his task effectively in such circumstances, and act in the best interests of his Principal.

It is, however, possible to negotiate a ship or a cargo on the basis of being **'subject open'** or **'subject unfixed'**. In this way the other side receives clear advice that alternative negotiations are being conducted, although some Principals will be unwilling to negotiate on this basis as the alternative business may take precedence, and they would be left with nothing to show for their time and trouble.

Nevertheless, with certain trades, for example, with Indian Government cargoes on certain occasions, working **'subject open'** is not unusual and where, say four vessels offer for what is quoted as one cargo (but may, in fact, turn out to be several cargoes on the same position from the same port), the most attractive offer may be countered to **'clean'**, the next on the basis of **'subject open'**, the third **'subject unfixed two'** and the fourth **'subject unfixed three'**. There may not be four separate cargoes and as, perhaps, ships 1 and 2 drop out during negotiations, it may be that successful negotiations are concluded only with ships 3 and 4, in such a way justifying what at first sight appears to be a rather tiresome procedure. It is, however, professionally unethical to misleadingly counter to another party on the basis of being **'subject open'** when not, in fact, under offer to anyone else.

3.5.3 Indications

Having found a potential ship to carry his Principal's cargo the Broker involved will normally gather additional data in an effort to ensure that the opportunity is really of interest and workable with a reasonable chance of success. Indications of fixing levels may be exchanged, and these may be made in the form of offers by including dates when a ship or a cargo may be available, the freight rate a principal is prepared to pay or to accept, the cargo quantity, etc. There may even be a **'counter indication'** or an indication said to be **'firm'**.

However, **an indication is not an offer. It is not binding on the party making it, and several indications may be made for various cargoes or ships at one and the same time**. An indication is merely an advice of the 'approximate' terms and conditions upon which a Principal is prepared to undertake business, or from which level that Principal is prepared to negotiate.

It must also be remembered that it is considered unethical to imply that a ship or a cargo is held 'firm' when it is not, in order to secure an offer or a counter-offer from a Principal and indications should not be abused in this way any more than should actual offers.

3.6 CHARTER PARTIES

It is common practice when advertising a cargo to include the type of charter party on which an eventual fixture will be based, e.g. Gencon CP, and certainly this should be the case when initially offering or counter-offering. It is, however, unusual for a contract to be based upon a blank copy of the named charter party form, it being normal practice to base negotiations either on a proforma contract prepared by Charterers including any special terms and conditions relevant to their business or, more commonly, for negotiations to be based upon terms agreed for a similar previous fixture, if possible upon a signed 'worked' copy of a previous fixture's charter party.

If a ship is in particular demand or is very specialist in character, the Owner may have his own form of contract that he will insist on.

It is usually only when negotiations are underway and have successfully reached perhaps, the **'main terms'** stage that the charter party upon which the Charterer wishes to base the fixtures is made available to the Shipowner and/or Owner's Broker. This may be due to the relative geographic locations of the parties involved, or down to a natural reluctance to go to the trouble of exchanging documents when it is by no means certain that the negotiations will show signs of reaching a successful climax and so warrant an exchange. It also may be considered poor negotiating tactics to appear too keen to give or to receive a proforma governing charter party at too early a stage in negotiations.

Most Charterers, Owners and Brokers now keep copies of Standard Charter Parties on computer together with the proformas customarily used in their trades. These can easily be transmitted by fax or E-mail and this has effected chartering negotiations by making the exchange of charter parties so much easier, the 'fax-machine' can be said to have brought about a fundamental change in chartering tactics by which a party purposely introduces the basic terms and conditions at an early stage in negotiations, thereby eliminating the 'main terms' stage altogether.

3.6.1 Timing

It is important that offers and counter-offers not only state the time by which a reply is due, but also the place where any reply must be made within that time limitation. Failure to follow this procedure may mean, for example, that a Principal replies in good time in, say London, with the other principals based in Singapore unaware of the valid counter-offer, and so negotiating and perhaps fixing elsewhere.

The time and place for reply to an offer must be quite explicit, e.g. "for reply in Singapore latest by 1500 hours local time 23rd June". Any counter-offer made in London to meet this deadline will have to be in sufficient time reasonably to permit it to be relayed to Singapore prior to 1500 hours local time in that place.

Beware of imprecise expressions such as 'For prompt reply' or 'For immediate reply'. The latter does not mean what it at first seems to say. An offer made through Broker(s) for immediate reply in fact means that time has to be allowed for contact to be made with the principal. He has to reply straight away but even using the 'most expedient means of communication available' it may take quite a while for the message to travel all the way there and back.

3.7 SUBJECTS

Charterers' offers and counter-offers are almost always made with **'subjects'** e.g. **'subject stem'**; **'subject receiver's approval'** or whatever. In practice even so-called firm offers have subjects contained in them, although strictly speaking they cannot then be firm offers. A true firm offer is one which is capable of being accepted by a simple affirmative with no further negotiation or clarification needed.

'Subject stem' is an expression about which there has often been debate as to its origin even its precise meaning. It can best be defined by example. Supposing a Charterer has a contract to buy a million tons of coal over a period in ships of around 50,000 tonnes. Obviously you cannot have such a quantity sitting on a quay waiting for a ship to be Chartered and so the Charterer needs to verify that the cargo can be brought down to the port to coincide with the proposed ship. If it is in order the Shipper will tell the Charterer that the 'stem' is confirmed so enabling the Charterer to lift that 'subject'.

The reason for 'subject receiver's approval' is for a similar purpose, the Charterers need to check whether a ship in that precise position can be accommodated.

Sadly both expressions are occasionally abused. There are cases where a fixture is made before the cargo is even bought, respectively sold, but those abusing accepted codes of ethics usually get found out and will be shunned by respectable Operators.

Under English Law there is no fixture until all **'subjects'** have been lifted and, from an Owner's point of view, it is therefore desirable to place a time-limit on the removal (i.e. the 'lifting' of any subjects agreed upon). This will have the effect of concentrating the efforts of Charterers to lift the subjects in good time or to risk losing the ship to other competing business. A time-limit on subjects also provides less opportunity for an unscrupulous Charterer to continue unobtrusively seeking cheaper tonnage whilst supposedly clearing the subject.

The time available to a Charterer to clear subjects is negotiable, like charter party terms, but should obviously be sufficient, reasonable and practicable, or else a Charterer may simply need to request extensions of time to comply with these requirements. This available time is, however, potentially capable of misuse by Charterers, and Shipowners are normally nervous about being too lenient by allowing too many subjects for indeterminate periods, especially when dealing with previously unknown and untested Charterers. On the other hand, Charterers may quite legitimately need a considerable length of time, especially when obtaining re-confirmation of a cargo's availability on certain dates in a remote corner of the world.

However, it is not always Charterers who put subjects on a negotiation. Where Charterers are unknown to Owners, it is quite likely that Owners will make any offer subject to 'approval of Charterers by Owners', or at least they will enquire of their background and history, probably seeking references from Shipowners with whom the Charterer has conducted business in the past. As a last resort, a Shipowner may insist on a bank guarantee in support of the Charterer, although this is expensive and frequently difficult to arrange, and is not usual.

Owners should be particularly wary where a Charterer is not named in a quoted cargo, being referred to perhaps as "FCC", short for "First Class Charterer". A definition of what is "first class" differs, of course, from person to person. Frequently there is nothing sinister about a Charterer not declaring his name behind an order, this being simply because the Charterer is hiding his involvement from market competitors, or, perhaps, because a Broker is quoting business passed to him from a 'Correspondence Broker' in whom he has faith will not deal with unscrupulous Charterers of a bad reputation, and is happy to re-quote the business prior to gaining a thorough knowledge of the background to the order. It is extremely unwise, however, for an Owner to agree to fix his vessel to an un-named Charterer.

There have been cases where a Broker has given an assurance that his Principals are first class to the other side and the so-called Principal has defaulted. There is more than ethics involved here because legal action has successfully been pursued against Brokers who have given such an assurance recklessly.

You do not even have to be one of the Brokers involved to risk action being taken in the case of negligent or recklessly given advice. You will learn about the civil wrong of tort in your law text. Sufficient to say that if someone asks for your advice and has right to consider you to be qualified to give that advice, even if the advice is given gratis, if the enquirer acts on your advice and it goes wrong, you may be in trouble. Unless the subject Charterer (or Owner) is very well known to you to be first class better by far to report on your experience, for example 'we fixed a ship to them on six months time charter and they paid the hires bang on time every month.' If you have no clear experience to report, you should suggest that the enquirer makes his own enquiries through more formal channels. Of course, if you have had a bad experience you should pass on the facts just the same but in the same way as you should not give an assurance of excellence if you are not absolutely confident, always remember that there are laws of libel and slander.

3.7.1 Negotiating

Once a firm offer has been made, all subsequent counter-offers should be prefixed in one of four ways:

1) "We decline Owner's/Charterer's offer and offer instead..."

2) "We accept Owner's/Charterer's last, except..."

3) "We repeat our last"

4) "We repeat our last, except..."

With parties engaged in serious negotiation, differences will gradually be eliminated and reconciled until either negotiations end in failure with neither side willing to concede on one or more issues or until agreement is reached, albeit with various 'subjects' still be lifted. Traditionally, this may be termed having reached agreement on 'main terms' or having reached the 'subject details' stage, leaving the charter party still to be negotiated between the parties. Ethically there is no reason why there should now be a serious impediment to reaching a firm fixture.

It may happen, however, that the charter party contains one or more terms which substantially affect the previously 'agreed' main elements of the negotiation. The seriousness of these 'details' may not be realised until negotiation on charter party terms is underway but it is incumbent upon Charterer's Brokers to ensure, if possible, that the original negotiations leading to agreement on 'main terms' contain **all** main terms. That would help to avoid disagreement over terms which substantially affect items already agreed, e.g. the freight rate. If agreement cannot be reached on major but simple issues such as cargo size, vessel's/cargo's available dates, freight rate, etc., there is little point in dealing with perhaps tedious and relatively minor charter party clauses.

Under English Law, however, there is no binding contract at the 'main terms' stage of negotiations, nor will there be any such agreement until each and every detail of the contract has been agreed and all subjects lifted. Legally, therefore, there is nothing to stop one or other of the parties renegotiating a feature of the 'agreement' reached, e.g. the freight rate, although, professionally, and unless justified by the discovery of a previously hidden 'major' item, this would be considered highly unethical.

As mentioned earlier, under present American Law, however, there may be a contract once 'main terms' have been negotiated and agreed, unless both sides decide to withdraw from the negotiations; unilateral withdrawal is not sufficient. Agreement reached on what may be interpreted as the 'essential' parts of a contract may well result in a legally binding fixture, even though a mass of relatively minor details have not even been discussed, let alone resolved, and even though numerous subjects remain to be lifted.

The solution to this potential problem would seem to be to elevate the 'subject details' stage from a legally insignificant process to an essential part of a contract. Negotiating on a charter party at an early stage so there is no distinction between the 'main terms' and charter party details is one method. However, if parties to a negotiation under American Law prefer not to be committed to what may legally be interpreted as 'fixture' before **all** details, major and minor, have been agreed, and **all** subjects lifted, they should make this patently clear by the use of appropriate wording.

An example of such wording would be "subject to Owner's/Charterer's full approval of the pro forma charter party dated.... with logical amendments thereto". It may be tempting in the heat of negotiations to use a short, easy phrase like "subject details" but, with American Law as it presently stands, this is not sufficient, and it is safer to get into the habit of being more explicit.

3.7.2   Summary

You have now covered the basics of freight markets, trading and negotiations. There is much to learn of a practical nature, but what you have read in this Chapter is intended to supplement and support your current or eventual working activities. In the next Chapter we will turn our attention to investigating and examining the world of dry cargo charter parties.

3.8   FREIGHT DERIVATIVES FOR DRY CARGO

A long time ago farmers had only one way to sell their crop. They had to travel to a market place where the price they received depended on supply and demand. Often Shipowners and Charters have likewise been restricted to trade their ships or cargoes on the prompt market, at market rates. Over the years farmers developed grain futures markets enabling them to value their crops before harvest and, since 1985, the shipping industry has had a similar tool available.

3.8.1   The Indices

In order to understand the mechanism, we need to see how the indices work.

In 1985 the Baltic Exchange began to publish a series of route-assessments of the prompt physical market. A group of independent broking companies submitted their votes daily on precisely defined routes. In addition to publishing the average of these votes or assessments, the Baltic Exchange also used a formula, by which the routes were weighted by importance, to produce one number. Initially this was called the Baltic Freight Index.

In the beginning the routes covered by the BFI covered a spread of handysize, panamax and capesize runs. But over time more and more routes were needed, so now the Baltic produces some 39 daily assessments (using some 24 broking companies world-wide), broken down into the various sectors. A full list is given in **Appendix 10** but suffice it to say that both the major wet (clean and dirty) and dry routes are now covered. The BHMI is concerned with handymaxes, the BPI with panamaxes and the BCI with capes. In addition the Baltic Dry Index is published, which is an average of the three dry indices. They are still produced in the original way i.e. the daily result of independent Brokers' assessments.

Will they change in the future? Certainly, Ships sizes change, trades change. Nothing is written in stone.

The indices have uses for lawyers, for underwriters, for researchers and in fact for assisting anyone who is seeking a historical guide to the market. The Baltic Exchange's indices are authoritative and remain the most fair and accepted gauges of the health of the shipping industry world-wide.

But the first use to which they were put was for a futures market called BIFFEX.

3.8.2   The Baltic International Freight Futures Exchange

The original BFI was given an arbitrary starting point of 1,000. The futures market decided, equally arbitrarily, to make each one point rise or fall in the index a value of US$10,000.00 of 'notional freight'. From then on it operated in the same way as any other open-outcry futures market, like oil or coffee. The hours of trading, the dates, the settlement, the contracts, the governing laws and the financial requirements were all laid down in detail. All trades were anonymous and guaranteed by the London Clearing House. An initial deposit was needed, and your account had to be topped up daily if it was in debt.

To start trading, a client had to open an account with a registered and approved Broker and, having met the necessary financial and documentary requirements, he could buy or sell based on the simple question: where will the index be on a particular date?

It is worth noting that the terms 'buy' and 'sell' are shorthand. The purelaser is not buying or selling a tangible asset you are giving direction to a number. For example an October contract 'bought' at 1,375 means that the client believes that the index will be higher than 1,375 at the end of October. For every 'bought' contract there must be a 'sold' one reflecting the opposite opinion.

BIFFEX had some very busy times but after 15 years its use was superseded by Forward Freight Agreements which had been introduced a few years earlier.

3.8.3   FFAs – Forward Freight Agreements

It became clear that the shipping industry appreciated the futures market but wanted to make contracts that were more specific than settling against a global freight index. In order to achieve this the format had to be changed.

Since 1991 it is also possible to hedge a forward position another way, by trading an FFA contract. FFAs were developed by H. Clarkson and Co Ltd, and are proving highly effective not just for Owners and Charterers, Traders and Operators but also offer the potential to banks, funds and other financial institutions for containing portfolio exposure.

FFAs are traded Principal-to-Principal - OTC (Over the Counter) as opposed to BIFFEX which is traded via an Exchange. The essential difference between FFAs and BIFFEX is that FFAs settle against a particular component rate, while BIFFEX settles against the BFI, the actual index number. There are broking houses with dedicated and legally registered staff who specialise in this service.

A Buyer (Charterer) and a Seller (Owner) agree to trade a FFA Contract. Through their FFA-Broker they will agree Route and Month and negotiate a mutually satisfactory price. The names of their counterparties are not disclosed to one another until the price and terms are agreed. Trades are not published. All deals are done on trust and in strictest confidence. When the contract expires (on settlement), if the agreed price is higher than the settlement price, the Seller will compensate the Buyer with the difference. If the fixed price is lower than the final settlement price, the Buyer will compensate the seller. Payment is in cash and is payable five business days following the date of settlement.

Every month forward is tradeable. Combinations of months and routes can also be considered, provided counterparties are available. Long term period can also be covered by taking the average of the four Time Charter routes as an FFA contract.

Normally an average of the last seven component rates of the agreed months are used for voyage and trip contracts, and all the components in the settlement month are used for period FFAs. But the format is so flexible that any agreement can be tailored if the two Principals are willing.

3.8.4 FFA Trading Example

– Date 22nd March 2003

– FFA Buyer. A Charterer has four cargoes from Nopac to South Japan, one cargo a month June to September. He fears the market may substantially strengthen for the September cargo and therefore wants to secure his freight, against potential adverse market movements.

– FFA Seller. A Panamax Shipowner has three vessels in the Far East, redelivering from various period charters in September. He would like to have a guaranteed income on at least one of his vessels, and is therefore looking to Sell a FFA.

The Owner is happy to lock in US$13,000/day forward in September. The Charterer is also happy as he has locked in a rate which is considerably less than the spot market.

– BPI Route 3a (Transpacific Round voyage) time charter.

– After a short negotiation a price is agreed between both parties at a rate of US$12,900/ day for a duration of 50 days.

– A commission of 0.25 pct (of the agreed price x duration) is payable by both parties to the FFA Broker that put the deal together.

– Settlement against Route 3A of the BPI as an average of the last 7 indices published in September 2003.

CONCLUSION – 13th April 2003

– The average of the two indices used for settlement is US$13,500.

– The settlement price being higher than the fixed price, therefore the FFA Seller pays the Buyer US$600 × 50 days duration = US$30,000 (payable within seven days).

– The Charterer is happy as he gets US$30,000 to offset against the higher rate he will have to pay for a vessel on the spot market. The Owner is happy as the market is higher than he anticipated.

– The problem with derivative markets of all types is that they are rarely confined to key players such as shipowners and charterers but will also attract speculators. The sort of win-win situation described above is a good example of the benefits of such a system but it must be added that where there are winners there are also losers and when the winner is a speculator and the loser a shipowner or charterer then the whole system begins to fall down.

– A lot of big names in shipping have had their fingers burnt by dabbling in derivatives and many have turned their back on them altogether. In other sectors of commerce trading in derivatives has led to massive price rises in essential commodities and there are calls for the activities of derivate traders to be curtailed.

3.9   SELF-ASSESSMENT AND TEST QUESTIONS

Attempt the following and check your answers from the text:

1.   Under what headings do the main practitioners in the dry cargo freight market fall?

2.   In what different roles may a dry cargo chartering Broker be acting?

3.   What are INCOTERMS?

4.   How many methods of ship employment can you list?

5.   For what items would a time charterer be responsible which would not be the responsibility of a voyage charterer?

6.   What is meant by 'breach of warranty of authority'?

Having completed Chapter Three attempt the following and submit your essay to your Tutor.

1.   Referring to the reporting style of **Appendix 8**, and using the data provided in **Appendix 9**, provide a freight market report of about 250 words.

State whether you are addressing your report to a "Shipowner" or to a "Charterer", advising your opinion of the best course of action.

The Shipowner has two 'panamax' vessels open 'prompt', one in Osaka the other in Rotterdam, and prefers the iron ore trade.

The Charterer has two early cargoes of iron ore to ship, both of about 100/150,000 tonnes, one from Dampier to Rotterdam and the other from Tubarao to Rotterdam.

2.   Some of the time charter fixtures mention payment of a ballast bonus. What do you understand by this term and give reasons why the Charterer does not merely agree to a higher daily hire rate for the ship.

Chapter 4

CHARTERING CONTRACTS

4.1 INTRODUCTION

In this Chapter we will examine the documents which control the whole chartering market and form the cornerstone of shipbroking life. So much of the practical life of a Broker revolves around the various requirements of charter parties that it is absolutely essential you understand them as fully as possible. No one expects every Broker to understand every charter party in detail, but Brokers should be aware of the basic structure of voyage and time charter forms, and should also be capable of nominating a suitable charter party for any particular commodity or trade.

Whilst in shipping almost anything is possible (provided it is legal) there are usually specific charter parties which relate to particular trades, and a Shipbroker should recommend and use these if possible, since most will have stood the test of time both in practical everyday usage and, as important, in legal dispute. An example of what can happen when the wrong form is chosen is given in Chapter Ten (The Jordan II case).

To help you in this aim, **Appendix 11** lists a selection of important dry cargo charter parties under the headings of various commodities.

As you can see from this list, some dry cargo charter parties in use today are around eighty years old and, although many during that period have grown unsuitable for the trade for which they were originally intended and/or the trade itself has become obsolete, leading to the discontinuation of use of those charter parties, some of these older forms have still a valid role to play and have been updated when and where necessary to keep step with market developments.

Even so, new dry cargo charter party forms are published from time-to-time and older ones revised and updated, and active in this field are two bodies that you will encounter in particular, The Baltic International Maritime Council (BIMCO), and The Association of Shipbrokers and Agents (USA) Inc (ASBA). BIMCO, based in Copenhagen, has an international membership and originated as a Shipowners' lobby group before expanding its Broker and Charterer membership in recent years. ASBA is an American organisation, based in New York and, as its name implies, is an association of Shipbrokers and Agents.

As will be seen in **Appendix 11**, other bodies are also active in drafting charter parties, some international (e.g. FONASBA) some national (e.g. UK Chamber of Shipping, now part of the General Council of British Shipping) and in some trades, the Charterers themselves have drafted the charter parties for their own commodities (e.g. S. African Anthracite Producers Assn.).

In general all these parties co-ordinate their activities with one another and in particular through the Documentary Committee of BIMCO. We have selected two forms which contain an illustrative structure in their printed versions, and which are of value for our purposes in this publication. The two selected are the MULTIFORM of FONASBA (The Federation of National Associations of Shipbrokers and Agents), (**Appendix 12**), as our voyage charter party, and the ASBATIME of ASBA (**Appendix 14**) for our time charter, supported by the AMWELSH (**Appendix 13**) and the New York Produce (**Appendix 15**), both of ASBA. More about these later. In the meantime we will start with examining charter parties in general terms.

A charter party, properly signed, by those authorised to do so, sets out in written form the contract that has been made between the Owner (or disponent Owner) and the Charterer. It factually records all the details of the agreement reached between the parties but you should always remember that the charter party is the memorandum of the agreement; the contract itself will have been made (as we have seen in Chapter Three) by word of mouth, fax exchanges or whatever. It can exist independently of the physical movements of the vessel and in some cases, especially in the fast-moving world of short-sea trading where a vessel may complete two or even three cargoes in one week, frequently the drafting of charter parties is some way behind physical events, and a ship may have loaded, carried the cargo and discharged, freight may have been paid and laytime calculated and settled even before a hard pressed Broker has set to work to draw up the contractual agreement, the charter party.

On the other hand, the availability of the charter party may be an essential for trading purposes, the release of letters of credit, etc. and it should be the aim of every Broker, no matter how hard pressed, to prepare a charter party as soon as possible following the successful conclusion of a negotiation. Just occasionally, the preparation of the charter party reveals an error in the negotiating process, and the sooner such errors are brought out into the open and reconciled the better for all concerned.

4.1.1 'Official Charter Parties'

Certain charter parties are 'official', in that they have been inspected and passed by an authoritative body, e.g: a chamber of shipping, whilst others have not been so treated or may have been found lacking in some respect. Certain organisations take it upon themselves on behalf of their members and, in the case of BIMCO, as a service to world shipping, to inspect and, where possible, to 'recommend' or 'approve' various forms, going so far as to themselves draft and issue some documents.

The explanation of certain varied words of recommendation at the head of some charter parties can be briefly described as follows:

> **Agreed or Trade:** The charter party wording has been 'agreed' between a body such as BIMCO (broadly representing Owners' interests) and a Charterers' organisation for a particular trade. The printed conditions of such a charter party may not be altered in any way without the express agreement of all the organisations drawing up the document, which is compulsory for all engaged in the particular trade.

> **Adopted:** Where a body (e.g. a Chamber of Shipping) 'adopts' a charter party that has been 'agreed' between say, a Charterers' organisation and BIMCO. An example is the POLCOALVOY charter party, adopted by the General Council of British Shipping. Such a body can also adopt a charter party that has not been 'agreed', should it approve of that document's contents, although in the latter case the clauses can be altered by mutual consent by contracting parties in the trade.

> **Recommended:** Where charter party text is liable to alterations in negotiations, although the wording of the printed text meets with the approval of the inspecting body, the form can be used as a 'recommended' document. An example is the GENCON charter party. (See **Appendix 20**).

> **Approved:** Simply an expression describing 'recommended', 'adopted', or 'agreed' charter parties.

> **Issued:** A charter party for which a group such as BIMCO is responsible for drafting and making available for use.

4.1.2 Charter Party Library

For those faced with the awe-inspiring task of studying popular dry cargo charter party forms, it will be found productive for the purposes of both examinations and practical trading, to examine such blank printed documents as can be obtained alongside final, negotiated and duly amended charter parties. In this way commonplace alterations, deletions and additions to printed wording can be observed and lessons learned for future negotiations. Additionally, for students and for practising Brokers alike, the maintaining of a comprehensive file of sample charter parties, both blank and worked examples, is an excellent habit and one which will repay the time and trouble involved many times over during a career in the industry.

In large centres such as London and New York, blank copies of most charter party forms can be obtained from specialist stationers supplying maritime documents, failing which local Shipbrokers or the organisation publishing the form may be able to provide guidance on its availability in particular areas. For those with Internet access copies of many BIMCO approved forms can be downloaded from the BIMCO website at www.bimco.dk

4.2   CHARTER PARTY WORDING

The wording of most charter parties (other than in 'agreed' documents) is used only as a basis for negotiation and, where necessary, the printed text is altered, deleted or added to, so as to reflect the specific agreement reached. To the amended 'main' form will usually be added various typed additional clauses, known also as riders, or as side clauses, and peculiar to the particular business. On some occasions, an addendum or a side letter, or two, will be added to the charter party, to record a particular clause or clauses that one or other of the contracting parties wish kept confidential from certain others who might subsequently refer to the charter party. For example, the rate of freight or hire may be treated in a confidential manner, with the main charter party clause referring only to a rate/hire 'as agreed', the actual figure decided upon appearing only in a detachable addendum or side letter to the charter party. Therefore, port agents, etc. would be unaware of the rate of freight/hire agreed upon, since they would need only the main charter party and rider clauses to perform their functions satisfactorily.

Occasionally, additional agreement(s) will need to be made subsequent to the fixture and the drawing-up of the charter party, and these subsequent agreements are normally recorded in additional addenda.

It is good practice to refer to the number of any *additional clauses* at the foot of the main charter party form, with such wording, for example, as *'additional clauses 29 to 55 inclusive, as attached, are deemed part of and are incorporated into this charter party'*. Such is not necessarily the case with addenda, however, and it may not be apparent to those reading the main charter party and additional clauses that other agreement has been reached. If addenda are drawn up, though, they should for good order's sake be accorded a reference number in numerical sequence, i.e: Addendum No. 1, 2, etc.

A side letter is an alternative to an addendum for recording agreements that both parties consider too sensitive for general perusal, e.g; the guaranteeing by one company of a sister company's performance of the contract. The general market feeling, however, is that a side letter is not quite so close to the heart of a contract (the charter party) as is a numbered addendum and perhaps, if legally tested, a side letter would not carry the weight of an addendum.

It is common practice in sea-trading, however, not to draw up a charter party from a blank form but to base negotiating upon a previous fixture, altering main terms and additional clauses alike as required. This system is both labour-saving and expedient, at the same time providing evidence to Shipowners and their Brokers that certain clauses they encounter in the charter party and perhaps find unattractive have been previously agreed by other Owners.

In certain cases, where chartering business is sub-let by a *head charterer,* the *sub-charterer* may be restricted to negotiating strictly on the basis of the *head-charter party,* using only clauses that are identical, termed back-to-back, with the main, governing contract.

Each charter party may differ in some particular aspect, some including peculiarities not seen in others. It is the task of the sea trader to be aware of the pitfalls and advantages of major charter party forms, and for Shipbrokers to advise their principals of these when conducting chartering, so that by adept negotiation the most favourable conclusion can be reached.

With some documents it is commonplace during fixing to negotiate that printed sections of text be deleted or amended in some way. These negotiations are always subject, however, to the relative strengths of the parties involved and, although one or other may be fully aware of the potential pitfalls of a certain clause, it may not be possible to alter it favourably if the other party is negotiating from a position of strength. Additionally, depending upon the particular circumstances of the voyage under negotiation, certain wordings may well have little effect whilst, for another voyage and another set of circumstances, the phraseology agreed upon may make all the difference between the success or financial failure of the venture.

But to start with a sea-trader owes it to himself and his principals to be at least aware of common charter party wordings and alterations so that act advantageously or otherwise to prospective ventures. Unfortunately, it is not possible to learn all of these technical peculiarities from books on the subject. Much must be learned from experience and from the advice of colleagues. Knowledge can also be gained from comparison between blank pro-forma and previously negotiated contracts, and from intelligent perusal of shipping newspaper and magazine reports of shipping disputes and legal decisions. Implications for chartering of legal decisions are reported in circulars issued by bodies such as BIMCO, P&I Clubs and the like, all essential reading for the sea-trader.

4.3 DRAWING UP CHARTER PARTIES

Once negotiations leading to a fixture have been concluded, it becomes the task of the Shipbroker acting for the Charterer to draw up the charter party, amending the printed text where necessary, and adding appropriate side clauses and addenda. Care should be taken to avoid repetition and the inclusion of irrelevant and unnecessary clauses which are liable to creep in if the fixture is based upon a completed charter party drawn up on a previous occasion. But nothing should be deleted, inserted or altered without the agreement of the Owner's Broker. It is also advisable to include the text of *all* clauses agreed upon, not merely to mention them. For example, if protective clauses are included, e.g. the Both to Blame Collision Clause, it is not really good enough to state that it is deemed to be included. It should actually be attached for all to read if required.

There are schools of thought on what should happen next. Ideally, before any person signs a charter party, it should be checked by all concerned so as to confirm their agreement with the contents. It is also polite to follow this course of action. However, where the parties are spread across the globe, this is impracticable and time-consuming. Of course, a fixture has been made verbally or in a series of telex messages or cables, and the charter parties existence or otherwise does not alter that agreement. But a charter parties prime function is to factually record an agreement in an easily read document, so as to avoid later misunderstandings or poor memory. Thus its early production is indeed desirable.

For practicable purposes, therefore, it is best that the Charterers Broker promptly prepares the document and either submits same to his Principal, or signs on his Principal's behalf under his authority, before despatching the half-signed original to the Owner's Broker, retaining working copies for his own and his Principal's use. Any errors which the Owner's Broker discovers upon checking the charter party should be discussed with the Charterer's Broker and, if necessary, rectified. Once content that the document before him factually represents all that has been agreed, the Owner's Broker should similarly arrange for his Principal to sign or should himself sign under appropriate authority.

It is then a matter of courtesy, the Charterer's Broker having drawn up the original document, for the Owner's Broker to provide whatever copies are required by the various parties to the contract, the original charter party usually being retained by the Owner.

But this procedure is by no means sacrosanct, and can be varied at the whim of the parties concerned, the above formula being suggested merely from the point of view of convenience and practicality.

There are several commercially available charter party editors that can be installed on office computers, and which can produce charter parties at the press of a button. Programs like this are very useful in busy offices and have dramatically cut the time taken to prepare a final charter party.

BIMCO, has developed an Internet based charter party editor, named "BIMCO's idea". It is built around a widely used word processing package meaning that most users will already be familiar with the layout and controls. Templates of BIMCO approved documents are kept and are available in a central, common storage, whereas edited documents are stored on a private area only accessible by the individual user who must pre-register and subscribe to the system

This ensures the integrity of the original BIMCO form and allows new forms to be added rapidly to the catalogue of available documents. Upon printing, the edited document is e-mailed to a pre-registered e-mail address in the shape of a pdf file. The document may subsequently be distributed by e-mail to the relevant parties. Another great advantage over the old, PC based BIMCO Charter Party Editor is that the application is not locked to one computer, but may be accessed by anybody in your organisation, from any computer, without the need for registering that particular PC with BIMCO.

4.3.1 Signing Charter Parties

Care should be taken by the Brokers when and if signing on behalf of their Principals to show the means of that authority, e.g.;

> By telex authority from
> MEGABULK UK CORPORATION, Monrovia

> For and on behalf of
> ABACUS CHARTERING LIMITED, London
> (as agents or Brokers only)

> **John Smith, Director**

It is important to include the wording: '...as agents (or Brokers) only', to illustrate clearly that the role of Abacus is not that of principal.

With such a qualified signature, a Broker will not be held personally liable for the performance of the contract unless there is a clause or wording in the charter party clearly showing that the Broker is in fact a Principal.

Addenda and side letters should be treated in the same fashion as charter parties, being signed by both parties, or their Brokers, in the manner described above.

Adding Originals

Occasionally, perhaps in agreements where documentary credits are involved, it may become necessary to produce two or more 'original charter parties'. In such cases, each document should bear its proper title, e.g: 'First Original', or 'Second Original'.

4.4 THE VOYAGE CHARTER PARTY

This document covers the largest proportion of any fixtures arranged on the chartering market, despite the trend in recent years for charterers to take more vessels on trip time charter terms than was once the case.

Whilst the following list of clauses is by no means exhaustive, it provides some idea of the normal clauses required in a voyage charter party for dry cargo vessels:

List of Voyage Charter Party Clauses

1.	Preamble	17.	Overtime
2.	Cargo Description/Quantity	18.	Shifting/Seaworthy Trim
3.	Loading Places	19.	Cargo Separation and Tallying
4.	Loading Orders/Rotation	20.	Dues and Taxes

5.	Discharging Places	21.	Ports Agents
6.	Discharge Orders/Rotation	22.	Bills of Lading
7.	Laydays and Cancelling	23.	Lightening
8.	Freight	24.	General Average
9.	Cost of Loading/Discharging	25.	Strikes
10.	Notice of Readiness/Time Counts	26.	Exceptions
11.	Loading/Discharging Rates	27.	Commissions
12.	Excepted Periods	28.	Protection Clauses
13.	Demurrage/Despatch	29.	Lien
14.	Notices	30.	Ice
15.	Ship's Gear	31.	War Risks
16.	Grab Discharge/Stevedore Damage	32.	Signature

Elements of a Voyage Charter Party:

We will now examine the items on the above list in the context of an actual printed charter party form, with reference to the text of the MULTIFORM Multi-purpose Charter Party 1982 as revised in 1986, which document you will find reproduced in **Appendix 12**, with occasional references to the AMWELSH charter party in **Appendix 13**.

The MULTIFORM Charter was produced by FONASBA in an attempt to create a modern and even handed, as between Owner and Charterer, general purpose voyage charter. It has unfortunately found little favour in the market perhaps because for those very reasons that make it an excellent study form.

You will probably find the best way of understanding the following references is to first read the relevant text in the MULTIFORM Charter Party and then the written commentary below.

1. **Preamble:** This can be extensive in some charter parties. In the MULTIFORM much of what may be found in preambles of certain forms is contained in clause 1. There are two important aspects of the brief MULTIFORM preamble, the place and date of the charter party.

    Place: This can be important as, in the absence of a clause to the contrary, the place where a contract is deemed to have been made may govern the law which is to be applied to that contract in the event of a dispute. So, if the place is London, English Law may very likely prevail. The place can be defined as where the contract is made, usually the domicile of the Charterer's Broker, not necessarily the abode of one or other of the Principals.

    For certainty so that a dispute can be heard under a particular jurisdiction, it is strongly advisable that a contract should include an **'exclusive jurisdiction clause'**, in other words, the charter party should state, for example, that **'English Law is to apply'**.

    Date: Equally important, the date to be shown is that by which fixture negotiations are concluded, with all subjects lifted, in other words, when all negotiating formalities are complete.

    Names and Domiciles of Contracting Parties: (Clause 1). The names of the Shipowner (or disponent Owner) and Charterer, and their domiciles i.e; their **'full styles'**.

    Name and Brief Description of Vessel: (Clause 1). The MULTIFORM allows for a more complete vessel description in the main, printed part of the form than many (e.g. compare with the AMWELSH), others utilising an additional, rider clause, to provide concise details relevant to the trade/cargo envisaged. The position of the vessel at the time the contract is negotiated is also important (see line 4) as this governs its likely readiness to load (see line 5). These lines are often treated very light-heartedly in contemporary negotiations and you will frequently encounter the simple word 'trading' after the printed word 'now' as in line 4. The courts, however, attach considerable importance to the accuracy of information about expected readiness to load and any substantial error in the stated position of the vessel can be considered misrepresentation. This could, therefore, be treated as a breach of condition entitling the Charterer to rescind the contract. In the absence of any more specific stipulation, the ship is obliged to proceed to the loading port with 'reasonable despatch'. It would not, for example, be right for a Shipowner who had fixed his ship with laydays and cancelling 1/20 July stating 'now trading and expected ready to load 3rd July' to slip in an additional short voyage and turn up on the 17th July instead of around the 3rd. The time span between laydays and cancelling is to cover the Owner against unforeseen delays and if the Owner has been reckless or deliberately misleading in the expected readiness of his ship, the Charterer would be entitled to claim damages for any loss attributable to the undue delay. The Charterer would not, of course, be permitted to rescind the charter unless the result of the breach was such as to frustrate the entire object of the contract.

In the last year or so, many owners have begun exploring the possibilities of slow steaming at one or two knots below normal service speed. This is done both to reduce fuel consumption for economic reasons and to reduce a ship's environmental impact (less fuel used means less CO_2 emitted). Unlike time charter parties where a ship's speed is warranted, voyage charters may not always contain references to the speed at which the vessel should complete the voyage.

The description of the vessel will usually include the normal service speed of the ship which some owners will reduce slightly as time elapses after the last drydocking due to the inevitable deterioration in performance over time. However, there is always an expectation that the ship will proceed at the fastest service speed commensurate with weather conditions and safety of the ship and cargo.

This issue has been tested many times in the courts and the accepted position is that there is an implied obligation that the Master should prosecute voyages with reasonable/due/utmost despatch. Most of the past legal judgements concerned instances of deviation or some other delay such as waiting for sapre parts or additional cargoes and the question of economic or environmental reasons has not really been decided upon legally.

It could be that slow steaming without consulting and agreeing first with the charterer, may open an owner up to claims for damages.

Condition of Vessel: (Clause 2). It is usual for a Shipowner (or disponent Owner) to confirm that a vessel is in a suitable condition safely and properly to undertake the contractual voyage (line 24).

2. **Cargo Description and Quantity:** (Clause 2). Commodity and nature of goods to be carried (e.g. in bulk or bagged); stowage factor (e.g. about 55 cubic feet per tonne); and either minimum/maximum quantity or cargo size margins and in whose option (e.g. 12,000 tonnes, 5% more or less in Owner's option).

3. **Loading Places:** (Clause 2). Names of loading place(s) and/or range (e.g. Bordeaux/Hamburg range); mention of number of safe berths/anchorages Charterers entitled to use at each place; whether vessel to remain **'always afloat'** or **'safely aground'**; maximum/minimum available drafts.

4. **Loading Port Orders/rotation:** (lines 31 to 34). Rotation can be very important, since extra steaming can be involved, adding to an Owner's expenses, whereas it might be essential for a Charterer to negotiate loading in a particular rotation so that ship availability fits in with cargo availability.

5.&6. **Discharging Places and Port Orders/rotation:** (Clause 3). The comments under 3 and 4 above apply.

7. **Laydays and Cancelling:** (Clause 4). The spread of dates during which a vessel is to present herself at the first (or sole) loading port. This spread should be entered in a contract, as well as conditions under which the contract can be cancelled in the event that the vessel is unable to meet those dates.

8. **Freight:** (Clause 5). The amount and currency of freight; to whom, where and when payable. The risk of vessel and/or cargo loss on passage in relation to freight should be specified, i.e; whether freight is deemed earned as cargo is loaded (as in the MULTIFORM) or upon delivery (e.g; as in the C ORE 7).

9. **Cost of Loading/Discharging:** (Clause 6). Which of the parties to the contract is to appoint and pay for cargo handling at each port. (See also Clause 11 of the AMWELSH).

10. **Notice of Readiness/Time Counting:** (Clause 7). An important clause in the calculation of Laytime, (see Chapter Six).

11. **Loading/Discharging Rates:** (Clause 8). The speed at which cargo handling activities are to be performed.

12. **Excepted Periods:** (Clause 8). Periods when cargo handling normally does not take place and, therefore, will not count in the computation of laytime unless work is actually carried out during such times 'when only time actually used shall count'. You will, later on, encounter charters where the loading takes place at highly automated terminals (e.g. iron ore) where there are no excepted periods and the abbreviated SHINC (Sundays and holidays included) will appear in the negotiations.

13. **Demurrage/Despatch:** (Clause 9). Daily amount of liquidated damages (demurrage) payable by a Charterer in the event a vessel is detained in port beyond the maximum permitted laytime, as well as any stipulations to despatch (at usually half the rate of demurrage) – see Chapter Six.

14. **Notices:** (Clause 10). A Shipowner/Master may be required to give comprehensive notices of a vessel's expected arrival at the first (or sole) loading port, failing which the Shipowner may face a penalty in the form of extra laytime allowed a charterer.

15. **Ship's Gear:** (Clause 12). A normal clause in dry cargo shipping, specifying that a vessel's gear will be maintained to a high standard and specifying what happens in the event of gear breakdown resulting in extra expense.

16. **Grab Discharge/Stevedore Damage:** (Clauses 14 & 15). Owners normally confirm that a vessel is suitable for grab discharge and formalities need to be set out in the event that a vessel suffers damage during the cargo handling processes.

    Frequently, however, Masters are required to notify Charterers or stevedores upon 'occurrence' of damage, even though this may not be discovered until overstowed cargo is unloaded at ports of discharge. It is therefore reasonable that the word 'occurrence' be replaced by 'discovery'.

17. **Overtime.** (Clause 17). Who is to pay for overtime.

18. **Shifting/Seaworthy trim:** (Clauses 18 & 19). Who is to pay shifting costs (if any) between berths, also whether time so used is to count as laytime. The vessel is to be left in safe seaworthy condition between ports. It is important to add in a clause of this nature that it is up to the Master to decide whether a vessel is in safe seaworthy trim or not. Silence on this point may lead to eventual dispute.

19. **Cargo Separations and Tallying:** (Clauses 13 & 16). Where a vessel is to carry various parcels of cargo, it may not be possible for all separations between the individual parcels to be 'natural' - i.e. separated by bulkheads and/or, in the case of tweendeckers, by tweendecks. The parties may need to agree between themselves on how parcels

loaded in the same compartment are to be separated – e.g. by polyethylene sheeting or by tarpaulins and on who is to supply and pay for this facility. The tallying (checking) of cargo as it is loaded or discharged is frequently an expensive operation and, if not carried out conscientiously, substantial cargo claims can arise for alleged short delivery, bad condition, etc. It is essential that some provision as to who is responsible at least for payment of tally clerks be entered in a charter party covering the loading of bagged or similar cargo.

20. **Dues and Taxes:** (Clause 20). This clause specifies which party to the contract is responsible for taxes which may be levied against the vessel and/or her cargo and/or the freight.

21. **Port Agents:** (Clause 21). In any charter party it is advisable that reference be made as to which of the parties is responsible for the selection of an Agent. It is important to remember that the Agent remains the servant of the Shipowner, and the Shipowner remains responsible for paying the port costs and the agency fee. Nevertheless, the appointment of an efficient Agent is also important to a Charterer, who will need to feel secure in the knowledge that proper liaison is being maintained between the Agent and, say, a cargo shipper. Consequently it is often the case that Charterers specifically negotiate that they have the right to nominate the Port Agents that will be appointed by the Shipowner.

22. **Bills of Lading:** (Clauses 22 & 33). The full import of these provisions will be better understood after reading Chapter Eight. For the present it is important to make sure that similar provisions should be contained in all voyage charter parties.

23. **Lightening:** (Clause 23). Where cargo lightening is necessary, a comprehensive clause covering all facets of this sometimes complex operation should be negotiated. The MULTIFORM and AMWELSH clauses between them cover several of these facets but not nearly all of them.

24. **General Average:** (Clause 26). A clause specifying where General Average (if any) is to be adjusted (e.g. 'in London') and/or paid, irrespective of the ports of call involved and the laws relating to GA e.g. 'as per York/Antwerp Rules 1974'. Earlier charter parties may refer in their printed text to York/Antwerp Rules 1950, which should be amended during negotiation to reflect the latest Rules. It is sometimes negotiated also that where a cargo involves voyages to/from the United States or United States Principals, the New Jason Clause be incorporated into the contract, dealing with General Average law and practice for adjustments made in the United States (see Clause 24 of the AMWELSH).

25. **Strikes:** (Clause 27). Both parties to a charter party have risks and liabilities in the event of a strike. Various clauses exist, some in far greater detail than in others. The MULTIFORM repeats the Strike Clause from the GENCON charter party, notorious for its confusing language and very much in the Owner's favour. Most strike clauses are in fact biased in favour of Charterers, placing the risk of strikes on Owners – e.g. compare the sweeping provisions of the AMWELSH Clause 9.

26. **Exceptions:** (Clause 28). The rights of contracting parties to cancel the charter party in case of events making its performance virtually impossible – e.g. Force Majeure or Acts of God.

27. **Commission:** (Clause 31). Specifies the amount and to whom commissions and brokerages are payable, usually adding that commissions/brokerages are payable on freight, deadfreight and demurrage.

28. **Protecting Clauses:** (Clauses 32 & 33). A set of clauses commonly included in the printed form of a charter party or as additional clauses. The New Jason already mentioned is one such clause (Clause 26). However, others have their roles to play, which are:

P&I Bunkering Clause: sets out Owners' rights to deviate for bunkers during the contractual voyage.

Clause Paramount: incorporates a set of rules into the contract (and into bills of lading issued under the contract), which govern the rights and responsibilities of the carrier. Appropriate amendment should be made to the older forms to ensure that the latest rules apply, the MULTIFORM updating the long established Hague Rules, to incorporate the Hague/Visby Rules of 1968. Other charter parties involving voyages to/from America and/or Canada should utilise either the USA or the Canadian Clauses Paramount (see the AMWELSH, Clause 24).

A new set of rules developed by the UN and now known as the Rotterdam Rules were made open for ratification in early 2009. If these rules attract an appropriate number of ratifications and are adopted into national legislation by states they are likely to become the new standard rules. While parties to a charter party are free to negotiate conditions applying, the Rotterdam Rules may well at some future time apply to bills of lading issued under the c/p.

Both to Blame Collision: covers an Owner's rights in respect of American Law in case of collision at sea.

29. **Lien and Cesser:** (Clause 24). Most charter parties contain a cesser and lien clause and the MULTIFORM (and AMWELSH Clause 21) are no exceptions.

30. **Ice:** (Clause 32). Depending on the trade involved, it may not be necessary for an ice clause to be included in a charter party, but where one is required, great care should be taken over its wording.

The MULTIFORM uses the BIMCO recommended GENCON ICE CLAUSE, which is widely reproduced in other charter party forms.

The object of an ice clause should be to prevent a Shipowner and his Master being left with no alternative but to attempt to proceed to a contractual destination irrespective of ice conditions, and to avoid damage that may be caused to ship and cargo as a result.

31. **War Risks:** (Clause 32). War risks clauses should be examined in detail as some are unfair to Shipowners, others to Charterers and/or patently unsuitable for the purpose intended. For example, the Chamber of Shipping War Risk Clauses 1 and 2 are some fifty years old, out of date, and silent on several important issues, one being cancellation rights in the case of an outbreak of war before or after a vessel's voyage to her loading port, or after arrival. Yet still the Chamber of Shipping Clauses are widely utilised.

A War Risk Clause should provide a Shipowner with the right to refuse to allow his vessel and her crew to enter or to remain in an area which has become dangerous due to warlike activity. To accomplish this objective, MULTIFORM uses the VOYWAR 1950 Clause, itself forty years old and although better suited to current needs, biased in the Owner's favour. BIMCO recommended their own Standard War Risk Clauses – "Voywar 1993" and "Conwartime 1993" and these represent the best current position.

32. *Signature:* **No charter party is complete without the signatures of or on behalf of the parties concerned:**

4.5 VOYAGE CHARTER PARTIES FOR SPECIFIC TRADES

A quick glance down the list of charter parties in **Appendix 11** will show various voyage charter parties under the headings, grain, coal, fertilisers, etc. As well as containing basic clauses as detailed in the above 'elements' section, each of these 'trade' charter parties has specific clauses that are of particular import for the commodity involved.

Grain: Appendix 17 contains the important NORGRAIN charter party, as revised in 1989. Readers of this text should look particularly at the following clauses that refer specifically to grain carriage related problems:

Clause 12 – Self-trimming/Wing tanks

14 – Cargo separations

15 – Securing of cargo/Bag bleeding

16 – Cargo fumigation

18 (e) – Cargo compartment inspection

It is usual in grain trading that full freight (or at least a substantial percentage) is paid before release of the Bill(s) of Lading by the Owners/Master to the shippers. The responsibility of paying the cost of loading can vary, being negotiable as either for Owners account and referred to as 'gross load' or for Charterer's (shipper's) account either referred to as 'free load' (free of expense to the vessel) or 'nett terms'. The NORGRAIN Clauses 10 and 11 leaves it to the parties to decide and to record the result of their negotiations.

Coal: The AMWELSH in **Appendix 13** is now the world's major coal charter party dealing not only with cargoes of coal from America (as the name implies) but with coal cargoes from elsewhere, e.g; Australia. The latest edition was revised in 1993 from the original version which, as the full name tells us, was an adaptation of the Welsh Coal Charter 1896 and some of the wording is over a century old.

Here loading costs are payable by Charterers; loading, dumping and spout trimming costs (see Clause 11). Dumping is specific to the practice in America of 'dumping' coal from railway wagons at the loading port.

Ore: Appendix 18 contains the OREVOY 1980 charterparty. There are various ore charters and we could have selected the long established MEDITERRANEAN ORE, the C ORE 7 c/p, but decided against this because of the old fashioned language employed and the references to obsolete ports and currency which, in any case, are nowadays widely deleted, so much so that the C ORE 7 is little more than a widely deleted main form with various individually designed riders attached.

However, some ore charters (including the C ORE 7) have the penalising provisions against the Owner discounting time lost due to shore disputes or machinery breakdown.

For relatively short duration deep sea voyages, it is often the case that freight is paid only after delivery of the cargo at the discharge port.

Ore is usually loaded in a wettened condition, and weight loss during the voyage as moisture evaporates and drains off may be considerable. Consequently, although the OREVOY is not very clear on this point, it is normally the case that Charterers negotiate the right to pay freight on either (1) the bill of lading quantity established at the loading port, (2) on the out-turn weight ascertained at the port of discharge, or (3) basis 'less half of one percent of the bill of lading weight, in lieu of weighing', frequently the latter.

Fertilisers: There are various fertiliser charter party forms. The one selected here in **Appendix 19** is the AFRICANPHOS 1950, widely utilised in the major trade involved around the export of bulk phosphate rock from West Africa (e.g. Kpeme) right round to North Africa (e.g. Sfax).

A peculiarity of this trade is that loading costs are frequently for the Shipowner's account (as per Clause 7) and loaded at a 'scale' rate established by the cargo quantity (see the scale inserted in Clause 8). This is described as 'Scale Gross Load' and costs are currently around US$ 2.00 per tonne loaded plus a percentage addition for value added tax. Occasionally the agreement may also allow for gross discharge.

There is a traditional 'turn time' applicable at the loading port, as expressed in Clause 6 of the charter party, and sometimes this applies also at the discharging port (see Clause 18). A new Ferticon c/p is currently being prepared by BIMCO and should be ready some time in 2008.

Other Commodities: Other commodities have specialised clauses in their charter parties, e.g; timber, and those students likely to be engaged in those trades should familiarise themselves with any peculiarities involved.

Factors specific to various trades will be found in 'CARGOES' as commodities are encountered upon reading the book. However, practitioners are advised to take seriously the suggestion of starting their own charter party 'library' adding to this as and when they come across new forms, which should be read through both for the sake of interest and to gain further knowledge.

4.6 THE TIME CHARTER PARTY

As we have seen from Chapter Three, time chartering can be sub-divided between period time charters perhaps involving several years and trip time charters, for one or several trips. There are no charter party forms designed purely for trip charters, an employment technique that has become particularly popular during recent years, trip charters being negotiated on standard time charter forms and adapted slightly where appropriate.

Although considerably fewer in number than the wide choice available for voyage chartering, there is an adequate number of dry cargo time charter forms for use in the industry, although by far the largest number of deep-sea dry cargo trips and periods are fixed on the basis of the New York Produce Exchange (NYPE) Charter Party, first drawn up as long ago as 1913. It has been updated since, most notably in 1981, when it was renamed ASBATIME. Nonetheless, by that time the 1946 version had become widely used and, to the basic printed text, many charterers had added over the years numerous side-clauses. It transpired that few Charterers were prepared to abandon their NYPE 1946 + side clauses charter party and so, despite the availability in the ASBATIME of a neater, more up to date charter party incorporating many of the previous NYPE clauses, and standard rider additions, the 'market' remains wedded to the NYPE 1946 c/p. It has again been revised in 1993 and renamed New York Produce Exchange Time Charter (NYPE 93) incorporating many of the side clauses commonly used in conjunction with the 1946 version, in the hope that this will create a more suitable replacement. While it is still too early to confirm that it is generally replacing the earlier versions, there is no doubt that it has met with great market interest.

For convenience we will examine the elements of a time charter party based on the ASBATIME (**Appendix 14**), you will also find the NYPE 93 form enclosed in the appendices (**Appendix 15**)

Whilst the following list is by no means exhaustive, it provides some idea of the normal clauses required in a time charter party for dry cargo vessels:

List of Time Charter Party Clauses

1.	Preamble	17.	Logbooks
2.	Vessel Description	18.	Supercargo
3.	Duration of Period/Description of Trip(s)	19.	Pollution
4.	Trading Intention/limits	20.	Salvage
5.	Cargo Intention/exclusions	21.	Laying-up
6.	Vessel Condition	22.	Arbitration
7.	Owners' Responsibilities	23.	Lien
8.	Charterers' Responsibilities	24.	Assignment
9.	Delivery and Re-delivery	25.	Exceptions
10.	Bunkers	26.	Requisitioning
11.	Hire	27.	Bills of Lading
12.	Off-hire	28.	Stevedoring Damage

13.	Vessel Performance	29.	Commissions
14.	Vessel Maintenance	30.	Protective Clauses
15.	Cargo Claims	31.	Signature
16.	Master/Officers		

1. **Preamble:** Contrary to the MULTIFORM and the AMWELSH, the preamble of the ASBATIME is lengthy, taking up most of the first page of the charter party, and covering a wide range of subjects within its text, not least the place where the contract is made, the date of the charter party and the names and domiciles of the contracting parties. (NYPE 93 follows the same pattern.)

2. **Vessel Description:** (Preamble lines 5/23). Depending upon the complexity of the intended trade, the description of the vessel may be more or less as for voyage charter parties, with the important addition of speeds and bunker consumptions. For the sake of clarity, it is also advisable to include clarification of the term 'good weather conditions' (in line 19), usually with reference to weather and sea conditions (e.g: Beaufort Wind Scale and, perhaps Douglas Sea State see NYPE 93 and Chapter Nine) against which factors a vessel's performance should be measured. Not forgetting the vessel's position and readiness (line 23) which is as important to a time charterer as to a voyage charterer.

3. **Duration of Period/Description of Trip(s):** (Preamble lines 27/30). The duration of a period time charter should be entered, together with a margin either side of the formal period, e.g; '15 days more or less, at Charterers' option'. The parties can agree an exact redelivery date, but in practice this is difficult to comply with and, in the event of legal disputes, most courts would imply a reasonable margin.

    For trip charters designed for specific voyages, it is commonplace to insert an approximation of the voyage duration, e.g: '45 days', although this is normally qualified by the addition of the words 'all going well' or 'about' or 'without guarantee'. (Here a word of warning for Shipowners and their Brokers. Legally 'about' will be given a reasonable implication. An actual duration of '50 days', for example, could be interpreted as 'about 45 days'. However, 'without guarantee' means exactly that. In effect redelivery after only '10 days' is legally satisfactory).

4. **Trading Intentions/limits:** (Preamble lines 57/62 – Clause 6). The areas of the world in which the vessel is to be employed should be entered, e.g: 'world-wide, but always within Institute Warranty Limits' (see Chapter Nine), as well as listing those countries and parts of the world specifically excluded from the permissible trading area. Where there is insufficient space to type in the full agreed data, it may be necessary to include the same in a rider clause, using blank lines in this part of the charter party to refer the reader to the relevant rider clause.

    This also becomes a logical point in some charter parties to include limitation to the effect that a vessel must trade always between 'safe berths and ports', usually 'always afloat'.

5. **Cargo Intention/exclusions:** (Preamble lines 45/56 – Clause 12). Include details of cargoes which can and those which cannot be carried (see reference to cargo exclusions in Chapter Two). Trip time charters often specify the actual cargo to be carried although, if this is only an 'intention', a cargo exclusions clause must still be included.

6. **Vessel Condition:** (Preamble – lines 8/9 and lines 41/454). Just as for voyage charter parties, an undertaking by the vessel's Owners that the vessel is in good condition.

7. **Owner's Responsibilities:** (Clause 1). Lists what an Owner is to provide.

8. **Charterer's Responsibilities:** (Clause 2). Lists what a Charterer is to provide.

9. **Delivery and Redelivery:** (Preamble lines 34/41, Clauses 28 and 34). Places of delivery/ redelivery, laydays/cancelling, notices to be given by Owners prior to delivery and by the Charterer prior to redelivery.

10. **Bunkers:** (Clause 3). It is common practice for time charterers to take over and pay the Owner for bunkers remaining onboard a vessel upon delivery onto time charter, and for Owners to act similarly upon redelivery, the quantities of fuel, diesel and/or gas oil, and the prices per tonne of each, being negotiated when fixing. It is often the case that about the same quantities and prices prevail at both ends of the time charter, although occasionally one side or the other benefits by shrewd negotiation, and obtains either inexpensive bunkers or sells at a good profit.

    With some trip-charters of short duration, however, this system of taking over and paying for bunkers remaining onboard may prove unnecessarily cumbersome, and it may be arranged that Charterers supply sufficient bunkers for the trip at their own expense, or that they pay an Owner for only the estimated quantity of bunkers required for the trip out of the total remaining onboard. Balances in one side's favour or the other are settled upon completion of the time charter in the financial reconciliation.

    The grade and quality of bunkers supplied to a vessel has developed during the 1980's into a subject of considerable importance. The wording of the printed ASBATIME does not reflect this importance, however, restricting itself to just a brief reference in the preamble, lines 15/18. Almost certainly an additional rider clause will be required, which contains a full specification of the quality of bunkers that must be supplied to a time chartered vessel and this has been addressed in NYPE 93, Clause 9.

11. **Hire:** (Clauses 4, 5 and 29). Amount, when, where and to whom hire is payable, and arrangements for other payments, less deductions for items such as port expenses and cash for the Master. Agreement for procedure in case of late payment of hire. (The subject of time charter hire is dealt with at length in Chapter Five).

12. **Off-Hire:** (Clause 15). Provisions leading to off-hire situations, e.g; poor performance; strike of crew; dry-docking; etc., and appropriate deductions from hire payments. (See also Chapter Five).

13. **Vessel Performance:** There is no especial stipulation about vessel performance in the ASBATIME which, in common with most dry cargo charters penalises through its off-hire provisions (see Clause 15) for poor performance but, in contrast to tanker time charter parties, does not reward dry cargo Owners in the event that their vessel performance exceeds the contractual speed and/or consumes less bunkers than specified. There is a valid case for dry cargo time charterers to copy tanker traditions and to enter in the charter party a range of speeds and consumptions, say from 8 knots up to 15 knots, in both laden and ballast conditions. Ideally a Master should be given specific instructions at the commencement of each voyage leg as to a Charterer's performance requirements, and failure to perform as per charter commitments should be penalised whereas extra performance should be rewarded.

14. **Vessel Maintenance:** (Clauses 20 & 21). The ASBATIME restricts its comments to dry-docking and to ship's gear. Yet there might well be additional rider clauses depending on the complexity of the ship type and/or trade involved, e.g; a reefer or a logger.

    For trip charters it is customary to delete the dry-docking clause and replace it by a simple statement such as 'no dry-docking during this time charter, except in cases of emergency'.

15. **Cargo Claims:** For their mutual benefit, it is important that time charterers and Owners of time chartered vessels reach an understanding on how cargo claims (if any) will be handled, which of the two is to handle them, and under what authority. Clause 30 of the ASBATIME sets out a very brief division of responsibility but many time charter parties draft a rider clause incorporating into the charter party the detailed NEW YORK

PRODUCE EXCHANGE INTER-CLUB AGREEMENT. The latest revision being dated 1996. The provisions of this document will be considered in reasonable detail in Chapter Eight and the Agreement itself will be found under **Appendix 34**.

16. **Master/Officers:** (Clauses 8 & 9). The duties of a ship's Master are defined and it is spelt out that although a Master is the Owner's legal servant he must act under the orders of the Charterers as far as the vessel's employment is concerned. It is frequently the case that a rider clause lists the duties expected of a time chartered ship's Officers and crew, whereas Clause 9 is a universal clause giving the Charterers rights should they feel that the Master and/or his Officers are not carrying out their responsibilities towards the Charterers in a reasonable manner.

17. **Logbooks:** (Clause 11). Another protection clause for Charterers' interests. In fact, it is frequently the case that Charterers add a clause, or wording to this clause, that they have the right to check a vessel's performance by reference to a specialised weather routing company, e.g; Oceanroutes, and in the event that the logbooks and the independent reports disagree, the independent reports take precedence over the logbooks. This is important in respect of off-hire claims and vessel's performance.

18. **Supercargo/Victualling:** (Clause 10). Spells out Charterer's right to appoint a supercargo and the costs of exercising this right with regard to meals and accommodation. A right not exercised very frequently, but an invaluable means not only of watching over a time chartered ship's performance, but of providing training to a Charterer's personnel.

    The second part of the clause deals with meals which are to be provided by the Owners, and the cost of these meals.

19. **Pollution:** (Clause 38). Many states are becoming extremely conscious of pollution of their waterways and coastlines and merchant Shipowners must ensure that their vessels comply with a host of international and national legislation in connection with this subject. Not only does this affect tankers. The cost of cleaning up and fines levied following pollution can be considerable, even if caused by, say, a dry cargo ship's ruptured bunker tanks. Contracts should therefore specify the rights and responsibilities of the parties, as well as listing the certificates that the contracted vessel is expected to carry.

    P&I Clubs usually provide insurance cover for entered vessels against oil spillages and resulting fines and clean-up expenses. Certain states, however, may insist that Owners of all vessels calling at their ports (dry cargo as well as tanker ships) provide evidence of financial responsibility for pollution liability in case of oil spillage, such evidence being usually in the form of a certificate of financial responsibility. Potential amounts demanded as security can be huge and entail the tying-up of immense sums of capital against relatively small risks of pollution.

    As a result, P&I Clubs do not encourage states to insist on their own, individual demands for security, instead providing dry cargo Owners with just the United States Federal Water Pollution Control Act Certificate. Further P&I Club assistance with certification to comply with any requirements of individual governments is not possible. Consequently, Owners should not agree time charter party clauses that provide for same.

20. **Salvage.** (Clause 19). It seems fair that expenses and rewards in cases of salvage should be shared, and this is normal practice.

21. **Laying-up:** (Clause 37). Unlike tanker time charter parties it is only rarely that dry cargo Owners and time charterers consider the risks of a vessel laying-up through lack of employment. For a trip-charter this is, of course, not necessary, but for lengthy period employment, this attitude should be carefully reconsidered. What most dry cargo time charter parties do include, however, is reference to what happens if a vessel is detained in port for periods in excess of 30 days.

22. **Arbitration:** (Clause 17). An essential part of any contract. The ASBATIME specifies New York, since the charter party is drafted and published by a body resident in New York. Frequently, however, this clause is either deleted and replaced by a rider arbitration clause specifying some other venue, or the reference to 'New York' in the clause wording is replaced by, say 'London'.

23. **Lien:** (Clause 18). Just as an element of voyage charters, see above, each party's right of lien must be considered and stipulated.

24. **Assignment:** (Preamble lines 31/33). Defines a Charterer's right to sub-let the vessel to another Charterer.

25. **Exceptions:** (Clause 16). Similar to the voyage charter clause.

26. **Requisitioning:** (Clause 33). Arrangements in the event a vessel be requisitioned by the government of her Flag State.

27. **Bills of Lading:** (Clause 8). Specifies the manner in which bills of lading are to be drawn up, the signing of same, and protection for an Owner in case of paper inconsistencies.

28. **Stevedore Damage:** (Clause 35). Provision for notification of stevedore damages and repairs.

29. **Commissions:** (Clauses 26 & 27). Specifies amount and to whom commissions and brokerages are payable.

30. **Protective Clauses:** You will recognise most of the protective clauses from the above comments under the elements of a voyage charter party, including, Clauses Paramount; New Both to Blame Collision and the New Jason. It is important, however, that only War Clauses designed for time charter parties are used, not voyage clauses. In case of a major war between the so-called 'superpowers', or involving nations connected in some way with the charter party, the contract may become null and void. It is common practice to incorporate a clause to this effect, listing the nations involved and spelling out the rights and remedies of the parties in the event of such war-like activities.

There is also protection for an Owner (see the last paragraph of Clause 16) for the vessel to have various 'liberties'.

As in the voyage charter party counterpart, the object of a time charter ice clause should be to prevent a Master being left with no alternative but to proceed to a contractual destination irrespective of ice conditions. Clause 24 achieves this to a certain degree.

The advent of the ISM and ISPS Codes introduced by the IMO has led BIMCO to draft new protective clauses aimed at setting out the rights and responsibilities of both parties in relation to the safe management of ships and security issues.

31. *Signature:* Not to be forgotten!

4.7   THE BAREBOAT CHARTER PARTY

Bareboat chartering, or 'chartering by demise' as lawyers call it, is the contracting for the lease of a vessel, whereby the Owner charters away the ship to another party who, in turn, assumes more the role of Owner than Charterer, the vessel coming under the complete control of the bareboat charterer, who has to supply everything including Master, officers and crew.

The true Owner assigns to the bareboat Charterer all responsibility for operating the vessel, and thus entitlement to any profits (or losses!) the ship may make, in return for an agreed and regular payment of hire. Naturally, such a method of period employment is designed for years rather than for months, and bareboating serves the admirable purpose of allowing persons who are not experienced in shipping to invest in a ship without the responsibility of organising its day-to-day affairs, at the same time permitting those with experience and an entrepreneurial spirit to assume the role of an Owner without the necessity of raising finance to purchase a vessel.

Indeed bareboat chartering is in effect a way of financing shipowning. The bareboat Charterer can register the ship under the flag of his own country, even if that is different to the actual Owners. To the outside world the bareboat Charterer of a vessel is seen as the Owner.

BIMCO designed two bareboat charter parties in the 1970's to meet increased demand for suitably worded contract forms; one intended for the bareboating of existing vessels (with or without mortgages), the BARECON A, the other for newbuildings financed by a mortgage, the BARECON B. Recently reflecting changes in bareboat practice with particular regard to 'flagging out' and the registration of mortgages under 'off-shore' ship registries, a BIMCO documentary sub-committee designed a new bareboat charter party, incorporating the updated BARECON A and BARECON B provisions into one form, the BARECON 89, together with optional sections.

Although a system of vessel employment of which it is important to have a general knowledge, it is not essential in a book of this nature for readers to have as detailed an understanding as for voyage and time chartering. Consequently, the BARECON 89 charter party text is included under **Appendix 16** and whilst it is recommended that the largely self-explanatory clauses be studied, there is not the need for analysis of the elements of a bareboat charter party in the same way as for voyage and time charterparties described above.

4.8   USEFUL TERMS AND ABBREVIATIONS

Commercial shipping is awash with terms and abbreviations. On occasions, the speed of negotiations is such that much laborious effort can be saved by utilising such a system, but only if both sides have the same understanding of the term of abbreviation used!

Some terms have already been used and explained in the Chapter to date. Others that are usefully remembered are:

AA:	**Always Accessible** In connection with the berth of the ship, this signifies that the charterer is obliged to secure a berth that is able to be reached immediately on arrival. For tankers the term **Reachable on Arrival** is more commonly used.
OR	**Always Afloat:** Signifies that at the berth there will always be sufficient water to prevent the ship from 'touching bottom' at any time.
AAAA:	**Always Accessible Always Afloat:** Combination of the above terms often used when negotiating to qualify the description 'Safe Berth'.
APS:	**Arrival Pilot Station:** Signifies a location, on arrival at which a vessel will deliver on to a time charter. Of advantage to a Shipowner when compared with TIP, which see.
BB:	**Below Bridges:** Indicates agreement for a vessel to proceed to that section of a port or a river/canal that is *'below bridges'* in other words below the place(s) where height restrictions would prevent a vessel navigating beneath certain overhead obstructions.
	e.g; 'Vessel to discharge at one safe berth River Thames, below bridges'
OR	**Ballast Bonus:** A lump sum amount paid to a Shipowner, usually as a reward (a *bonus*) for positioning his vessel at a certain place as a prerequisite for her delivery on to time charter, e.g. for a ship ex-Mediterranean Sea, *'delivering*

United States Gulf for a time charter trip to the Far East at US$5,000 daily, plus a ballast bonus of US$100,000'. Occasionally paid as a reward for accepting redelivery from time charter in an unfavourable position.

A Ballast Bonus may be *nett* (i.e. free of address commissions and brokerages) or *gross* (i.e.; subject to deduction of brokerage and address commission). (See Chapter Five).

BBB: **Before Breaking Bulk:** Freight not to be paid until after arrival at the discharge port but before commencement of unloading – i.e.: *before breaking bulk.* (See Chapter Six).

BWAD: **Brackish Water Arrival Draft:** Refers to either available water at a port or, more usually, to a ship's maximum draft on arrival at a port on the basis of *brackish water,* a mixture of saltwater and freshwater, such s would be experienced in an estuarial port, e.g.: berths alongside the River Clyde.

CD: **Customary Despatch:** See CQD

OR **Chart Datum:** Water level calculated on the lowest tide that can conceivably occur, and used as a basis for chart measurements. Such a low tide is known as the *Lowest Astronomic Tide (LAT),* and presupposes that, at the very worst, there would always be that depth of available water at that particular spot.

CFR: **Cost and Freight:** Goods are to be sold on the basis that the seller arranges their sea borne transportation and delivery to the buyer.

CHOPT: **Charterer's Option:** May refer, for example to Charterer's option to discharge at a number of ports e.g;. *'up to three ports Taiwan, in charterer's option'.* Or perhaps relative to a cargo size margin, e.g.; *'10,000 tonnes, 5 per cent more or less chopt.* (See MOLCO).

CIF: **Cost, Insurance and Freight:** As for CFR, except the seller will also insure the goods.

COA: **Contract of Affreightment:** See Chapter Four.

COP: **Custom of Port:** Can be applied to many aspects including nominating of berths, method of loading or discharging, method of delivering or receiving cargo.

CQD: **Customary Quick Despatch:** The vessel is to be loaded or discharged as quickly as is customary and possible.

CVS: **Consecutive Voyages:** A series of consecutive voyages, usually laden from Port A to Port B, returning in ballast condition, and so on until completion of final cargo discharge.

DFD: **Demurrage/Free Despatch:** An expression confirming that a Shipowner may be entitled to demurrage for port delay to his vessel, but that no despatch is applicable in case laytime is saved, e.g. *'$2000 Demurrage/ Free Despatch'.* Common in short-sea and other trades where turn-round in port is speedy; for example, ro-ro vessels.

DHD: **Demurrage/Half Despatch:** More frequently encountered than DFD in deep-sea trades, where despatch earned is agreed to be at half the daily rate of demurrage.

DOP: **Dropping Outward Pilot:** Signifies a point of delivery onto or redelivery off time charter, following a vessel's sailing from a port.

DLOSP: **Dropping Last Outward Sea Pilot:** As DOP but more clarified. In some ports as many as four pilots may be used on the outward passage. This term indicates that all acts of pilotage must be complete.

DWAT: **Deadweight All Told:** The total deadweight of a vessel at any time, or estimated against a particular draft. Includes cargo, bunkers, constant weights, etc.

DWCC: **Deadweight Cargo Capacity:** An estimate of the actual cargo intake against a particular draft, allowing for bunkers, constant weights, etc.

EIU: **Even if Used:** Signifies that time spent on cargo working in excepted periods, e.g.; during a holiday, will not count as laytime, even if used.

ETA: **Estimated or Expected Time of Arrival.**

ETC: **Estimated or Expected Time of Commencement, or Estimated or Expected Time of Completion.**

ETD: **Estimated or Expected Time of Departure**

ETS: **Estimated or Expected Time of Sailing**

FAC: **Fast As Can:** Another laytime term, under which the ship concerned is to load or discharge itself (e.g.; for a 'self-discharger') as fast as it can manage. May be qualified by including COP (see above). The ship must load or discharge as fast as it can manage but subject to the normal method of delivering or receiving cargo.

FAS: **Free Alongside, or Free Alongside Ship:** Goods to be brought alongside the carrying vessel at the port of loading, free of expense to the carrier

FCA: **Free Carrier:** Cargo to be delivered by the seller into the charge of the carrier at a place nominated by the buyer or carrier.

FCL: **Full Container Load**

FD: **Free Despatch (See DFD)**

F(DF)DEDVAOCLONL:

Freight (Dead Freight) Deemed Earned on Departure, Vessel And Or Cargo Lost Or Not Lost: This somewhat unwieldy expression is often used to clarify the freight rate. It signifies that even if the vessel or its cargo is lost at sea the charterer is obliged to pay the full freight.

FIO: **Free In and Out:** Cargo to be loaded and discharged free of expense to the carrier.

FIOS: **Free In, Out and Stowed:** Cargo to be loaded, stowed and discharged free of expense to the carrier, for bulk commodities.

FIOST: **Free In, Out, Stowed and Trimmed:** Certain commodities require both stowing and trimming, e.g.; scrap metal in bulk. This term ensures that none of the loading, discharging stowing or trimming expenses will be for the account of the carrier. For similar terms for some goods, traders must be even more explicit. For example, with motorcars, equivalent terms would be used so as to read 'free in, out, lashed, secured and unlashed'.

FIOSPT: **Free In, Out and Spout Trimmed:** Free-running cargo, e.g.; bulk grains, to be loaded, spout-trimmed (i.e. trimmed by means of manoeuvring the loading spout) and discharged, free of expense to the carrier

FHEX: **Fridays and Holidays Excepted:** Laytime will not count during Fridays and Holidays

FHINC: **Fridays and Holidays Included:** Opposite to FHEX. Laytime counts during Fridays and Holidays, which are to be considered as working days

FOB: **Free onboard:** Cargo to be delivered onboard free of cost to either the buyer or carrier

FOW: **First Open Water:** Refers to the earliest possible resumption of trade to an ice-bound port or area, e.g.; to load FOW Churchill, Hudson Bay.

FP: **Free of Pratique:** The vessel has been approved by the port medical authorities as not having any sanitary disqualifications that would prevent her from proceeding to the berth and commencing operations.

FWAD: **Fresh Water Arrival Draft:** See BWAD. Relevant to trading in freshwater areas, such as prevails in the Panama Canal

Gross Terms: Under which the carrier has to arrange and pay for cargo-handling, although laytime will probably apply. The opposite to Nett Terms

HAT: **Highest Astronomic Tide:** The opposite to Lowest Astronomic Tide – see Chart Datum

HWOST: **High Water on Ordinary Spring Tides:** The opposite to Low Water on Ordinary Spring Tides see LWOST on next page.

ISM: **International Safe Management Code:** A mandatory requirement for ship operators to demonstrate that their vessels are being operated in a safe manner and in accordance with internationally accepted codes and conventions. Vessels may be detained by Port State Control Authorities for breaches of this code. Although the code applies to the operation of the ship and is therefore controlled by the owner or manager, many actions of Charterers can have an effect on its proper operation onboard.

ISPS: **International Ship and Port Facilities Security Code:** A mandatory requirement applying to both ships and ports. The aim of the convention is to combat terrorist threats and criminal activities. All ships, shipping companies, ports and terminal operators must demonstrate effective procedures are in place to improve security. As with the ISM code its practical operation can be affected by chartering issues.

IWL: **Institute Warranty Limits:** (Navigational Limits) Geographical limitations to permitted trading areas, drawn up and imposed by underwriters, and commonly applied throughout the maritime world. Owners wishing their ship to proceed outside these limits (e.g.; to the Great Lakes at any time of the year; or to the Northern Baltic Sea in winter) must usually obtain permission from their underwriters to 'hold covered' their vessel against payment of an additional premium

LAT: **Lowest Astronomic Tide:** See Chart Datum

L/C: **Letter of Credit:**

OR   **Laydays/Cancelling:** A spread of dates, e.g.: *'Laydays 1st September/ Cancelling 15th September'* between which dates a vessel is to present for loading. Too early and she will probably have to wait. Too late and she risks being cancelled by the Charterers

LCL: **Less than Full Container Load:**

Liner Terms: The responsibility and cost of loading, carrying and discharging cargo is that of the carrier, from the moment the goods are placed alongside the carrying vessel in readiness for loading, until discharged alongside at their destination. Time spent cargo handling is also at the carrier's risk

LO/LO   **Lift on/Lift off:** A term describing the method of loading and discharging cargo by ship or shore gear

LT: **Long Ton:** A ton of 2240 pounds, equivalent to 1.016 metric tonnes

LWOST: **Low Water on Ordinary Spring Tides:** A measure of water depth at the low water mark on ordinary (i.e.; not exceptional) Spring tides, see Chart Datum and MLWS

MHWS: **Mean High Water Spring:** and

MLWS: **Mean Low Water Spring:** Average depth of water available at the times of low and of high tides during periods of Spring tides. Some charts are calculated against these 'averages' rather than based on chart datum

MHWN: **Mean High Water Neaps;** *and*

MLWN: **Mean Low Water Neaps:** Average depth of water available at the times of low and high tides during period of Neap Tides

Min/Max: **Minimum/Maximum:** Refers to a fixed cargo size, e.g.; *'10,000 tonnes min/max'*

MOL: **More or Less:** Refers to a cargo size option, say *'10,000 tonnes, 5 per cent more or less',* usually clarifying whose option to select the final cargo size e.g.;

MOLCO: **More or Less Charterer's Option: or,**

MOLOO: **More or Less Owner's Option**

MT: **Metric Tonne:** A tonne of 2,204 pounds or 1,000 kilograms, equivalent to 0.9842 long tons

OR   **Measurement Tonne:** Used in the liner trades and equal to 1 cubic metre or in trades still using imperial measurement 40 cubic feet (although this latter is now almost in disuse)

NAABSA: **Not Always Afloat But Safely Aground:** Most Owners (especially of deep sea vessels) will stipulate that their ships proceed only to ports where there is sufficient water to remain *always afloat,* so as to avoid the risk of hull damage. There are areas and ports, however, where water depth is restricted but, the bottom being soft mud, it is customary for ships to safely lie on the bottom at certain states of the tide., e.g.: River Plate. In such a case, Owners will probably agree to proceed NAABSA

NAV Limits: (See Institute Warranty Limits).

Neap Tides: The opposite to Spring Tides (see Spring Tides on page 90). Neap Tides occur when the tidal range is at its lowest, in other words during periods of relatively low high tides, and of relatively high low tides. A vessel that is prevented from berthing or from sailing with a full cargo or, in deed, is trapped in a berth by the onset of neap tides, is said to have been 'neaped'

Nett Terms: Opposite to Gross Terms. Cargo handling is the responsibility and for the account of the Charterer or the cargo seller.

NOR: **Notice of Readiness:** See Chapter Six

PPT: **Prompt:** Indicates that a cargo or a ship is available promptly

ROB: **Remaining Onboard:** Refers to cargo, bunkers or freshwater remaining onboard a ship at any particular time

RO/RO: **Roll On/Roll Off:** A term indicating that cargo is to be driven on at the loading port and driven off upon discharge, e.g.; a car carrier. Also used to describe a type of vessel specialising in such trades (See Chapter One)

SA: **Safe Anchorage**

SB: **Safe Berth**

SHEX: **Sundays and Holidays Excepted:** Means that laytime will not count during Sundays or Holidays

SHINC: **Sundays and Holidays Included:** Opposite to SHEX. Laytime counts during Sundays and Holidays, which are considered to be normal working days.

Both SHEX and SHINC are often extended to cover Saturdays in which case they are written SSHEX or SSHINC as appropriate

SP: **Safe Port:**

Spot: Indicates that a ship or a cargo is immediately available

Spring Tides: The height of a tide varies (being influenced by the phases of the moon). Approximately twice a month, tidal levels attain their highest high water and lowest low water marks, being termed Spring Tides. The difference between high and low water is called the tidal range and this range is therefore at its greatest during spring tide periods. Because of greater available drafts during spring tide periods, when ships can enter and leave around the high water time more deeply laden than otherwise, some ports experience a far greater volume of traffic than normal, being termed *Spring Tide Ports*. An example is Goole, on the River Ouse, in North-Eastern England (See Neap Tides)

Stem: Refers to the readiness of cargo and is often a prerequisite to the fixing of a vessel, e.g.; *'subject stem'* (i.e.; subject to the cargo availability on the required dates of shipment being confirmed).

SWL: **Safe Working Load:** Refers to lifting capacities of cranes or derricks

SWAD: **Salt Water Arrival Draft:** As for brackish water (see BWAD on age 86), except that the prevailing water is saline.

T/C:	**Time Charter**
TIP:	**Taking Inward Pilot:** Signifies a location on arrival at which (but only upon taking aboard the pilot a ship delivers on to her time charter. Of advantage to a time Charterer when compared with APS (see APS on page 85) as, in the event of a suspension of the pilotage service, or of late boarding by a pilot, the risk and expense of delay is that of the Shipowner.
Under Hook:	Cargo will be brought alongside the carrying vessel, i.e.: under her 'hooks', free of expense to the cargo buyer or the carrier
UU:	**Unless Used:** Sometimes qualifies terms such as SHEX, signifies that if work is done during an excepted period laytime will count.
WCCON:	**Whether Customs Cleared Or Not**
WIBON:	**Whether In Berth Or Not**
WIFPON:	**Whether In Free Pratique Or Not**
WIPON:	**Whether In Port Or Not:**
	All the last four terms are connected with the question of when the ship can be considered as 'arrived' and so present a NOR. In cases when all four apply the abbreviation WWWW is used instead.
W/M:	**Weight Or Measure:** The method on which liner cargo may be charged
WP:	**Weather Permitting:** See Chapter Six
WVNS:	**Within Vessels Natural Segregation:** Used for tanker chartering. When accepting a cargo that may consist of different grades or products the amount of each that can be carried will depend upon the ability of the vessel to segregate the grades/products.
WW:	**Weather Working:** See Chapter Six
WW Ready:	**When and Where Ready:** Refers to a position where a vessel will be handed over to buyers or will be delivered on to/redelivered off time charter.

The above list, although long, is by no means exhaustive of the abbreviations used. There are also in common use various abbreviations for cargo types e.g. TSP - Triple Super Phosphate (a type of fertiliser).

For further abbreviations and terms refer to *Dictionary of Shipping, International Business Trade Terms and Abbreviations* - Branch - Publisher: Witherby Seamanship International.

4.9 SELF-ASSESSMENT AND TEST QUESTIONS

Attempt the following and check your answers from the text or appendices:

1. Who pays for the cost of loading when 'gross terms' apply?

2. What charter party form would you expect to use for a cargo of coal from Australia?

3. Name four bodies active in drafting charter party forms.

4. What effect does an Ice clause have?

5.   What are the essential differences between delivery and redelivery surveys for Time Charters and Bareboat Charters?

6.   What is the current name of the revised ASBATIME charter party?

7.   To whom is the ship's Master responsible under a Time Charter?

8.   What is the legal name used to describe bareboat chartering?

Having completed Chapter Four attempt the following and submit your essays to your Tutor:

1.   It is Friday afternoon in London and your Principal, a Charterer, has given you full authority to fix best possible within that evening the M.V. "SEA ROBIN", 60,000 dwt built 1978 single deck, gearless bulk carrier, for the carriage of coal from the US Gulf (where the "SEA ROBIN" is open spot) to the Charterers berth in Holland.

     Draft your opening offer and the subsequent negotiations resulting in a fixture.

     Discuss the events that could have led to such an urgent situation occurring.

2.   Assume that it is your responsibility to give instructions to the Master of a ship which has just been Voyage chartered under OREVOY (see **Appendix 18**). You will arrange for a copy of the charter party to await him on arrival at loading port. What information do you consider you must give him before he gets there?

Chapter 5

FINANCIAL ELEMENTS OF CHARTER PARTIES

5.1 INTRODUCTION

The whole purpose of Shipowners arranging to carry goods in their vessel(s) is to earn sufficient income to operate their enterprise successfully and, hopefully, to make a profit. Charterers, on the other hand, are anxious to move their cargoes at the lowest possible unit price commensurate always with safe delivery. It follows, therefore, that close attention must be made in all shipping contracts, not only to the amount of income involved and to its calculation, but also to the methods and times of payment, and to the various risks of the parties involved.

For voyage chartering, income will result from freights, deadfreights and from the calculation of laytime, whilst for time chartering, income will result from payment of hire. In each case, however, there are various additions and deductions where need to be taken into consideration to achieve an accurate calculation of income and, in this Chapter, we will be examining these aspects in some detail.

5.2 VOYAGE CHARTERING

Currency: In most cases, freights are paid in United States dollars, the currency of international shipping, but this is not always the case, particularly for short-sea and coastal shipping where local currencies applicable to the trade are frequently used.

Risk of loss of freight: Usually the occasion on which freight is deemed to be earned is specified in the contract of carriage, otherwise it is legally construed as '**a reward payable upon arrival of the goods at their destination, ready to be delivered in merchantable condition**'. Freight would then be payable concurrent with delivery of the goods at the discharge port(s), and a consignee would not normally be entitled to take delivery of the goods until the freight had been tendered.

It follows that, unless otherwise specifically agreed, the risk of losing the freight before safe delivery of the cargo falls upon the Carrier or Shipowner. The party at risk should therefore prudently seek cover against potential loss of cargo (and therefore of freight entitlement) from the insurance market, where freight insurance is normally available at a modest premium, adjusted by the risks involved such as age of ship, duration of voyage, etc.

Frequently, however, Shipowners negotiate that freight '**deemed earned upon loading**' or '**freight payable on shipment**,' in which case the risk of losing the cargo and being liable to pay freight (even without receiving the goods) becomes that of the Charterer, who is left to make appropriate insurance arrangements instead of the Shipowner.

This risk of loss of freight is independent of when freight is physically paid. Therefore, even if freight is paid in accordance with a charter party term stating that '**freight to be paid within seven days after signing and releasing bills of lading**,' in the event of a total loss of ship and cargo, say fifteen days into the voyage, freight might have to be returned to Charterers if the risk of loss was deemed to be the carriers. As a result of this, some carriers will put the issue beyond doubt by including in their contract the words such as: '**freight deemed earned upon loading, discountless and non-returnable, cargo and/or vessel lost or not lost**'.

It is essential, therefore, that care be taken with even the printed words of commonplace charter parties in this respect.

The 1976 version of BIMCO's Uniform General Charter Party, the GENCON states, for example that **'The freight to be paid in cash without discount on delivery of the cargo at mean rate of exchange ruling on day or days of payment, the receivers of the cargo being bound to pay freight on account during delivery, if required by Captain or Owners'.** On the other hand, the MULTIFORM **(Appendix 12)** deals with this aspect in Clause 5, by using the wording **'freight shall be deemed earned as cargo is loaded onboard and shall be discountless and non-returnable, vessel and/or cargo lost or not lost'.** It follows that under the terms of the 1976 printed GENCON, the risk of loss of freight is that of Shipowners and under the MULTIFORM that of Charterers, and so the appropriate party must insure accordingly. The 1994 version of GENCON provides an option to be exercised in Clause 4 between 'prepaid' and 'on delivery'.

Where Freight payable: It is extremely rare for a freight payment to be made simply by writing a cheque and mailing it. The Shipowner will want the money in his bank account available to meet his financial commitments at the time stipulated, not several days later. Pause for a moment with your calculator at hand. A 'capesize' bulk carrier fixed at around $10 per tonne at a time when bank overdrafts are at 10% per annum and you will find that if the freight is not in the right place at the right time then something in excess of $10 per hour is being lost, lost until the money is in the right place.

It is usual for freight and hires to be paid by means of a transfer of funds from the Charterer's bank to the Owner's. Even this can take time and so it is important for the charter party to state where as well as when the funds have to be credited to the Shipowner's bank account. Many charter parties leave it to the contracting parties to incorporate the arrangements they require, e.g.; the AMWELSH **Appendix 13)** Clause 2, but others demand more specific information, e.g.; the OREVOY Box 29 **(Appendix 18).**

When Freight payable: Voyage freight may be payable in advance, e.g: **'fully prepaid',** or upon reaching its destination, e.g; **'upon right and true delivery'.** It may also be paid at some time during a vessel's voyage, e.g; **'within seven banking days of signing and releasing bills of lading',** or at the destination but prior to discharge, e.g; **'before breaking bulk',** (abbreviated as 'bbb' in negotiations).

Voyage freight is also frequently paid in stages. It is commonplace for a majority of the freight, say 90% to be paid during a voyage, with the balance within a set period after discharge has been completed, together with adjustment for demurrage or despatch owed by one party or the other. For example: **'Ninety percent of freight to be paid within five banking days of signing and releasing bills of lading marked, "freight payable as per charter party", balance to be paid within one month of completion of discharge, duly adjusted for laytime used during loading and discharging operations'.**

(With reference to 'Laytime' in the above paragraph, readers should note that this important subject will be examined in detail in Chapter Six).

How Freight is Calculated: Freights are paid usually against the quantity of cargo loaded, often on a tonnage basis, but occasionally in accordance with cargo volume or ship capacity. So, freight for a bulk cargo, e.g; coal, will very likely be paid at a rate of US$ per long ton or per metric tonne (see AMWELSH, lines 15/16). It is important, however, to specify how the cargo quantity is to be established.

Often this will be achieved by **'shore measurement',** from which a **'bill of lading weight'** is obtained, and on which freight is based. Sometimes, though, shore instruments are suspect perhaps non-existent, and cargo/bill of lading tonnage, **'intaken weight',** is calculated by means of **'ship's draft survey'.** In some trades there may be a discrepancy between shore cargo figures and cargo intaken quantity estimation as assessed by ship's draft survey. Provided such discrepancy is of relatively minor proportions, the problem may not be serious but, given the high value of certain commodities, a substantial difference between these two sets of figures calls for immediate and closer investigation.

On some occasions, freight is to be assessed on **'cargo outturn quantity'** at the port(s) of discharge and again, this quantity may be calculated by means of shore gauges or by ship's draft survey. Where **'draft surveys'** are involved, often a charter party will include a clause specifying that the Surveyor will be independent and also that the ship's Officers are to provide every assistance to the Surveyor to the extent of providing ship's plans and refraining from pumping water or bunkers during the survey itself.

In certain trades, e.g; for iron ore, where cargo is liable to suffer from weight loss (due principally to the evaporation of moisture) during transit, it is common to give Charterers the option to abide by loaded figures on which to base freight calculations, or to weigh the cargo upon its discharge. As a further alternative, a Charterer may negotiate the right to deduct from freight a percentage off the bill of lading weight obtained at the loading port, say 0.5%, **'in lieu of weighing'** cargo upon discharge. In most trades this is now an option which is rarely exercised but the clause survives and so the 0.5% becomes just another 'picking'.

5.2.1 Cargo Size

Occasionally a Shipowner undertakes to carry an exact cargo size, e.g; **'40,000 tonnes minimum/maximum coal in bulk, stowing around 47 cubic feet per tonne'**, but often a margin is negotiated to enable a Master to maximise his ship's lifting (which will vary depending upon the quantity of bunkers she has onboard), e.g; **'40,000 tonnes coal in bulk, 5% more or less in Owner's option'.**

It may be that this margin is at **'Charterers' option'** although such an arrangement precludes the certainty that the vessel's Master can maximise his cargo lifting, and means that the owner must estimate on the minimum cargo quantity when calculating the viability of such a prospective future. Where a Shipowner contracts to load or a Charterer to provide **about** a certain quantity, e.g: **'about 10,000 metric tonnes bagged fishmeal'**, the word **'about'** is construed to mean within, say, a reasonable margin of (say) 5%; in other words, between 9,500 and 10,500 tonnes.

However where the word **'about'** is replaced by **'without guarantee'** (usually abbreviated to WOG in charter negotiations) it means just that. There is **'no guarantee'** and the cargo can legally be of any size.

Occasionally a stated margin is agreed, e.g: **'30/32,000 tonnes'.** Here it is understood that the cargo to be loaded and/or supplied will be between 30,000 and 32,000 tonnes of cargo and, to make matters absolutely clear, the words **'minimum/maximum'** or similar might be added, e.g: **'within 30/32,000 tonnes min/max'** whilst the additional phrase **'in Owners/ Shippers'** option' defines whose right it is to decide upon the exact cargo quantity within the agreed limitations.

While an Owner will usually be looking to maximise a ship's intake there are other elements to consider. On no account must the ship's maximum dwt be exceeded, nor must the loadline be submerged at any point during the voyage. Remember that even if a ship starts its voyage in a zone where cargo intake can be maximised, the ship may have to pass through another zone during the voyage. Sometimes a ship may have to sail with empty holds for safety reasons because to do otherwise would mean part cargoes in one or more holds that might be liable to shifting.

5.2.2 Alternative Means of Calculating Freight

On other occasions, however, the likely loaded commodity may be difficult to calculate in advance. In such events, there are alternatives open to the negotiating parties:

1. The onus can be shifted from the Shipowner to the Charterer and freight paid on a **'lumpsum basis'.** Here it is up to the Charterer to see that the maximum cargo is loaded in his own interest, consistent always with the vessel's maximum permitted draft and her safety. There is, of course, no financial advantage to the shipowner from maximising cargo intake in this case.

2. Where the cargo consists of awkward shapes and sizes, e.g;. general cargo, or where it is uncertain just what can be fitted into a ship's various shaped cargo compartments for a uniform-style commodity e.g; packaged lumber an alternative is for freight to be calculated on either the **'available cubic capacity'** of the ship's cargo compartments, or on the **'cubic quantity of cargo loaded'.**

5.2.3 Deadfreight

Should a Charterer/Shipper fail to provide a full cargo in accordance with that described in the contract of carriage, a Shipowner can claim **'deadfreight'** which is a form of damages being computed on the basis of loss of freight, less any expenses which would have been incurred in earning it, e.g; stevedores' costs and less any advantage taken by the Owner from the deadweight unexpectedly available, e.g: extra bunkers. Deadfreight is added to freight earned and, likewise, is usually liable to appropriate commissions and brokerages.

5.2.4 Freight Taxes

The authorities of some (principally developing) nations levy taxes upon freight deemed earned on outbound cargoes (and a few on inbound cargoes as well). It is the recipient of the freight who is liable to pay this tax, not the party paying same, and therefore this charge is frequently levied against the Shipowner, being usually added to port disbursements incurred by the vessel concerned, and collected via the offices of the Port Agent.

Consequently, appropriate allowance for freight tax must be made in voyage estimates and subsequently in freight rates negotiated by Shipowners. Furthermore, mention of any freight taxes should be made in charter parties and contracts, clearly specifying which of the contracting parties is ultimately responsible for payment of such charges, as, even though in the first instance the recipient of freight is liable for payment of taxes, it may be negotiated that a shipper or charterer is ultimately responsible and must in due course reimburse a carrier for expenditure so incurred.

Some governments which impose taxes on freight negotiate bilateral agreements with other governments under which ships registered in certain nations are exempt or partially exempt from such charges, and it is necessary to all concerned in negotiating ocean voyages to check carefully first whether freight taxes are likely to be levied and, secondly, which nation's ships, if any, are exempt. This can be clarified via the good offices of an Agent in the port(s) involved or perhaps more simply in BIMCO's 'Freight Tax' booklet, although, being an annual publication, this may be slightly out-of-date for the particular case under review.

It is essential to clarify the exact circumstances under which vessels will be exempt from freight tax. It may be that Greek flag ships, for example, are exempt under one particular nation's regulations, providing only that the freight beneficiary resides in Greece. A Greek flag ship owned ostensibly by a Liberian corporation (even though the shares in that corporation are held by Greek nationals) would not qualify for exemption; whereas if the vessel was time chartered to a Greek resident, individual or corporation for the voyage in question, as disponent Owner that resident or corporation might very well qualify for exemption.

Bills of Lading: These documents will be examined in Chapter Eight. However, mention should be made of the clausing of Bills of Lading in relation to freights. Sometimes letters of credit between the seller and buyer of a cargo stipulate that Bills of Lading are to be claused **'freight prepaid',** and a buyer is then entitled to assume that freight has indeed been paid when the bills eventually come into his possession. It can, in fact, be tantamount to fraud to reach an alternative agreement between seller and Shipowner/Carrier and mark bills of lading **'freight prepaid'** where none, or only partial freight has been paid.

Not only that, if a Shipowner releases bills marked **'freight prepaid'** before receiving any or all freight, that Shipowner is in effect admitting receipt of all freight and may find extreme difficulty in obtaining any balance, whilst being obliged to deliver the cargo in full to the receiver/holder of the bills. There can be no objection to clausing of bills such as **'freight payable as per charter party',** and it is surely better for a Shipowner or his port agent to retain bills of lading marked **'freight prepaid'** until the freight is actually received.

Although, as we have seen from Chapter Four, most voyage charter parties give a Shipowner/ Carrier a lien on the cargo for non-payment of freight and deadfreight (see clause 24 of the MULTIFORM), this will not apply if the Shipowner has released 'freight prepaid' bills of lading.

Sometimes Charterers offer to issue a **'letter of indemnity'**, indemnifying Shipowners for issuing **'freight prepaid'** bills without physical receipt of the freight. Depending on their trust of the Charterer, some Shipowners accept such a letter, but wise ones demand that it is countersigned by a first class bank.

5.3 COMMISSIONS AND BROKERAGES

A Shipbroker's income from voyage chartering is based on a percentage of the gross freight payable to a Shipowner, and this income is payable by that Shipowner to all the Brokers involved in the fixture. In addition, each Shipbroker may be entitled to an equivalent, percentage of the gross amount of any deadfreight although, since deadfreight is, in fact, payment by a Charterer of damages for failing to produce an entire, contracted cargo and not strictly a freight entitlement by the Shipowner, a Shipbroker's right to receive income based on deadfreight must be specifically recorded in a charter party. It is also normal practice for Shipbrokers to be entitled to receive income in the form of a percentage of any demurrage that might accrue after the calculation of laytime, although this too has specifically to be recorded.

A Shipbroker's income is usually termed **'brokerage'** to distinguish it from **'commission'** or **'address commission'** used to describe a Charterer's negotiated entitlement to a discount on freight payment, ostensibly to cover expenses incurred as a result of employing tonnage to carry the goods. In fact the practice of deducting **'address commission'** from freight, deadfreight and/or demurrage, is one peculiar to the dry cargo trades and is rarely, if ever, encountered in the 'wet' or tanker trades.

In deep-sea markets, brokerage normally amounts to 1.25% of gross freight, deadfreight and demurrage, and is payable by a Shipowner from sums received to each Broker involved in a transaction, although it frequently occurs that a Charterer will deduct an appropriate amount from freight payment to the Shipowner and undertake to pay the brokerage direct to his own and/or to other Brokers involved. Therefore, for the involvement of two brokers, 2.5% brokerage is payable, 3.75% for three and so on. This varies, however, and a Broker regularly and exclusively employed by a particular Shipowner or Charterer may agree to a brokerage of, say, only 1%. Alternatively, if that Broker undertakes to handle all the post-fixture work on behalf of that Owner or Charterer, his brokerage may be increased to, say, 2%, to cover the costs of the extra time and expenses involved. Furthermore, a Broker involved in transactions of relatively small value, say a short-sea Broker, may be entitled to a higher basic brokerage than 1.25 %, say one third of 5% or 2%.

Address commission also varies in amount. A few Charterers do not apply it at all whilst a further few negotiate as much as 5%. The total commission (i.e. address commission plus brokerages) due on dry cargo business may vary from as little as 1.25% to as much as 7.50% perhaps even more. The norm for deep-sea dry cargo business is around 3.75/5%, although for certain trades, e.g; sugar business, it is traditionally higher at 6.25%, and other traditionally less, e.g; The World Food Programme, of the United Nations, at 1.25%.

Whatever the amount of total commission, however, it is a matter for assessment in the appropriate freight rate, just as for any other factor, e.g; port time. Shipowners must obviously take the total amount into consideration when negotiating freight levels, as it is on net income that returns and profits/losses are calculated.

Although in certain cases these brokerages may seem generous, it should be remembered that a Broker's income very much follows the fluctuations of the freight market in which he or she is involved. The lower the freight rates, the harder it is necessary to strive to fix business and the lower the return if successful, based as brokerage is on depressed freight rate levels.

Furthermore, a Broker receives income only if successful. All those failures and near misses, even though costly in terms of time and expenses, count for nothing unless a confirmed fixture results.

Nevertheless, a Broker may be able to gain some protection in the case of 'non-performance' of confirmed business, as is provided, for example, in the GENCON charter party, which states: **'In case of non-execution at least 1/3rd of the brokerage on the estimated amount of freight and dead-freight to be paid by the Owners to the Brokers as indemnity for the latter's expenses and work. In case of more voyages the amount of indemnity to be mutually agreed'.** Few printed charter parties are so generous, however, and it behoves brokers to endeavour to persuade principals to cover them against the financial expenses and time involved in the case of cancellation of a negotiated fixture.

It should also be noted that a Broker may have great difficulty in pursuing a claim against a Shipowner, for example, for non-payment of brokerage. Until 2000, under English law Brokers were unable to sue for brokerage as they were not party to the contract between the Charterer and Shipowner even if they were fully responsible for negotiating and drawing up the charter party. That position was changed following a case brought under the Contracts (Rights of third parties) Act of 1999 when it was ruled that they could sue for brokerage written into the charter party. The act brought English law into line with that of most other major shipping nations but chartering is of course a global activity and some Brokers may not be able to rely on such legal assistance. Help might be at hand through underwriters of professional indemnity insurance schemes (see Chapter Ten) or through the offices of bodies such as the Baltic Exchange or BIMCO, the defaulting Shipowner perhaps being shamed into paying it if faced with adverse publicity resulting from non-payment.

Some Shipowners are better than others at paying brokerage, settling sums as and when they become due, e.g; paying 90% of brokerage once 90% freight has been received. Others are extremely tardy, only paying the first and only sum of brokerage months after completion of the voyage(s) concerned and, of course, even longer after the fixture was confirmed.

Also, in some cases Charterers negotiate that the full, 100% of address commission and, perhaps, brokerage, is deductible from any advance freight paid to a Shipowner.

It is also important for Brokers to enter their entitlement to brokerage into the charter party signed by both Principals because then at least a miscreant Shipowner cannot deny being aware of brokerage due.

5.3.1 International Brokers Commission Contract (See Appendix 21)

FONASBA have produced a standard form of agreement (recommended by BIMCO) to be made between the Shipowner and the Broker under which the Owner agrees to pay the Broker the commissions due under the relevant charter party. This form creates a separate contract between the Owner and Broker under which the Broker could sue for his brokerage under English Law.

5.4 TIME CHARTERING

Much of that which has been written above under the heading "Voyage Chartering" applies also to "Time Chartering". There are naturally, however, substantial differences in the calculation of freight applicable to voyage chartering, and hires applicable to time chartering.

How Hire is calculated: Time charter hire is commonly calculated and described in dry cargo charter parties as a daily rate, e.g; US$ 8,000 daily. To this is applied a pro-rata adjustment for part of a day. Therefore a vessel on hire for 10 days 12 hours, in other words for 10.5 days, would be entitled to gross hire of US$ 84,000.

For hire paid **'semi-monthly'** (i.e. 15 days in advance for a thirty day calendar month) gross hire would amount to US$ 120,000 (US$ 8,000 × 15), or US$ 240,000 for the full calendar month.

An alternative but less utilised method of calculating hire is to base the same on a vessel's deadweight tonnage per calendar month. For a 40,000 tonne summer deadweight bulk carrier, the equivalent time charter rate to US$ 8,000 daily can be calculated as follows:

US$ 240,000 ÷ 40,000 sdwt = US$ 6.00 per sdwt tonne.

However, the duration of a 'calendar month' varies month-by-month. One month it will indeed consist of 30 days, another of 31 or even 28 days. Consequently, it is normal to use as a factor in such calculations, the average number of days in a calendar month allowing, of course, for the leap year. An average calendar month will therefore be found to exist of 30.4375 days, and this will give a slightly different daily value to our bulk carrier:

40,000 tonnes sdwt × US$ 6.00 per tonne ÷ 30.4375 = US$ 7.885.01 daily.

The ASBATIME charter party (for example) allows for either method of hire calculation in clause 4.

When Hire is payable: In nearly every case, it is agreed that hire is payable in advance i.e. monthly, or semi-monthly, or every fifteen days in advance. The ASBATIME, Clause 5 selects 'semi-monthly in advance' but, in the interests of easy accounting, convenience and certainty, it is common practice to pay hire every fifteen days in advance, which continues to allow for subsequent equal payments irrespective of whether a calendar month comprises 28, 29, 30 or 31 days. For the period leading up to redelivery, when there will probably not be an entire 'semi-monthly' period outstanding, Charterers are normally reluctant to pay hire in excess of that which is estimated to be due. Nevertheless, the ASBATIME, in common with most other time charters, stipulates that 'hire shall be paid for the balance day by day as it becomes due, if so required by Owners'.

Where Hire is payable: Just as for voyage chartering and the payment of freight, time charter hire has to be transferred in good time from the Bankers of a Charterer to the bank account of a Shipowner. If this hire does not arrive in time, then technically the Charterer is in breach of the contract and the Shipowner has a case for withdrawing his vessel from the Charterer's employ.

In fact, it is not as simple as that because, in a legal sense, the Shipowner has to show that the Charterer consistently paid late and had been consistently warned that the Owner was contemplating withdrawal. One has to realise that for every defaulting Charterer who misbehaves because of stringent financial problems, there may, at certain stages of the freight market, be a Shipowner who is anxious to find any excuse to withdraw his ship from a time charter commitment at a low rate of hire to take advantage if possible of higher freight and hire levels elsewhere.

The object of a well drafted time charter party should be, as far as possible, to remove any temptation for potential miscreants to misbehave. Whilst hire is to be paid and received by the Shipowner's bank in advance at agreed intervals, and the time charter party should clearly state this, so it has to be realised that inevitably banks will occasionally accidentally delay transfers of moneys or misroute that money. It is typical to insert a side clause requiring owners to give some notice of any intention to withdraw their vessel, thereby providing an opportunity for time charterers to make amends or to remedy any banking error, e.g; a **'period of grace'**. In fact the ASBATIME includes a suitable optioned clause in Clause 29 of that charter party.

Ballast Bonuses: (Already referred to in Chapter Three). Where some ships deliver onto time charter some distance from their original position, their Owners may negotiate a positioning bonus to cover time and expenses (e.g. bunker costs or canal tolls) incurred between departure from the original position to the vessel's delivery under the new employment. (Very occasionally, if a time charterer redelivers a vessel in a poor position relative to following employment opportunities, it may be possible for an Owner to negotiate a redelivery positioning bonus, although this is not very common). Such a lumpsum payment, however, whether applicable to delivery onto or redelivery off time charter, is termed a **'ballast bonus',** and a delivery ballast bonus is usually payable in full together with the first hire due under a new time charter.

Payments in respect of hire are usually subject to a discount for address commissions and/or brokerages (just as for freight), but not so in respect of bunkers or canal tolls. Consequently, with ballast bonuses containing elements of both hire and voyage expense reimbursement, the question arises as to whether such bonuses should be paid **'gross'** (i.e. liable to deduction for commission/ brokerage) or **'nett'** of such deductions.

In practice it all depends on the negotiating strength of each party and the state of the freight market. In some cases ballast bonuses will be nett and in others they will be gross. It is not unusual, even, for ballast bonuses to be nett of address commission but gross of brokerage.

Bunkers: As we have seen in Chapter Four, when a vessel delivers on time charter, the Charterers will normally take over the bunkers remaining onboard the vessel at that time, and reimburse the Shipowner accordingly. Payment is usually made with the first hire payment.

On redelivery, the reverse process takes place, with Charterers estimating the quantity of bunkers remaining onboard on redelivery and deducting the equivalent monetary value from the final (or penultimate in the case of large quantity of bunkers) hire payment.

Adjustments in both cases are able to be made upon receipt of delivery and redelivery survey reports.

Delivery and Redelivery: When a vessel delivers on to time charter, not only does the 'time charter clock' start to tick, but it sets in motion also the payment of the first hire and any additional sums such as for bunkers remaining onboard at the time, and ballast bonus. It is therefore essential that copies of the survey reports signed and witnessed by the Master and port Agents and, if available, by a Charterer's representative such as a supercargo, be distributed to all concerned. In this way the accounts procedures can avoid being unnecessarily complicated.

It is also vital to specify whether delivery and redelivery times will be recognised as being as per local times or as per some convenient 'standard' time, such as Greenwich Mean Time (GMT). If the charter party is silent on this aspect, English Law will assume that actual 'elapsed time' will apply to the time charter period, i.e. as if a stop-watch was started on the bridge of the ship upon delivery only to stop upon redelivery (and, of course, for any off-hires). If local time is specified, however, one party or the other might 'benefit' by gaining time by application of time zone changes. You can work it out for yourself with an atlas showing time zones and can calculate whether a ship moving east/west or west/east is to the advantage of a time charterer basis 'local time'. With GMT or equivalent, there is no advantage to either party and this, therefore, is to be recommended.

The beginning of a time charter is a relatively easy point to determine, the ending or redelivery is less certain. This is because final voyages can terminate earlier than expected or over run sometimes by quite considerable periods.

It has generally been accepted that if the Charterer fixes the vessel on a final voyage that will exceed the agreed duration of the c/p, the Owner has the right not to allow the voyage to proceed. It has also been generally accepted that when a vessel is redelivered late the time charterer must continue to pay the Owner up to the time of redelivery either at the hire rate agreed in the c/p or at the market rate if this is above the c/p rate.

This generally accepted idea was almost turned on its head in the case of the *Achilleas* which was finally decided in the British House of Lords in 2008. Earlier, arbitrators and other courts had allowed a case by the Owner that the Charterer should compensate for a following cancelled charter at a high daily rate caused by the late redelivery of the vessel. Because of the delay, the Owner was forced to renegotiate the following charter as the vessel missed its cancelling date and was obliged to accept a substantially reduced daily rate as a consequence. If the law lords had not allowed the Charterer's final appeal, the late delivery would have cost the Charterer in excess of $1.5 million. However, the case did serve to illustrate that new areas of dispute are still possible despite the long legal history and case law surrounding charter parties.

Another case resolved in 2008 also concerned a late delivery but this time the vessel was operating on a trip charter that both parties had only expected to last a few weeks. Because of delays at the discharge port the ship was finally delivered more than a whole year after the Owner initially expected the voyage to be completed. The Charterer did however continue to make payment as required under the trip charter and so the Owner's attempt to force the ship to discharge elsewewhere was rejected as were the later legal claims for damages due to detention.

Additions to Hire: Quite apart from ballast bonuses, there may be other additions to hire payments made from time to time. In Chapter Four, under the section dealing with elements of time charter parties, readers will recall, for example, the clause concerning (1) supercargo accommodation and (2) port employees' meals. In addition there may be claims from the owner for (3) radio message expense reimbursement, for communications necessary on behalf of time Charterers, as well as for (4) gratuities expended on Charterers' behalf to certain employees at ports of call. Finally (5) a time charter invariably insists upon the vessel being redelivered 'in like good order and condition' as when she was taken over by the Charterer. This would, therefore, mean that the time charter would be required to employ labour to clean the ship's holds and she would remain on hire all the time this was taking place. Hold cleaning can sometimes be quite easily done by the ship's crew on the ballast passage to the next loading port and quite often the Charterer is able to negotiate the right to redeliver the ship without that final cleaning. The *quid pro quo* for this concession is usually a lumpsum **'in lieu of cleaning'** payable with the balance of outstanding hire. All these need to be costed, vouchers supplied and claims made.

The Charterer is obliged to make good any damage to the vessel done by stevedores and others servants of the Charterer during the period of the charter. Quite often this damage is minor in nature and to delay the ship while repairs were made could be expensive. Frequently the parties agree that the Charterer pays over a sum of money that the Owner will use to put matters right when the vessel is in dry-dock or undergoing more extensive repair work.

Deductions from Hire: As we have already seen, just as for freight, hire is subject to deductions for:

1. **Address commission and/or brokerage.** However, hire is also subject to other deductions:

2. **Port disbursements.** Quite often the Owners of a time chartered vessel will avoid appointing a Port Agent to attend on their behalf, relying instead on the time Charterers' Port Agent and reimbursing any expenses the time Charterer and/ or the Port Agent may incur, (e.g. cash to vessel's Master, chandlery bills, crew leaving or joining etc.) by means of a routine deduction from hire. Most time charter parties give Charterers a 'reward' for carrying out this service by payment of a percentage based on the amount involved. In the ASBATIME **(Appendix 14)** lines 128/132, this 'reward' amounts to 2.50% commission on any such advances.

   A particular port disbursement that causes some disputes is waste disposal charges. Few Owners object when they actually dispose of ship's waste but some ports levy the charge regardless and in such cases the dispute is over whether this is an expense that should be paid for by the Owner or the Charterer.

3. **Domestic bunkers.** Bearing in mind that ASBATIME although intended and marketed as a replacement of the New York produce exchange time Charter 1946, is rarely used, and is used here only for ease of illustrating the elements of a time charter and particular clauses, it is important to draw readers' attention to an omission in regard to domestic bunkers. Reference to the NYPE 46 form, Clause 20, will reveal that **'fuel used... for cooking, condensing water, or for grates and stoves to be agreed as for quantity, and the cost of replacement same, to be allowed by Owners'.**

No mention of this 'domestic fuel arrangement' is contained in the ASBATIME or NYPE 93. Nevertheless, and despite the old fashioned language introduced originally when steam-powered vessels were the norm, it has been legally upheld under English Law during the 1980's that the spirit of this clause applies in principle also to modern diesel-engined ships. Consequently, providing agreement can be reached as to quantity (usually by a pre-calculation during fixing negotiations) and no matter what charter party form is being used, Charterers can negotiate entitlement to an allowance for a vessel's domestic fuel consumption for heating, lighting, cooking, etc. and this is usually deducted in the form of a lumpsum payment from hire.

4. **Off Hire.** Clause 15 of the ASBATIME provides a valuable summary of some of the many reasons why a Charterer will be entitled to place a time chartered ship **'off- hire'**. Whilst a time chartered vessel will remain **'on-hire'** whilst fully at the service of Charterers for the purpose in hand, inevitably, even for the best run vessel, a time will come when that ship will be placed 'off-hire'. Such occasion may occur through mechanical break down, either of a ship's motive power or cargo gear, or it may be that the vessel has to deviate from her course to land a sick seaman. An off-hire clause normally covers such eventualities fully and there should be no reason for any differences of opinion. However, much the same as when a vessel delivers on time charter at sea instead of at a convenient and easily identifiable place, such as 'dropping outward pilot Elbe No. I', it may be very difficult to establish the exact limits of off-hire and, consequently, the equivalent amount of hire.

One situation which can be considered under the same heading as 'off-hire' is that of **poor performance** when the Charterer claims that the vessel has failed to perform in terms of speed and fuel consumption as provided for in the charter party. Most modern ships are able to provide a range of combinations of speed and fuel, allowing Charterers to select whichever combination is most suitable for their purpose. They may for example have a tight schedule to meet in which case they will want the highest speed even though this means higher fuel costs. Conversely time may not be so important and economical use of bunkers is preferable. However, whichever speed range is selected the charter party will specify that such a speed and consumption is only achievable in fair weather conditions. In a dispute over speed and consumption the Owner will claim the weather was at fault whilst the Charterer will argue otherwise and demand financial compensation for the alleged poor performance.

As we have seen in Chapter Four, it is usual for a vessel's log books to be made available to a time Charterer and it may well be that it is also agreed that in such disputes, reference will be made to an outside body such as Ocean routes, to assess whether a vessel performed poorly or not and, if so, the financial extent of the poor performance.

With tanker chartering, it is often the case that the Owner of a tanker exceeding the stipulated time charter performance, is rewarded by payment of extra hire reflecting the financial extent of the better performance. Only rarely is this the case with dry cargo chartering, although there is no reason why dry cargo ships should not be similarly assessed. In fact, although it would create an additional workload for those entrusted with performing the calculations, with the aid of computer technology this is no longer the chore it once was, and there is less reason for Shipowners to misdescribe their vessels during negotiations leading to a fixture, if they are to be rewarded any way for enhanced performance in accordance with the time charter value of their vessel. Consequently, there is every reason to 'borrow' one of the tanker industry's good ideas.

Lines 190 to 195 of the ASBATIME refer to diversions from a vessel's planned course, and it is necessary for those involved in this area of shipping to familiarise themselves with simple **deviation** calculations used to assess the costings of off-hire incidents. In the following example, let us assume that our vessel is deviating to land a sick seaman (the cost of which, incidentally, should be covered under the terms of an Owner's P&I insurance cover) or, perhaps, is proceeding to a dry-dock for routine repairs. Let us also assume that both incidents are clearly off-hire and the only problem is for the parties to calculate the time spent off-hire and the quantity and cost of excess bunkers consumed.

Example One

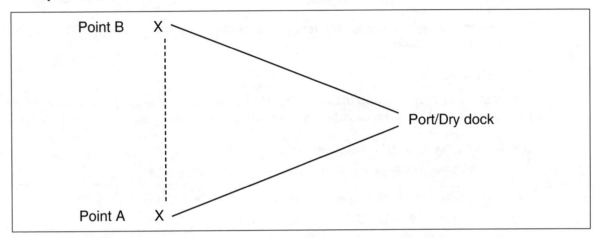

The deviation is normally calculated by the Master and sent directly to both his Owners and Charterers or to Charterers via his Owners and will cover extra time and bunkers used. From the actual time used to deviate from Point A to Port/Dry-dock and to return to Point B (including all time spent in Port/Dry-dock) must be deducted the estimated time that would have been taken if steaming as per time Charterers' instructions from Point A to Point B direct. The difference is off-hire. These figures can be checked by time Charterers, even if they employ noone with seagoing experience, by dextrous use of marine distance tables which, although possibly not entirely accurate, will give a close approximation.

Fuel and diesel oil consumption can be checked by applying C/P bunker figures to the speeds used in the deviation calculations, compared with distances involved.

Using the example, and assuming that the distance between each point is 312 nautical miles and that the ship spent five days in port both dry-docking and repairing alongside the shipyard facilities, and given that the Charterer's instructions were for the ship to proceed at 13 knots on a consumption (as per charter party) of 20 tonnes fuel oil daily at sea we can estimate:

Example One

(Ship's speed: 13 knots (13 × 24 hours)			=	312 NMPD)
Deviation:	Point A to Port:	312 nm.	=	1 day
	Port to Point B:	312 nm.	=	1 day
	Time in Port:		=	5 days
	Total Deviation		=	7 days
	Less Point A to B:	312 nm.	=	1 day
	Off-Hire		=	6 days

Bunker Consumption:

F/O	Point A to Port:	20 tonnes
	Port to Point B:	20
		40
Less	Point A to Point B	20
		20 tonnes F/O
D/O: say 1 tonne D/O per day		(as per c/p)
Off-Hire 6 days thus:		6 tonnes D/O

The above example is obviously very simple but the principle is exactly the same for more complicated calculations.

Example Two

A vessel en route from Cape of Good Hope to Fremantle deviates to Durban to collect urgently needed spare parts. To calculate approximate off-hire and extra bunker consumption:

Distances according BP Distance Table:

i) Cape of Good Hope/Fremantle 4,670 NM.

ii) Cape of Good Hope/Durban 755

Durban/Fremantle 4,241   4,996

Deviation: 326 NM.

Assuming vessel's speed and consumption as per Example One:

326 ÷ 312 = 1,045 days off-hire

1,045 × 20 tonnes F/O = 20.09 tonnes F/O

+ 1,045 tonnes D/O

5.5   SELF-ASSESSMENT AND TEST QUESTIONS

Attempt the following and check your answers from the text:

1. How can Charterers protect themselves against the risk of loss of freight during a voyage if freight is deemed earned by a Shipowner upon loading of the cargo?

2. As a Broker, what means would you employ to encourage prompt payment of your brokerage after fixing a vessel?

3. List the reasons you can identify for a vessel to be placed off-hire.

Having completed Chapter Five attempt the following questions and submit your essays to your Tutor.

The bulk carrier *'Albatross'* has performed a voyage charter followed by a time charter. You have now received the final papers for both employments and are in a position to draw up final statements for each using the following data, and producing the balance due:

1)   VOYAGE

Loading Aqaba
Discharging Montoir

Cargo: 21,475 tonnes bulk phosphate
Freight: US$ 21.00 per mt.
Address Commission: 2.00%
Brokerage: 2.50%
90% Freight paid in advance
Total Despatch at Aqaba: $ 9,500.00
Total Demurrage at Montoir: $ 12,250.00

2) TIME CHARTER

Delivery dop Montoir 15th March 0600 hours GMT
Redelivery dop Madras 30th May 1800 hours GMT
Bunkers on delivery: 495 tonnes f/o and 53 d/o
Bunkers on redelivery: 450 tonnes f/o and 47 d/o

Bunker prices both ends: US$ 105 per mt. f/o US$ 165 per mt d/o

Hire: US$ 8,000 daily
Address Commission 2.5%
Brokerage 3.75%

Domestic Consumption: 0.25 tonnes d/o daily at t/c price.

Owner's port disbursements (at 2.5%):

Hamburg	US$ 4,250
Rotterdam	5,000
Suez Canal	2,500
Bombay	3,750
Madras	1,500

Radio Messages:

March	US$ 525
April	750
May	225

Meals and Gratuities:

	Meals	Gratuities
Hamburg	NIL	US$ 200
Rotterdam	50	225
Suez Canal	25	900
Bombay	550	250
Madras	525	225

Hire Payments:

15th March	US$ 112,500.00
30th March	112,500.00
14th April	112,500.00
29th April	112,500.00
14th May	20,000.00

Payment for Bunkers on Delivery: US$ 58,620.00

Chapter 6

LAYTIME

6.1 INTRODUCTION

Laytime is the time permitted in a contract for loading and/or discharging a voyage chartered ship. If this permitted time is exceeded, the Owner or Operator of the ship will be entitled to damages. These damages are normally agreed to be 'liquidated', that is to say that a daily sum (or *'pro-rata'* for part of a day) will be negotiated in the form of 'demurrage', payable for each day or part day of delay.

The demurrage rate is usually freely negotiated by the parties concerned during the fixing stage and will reflect market conditions prevailing then. Of course matters can change during the course of the voyage but under most charter parties the rate of demurrage will not alter. Some charter parties, Gencon 76 is a good example, restrict the period in which the demurrage rate applies. If the vessel is still delayed beyond this period the Owner can claim **'damages for detention'** instead of demurrage.

Unlike demurrage, damages for detention will need to be proved, i.e; the basis on which they are calculated must be related to the actual loss of the Owner and generally they will need to be sanctioned by a court or arbitration. Where the freight market has increased dramatically the damages may well be more than the demurrage that would otherwise have been paid but conversely in a poor market they may be less. An Owner who can show that a following, but previously agreed, contract has been cancelled will clearly have a good basis on which to claim damages for detention.

Given that proving damages for detention might be a complicated matter it is easy to see why most charter parties, including the Gencon 94, do not contain provision for any penalty other than demurrage. Interestingly the Gencon 76 form, which is still widely used, gives the Owner a right of lien on the cargo for damages for detention and that would surely expedite approval of the damage claim.

If a vessel finishes before the allowed time, or **'laytime',** has been used, a Charterer may be entitled to a 'reward' in the form of payment of **'despatch'** money, usually payable at half the daily rate of demurrage.

Laytime calculating is not an activity to be undertaken lightly. There may be considerable sums of money at stake, which will have a noticeable effect on a ship's profitability, or on a Charterer's income.

The calculation of laytime can be divided into 'Seven Stages':

1. Read the relevant clauses in the governing *'contract'.*

2. Obtain the *'statement of facts'.*

3. Determine how much laytime is available, i.e. its *'duration'.*

4. Establish the *'commencement'* of laytime.

5. Allow for *'interruptions'* to laytime.

6. Establish when laytime will cease, i.e. *'cessation'*, and,

7. Calculate how much *'despatch'* or *'demurrage'* is payable.

6.2 CONTRACT

The relevant charter party or the sales contract should specify laytime terms, so that by referring to the contract in relation to the details supplied by the Statement of Facts form, a 'time sheet' can be drawn up which shows whether the allowed laytime has been exceeded or is not fully used. The interpretation of many of these clauses and their true significance is almost an art in itself, and careful wording needs to be employed in the drafting of laytime clauses, guided by knowledge of specialised case law on the subject.

6.3 STATEMENT OF FACTS

One of the prime functions of a Port Agent is to produce a written record of events occurring during a vessel's port visit, this is sometimes referred to as a **'port operations log'**. Thus are recorded a ship's arrival date and time: when berthed or shifted to another berth; worked cargo, bunkered and departed; the time **'notice of readiness'** was tendered and accepted; weather conditions; and whatever else is relevant.

No matter the reason for a vessel's visit to port, whether it is for dry-docking or repairing; bunkering; cargo working; whether on voyage or time charter; a Port Agent should produce a **Statement of Facts** form to be forwarded to his Principal upon the vessel's departure. Many Port Agents use their own in-house designed form for this purpose, but a standard document which can be used at any port, world-wide, is available from BIMCO, and can be used if the agent or his Principal so wishes (see **Appendix 22**). It will be from this that a Time Sheet (such as in the form of **Appendix 23**) will eventually be drawn up.

It is good practice for Principals to brief a Port Agent fully about operational and chartering matters before a vessel's arrival in port. If possible the Port Agent should be sent a copy of the charter party/sales contract for perusal and guidance. In this way the Agent should be aware of information ultimately needed to be incorporated into the Statement of Facts form.

To avoid unnecessary dispute, interested parties to a vessel's visit to port, e.g. the ship's Master, Port Agents, Shipper/Receiver, should sign the completed Statement of Facts form. There should rarely be any objection to signing that document if it sets out to be simply what its name implies, a Statement of Facts. It is in the laytime interpretation of those facts that disputes are likely to arise, not in the recording of events. If, however, one or other of the parties has an objection to the contents of a Statement of Facts form, it should be signed 'under protest', a statement being added, clarifying the reason(s) for the objection.

Some Agents provide an Internet-based service that allows Owners and Charterers to access a running Statement of Facts while the vessel is working in port. The more sophisticated systems allow the information to be moved electronically into computer laytime calculation programs.

6.4 DURATION

Duration of laytime can be sub-divided into three categories:

1. Definite

2. Calculable

3. Indefinite

6.4.1 Definite Laytime

The simplest of the categories, specifies how many days/hours are allowed, whether for loading or for discharging, or for both activities, the latter sometimes being known as for **'all purposes'**. Terms might be: 'Cargo to be loaded within five weather working days of 24 consecutive hours', or seven working days of 24 consecutive hours, weather permitting, for all purposes'.

6.4.2   Calculable Laytime

In these cases periods of definite laytime as described above can only be established once a calculation has first been carried out, based on factors contained in the contract and in the Statement of Facts form.

Calculable laytime can be sub-divided into two further sub-sections:

Tonnage Calculations: Tonnage calculations are the most common types of calculable laytime. A contract will state that a vessel is to load and/or discharge at a set rate of tons/tonnes per day/hour. For a ship loading 40,000 metric tonnes of cargo, minimum/maximum, at a rate of 10,000 tonnes daily, there will be four days of laytime available to her Charterers.

However, it might be that the ship's Master has a margin within which to load, e.g. 40,000 tonnes/5% more or less. Therefore, if the ship eventually loaded 41,258 tonnes of cargo, available laytime can be assessed as follows:

41,258 tonnes) 10,000 tonnes daily = 4,1258 days.

4,1258 days equates to 4 days 3 hours 1 minute in the following manner:

	D	H	M
4.1258			
-4.0000	4	00	00
0.1258			
-0.1250	0	03	00
0.0008			
-0.0007	0	00	01
	4	03	01

A table giving the decimal parts of a day to help in calculations of this kind will be found in **Appendix 24.**

Hatch Calculations: Are more complicated than Tonnage Calculations, but occasionally need to be performed: Nonetheless, there are well-established procedures to assist.

Let us assume that general cargo vessel 'HERON' is discharging bagged wheat flour on the basis of:

i)   a discharge rate of 175 tonnes **per hatch** daily,

ii)   total cargo of 7,000 tonnes,

iii)   1,575 tonnes cargo in the largest cargo compartment, and

iv)   vessel has five (5) hatches.

'Per Hatch daily': The vessel is to be discharged at 175 tonnes per hatch daily.

Thus 5 (hatches) × 175 tonnes = 875 tonnes daily,

Thus 7,000 tonnes cargo) 875 = 8 days permitted laytime.

'Per Workable Hatch daily': Where the terms 'workable', 'working' or 'available hatch daily' are introduced, complications set in. To be 'workable' under English Law, a hatch must be capable of being 'worked', that is to say, there must be space beneath that hatch at the loading port, and there must be cargo under the hatch at discharge port.

Taking the above example of the 'HERON', as each hatch is emptied, the discharge rate would reduce by multiples of 175 tonnes daily, until all holds become empty one by one. This is, however, a cumbersome and sometimes complicated method of calculation, and English law procedure lays down a simpler alternative which is followed in such cases. First, it is necessary to establish the 'largest' unit of cargo in the vessel. Reference to the 'stowage plan' shows that 1,575 tonnes contained in No. 3 hold and tweendeck beneath No. 3 hatch constitutes the 'largest' unit.

Therefore, 1,575 tonnes) 175 daily = 9 days laytime overall.

However, where the largest unit of cargo is served by two or more hatches, the unit tonnage must be sub-divided. Assuming two hatches served No. 3 hold and tweendeck, for example, 1,575 tonnes would first be divided by two before applying the factor of 175 tonnes daily. In that case, the largest indivisible cargo unit would become the 1,500 tonnes contained in No. 2 hold and tweendeck, and the laytime duration calculation would then be:

1,500 tonnes) 175 daily = 8.571428 days laytime.

(8.571428 days can be converted to days, hours and minutes by using the table in **Appendix 24).**

6.4.3   Indefinite Laytime

Occasionally, an Owner or Operator will agree for his ship to be loaded or discharged as per 'Custom of the Port (COP); 'Customary Despatch' (CD); 'Customary Quick Despatch' (CQD), or 'Fast As Can' (FAC) terms.

The common factor with these terms is that all provide a shipper or receiver with an 'indefinite' period during which to perform cargo operations, although they must act 'reasonably'. It is 'unreasonable', for example, for cargo not to be available upon a vessel's arrival within agreed laydays, and in such a case, the Owner or Operator of the ship would normally become entitled to reimbursement by 'damages for detention'. But risk of bad weather, port congestion, and any other problems are all for the Shipowner/Operator to bear.

'Fast as can' applies normally to ships that have their own gear and can load or discharge without use of shore equipment and stipulates that the cargo will be loaded and/or discharged 'as fast as the vessel can', often adding a further stipulation that Charterers or Shippers/ Receivers must be able to 'deliver' or 'take-away' cargo at a particular daily tonnage rate.

6.4.4   Deadfreight

Where only part of a contracted cargo can be supplied and, consequently, where 'deadfreight' becomes payable to a Shipowner/Operator as a result, under English law laytime is applied only on the portion of cargo actually loaded. Therefore:

i)   contracted cargo:- 10,000 tonnes min/max

ii)   loading rate:- 2,000 tonnes daily

iii)   cargo supplied:- 7,000 tonnes

iv)   deadfreight:- 3,000 tonnes (10,000 - 7,000)

v)   laytime:- 7,000/2,000 = 3.5 days.

However, also under English Law, a Shipowner/Operator claiming deadfreight must return to the Charterer any benefit received. Two laytime calculations should be carried out, one based on actual cargo loaded/discharged and the other on the original cargo that should have been loaded/discharged. Any difference in the Owner's favour should be credited to the Charterer in return for payment of deadfreight.

In the above case: Actual laytime 3.5 days.

Original laytime 10000 tons/2000 = 5 days.

Laytime saved to be credited against deadfreight 1.5 days.

American law is more straightforward in cases of deadfreight, calculating laytime on what has been loaded, plus tonnage equivalent to the deadfreight paid by Charterers.

6.5   COMMENCEMENT

For laytime to have 'commenced', a vessel must have 'arrived' at the place where cargo operations are to be performed (1) **'arrival'**: must be physically able to undergo cargo operations (2) **'readiness'**; and have dealt with (3) **'contractual commitments'**.

Arrival: Laytime is a subject which lends itself to dispute, and the definition of whether or not a ship has 'arrived' in a laytime sense may sometimes be legally extremely complicated, there being much English Law on the subject. Simply, to have 'arrived' at a port, a vessel must have reached either the loading/discharging place or, should that place be busy, the normal waiting place.

Furthermore, a ship's Master or Agent must have tendered Notice of Readiness, in accordance with the contract requirements (e.g; 'within office hours, Mondays to Fridays').

Notice of Readiness can be given orally, but usually a written form is used, an example of which can be found in **Appendix 25.** It is an important function of a Port Agent to assist a ship's Master in tendering notice of a ship's arrival, and also to ensure that shippers/ receivers officially 'accept' the vessel's Notice of Readiness, accomplished usually by signing and timing acceptance on the notice form, although many Shippers/Receivers or Charterers' nominated Port Agents, will 'accept subject to charter party terms and conditions'.

Readiness: A ship must be physically capable of performing cargo operations, e.g; at a loading port, holds must be cleaned and prepared for receiving cargo and, if the contract so specifies, holds must be inspected and declared suitable by an appropriate authority before Notice of Readiness will be accepted.

Contractual Commitments: Contracts usually state that before laytime commences, a vessel must, (a) have been 'entered' at the local custom house and (b) be in 'free pratique' (given the go ahead to proceed by the port health authority).

Congestion: In case cargo berths are occupied upon a vessel's arrival, contracts usually specify that Notices of Readiness can be tendered from a 'normal waiting place', 'Whether in Berth, Or Not' (WIBON); 'Whether In Free Pratique, Or Not' (WIFPON); and 'Whether Custom's Cleared Or Not' (WCCON). It is normal that time spent in eventual shifting from the waiting place to the first cargo berth will not count as laytime.

Turn Time: This occurs at certain ports where ships wait their 'turn' to load/discharge. When waiting turn, laytime will not usually count. Sometimes 'turn time' is limited, say to '48 hours', laytime commencing once this period has elapsed, or earlier if cargo operations begin within that period. Where no 'turn time' limit is specified, the risk of excessive delay is that for a Shipowner. When markets are in their favour, some Charterers attempt to impose 'turn time' conditions into a charter party, even though there is no such custom for the same at the ports involved, e.g; '36 hours turn time both ends'.

Commencement: Once a vessel has arrived at a port, complied with all formalities and contractual commitments, and tendered Notice of Readiness, laytime will commence in accordance with the contract terms, e.g; 'at 07.00 hours next working day', or '12 hours following tendering and accepting Notice of Readiness'.

It is important to remember that the commencement of time counting and the commencement of actual loading or discharging can, under certain circumstances, be quite different. Take, for example, a charter party with 36 hours turn time 'even if used' also Sundays and Holidays excepted 'even if used' and Notice of Readiness to be given during normal office hours. Such a ship could arrive at, say, 6 pm on a Friday, work the entire weekend and time would not commence to count until 36 hours after 8 am Monday. Such a ship would have been working for over four days before time even commences to count. Vital, therefore, to ensure also that Notice of Readiness is handed in at the earliest permissible moment. Never think that as work has already started a Notice of Readiness is not needed.

6.5.1 Arrival Before Laydays

Providing a ship arrives at a loading port within the laydays before the cancelling date, the Charterer is obliged to produce a cargo for it. He is not obliged to produce any cargo before the laydays if the ship arrives early.

Even though the Charterer is under no obligation to provide cargo, the Owner can present an immediate Notice of Readiness and time will begin to count in accordance with the terms of the charter party. In such a case, the exceptions to laytime, in addition to those agreed upon, will include any time up to the first time and date mentioned in the agreed laydays.

Effectively this situation means that the time lapse between presenting a Notice of Readiness and time starting to count that would exist under more normal conditions disappears.

As an example the laycan for a ship on a Gencon 76 may have been agreed as Wednesday 8th April – Tuesday 14th April. The time to count from 1400 if NOR delivered in office hours before noon and 0800 the next day if delivered after noon. A rate of 5,000 tonnes per day WP was agreed for cargo handling.

Had the ship arrived on Wednesday 8th at 07.45, the NOR would have been tendered at 09.00 and time and time started to count from 14.00 that day. But if the ship arrived on Friday 3rd April at 11.00 and tendered immediate notice time would start to count at 14.00 on Friday 3rd. None of the time up to 00.01 on Wednesday 8th would count either because it was a weekend (excepted under the terms of the c/p) or because the time was before commencement of laydays.

But as soon as Wednesday 8th arrived the laytime clock would start to run, and unless the weather prevented any work it would do, say at 0001. A whole 14 hours earlier than the Charterer may have counted on. Some Charterers have countered this advantage for the Owner by demanding a clause that prevents the NOR being presented before laydays.

6.5.2 Interruptions

Once laytime has commenced, unless a vessel's cargo handling equipment breaks down, it will continue unhindered until the completion of cargo operations, or until laytime expires or demurrage commences. Nevertheless, contracts frequently include express clauses interrupting laytime in the event of:

5.1 Weekends and holidays
5.2 Shifting between berths
5.3 Strikes
5.4 Bad weather
5.5 Breakdowns

Weekends and holidays: If these are to interrupt laytime, the contract can be said to be on 'SHEX' terms (Sundays and Holidays Excepted), or on FHEX terms (Fridays and Holidays

Excepted) if in Moslem countries. Should weekends and holidays count as laytime, the contract can be said to be based on SHINC (Sundays and Holidays Inclusive), FHINC in Moslem countries. The terms SHEX and SHINC came into use when Saturdays were considered part of the working week. Nowadays of course Saturday is also a non-working day and the terms have been altered slightly to SSHEX and SSHINC, sometimes Brokers refer to this as 'full' SHEX or SHINC as the case may be when talking to each other.

Normally a charter party will specify the actual time before a holiday or a weekend that laytime is to be suspended, e.g; 'from 18.00 hours on the day preceding a holiday'. If no such time is specified, laytime is usually suspended from midnight on the day preceding a holiday.

In the same way a charter party will normally specify the actual time of resumption of laytime following a holiday or weekend, e.g; 07.00 hours Monday. If no such time is specified, laytime will usually recommence at 00.01 hours on the day following a holiday or weekend.

If cargo work is performed during an excepted period, laytime will not normally count, unless the contract allows it to, e.g; 'time not to count during weekends, **'unless used'**. Alternatively, a contract may emphasise that 'time used during weekends is not to count, **'even if used'**. Occasionally, agreement is reached that 'actual time used during weekends is to count as laytime', or even 'half time actually used to count'. It may also be agreed that the period between Notice of Readiness being tendered and the commencement of laytime may count as laytime 'if actually used'.

Shifting between berths: It is common practice for contract wording to permit loading/discharging at more than one berth or anchorage at each port. Consequently, time spent shifting between berths/anchorages is normally taken to be for Owners' account. However, should the agreed number of berths/anchorages be exceeded, it becomes reasonable that the shifting time involved should count as laytime, and that the expenses involved, e.g; towage and pilotage, should also be for the account of the Charterers.

Strikes: There is nearly always an express clause in a contract to the effect that delays due to shore strikes are not to count as laytime.

Bad Weather: Clauses in a shipping contract referring to bad weather interruptions of laytime at one time could be divided into two types, 'weather working days' and 'days, weather permitting'. For many years it had been accepted that the former expression favoured Charterers and the latter favoured Shipowners.

In cases of 'weather working days', laytime does not count during periods of bad weather that interrupt loading or discharging, nor (and this is the important factor) does laytime count when bad weather occurs during a working day even if, had the weather been fine, no attempt would have been made to work. 'Weather working day' describes a type of working day. It does not matter whether the vessel was actually working or not.

It follows, therefore, that even if a ship is not actually on the loading (or discharging) berth, for example because it is occupied by another ship, if time has started to run and bad weather occurs during a working day, that time will not count against Charterers as laytime.

Take note of the word 'working' day (we will be studying this a little more deeply later in the Chapter). A working day not only refers to a day when work normally takes place, it is also that **part** of the day when work is normally done in the port in question. If, therefore, the word 'working' is not qualified in any way, the bad weather would have to occur during the port working part of the day for it to be deducted from the laytime.

Conversely, where the charter party reads 'working day of 24 consecutive hours' (which is now more normal), then bad weather occurring at any time (once laytime had started to run) would be deductible even if the Charterer had no intention of working during such a period.

In cases of 'days, weather permitting' it was understood until 1982 that only working time **actually interrupted** by bad weather would fail to count as laytime. All this, however, was before the case of the 'VORRAS' in that year. That vessel was a tanker and the judges of the English Court of Appeal had to determine the meaning of the term '72 running hours, weather permitting, Sundays and holidays included...', where the vessel was kept from a loading berth for some days owing to bad weather. They held that bad weather at the time was such as to prevent the loading of a vessel of the 'VORRAS' type and as such, laytime should not count. In other words, that decision on a tanker has effectively eroded the long-held and sacred distinction in the dry cargo market between 'weather working' and 'weather permitting'.

Frequently in modern charter parties one will still encounter either the terms 'weather working' or 'weather permitting', although under English Law, at least, there is effectively now no difference. However, both will probably refer in the same clause to **'days of 24 consecutive hours'**, a similar expression to the **'running hours'** used in the case of the 'VORRAS'. The word **'consecutive'** is, in fact, extremely important, having evolved over very many years in order to avoid costly disputes.

Where the term 'days of 24 consecutive hours' is incorporated into a charter party's laytime provisions, and this is the term used in almost all modern dry cargo charterparties, it in effect means that a laytime day will run continuously for 24 hours each day, unless specifically interrupted by some charter party factor such as a weekend or holiday, bad weather, or a strike. It is of no consequence whether the 'working day' of a port is of less than 24 hours. The parties to the contract have agreed, in effect, to ignore port 'working days' and to define a 'laytime day' as running continuously for 24 hours, except for any specified interruptions.

Once the practitioner of dry cargo laytime can fully understand this point, the effect of interruptions on laytime should cease to be a mystery.

Where the words '24 consecutive hours' do not appear, as occasionally happens by intent, although perhaps more often by mistake, variations in today's practices may arise.

The term 'weather working day' on its own without qualification is indeed affected by the number of hours actually worked in a port. Should bad weather occur outside working periods in the normal, non-working and otherwise idle time, laytime will not be affected. However, if bad weather occurs in normal working time, even if the vessel was idle at the time, laytime will be interrupted and the degree of interruption has to be reached by apportioning working time in a port against a 24-hour day.

Assuming port labour works a 12 hour day, from 07.00 hours until 19.00 hours:

					Laytime Used
Day 1: worked	0700/1900	=	1.0 day	=	24 hours
Day 2: worked	0700/1900				
rain	2200/2400	=	1.0 day	=	24 hours
Day 3: rain	0001/2400	=	0.0 day	=	0 hours
Day 4: rain	0700/1900	=	0.0 day	=	0 hours
Day 5: worked	0700/1300				
rain	1300/1900	=	0.5 day	=	12 hours
Day 6: worked	0700/1000				
rain	1000/1900	=	0.25 day	=	6 hours
Day 7: rain	0700/1000				
worked	1000/1900	=	0.75 day	=	18 hours

Since the case of the 'VORRAS', the term 'working days, weather permitting' should be taken to be the same as for the above example, and the terms 'weather working days of 24 hours' and 'working days of 24 hours, weather permitting' (i.e. without the all important 'consecutive') must also be treated in the same manner.

Breakdowns: It is reasonable that if a vessel's gear is being used and it breaks down, laytime should not continue during the period of breakdown. It may be that, for example, one crane out of four has broken down and, in such a case, apportionment of the degree of loss must be carried out. In that relatively simple example, laytime would continue at a rate of 75% until the crane is repaired.

There are, however, shore breakdowns, and it may be that the Shipowners have knowingly or unwittingly assumed responsibility for these in their contract. Some charter parties exclude time lost due to stoppages of shore machinery "beyond the Charterers control", which means just that under English Law. A shore crane breakdown that is judged to be 'beyond Charterers' control' (i.e. Charterers do not own or otherwise 'control' the crane) such a breakdown will, therefore, interrupt laytime. Under American law it may be that the alternative view would be upheld, in the Shipowners' favour, although that is not completely certain.

While most modern revisions have removed this wording, there are still several widely used forms containing this expression or another to similar effect.

6.6   CESSATION

Generally, dry cargo laytime ceases simultaneously with the termination of cargo operations, i.e; as loading is completed. Occasionally, however, special cargo work such as trimming, lashing or securing will be necessary, the time for which would reasonably be added to laytime.

Most charter parties are silent also on the effect on laytime of time taken for reading drafts, perhaps an essential activity before bill of lading weight can be assessed. Usually, Charterers will recognise this activity as essential and include the same as laytime, especially since it normally involves a relatively short time. Every now and then, however, a draft survey is seriously impeded by, for example, bad weather, and there might well be a dispute between the parties unless the contract specifies whether time devoted to ascertaining a vessel's draft should count as laytime or not.

6.7   CALCULATION

This can usefully be sub-divided into the following categories:

Damages for Detention
Demurrage
Despatch
Averaging Laytime

But before examining each of these four categories, it is important at this stage to examine 'time sheets'.

Armed with a Statement of Facts and the relevant charter party, the calculator having reached this 'seventh stage' can move on to using a 'time sheet' to compile the laytime calculation.

A time sheet is a document showing laytime utilised, taking into account all the factors mentioned in this Chapter, before arriving at a balance of despatch money in favour of Charterers, or demurrage money in favour of Owners/Operators. They are based on information supplied from the Statement of Facts as interpreted by the relevant laytime clauses in the governing contract, themselves interpreted by knowledge of the law relating to laytime.

As in the case of Statement of Facts, BIMCO produce a standard time sheet form which is available for use world-wide, and this is reproduced under **Appendix 23**.

6.7.1 Damages for Detention

If Charterers fail to abide by the provisions of a contract and, as a result, permitted laytime is exceeded, Shipowners are normally entitled to reimbursement for their loss, if any. One method of reimbursement could be by claiming 'damages for detention', however this could be a lengthy and costly legal exercise. Consequently, most parties to a shipping contract avoid the problem by negotiating a daily level of 'liquidated damages', i.e; 'demurrage', for the time spent in excess of agreed laytime.

6.7.2 Demurrage

When all permitted laytime is used before the completion of cargo operations, and the parties to a contract have foreseen this possibility, it is usual that a governing contract will provide for demurrage to be paid to the Shipowners. The amount of demurrage is negotiated with the contract and is usually described as '$...per day' or *pro rata* for part of a day. (Very occasionally demurrage might be described as '$ x cents per ton' but in such a case it is vital to establish whether the 'ton' refers to a summer deadweight tonnage of the ship involved, or 'per cargo ton', or 'per registered ton', and whether metric or long, gross or nett).

Usually address commissions and brokerages are deductible from demurrage payments, just as in the case of freight or deadfreight but this has to be clearly stated in the commission/brokerage clause(s).

Demurrage is intended to reflect the daily running cost of a vessel, including port bunker consumption, and where applicable, a reasonable profit level. Shipping being a free market, however, and exposed to market forces and necessities, there may be occasions when Shipowners accept low or negotiate high demurrage rates.

Once laytime has been fully used, demurrage should normally run continuously, night and day, weekend and working period, with no interruptions until cargo work is completed **unless** the contract expressly provides otherwise, e.g: 'shifting time from anchorage to berth not to count as laytime or as time on demurrage'. Normally, however, laytime interruptions such as bad weather, weekends and holidays, will not interfere with demurrage time, although breakdowns on a vessel affecting discharge will interrupt demurrage time. Given these exceptions, it can usually be said that the much used shipping expression 'once on demurrage, always on demurrage' means what it says.

6.7.3 Despatch

It is very often agreed that if a vessel completes cargo operations within the available laytime, the Charterer will be rewarded by the payment of despatch money, which is normally set at half the daily rate of demurrage.

It should be borne in mind, however, that a few Charterers negotiate that daily despatch is the same as daily demurrage, while, by contrast, for vessels that normally might expect a fast turn-round in port, e.g: ro-ro ships, car carriers, or coasters, it is not at all unusual for the contract to specify 'free despatch', i.e; no despatch at all.

However, no address commissions or brokerages are payable on despatch money.

Where despatch is payable, it can be sub-divided as being payable on:

1. All time saved, or on

2. Working time, or laytime saved.

It is perhaps easier to understand despatch on 'all time saved' by the use of an example.

The *'HERON'* completes loading at 12.00 hours on a Friday, her charter party being 'per weather working day of 24 consecutive hours, Saturdays, Sundays and Holidays excepted, even if used'. Therefore, laytime would be suspended in normal circumstances from Friday 24.00 hours through to Monday 00.01 hours.

At 12.00 hours on Friday there are three days of laytime remaining and, since the term 'all time saved' means exactly what it says, the calculator of laytime has to base figures on the hypothetical case that "if the vessel had not completed loading on the Friday at 12.00 hours, but had remained in port working cargo when would laytime have been fully used"?

Despatch would be calculated in the following fashion:

	'All time saved'	**'Laytime'**
Friday	1200/2400 hours	12 hours
Saturday	0000/2400	0 hours
Sunday	0000/2400	0 hours
Monday	0000/2400	24 hours
Tuesday	0000/2400	24 hours
Wednesday	0000/1200	12 hours
	5 days	3 days

Allowing for the weekend that has been 'saved' by the Charterers due to their finishing before the expiry of permitted laytime, they have in effect 'saved' the Shipowner some five days and, under 'all time saved' terms, are entitled to five days despatch.

Using the same example, but on the basis of 'working time' or 'laytime saved', only the three remaining days of laytime would apply as despatch, despite weekends or holidays or bad weather or any other factor occurring once the ship had departed.

The question remains, however, is 'working time saved' the same as 'laytime saved'? With laytime described as 'a day of 24 consecutive hours' it will be the same. Otherwise, if one is involved in apportioning 'working time' in the manner shown under Section 6.5, then despatch should be apportioned in the same manner.

You will readily see that 'despatch on all time saved' favours the Charterer whilst 'laytime saved' or 'working time saved' is better for the Owner; the 'fairness' of one versus the other is a perpetual debate. The Owners naturally say that as laytime excepts certain periods like Sundays and holidays, then despatch should be on the same basis. The Charterer counters this by arguing that a ship is earning all the time she is at sea regardless of which day of the week it is so that getting the ship to sea that much quicker should reward the Charterer for every day without exception.

One final word about despatch; it should be borne in mind that some markets (e.g. bulk sugar) are based on laytime far in excess of the time actually required to perform cargo operations. It is, therefore, important for Shipowners to take this into account when negotiating business and to reflect the 'saved' time as a 'despatch expense' in a voyage estimate.

6.7.4   Averaging Laytime

This is an overall title which should in reality be sub-divided into:

Normal (or 'non reversible') laytime

Reversible, and

Average

Normal or Non-reversible Laytime: If nothing is specifically mentioned in the contract, and where loading and discharging port laytime allowances are separately assessed, it can be taken that laytime is 'normal' or 'non-reversible'. Laytime for loading port(s) and for discharging port(s) are assessed entirely separately and it is possible even to calculate, claim, negotiate and settle the load port(s) despatch/demurrage sums before even a vessel has reached her discharge port(s).

Reversible Laytime: Where allowance for both the loading and discharging ports are added and calculated together. Either the contract may openly be on 'reversible' terms without actually stating so, e.g; 7 days, **'all purposes'**, or '16 **total** days', or there may be an express clause giving the Charterers the right or the option to apply reversible conditions if they so wish, in other words, if they calculate it to be in their favour to do so. Any laytime saved from the loading ports can be carried forward and added to laytime allowed at the port(s) of discharge.

Average Laytime: This a rises where separate calculations are performed for the loading and for the discharging ports, with the final results for each being combined in order to assess what is finally due, e.g; two days demurrage at load port would be cancelled out by two days despatch at discharge port, even though the daily value of demurrage may be twice that of despatch.

At first sight it may appear there is no difference between the application of reversible and average laytime. In fact, differences can arise and, with the same basic facts, it is possible to reach three different results by applying each of the above alternatives.

Laytime Definitions: Appendix 26 contains the 'VOYLAY Rules 1993' in which laytime terms have been defined by a group of distinguished international shipping practitioners. It may be found useful in everyday laytime calculating. One word of warning, however. The definitions relate to international practice and not necessarily to a particular code of law. There may be slight but significant differences between the definition appearing in this document from legal practice in a particular country.

It should also be noted that the rules do not automatically apply to every fixture made. Willing parties can however ensure that this is so by merely adding a short clause to the effect that in the event of a dispute the Voylay rules are to apply in interpreting particular words or phrases.

A study of the rules would show that the very first elements to be defined are 'port' and 'berth'. This is particularly relevant because many charters specify particular berths for loading or discharging while others only mention the port.

If the Charterer intends to work the ship at a specific berth it may be in his interest to name the berth and so make the fixture a 'berth charter'. There are many reasons why the Charterer may want to nominate a particular berth but from a practical point of view as regards laytime the important difference between berth and port charters is that if a named berth is not available for a reason in which time would not count (such as neap tides) then the risk of incurring demurrage is lessened. Under a port charter time would count if other berths within the port were not affected by the tidal reason stated.

This Chapter is designed to provide you with an introduction to this most complicated of subjects. This Chapter will not, however, have made you an expert. That can only come with experience (some bitter) and by extensive reading. There are probably more arbitration and court cases connected with 'time counting' than any other single aspect of charter parties. You need to keep up-to-date by reading newspaper and magazine articles. For example, in addition to the (many say perverse) judgement in the case of the *'Vorras'* referred to earlier, an apparently simple dispute recently went all the way to the English House of Lords. This concerned the *'Kyzikos'* which had been fixed with time commencing to count 'whether in port or not', 'whether in berth or not', 'whether in free pratique or not' and 'whether cleared at the Customs House or not'. She had to wait for the berth to become free so time started to count but when the berth became available, the ship was unable to move immediately because of fog. The Charterers argued that bad weather impeding navigation was a ship's concern so time should not count between calling the ship onto the berth and her actually getting there including the delay caused by the fog. The Owners contended that had the Charterers not been tardy in providing a ready berth, the fog would not have caused any trouble. In the event their Lordships ruled in Charterer's favour. By no means every commercial/shipping person agreed with that decision.

6.8 SELF-ASSESSMENT AND TEST QUESTIONS

1. Work out the laytime allowed for the following vessels on the basis of 'per hatch daily' and 'per workable hatch daily' under English Law:

   Vessel *'Lark'* to be discharged at 340 tonnes per...
   6 holds/6 hatches

   1. 2120T; 2. 2620T; 3. 2700T; 4. 2720T; 5. 2680T; 6. 2460T.
   Vessel *'Pigeon'* to be discharged at 1500 tons per...
   4 holds/7 hatches (twin Nos 2, 3 and 4 holds).

   1. 9200T; 2. 17,800T; 3. 22500T; 4. 24000T.

Attempt the following and check your answers from the text or appendices:

2. What are the seven stages to be taken into consideration when calculating laytime?

3. What is the difference between a Statement of Facts and a Time Sheet?

4. What is 'Free Pratique'?

5. What is the effect on laytime calculations when deadfreight is involved?

6. What events can interrupt laytime counting?

7. Does time continue to count if shore cranes break down?

8. What is (a) demurrage and (b) despatch?

9. What is meant by 'Reversible Laytime'?

10. What is D.R.I, and what are the problems associated with its carriage?

11. On what conditions would a Shipowner probably insist before agreeing to carry ferro-silicon?

Having completed Chapter Six attempt the following and submit your answer to your Tutor.

Set out a detailed Time Sheet and calculate Demurrage or Despatch for M.V. *Osprey* from the Statement of Facts in **Appendix 22**.

C/P stipulates: 'Laytime to commence at 13.00 if Notice of Readiness given before Noon, at 07.00 next working day if given after Noon: notice to be given in ordinary office hours'.

'Laytime shall not commence to count before holds are passed as clean by Shippers' Inspector'.

'Cargo to be loaded at the rate of 5,000 metric tons per weather working day of 24 consecutive hours'.

'Time from 17.00 Friday or the day preceding a holiday to 08.00 Monday or next working day not to count unless used (but only actual time used to count) unless vessel already on demurrage'.

'Demurrage US $5,000 per day and *pro rata*/Despatch at half demurrage rate on laytime saved'.

(NB: Appendix 24 will help convert decimal parts of a day to hours and minutes, and vice versa.)

Chapter 7

VOYAGE ESTIMATING

7.1 INTRODUCTION

Voyage estimating is an important skill for all persons engaged in the activity of dry cargo chartering, whether from an Owner's or a Charterer's perspective, even for competitive Brokers.

It is common these days for Charterers to undertake contracts, to relet tonnage and to take in vessels not owned by them, on voyage or on timecharter, whereas competitive Brokers need the ability to evaluate potential business, to enable them to present outwardly unattractive cargoes and vessels in their true light. So it is not only those closely associated with the control of tonnage that need the knowledge and ability this Chapter sets out to help you acquire.

The first essential in voyage estimating is to examine the subject heading itself. Despite the reference to 'voyage', voyage estimating will inevitably include the realistic valuation of time charter trips, since these are rarely as financially straightforward as they first might appear. The work 'estimate' speaks for itself and, whilst we have no wish to promote inaccuracy, it is necessary to point out that ships do not run like clockwork and it is, therefore, impossible to calculate to perfection. That is not to suggest that your aim should be less than total accuracy, and it is essential to do your best towards achieving a realistic appraisal of the potential worth of any proposed venture.

You should always compare a final 'estimate' with the eventual 'results' of a voyage or trip, so that any procedural shortcomings can be identified, and future errors avoided.

For voyage estimating it is essential to have a knowledge of maritime geography, with particular regard to distances and permissible loadlines (see Chapter Nine). There are several commercial distance tables available to assist with distances involved and one of these should always be used when embarking on a full-blown voyage estimate. To start such an exercise using a guess for the most fundamental piece of data would be very foolish; there is a great deal of sense in the dictum 'don't remember the fact remember where to find it'.

Having said that there will be times when you will want to do a 'back of an envelope' type of estimate perhaps to compare quickly two pieces of business and so it is useful to have a fairly accurate idea of major world maritime distances, from which basis one can usually estimate cross voyages. Perhaps the best method is to divide the world into areas (somewhat naturally this tends to fall into oceans) and then learn and remember a number of strategic mileages across each area.

There is a division of thought on whether you should learn actual distances or think in terms of days 'steamed' but, since most professionals tend to think in terms of days, the latter is perhaps the more favourable alternative. As a guide, a speed of 14 knots works out almost exactly three days per 1000 nautical miles (i.e. 14 knots × 24 hours × 3 = 1008 nm) and, on this basis, it is relatively easy to remember that, for example, a transatlantic voyage between the US Gulf (say New Orleans) and Rotterdam takes fifteen days in good weather, whilst that between USNH (United States, North of Cape Hatteras), say Hampton Roads and Rotterdam, lasts for eleven days in good weather. Under this relatively simple system, representative voyages can be calculated and memorised. Provided you remember to correct the time allowed in accordance with various speeds, this should make the task much easier than otherwise might be the case.

Having established a method of calculating the length of a sea-passage, we can next consider the basic elements of a voyage estimate and produce a 'skeleton' on which to hang the 'flesh' of any particular calculation. But before we start examining the make-up of an estimate it is as well to determine just how it will be produced.

7.1.1 Computerisation

As in many walks of life, there are now some very sophisticated and 'user-friendly' voyage estimating programmes available for general use, or even astute colleagues who can use their computing talents to design personalised programmes 'in house'. Nevertheless, it is vital that those setting out diligently to learn about voyage estimating learn the basics and that is made very much easier by starting with hand-produced calculations prepared by no more sophisticated a method than brainpower, pencil and paper, aided where necessary, by a pocket calculator.

The aim should be for those new to voyage estimating to build up confidence by the knowledge that if necessary and the computer 'goes down', a relatively accurate voyage estimate can be hand-produced in reasonable time.

7.1.2 Estimate Form

It will help you considerably in producing consistent estimates to use a standard estimate form for each calculation. **Appendix 27** provides a sample form containing all the necessary elements, and it may be that you will discover that form provides you with all that is required for successful voyage estimating throughout your career.

Not only that, but the form neatly sub-divides into the five stages of voyage estimating:

1. Itinerary
2. Cargo Quantity
3. Expenses
4. Income
5. Result

A voyage estimate consists broadly of income minus expenditure, like any profit and loss account. Which form of procedure you use is, however, a matter of personal preference, but all can be classified under the heading of **'method'**. It is easy to reduce an estimate to the back of an envelope and, indeed, there may be isolated occasions when speed of negotiating will make this a necessity. But if all the various elements are set out in front of you, it is far more difficult to overlook the odd, important item, which can make all the difference between profit and loss. So whether you intend to undertake voyage estimates regularly or simply for the initial purposes of this course, select a suitable form and use it constantly.

However, an estimate can quite adequately be made on plain paper. The vital thing is to acquire **'method'**. In this Chapter, therefore, we will be following the stages listed above and, indeed, the later examples are used on that system.

7.2 STAGE 1: ITINERARY

This first stage of any voyage estimate maps out the proposed employment and can itself be sub-divided into:

1. Voyage plan.
2. Duration, and
3. Bunker consumption

This will enable you to see at a glance just what is to be estimated, and can be called the 'itinerary'.

Of course you will need to know details about the vessel itself, its deadweight and drafts, cubic capacities and speed and consumptions of fuel oil and diesel oil. Perhaps more, depending upon the complexity of the calculation that is required or the commodity to be carried.

The most important point is always to work in the same way, so as to avoid confusion, and it is recommended that the commencement of a voyage should always be from the place where the vessel completes discharge of her previous cargo, allowing for the time and costs spent leaving the last discharge port to be charged to the previous voyage. In this manner, the first part of the voyage will be a ballast leg, commencing with dropping the outward port pilot, unless the Shipowner or Operator is fortunate enough to find a cargo from the port in which the vessel has just discharged. A few estimators commence their estimates at a loading port and follow the laden passage with a theoretical ballast leg back to the same loading port. However, since tramp dry-cargo vessels rarely proceed again on the same voyage, this is hardly a practical alternative to the more logical method of commencing from where a vessel is open and seeking next employment i.e. upon completion of the previous employment.

Turning once again to the blank sample estimating form and with distance tables to hand, it is not difficult to estimate the length of ballast and laden voyage legs, to plan out the sea-time and routes of the estimate, and to fill in the appropriate boxes.

When attention is directed at port times, however, immediate difficulties are encountered. Unlike tankers, dry cargo voyages vary enormously in their port time content. The difficulty is that often one cannot calculate port time until cargo quantity is known, and cargo quantity cannot be calculated until an assessment is made of the bunker quantity remaining on board at strategic points in the proposed voyage, and this cannot be properly calculated until voyage duration is assessed. Fortunately, even when working all cargo gear, dry cargo vessels normally consume very small quantities of bunkers in port and so port bunker consumption can largely be overlooked for the purposes of cargo quantity estimation. Nevertheless, it may sometimes be necessary temporarily to postpone completion of the itinerary section of an estimate until the cargo calculation in Stage 2 has been concluded.

Be very careful also over the route selected. Sometimes there are alternatives and only a marginal difference will tilt the balance in favour of one route or another. Bad weather at certain times of the year; high canal tolls on one route; cheaper bunkers on another. All factors must be considered. As an example, consider for a moment the alternatives for an estimator of a vessel proceeding from the *United States Gulf* (say, from New Orleans) to *Singapore.*

Alternative 1: Via Gibraltar and the Suez Canal   11461 miles
Alternative 2: Via Panama Canal   11905 miles
Alternative 3: Via Cape of Good Hope   12951 miles

On the face of it, Alternative 1 seems the better selection. But this is to overlook the cost of canal tolls and allowances for canal transit delay in comparison with the longer but probably cheaper Cape of Good Hope route. But is time of the essence? Is it necessary to complete the voyage as quickly as possible? In which case the estimator may have little choice but to proceed by the shortest, more expensive route.

Speed may, in fact, be an important factor. In some cases it may be more cost-effective to proceed more slowly and to economise on bunkers. Particularly this might be so where bunkers are expensive and freight rates are low, *or* in coastal estimating, where voyages are frequently dependent on tidal depths. There may be little point in steaming full speed, only to have to await a suitable tide for some hours following arrival off port. On the other hand, if an early arrival off a port means the Master can tender Notice of Readiness that much sooner, it may still be more cost advantageous to proceed at full speed.

Canal transit duration must also be calculated. Although usually without incident, occasionally the transit of vessels through canals is seriously disrupted, and although there is usually little notice of such events, sometimes it is common knowledge that delays can be anticipated and their effect should be taken into account.

Multiple ports, where a vessel has to call at, say several loading and/or discharging ports, calls for extra time to be allowed for delays in entering and leaving each port.

Bunkering calls can on occasion be lengthy, but generally it is appropriate to allow an extra half day (plus idle port consumption of bunkers) in an estimate.

Bad weather does not normally affect the drafting of a voyage estimate unless it is certain from the nature of the trade that delays will be experienced, either at sea or in port.

Bunker consumption, when all distances and times are calculated, it should be possible to calculate estimated bunker consumption both at sea and in port, and to conclude this stage of the estimate, although allowance must also be made for a vessel's Bunker consumption through the confined waters of a canal, as this may bear little resemblance to normal consumption whilst steaming in unobstructed waters at sea.

7.3   STAGE 2: CARGO QUANTITY

As we have seen, cargo quantity may substantially affect time spent in port by a dry cargo vessel, and it may first be necessary to calculate this before being able to enter port time in Stage 1 above.

On the assumption that there are no **draft limitations** anywhere on a voyage, it may be sufficient just to know a vessel's available **deadweight** in order to assess cargo capacity, otherwise adjustments must be made in accordance with available draft. From the eventual available tonnage must be deducted the vessel's **constant weights** (consisting of stores, freshwater, lubricants, spares, even the weight of the crew). A vessel's constant weight is rarely critical but must be accounted for. (For vessel of around 15/25,000 tonnes sdwt it will be about 250/350 tonnes and, for vessels in excess of, say 35,000 tonnes, some 4/500 tonnes).

The other important deduction is that of **bunkers** remaining on board a vessel, and here it may be necessary to obtain appropriate data from the vessel's managers or from her Master. Bunker calculation can be extremely complicated and we will examine this in more detail later in this Chapter.

Suffice at this stage of the Chapter, to be aware of bunkers constituting a major consideration.

In the meantime, let us assume we have reached a suitable figure for **deadweight cargo capacity.** Regrettably this is not the end of the problem. Our vessel may be able to lift the weight of 'x' amount of tonnes of cargo, but has she the space to contain it? It is at this point that the importance of cargo stowage factors we first met in Chapter Two enters into our consideration.

In theory, by dividing a vessel's grain or her bale capacity by the stowage factor of the cargo to be loaded, we reach **volume capacity.** This maximum amount of cargo that can be carried within available cargo compartment space must then be compared with the available cargo weight. The smaller quantity is the restriction with which the vessel's operators must comply. It is normally the available deadweight which proves to be the limiting factor but, occasionally, a high stowing cargo such as coke or certain agricultural products will restrict tonnage intake. Also it may be necessary to load several grades or types of cargoes, each requiring a separate cargo compartment and possibly causing, therefore, an inability to use all a ship's cargo space. The voyage estimate form provides space for draft, deadweight and cubic capacity calculations under the appropriate heading.

Finally, it may be that a vessel cannot be laden to her full available draft at the port of loading, because of the necessity of crossing restricted **loading zones** en route to the port(s) of discharge. A vessel cannot enter a winter line, for example, when loaded to summer marks and thereby submerging winter freeboard. The 'cargo calculations' section of the 'estimate form' makes allowance for loadline considerations and for deductions from the appropriate deadweight tonnage of bunker quantity remaining on board, and for constant weights. However, knowledge of loadline zones is essential. Maps can be obtained showing these, and the subject is covered in Chapter Nine of this book.

Time in Port Which brings us back to Stage 1 since, knowing the cargo quantity as well as the loading/discharging rates per day of the proposed cargo, it is now possible to deduce port time with some accuracy, to enter the information in the appropriate boxes of the estimate form, and to calculate port bunker consumption. However, as always it seems, there may be further pitfalls to avoid. As we have seen from the previous Chapter on Laytime, weekends and holidays will frequently not count as laytime in dry-cargo shipping and, in fact, dry cargo ships are often left idle and unworked during such periods. Moreover there may be weather delays, the effect of which it may be reasonable to anticipate and to allow for by an adjustment in expected port time. Let us take an example:

'm.v. *"Kingfisher"* is to load 35,000 tonnes of cargo, the c/p loading rate being 2,500 tonnes per weather working day of 24 consecutive hours, Saturdays, Sundays and Holidays excepted.

By dividing 35,000 by 2,500 we calculate that the loading time allowed to charterers is 14 days. This calculation, however, is to be conducted on the basis of 'SSHEX' terms.

Therefore, if we exclude Saturdays, Sundays and Holidays we are left with approximately a five day week, and the 'real' permitted laytime approaches three weeks. If allowances are made also for notice time and for some other interruptions, it will become realistic to allow some 20/21 days in port for loading.

If loading is to take place over some important public holiday e.g. Christmas and New year, or in Muslim countries, during the fasting period of Ramadan, even more port time should be allowed.

As a rule of thumb there is no 'magic formula' that can be used to calculate overall port time in normal 'SSHEX' circumstances, and that is to multiply the original figure by a factor of 1.4. Thus, taking the *'Kingfisher',* 35,000 tonnes divided by 2,500 = 14 days × '1.4' = 20 days, and that latter figure should be entered in the estimate 'box' under loading port time, on which loading port bunker consumption should be based.

Alternatively, if allowed time is described as 'SHINC' not 'SSHEX', less allowance will be needed, perhaps fifteen days maximum. Even with 'SHINC' terms, however, there will be inevitable delays on arrival, for shifting, waiting for tides, etc.

This 'system' is perfectly adequate for most occasions and, in general, the full time allowance should be placed in our estimate form and allowance for demurrage and/or despatch should be ignored. Unfortunately, very little is straightforward in shipping, and different criteria have to be used for what are termed **'demurrage'** or **'despatch'** trades.

Demurrage Trades Every now and then a cargo occurs where those involved are fully aware that laytime will be exceeded and demurrage will accrue. In such a case, full estimated port time should be calculated, including full allowance for weekends and holidays occurring during laytime. In this way the realistic overall voyage time will be recorded in the estimate and, from an assessment of full laytime (plus allowances for weekends and holidays as shown above) demurrage can be calculated. This anticipated 'demurrage income' should then be incorporated with 'freight income' (perhaps being entered in our voyage estimate form in the second line of the 'gross freight' box).

To this should be applied commission (as for freight) and after this the nett amount should be added to nett freight.

Despatch Trades There are certain trades, bulk sugar is one, where it is well known in the dry-cargo freight market that ships habitually load (or discharge) well within their permitted laytime and, indeed, shippers (or receivers) expect to earn considerable despatch money. In order to ensure that an estimate for a 'despatch trade' shows a realistic result, the actual expected port time should be entered in the itinerary section, with the amount calculated to be payable for despatch entered as an expense.

7.4   STAGE 3: EXPENSES

This third stage is where all the various costs that can be foreseen are collated and analysed. The voyage estimating form in **Appendix 27** lists various headings, and here will be found spaces for obvious costs such as port disbursements and canal tolls, as well as the not so obvious regarding extra insurance premiums, stevedoring costs, etc. Perhaps the major cost item, however, will be found to be that of bunkers.

Bunkers Bunkering a vessel is an art, and no two voyages are likely to be exactly the same, due to seasonal changes, price fluctuation, and the need to balance fuel prices against freight income. It can sometimes be more financially beneficial to take less cargo in a port where bunkers are cheap and to fill up with bunkers instead. You must also take into consideration limitations imposed by loadlines against the need or desirability to take bunkers en route.

At first glance, it may seem advantageous to call frequently at bunkering ports to shorten the intermediate steaming time and bunker quantity requirements, thereby maximising cargo intake. But no Shipowner willingly puts into port unless absolutely necessary, because of the extra time, risk and expense involved. 'A ship earns money only when laden and at sea' is a very accurate maxim.

However, in this era of wildly fluctuating bunker prices, often purely as a result of unexpected political decisions rather than because of discernable economic trends, bunker programming is not the straightforward task you might otherwise expect. The best advice in practice, is to obtain representative prices en route if time permits, otherwise to base the estimate on the price and quantity required at the loading port and to treat cheaper bunkers discovered later in the voyage as a bonus.

Where a vessel is likely to spend some time in port, where bunkers are difficult and/or expensive to obtain, it is essential to pre-plan your strategy and to arrive with sufficient quantity on board.

Safety surplus quantity will be needed and the amount required for this purpose will need to be judged by experience and knowledge of the conditions likely to be encountered and the availability en route of alternative bunker supplies.

Another factor affecting bunkers is the increasing regulation for environmental reasons.

Under the MARPOL Convention, member states acting alone or in concert can apply to the IMO for special areas called emission control areas (ECAs) to be established around their coasts. These ECAs are primarily concerned with sulphur oxide (SOx) reduction. Two have been established in Europe, one in the Baltic Sea and the other covering parts of the North Sea and the English Channel. In 2010 an ECA covering US and Canadian waters was established. That ECA extends up to 200 nautical miles along most of the US and Canadian coasts. France joined as a co-proposer on behalf of its island territories of Saint-Pierre and Miquelon, which form an archipelago off the coast of Newfoundland.

In addition to the IMO ECAs, individual states can enact local laws. The EU for example has directed that only very low sulphur fuels can be used in ports in the EU.

In the SECAs where ships cannot use standard fuels with normal sulphur contents, they are obliged to either operate on auxiliary engines or burn low-sulphur fuel in the main engine.

Because sulphur is only found in residual fuels (IFO and HFO) some believe that a wholesale switch to distillate fuels such as MDO or MGO will be the best action to take. This might seem an attractive idea but distillate fuels are almost twice as expensive as residual fuels and the refining companies do not have sufficient capacity to produce them in the quantities that would be needed. Neither do they have the capacity to remove sulphur from residual fuels without increasing the cost of the end product. Engine makers and other equipment suppliers are developing devices aimed at removing the harmful gases from the exhaust allowing ships to continue burning residual fuel oils.

From the operators point of view, the location of ECAs need to be taken into account when routeing ships or fixing their employment. If a ship is to load or discharge in a ECA or even pass through one, then it must carry sufficient supplies of the low-sulphur fuel needed. This means that one of the ship's bunker tanks must be dedicated to low-sulphur fuel or a call will need to be made at a bunkering port to take on supplies of the fuel on the edge of the SECA. To further complicate matters, ships' engines may not able to make rapid changes to the fuel in use and there may be a change-over procedure that will need to be followed which can take several hours to complete.

Port charges cannot easily be assessed without experience, and most companies will keep records of previous calls to assist them. Organisations such as BIMCO provide valuable information on many ports, but probably the most reliable method is to contact an Agent at the port in question, asking for a proforma disbursement account based on the relevant pertinent data of your vessel. Ethically, of course, such an enquiry should be directed to the Agent who will be appointed if that (or other) business is successfully concluded.

7.5   STAGE 4: INCOME

Knowing your cargo quantity, the freight rate and total commissions and brokerages, it is a relatively small step to calculating nett freight, adding demurrage where this is applicable.

7.6   STAGE 5: RESULT

By the application of Expenditure to Income and taking into account the total number of days shown in the Itinerary, a Result in the form of the **Gross Daily** can be calculated. From this figure can be deducted a vessel's daily **Running Costs,** if desired, leaving the **Nett Daily.**

For easier negotiations additional calculations provide the Gross Daily adjustment figure for each 10 cents variation in freight rate, whilst the final box in the voyage estimate form provides space for the timecharter equivalent rate to the gross daily return to be shown.

Freight Taxes and Bill of Lading Weight Adjustments: Freight Taxes were explained in Chapter Five. In voyage estimating they are considered an expense, but they are not a fixed expense. Calculated as they are on the basis of a percentage of the total freight, if treated as a fixed amount and included in the Expenses section, the estimator has constantly to adjust the figure as negotiations proceed and as the freight rate alters. Consequently, the best solution will be to consider a freight tax along with commission and brokerage, adding the three items together and deducting same from Gross Freight.

The same strategy applies to deductions from bill of lading cargo weights 'in lieu of weighing'. A deduction of, say, 0.5% can simply be added to commission/brokerage for ease of application.

7.7   TIME CHARTER ESTIMATING

As the practice of Charterer's taking vessels on time charter for trips has become widespread, the need has arisen to estimate the daily profit of this type of employment in the same manner as for voyage charters in order to compare the two alternatives. Chapter Five, in fact, showed how to compare time charter rates expressed in terms of a daily amount with those shown as per summer deadweight tonne.

Many merchants prefer the relative simplicity of voyage chartering, not having the organisation to enable them successfully to operate time chartered vessels. There are others, however, who frequently employ vessels on time charter trips as an alternative, where they calculate a saving in overall costs. Consequently, it is vital to be able to estimate the real 'nett' cost of timechartering and compare it with the voyage chartering alternative.

Fortunately, trip time chartering estimation is a relatively straightforward exercise; in many cases it being necessary only to deduct commission and brokerage from the gross daily hire for a ready comparison with an alternative voyage result. Care must be exercised, however, over items such as domestic fuel costs, hold cleaning payments, bunker price differentials, etc. where these are not totally realistic.

The real problems arise with time charter estimating, where a vessel is not taken on hire immediately after her previous employment, and allowance has then to be made not only for the time lost to her owners whilst the vessel is unemployed, but also for bunkers consumed during that period. Even here, the resulting calculation is not difficult if total income and expenditure is considered carefully and applied to the number of days for the entire venture.

As we have already seen in Chapter Five, depending on the strength or weakness of the freight market, a Charterer may pay an Owner a 'ballast bonus' towards the expenses of positioning a vessel for delivery on to a time charter or, very occasionally, for redelivery a vessel in an unattractive position, facing the Shipowner with a ballast voyage to regain a place where suitable employment can be obtained.

But whether Shipowners have to finance a ballast run before or after a trip time charter from their own pocket or with the aid of a ballast bonus paid by a time charterer, the principle of how to account for this in estimating terms is very much the same. All income, time charter hire and ballast bonus, must be added together and compared with all expenses, perhaps bunkers and tolls for a positioning canal transit. The result divided by the total number of days overall provides us once again with a 'gross daily', on the basis of which the venture can be judged financially and compared, perhaps, with a voyage alternative.

When freight markets are weak, Charterers frequently succeed in negotiating ballast bonuses that do not reflect the real cost to an Owner of positioning a vessel. Conversely, when freight markets are strong, a Charterer may have to pay far more than that real cost. Such are the essential elements of a free market, but it does mean that time charterers and their Brokers as well as Shipowners must be financially astute and capable of performing accurate ballast bonus calculations when called upon to do so.

Other Voyage Estimating Techniques: Voyage Estimating is a science and, as with any science, there are techniques (such as 'back-hauling' and 'voyage equalisation') that the astute perform from time to time to provide more realistic guidelines to better overall profitability. This Chapter has taught only the basics. Do not therefore leave this Chapter with the impression that you now know all that it is necessary to know. You should no longer be an amateur, but you will not be an expert. Nevertheless, based on what you have read so far and with the aid of the following examples, you should by the end of this Chapter be able to deal competently with most calculations that come your way.

7.8   PRACTICAL EXAMPLE

Let us now carry out a voyage estimate. This particular one concerns a choice of voyage routes for the operators of a panamax bulkcarrier, the *'Curlew'*, necessary to discover which of two (or possibly three or four routes) provides most profitability. If you turn to **Appendix 28,** you will find a typical estimating problem set out in detail and giving all the information required in order to carry out a calculation, the kind of calculation performed every day of the week by a busy market practitioner. In the real market, though, it will be necessary for an estimator to seek and to gather relevant and vital data from all over, both from 'in-house' records, from reference books, and from outside sources. Here, however, all information required to complete the estimate is provided, as would be the case, of course, for an estimating question set in an examination.

If you refer now to **Appendix 29,** you will see a suggested answer for one alternative set out in detail on the same estimating form as recommended for use and illustrated in **Appendix 27**.

Let us now follow the way this estimate should have been prepared and, to help you, it may be found convenient (but not essential) to have beside you an atlas, a loadline zone map and distance tables.

1. First carefully read the information provided in **Appendix 28.** The operators of the *'Curlew'* have fixed a cargo of coal for shipment from Australia to the Continent, the applicable freight rate being US$ 30.00 per tonne. The problem is that there is more than one route back from the loading port of Newcastle (New South Wales) to Rotterdam. One alternative is south-about round Australia and then westwards across the Southern Indian Ocean to the Cape of Good Hope. Thereafter the vessel would head northwards across the Atlantic Ocean and on through the Channel to the discharge port of Rotterdam.

2. A second alternative is once again to proceed south-about round Australia but to then proceed northwesterly, across the Indian Ocean to the Red Sea, via the Suez Canal, through the Mediterranean Sea and northwards around the Iberian Peninsular and via the Channel to Rotterdam.

3. A third alternative would be to proceed to the Suez Canal northwards around Australia, but this will entail passage between the Great Barrier Reef and the Australian Mainland and through the dangerous and shallow waters of the Torres Straits. A pilot would need to be hired and cargo would be cut out because of the draft limitation.

4. A fourth alternative is to proceed easterly from Newcastle, across the southern Pacific Ocean, aided by westerly winds, and around the southern tip of South America, either around notorious Cape Horn or through the Magellan Straights, and then northwards across the Atlantic Ocean to Europe and to Rotterdam. Ships facing this route must take into consideration the likelihood of bad weather around the South American Continent, and the distance is somewhat further than other choices.

Thus the selection is really between Alternatives One and Two. Alternative One is the longer in duration and made even longer by the fact that the vessel will very likely experience strong headwinds for the entire passage between Southern Australia and the Cape of Good Hope, and these winds, 'The Roaring Forties', will probably add around two days extra steaming to passage time calculated from distance tables. However, against this, Suez Canal tolls in Alternative Two will be an expensive consideration. It is therefore necessary to perform two estimates, one for each of Alternatives One and Two, to enable the right choice to be selected.

ALTERNATIVE ONE via South Australia and Cape of Good Hope

a) Let us start with Alternative One, and the first task should be to **include** in the estimate **details of the cargo and of the ship.** This will refresh the memory immediately before the start of calculations and also be useful for future reference. It is assumed that the vessel's optimum speed on the basis of the freight market and current market bunker prices is 14 knots in either ballast or in laden condition, and this data is entered. (Note that fuel oil consumption at sea is described appropriately for ballast or laden condition at 14 knots).

b) The **voyage itinerary** can be calculated by reference to mileages between Osaka and Newcastle (NWS) and between Newcastle via the Cape of Good Hope to Rotterdam. To this must be added the aforementioned allowance for anticipated strong head winds between Newcastle and the Cape of Good Hope.

The mileages can be divided by 336 (nautical miles daily at 14 knots) and the resulting days and decimal parts of a day rounded up to the next whole figure. (NB. For short distances, say one and a half days, this may not be realistic and the entry best made as 1.5 days, but for long voyages as in this case, it is perhaps simpler and just as accurate to round up as suggested).

Bunker consumptions can be obtained by multiplying the daily bunker consumption against the days duration of each voyage leg. Therefore 13 days (from Osaka to Newcastle) × 36 tonnes daily (when in ballast condition at 14 knots) = 468 tonnes.

Port Consumption might have to wait until cargo quantity has been established. In this case, however, where a very fast daily tonnage loading rate of 20,000 tonnes is involved, an approximate port time can be calculated on the assumption that around 62,500 tonnes cargo should be loaded, therefore:

> 62,500 mt/20,000 = 3.125 days × 1.4 ('magic formula' 7) 5 to allow for weekends and holidays) = 4.375 days.

> 4.375 days rounded up to the nearest 'whole' day, to allow for notice time, etc. = 5 estimated port days at Newcastle.

Rotterdam discharge is based on 'SHINC' terms, not on 'SSHEX' as at Newcastle. Therefore:

> 62,500/20,000 SHINC = 3.1215 days, which rounded up to allow for notice time, etc. = 4 days.

> 5 days (Newcastle) + 4 days (Rotterdam) = 9 days × 2 tonnes diesel oil daily in port = 18 mts. (Most panamax vessels are 'gearless', the *'Curlew'* being no exception. Thus port consumption for these ships is always basis gear being 'idle' and does not differ whether the vessel is loading or discharging.

Rotterdam is located in the North Sea SECA and also an EU port, so the requirement to burn low sulphur fuels will apply at sea and in port. However for the purpose of simplifying this calculation it can be assumed that the low-sulphur bunkers needed to meet the rules are available at the same places and prices as 'normal' bunkers.

It is now possible to complete the Itinerary boxes of the estimate and to see that the proposed voyage is expected to take 62 days and the vessel to consume 2068 tonnes fuel oil and 124 tonnes diesel oil. (This should be the figure in your own calculation at this point, not that shown in **Appendix 28.** The difference will become evident later on.)

c) For **cargo calculations** it is necessary to consult the load line zones map. The port of Newcastle is in a permanent summer zone and this zone stretches all the way to Southern Africa and up into the Atlantic ocean. There is a permanent tropical zone straddling the Equator as far northwards as the Canary Islands before a transitting vessel re-enters a permanent summer zone. So far there is nothing to prevent a vessel loading to her summer marks as an intervening tropical zone is no hindrance. Problems only set in with the vessels reaching the northwestern tip of the Iberian Peninsula, near Vigo, where the next zone may remain as a summer area for part of each year or be classified as a winter zone for the remainder of the year, the affected area reaching all the way to Rotterdam and beyond. Thus at certain times of the year a northbound vessel adjacent to Vigo will be crossing from a summer into a winter loadline zone and her Master/Operators will have to ensure that winter marks are not submerged.

In our case we are told that the *'Curlew'* is loading at Newcastle during April. Consequently, by the time she reaches the area of Vigo in May/June, the zone will be summer, and the effect of a winter zone can thus be disregarded. At other times of the year it may be necessary for an estimator to calculate whether the winter zone will affect the cargo quantity that can be loaded at Newcastle or not. To do this one has to ascertain whether the ship will have burnt off enough bunkers to raise her draft to winter marks and the way to do this is to run figures backwards from Vigo by calculating the distance back to Newcastle or to the previous bunkering port, and the vessel's anticipated bunker consumption for that part of her voyage. This consumption tonnage is then added to the vessel's winter deadweight, and the result equals the quantity of cargo the vessel can load at Newcastle, always providing this does not exceed the vessel's summer deadweight. In other words, if the estimated bunker consumption exceeds the difference between the winter and summer deadweight, the summer deadweight remains the restricting factor. (It is possible, of course, to increase cargo lifting by bunkering en route, say at Cape Town or in the Canary Islands, but usually the value of extra cargo loaded in this way does not compensate for delay and even the slight deviation to collect bunkers).

Thus we know in the case of the 'Curlew' that the vessel can load to summer marks at Newcastle, but no further. From this tonnage, of 64,650 metric tonnes, must be deducted constant weights and bunkers carried on board before cargo lifting can be calculated. Constant weights, we are told, amount to 500 tonnes for the 'Curlew', but bunker assessment again requires the estimator's skill.

It is not sufficient solely to determine the mileage from Newcastle to Rotterdam, to calculate the voyage days and to multiply this by the daily bunker consumption of the 'Curlew', calling this sufficient bunkers for the voyage. The ship will be required to carry a **safety surplus** of bunkers in case the voyage is lengthened by any unforeseen eventuality. This safety surplus varies depending on expected weather conditions but should never be less than, say, 15%, but can be influenced by the scarcity or wide selection of ports en route from which bunkers can be taken in emergency. Even where bunkering ports are available, however, it is sensible policy to be self-sufficient in bunker matters, because you can never be certain that supplies will be available when needed, or available at a realistic price. To deviate and delay for expensive bunkers is not prudent ship operating and it is far more sensible to take an appropriate supply of surplus bunkers, tailored for the proposed voyage, even if this means a slight reduction in cargo intake.

So let us study the voyage before us. As we have seen, bunkers are available in both Cape Town and in the Canary Islands, both recognised bunkering stations. We have checked, however, and discovered the following prices available en route:

	Fuel Oil US$	Diesel Oil US$
Osaka	520	820
Newcastle	550	825
Cape Town	500	815
Las Palmas	510	775
Rotterdam	500	750

The cheapest fuel oil is available at Cape Town and, at the end of the voyage at Rotterdam, where inexpensive replenishment can be obtained for the following voyage. As a rule of thumb it can be seen that the deviation to Cape Town will only be slight but the savings for every tonne of fuel oil taken on at Cape Town instead of at the commencement of the voyage at Osaka would amount to US$ 20. Approximately a third of the voyage remains at Cape Town, and a third of the total fuel oil required, 689 tonnes (2068 ÷ 3), would save the 'CURLEW's operators about US$ 13,750 (689 × US$ 20). Port costs at Cape Town will be about US $2,500, the deviation is barely noticeable, and the delay to be expected only about half a day. Consequently, it must be worth calling at Cape Town for fuel oil, since the daily voyage value is very unlikely to reach US$ 22,500 (US$ 13,750– 2,500 = 11,250 × 2 half days) on this particular voyage. Not only that, extra cargo can be taken at Newcastle, and if bunker prices at Rotterdam show signs of increasing by the time the vessel reaches Cape Town, extra bunkers can be purchased.

So we take sufficient bunkers at Osaka safely to reach Cape Town via Newcastle, and there the balance safely to reach Rotterdam. But what about our safety surplus? Study the atlas. There is no need to take safety surplus for the Osaka/Newcastle leg. If the worst comes to the worst after a difficult ballast voyage, extra bunkers can be taken alongside at Newcastle. The problem is the long stretch of 6,545 miles from Newcastle to Cape Town, made even longer by the strong head winds of the Southern Indian Ocean. A surplus of 15 percent on top of an extra two days consumption should be sufficient.

			Fuel Oil Tons	Diesel Oil Tons
1.	Osaka/Newcastle	13 days	468	26
2.	Newcastle/Cape Town	20 days	800	40
3.	Adverse Weather:	2 days	80	4
4.	Safety Surplus (15% of 20 days)		120	6
		Total	1468	76

It is assumed in estimating that a safety surplus will not necessarily be used. It must be allowed for in the calculation of cargo intake, etc. but not costed as one cannot be certain it will be used but will be taken forward to the next voyage in the form of a credit. (This estimate is slightly unusual as we are assuming the vessel is completely empty of bunkers at the start of the voyage in Osaka). You can therefore expect that the safety surplus of 120 tonnes f/o and 6 d/o will remain on board upon arrival at Cape Town. Since the voyage leg from Cape Town to Rotterdam is less than from Newcastle to Cape Town, there is no need to take any further safety surplus supplies at Cape Town, but simply to cost the extra bunkers required to reach Rotterdam, some 19 days away.

You will note that our itinerary has adjusted since our original figures. Not only do we have an extra half day's delay to account for at Cape Town, our policy of rounding decimal parts of a day up to the next full day has 'increased' our voyage by one day. We now have a voyage of 63.5 days, a fuel consumption (not counting safety surplus) of 2,108 tonnes and a diesel consumption of 127 tonnes.

But we can at least conclude the cargo part of our calculation as our bunker quantity at Newcastle can be estimated at:

	Fuel Oil	Diesel Oil
Newcastle/Cape Town	800	40
Adverse Weather Allowance	80	4
Safety Surplus	120	6
	1000	50

Thus cargo can be calculated as: – 64,650 tonnes (per sdwt)

less: Constant weights:	500	
Bunkers:	1050	1,550

Cargo Intake	63,100 tonnes

One final word of warning before we go on to voyage expenses, and that is about diesel oil. A safety surplus of only six tonnes of diesel oil is in reality no safety surplus at all. In reality it would be normal to carry around 50 tonnes spare. Thus our cargo should be reduced from 63,100 to 63,050 tonnes.

d) So we have already made a good start to calculating **voyage expenses** by solving the problem of calculating bunker costs. We know that 1,468 tonnes fuel oil is to be purchased in Osaka and the remaining 640 tonnes in Cape Town. An overall cost of US$ 1,083,360.

For the ship's diesel oil requirements allowing a safety margin of 50 tonnes means that the procedure is a little changed. To reach Newcastle the ship needs to use 26 tonnes, a further 10 tonnes will be used during the loading there, and 40 tonnes plus 4 tonnes bad weather allowance on the voyage to Cape Town. In all this amounts to 80 tonnes, but we still need around 50 tonnes safety surplus which would bring the total to 130 tonnes. This is almost identical to the amount needed for the whole voyage (127 tonnes) and since prices are US$ 5 cheaper in Osaka than Newcastle it is better to buy the whole lot there.

Although that will leave us with almost no safety surplus on arrival at Rotterdam we can of course take on more diesel oil at Cape Town where prices are even lower than in Osaka. Not that that will affect the outcome of the estimate because we will use all of the diesel bought at Osaka during the voyage leaving any oil bought in Cape Town to carry forward to the next voyage.

The cost for diesel is therefore US$ 104,140 which together with fuel oil costs gives a total bunker bill of US$ 1,187,500.

As regards port costs, Newcastle disbursement, we are told, amount to US$ 50,000 and Rotterdam to US$ 60,000, with Cape Town amounting to US$ 2,500.

Thus, voyage expenses can be estimated to amount to US$ 1,300,000.

e) **Income** can be calculated by taking our anticipated cargo of 63,050 mt and applying the freight rate of US$ 30.00 per mt; thus a nett anticipated freight rate of US$ 1,796,925, after the application of 5% commission and brokerage.

f) The **result** can be ascertained by deducting US$ 1,300,000 expenses from nett income of US$ 1,796,925 and by dividing the result by the overall estimated voyage duration of 63.5 days which gives us US$ 7,826 daily. We are told that the **running costs** of the *'Curlew'* amount to US$ 4,500 daily, so **nett income** will amount to US$ 3,326 daily.

To calculate the value of each 10 cents on the freight rate, a useful aid during negotiations, it is necessary to adjust the freight rate by 10 cents, say to US$ 29.90 or to US$ 30.10, and run the figures through to either the gross or nett daily stage for comparison purposes with existing figures. The difference can be entered in the appropriate box.

Finally, the equivalent time charter rate can be expressed in terms of daily hire by taking the gross daily of US$ 7,826 and applying to it a factor representing the likely commission/brokerage payable. Therefore, basis a total of 5%:

US$ 7,826/0.95 = US$ 8,238 gross timecharter daily hire.

To convert this t/c hire rate into terms of US$ × per summer dwt tonne, you will need to refer to the calculations in Chapter Five.

7.9 SELF-ASSESSMENT AND TEST QUESTIONS

Having completed Chapter Seven attempt the following and submit your answer to your Tutor.

ALTERNATIVE TWO via South Australia and Suez Canal

(Please include your detailed workings with your answer.) All the information you need to know is provided in **Appendix 28** with the exception that bunker prices *en route* are:

	Fuel Oil US$/Ton	Diesel Oil US$/Ton
Jeddah	510	820
Suez	407	820
Algeciras	510	790
Ceuta	505	780
	All per mt.	

Assume port charges at each bunkering port are US$ 2,500, except Suez, where are assume no extra charges in addition to transit costs of the Canal. Allow one day for transiting the Suez Canal, and an extra half day if bunkering at Suez, and half a day if bunkering elsewhere.

Finally, if you find that this second alternative shows less daily return than the alternative one, remember that sometimes the Suez Canal Authorities can be persuaded to lower their canal tolls in order to attract business. What reduction would be required to produce the same daily return as for Alternative One?

The exercise you are asked to carry out compares the different routings for the same piece of business but voyage estimates are made for almost every cargo seriously contemplated by an Owner, generally before embarking upon firm negotiations. Estimates could, therefore, be used to compare one cargo with another, voyage business against time charter even (in the grimmest of times) comparing trading with laying up.

Judgement beyond the cold figures will also be needed because voyage A may work out very much better than voyage B on paper but that may be because voyage A terminates in an area where nearby following business is hard to find or non-existent so that a long ballast run will be needed to reach the next loading port.

Chapter 8

BILLS OF LADING AND CARGO CLAIMS

8.1 THE MATE'S RECEIPT

As cargo is loaded on board the vessel the shipper is entitled to be given some acknowledgement of the receipt of that cargo. Traditionally that was a Mate's Receipt signed by a ship's officer containing remarks as to the nature, quantity and condition of the goods concerned. These documents may, in fact, be prepared prior to commencement of loading, thereby providing advance information for ship's personnel about the cargo to be loaded, assisting stowage plans, and forming a convenient means of recording a cargo's good condition, or remarking upon its shortcomings. Such receipts also form valuable evidence of cargo quantity and quality.

Mate's Receipts are, however, merely receipts and not documents of title that can be exchanged commercially. They are released to shippers in return for cargo loaded and thereafter tendered to the Master or to the Owner's Agents in return for one or for a set of signed Bills of Lading.

Today the Mate's Receipt issued by the ship's command is in very many ports replaced by a document issued either by the terminal or port authority, or a shore-based tallying company identifying the cargo loaded on board. Many bulk cargo terminals have their own system for determining the quantity loaded. Where the Mate's Receipt is not used it is important that the ship's command identify clearly any reservations they have regarding quantity or quality to the Ship's Agent or shipper so that appropriate clauses may be placed on the Bills of Lading.

8.2 THE BILL OF LADING

A Bill of Lading (B/L) can be drawn up in a variety of ways and wordings, but it is nearly always prepared on a pre-printed form. This form may relate to a specific or to a general cargo trade, see **Appendix 30**, or it may be designed for liner services. Whatever its form, a Bill of Lading fulfils three basic functions:

1. A *receipt* for the cargo, signed by the Master or by the Owner's Port Agents on behalf of the carrier, with remarks as to the condition of the cargo;

2. A *document of title* to the cargo, by which means the property may be transferred to another party;

3. *Evidence of a contract* governing terms and conditions of carriage.

The Bill of Lading as a Receipt

This will show the quantity and description of the cargo loaded. It will usually include a wording such as 'weight measurement, quality and contents unknown, all particulars as declared by shipper'. This is because at the point of loading all the vessel's command can tell is that it has shipped on board a number of cases, drums, cartons, etc. or in the case of bulk cargo a quantity of a commodity, but is not competent to judge the actual composition of those goods. In the case of container or palletized traffic it is customary to state "container (or pallet) said to contain..."

This qualification has been in use for a long time and has commercial importance that has been tested in many legal disputes. However its continued use is being threatened for a very different reason. Since the terrorist attacks on the World Trade Centre in New York in September 2001, The US has aggressively promoted a string of security related issues at the

IMO and on a national level. As a result US Customs officials no longer permit Bills of Lading for US ports to carry this clause and demand instead a full description of the goods.

Commercial interests are trying to persuade the US to change their position but they are successful and the catch-all phrase allowed to retain its commercial purpose remains to be seen.

Unless there is some such qualification, a ship will be bound to deliver the quantity or number stated in the Bills of Lading, or face a claim from the consignees. (See later paragraphs on Cargo Quantity).

A Bill of Lading will also comment on the condition of the cargo, usually by saying "in apparent good order and condition". (See paragraphs on "Clean Bills of Lading").

As well as reference to quantity and condition the Bills of Lading will also give any detail necessary in order to identify the cargo. In the case of packaged goods this will consist of distinguishing marks and numbers.

Additionally the Bills of Lading will of course show the names of the shipper and consignees, the name of the ship; the loading port and the destination. There will also be some reference to the freight payment, either that it has been prepaid or that it has to be collected. Finally it will have the signature of the Master (often signed 'for the Master' by the Ship's Agent) and the date. The date can be very important, affecting, as it does, letters of credit and trading terms.

The Bill of Lading as a Document of Title

A Shipper can transfer ownership of goods by making the Bills of Lading over to a named consignee, or to the 'order' of that consignee, or by "endorsing" the Bills of Lading to another party. In fact, such transfer of ownership and the buying and selling of Bills of Lading is common practice in international trade and a Bill of Lading may change hands several times before it reaches the party who will eventually claim and take delivery of the cargo at the discharge port(s).

Where payment for the goods has been arranged via a documentary credit (often called a letter of credit) the Bills of Lading becomes vital in its other role as a document of title, namely as **security for payment.** Banks never want actual title to the goods, with all the responsibilities that also involves, but they do want the security of denying payment to a Shipper until satisfied that all the conditions of a contract of sale have been carried out and, of course, denying title to consignees until payment has been made by them to the bank concerned.

The Bill of Lading as Evidence of a Contract

Where consignments of Parcel or Liner Cargo are concerned, the actual contract may well be no more than a telephone conversation or a simple fax message (very occasionally a 'Booking Note') and so the Bills of Lading is often the only means of setting out the terms and conditions of carriage which are usually printed on the reverse side of the Bills of Lading form and so provide *evidence of a contract.*

In the case of homogeneous bulk cargoes, however, Bills of Lading should contain reference to (i.e; evidence of) the relevant charter party; adding, for example, that *"all terms, conditions and exceptions of charter party dated London... are deemed incorporated herein".*

Indeed, charter parties frequently contain wording to the effect that certain charter party clauses (e.g; Clauses Paramount) are to be fully incorporated into Bills of Lading issued thereunder, and it is particularly important that the charter party arbitration clause be incorporated into Bills of Lading as, failing this, a Bills of Lading holder may not be able to call for an arbitration against the carrier.

Should any of the terms of these two documents be in conflict, however, *those of the Bill of Lading will take precedence over those of the charter party.*

This may sound strange at first when considering how much work went into preparing the charter party, but remember the paragraph about the Bills of Lading role as a document of title. If, for example, title to a cargo has indeed been 'sold on', a new consignee would be quite remote from the original negotiations between the charterer and the Shipowner. What the consignee would have, however, is his *document of title* and that is what he paid money for and that is what he has a right to receive. Whilst, therefore, a Bills of Lading may incorporate the charter party it should not mean that it incorporates anything that is more onerous than that which is specifically stated in the Bills of Lading.

From all this, we can see that the main elements of a Bill of Lading are:

1. *Quantity* of cargo.

2. Accurate cargo *description and condition*.

3. *Date* of the bill of lading.

4. *Names of shipper and consignee.*

5. *Ports* of loading and discharge.

6. *Ship's name.*

7. *Terms and conditions of carriage.*

8. Payment of *freight*.

Bills of Lading at the Loading Port

A ship's Port Agent may be given the task of drawing up Bills of Lading, and if these are subsequently required for letter of credit transactions, it is useful that the Agent be supplied with appropriate details of that letter of credit so that all relevant material can be included in the wording.

All bills should be signed by either the ship's Master or by a duly authorised agent, in their capacities as servants of the Shipowner or of the disponent time-charter owner, i.e; the carrier. If time does not permit the ship's Master to sign the bills, a letter is usually drawn up giving the Port Agent appropriate authority to sign bills of lading (see **Appendix 31**). Alternatively, it may be agreed at the time of negotiating the charter party that *"charterers and/or their agents be authorised by owners to sign Bills of Lading as presented on Master's and/or on Owner's behalf, in accordance with mate's and/or tally clerk's receipts, without prejudice to this charter party"*.

There is an international agreement published by the International Chamber of Commerce (ICC) entitled Uniform Custom and Practice for Documentary Credits (UCP600) which sets out the requirements of banks and other parties handling Bills of Lading and the shipping documents related to documentary credits. UCP600 stipulates that Bills of Lading must be signed by the Master (giving his name in full) or by the carrier or his agent in a form that clearly identifies the carrier's name:

> e.g; Liner Agencies Co. as agent for the Carrier Bulk Shipping Ltd.

It is important also to *date* Bills of Lading correctly, and as per the date on which the complete cargo (in the case of an homogeneous commodity) or an individual item (for liner goods) is actually loaded. Where cargo is loaded later than specified in letter of credit transactions, Shipowners may be approached to sign pre-dated Bills of Lading, possibly against letters of indemnity to be issued by the shippers or charterers. In fact, the consignee may be well aware of the delay in loading and be happy with the suggested arrangement, which otherwise might involve time-consuming and tedious extra paperwork. Nevertheless, the wise Shipowner will consider such an approach very cautiously, perhaps contacting his P&I Club for advice, even in cases where he is convinced that all parties are fully aware of the circumstances.

In general the international P&I Clubs will not support owners issuing 'pre-dated' Bills of Lading. Letters of indemnity supplied by shippers under these circumstances are not legally enforceable.

A shipper may require the ship's Master to carry on the voyage an original Bill of Lading with the ship's papers, i.e. in the *'ship's bag'*, for handing over at the destination to a named consignee. In connection with this service, the Master may be asked also to issue the shipper with a letter, termed a *'disposal letter'*, confirming the arrangement.

This procedure was vital in the days of sailing ships when the cargo-carrying vessel could well reach the discharging port before any other means of physical communication. It become less important when steamships took over and fast mail ships could carry documents much quicker than the tramp. It is, of course, now becoming rare given the speed and reliability of airmail, but is still encountered in the short sea and coastal trades.

A relic of those early days which still persists, much to the perplexity of many people in the shipping industry, is that of issuing more than one original Bill of Lading (that is not counting several non-negotiable copies). You will see this in Appendix 8:1 where, just above the signature there is a dotted line where the number in the 'set' has to be entered. In the days of sail and the early steam era, one could quite understand the despatch of one original via fast mail packet, one in the ship's bag and one held back by the shipper in case the other two were lost. Today, when letters of credit are so often involved, the banks obviously want all the originals otherwise they lose their security, so the reason for a set of more than one is something of an historic anomaly.

Releasing Bills of Lading

Bills of Lading should not be *"released"* to shippers marked *"freight prepaid"* or containing any similar expression indicating that freight has been remitted to the Shipowner (or to the disponent owner in the case of a time-chartered ship) without that party's express authority so to do. The release of such bills without freight actually having been made places a Shipowner in a weak legal position, as he may well lose the right of lien on the cargo if subsequently this is needed in order to force payment of freight. Consequently, either freight should be fully prepaid, as indicated on the Bills of Lading, or alternative wording acceptable to all parties and to the letter of credit arrangements must be found. In order to give a Charterer the time to make necessary financial transactions, it is often arranged that freight is to be paid within so many days of the signing and/or the releasing of Bills of Lading by the Shipowner, and there should be no reason why, with sufficient foresight, letter of credit arrangements cannot be adapted to this system.

Cargo Quantity and Condition

It is important that cargo quantity and condition be adequately and correctly described in the Bills of Lading. *Quantity* of general or bagged/baled goods can usually be accurately assessed by *tallymen*, employed by either a Shipowner or shipper, or jointly by both, in which event the tally-clerk's receipt takes the place of the Mate's Receipt. With bulk homogeneous cargo there may be dispute between cargo quantity assessed by shore apparatus and by the calculations of ship's officers based on a draft survey. In some cases where shore apparatus is unreliable (or even non-existent) ship's draft measurement is the accepted means of assessing in taken cargo weight, and the basis therefore of any Bill of Lading figure.

Ideally, a draft survey should be performed by an independent surveyor and should commence with the vessel in ballast condition. The difference in draft when fully laden calculated against the ship's plans and allowing for bunkers and freshwater, etc. supplied and consumed in the meantime, will provide a fairly accurate measurement of cargo loaded.

Nevertheless, a reasonable assessment of cargo on board can be achieved even when commencing draft calculations with a laden vessel and, should a Master be faced with a substantial discrepancy between ship and shore figures, he should clause the Bills of Lading with *"ship's weight"* figures if possible, supporting these remarks with an independent surveyor's report or, failing this, certainly his Owners should strongly protest over the discrepancy.

The *condition* of most cargoes can be checked by tallymen or by ship's officers as loading progresses, and relevant comments entered in either tally or Mate's Receipts, and thereafter in Bills of Lading. But for certain commodities claims for damage can be so high that a fully fledged loading survey is necessary, in fact many P&I Clubs insist on this for unprotected steel cargoes for example.

A Shipowner's local P&I Club representatives may assist in arranging for a reputable surveyor to inspect all items presented for loading, recording damages apparent in the goods prior to loading (i.e; indentation or rust) and supporting same with colour photographs where deemed advisable.

Clean Bills of Lading

Irrespective of the actual condition of cargo, many letter of credit transactions call for *"clean"* Bills of Lading i.e; bills stating that goods described therein are in *"apparent good order and condition":* with no additional or alternative wording indicating deficiencies in the goods. Unfortunately, difficult though it may be for shippers, a carrier cannot agree to issue clean Bills of Lading when cargo is not in good condition, even where letters of so-called indemnity are offered by the parties concerned. Bills of Lading must accurately reflect the actual condition of the goods, and to do otherwise is to act fraudulently.

Purchasers of a cargo rarely have the opportunity to examine it and to assure themselves of its good condition. Instead they must rely upon descriptions of quality and of quantity as entered in Bills of Lading. Despite a clean Bill of Lading indicating cargo to be unblemished, should goods be defective in some way, the consignee (as an innocent party to a fraudulent act) has the right to claim redress from the carrier, or to assume that the cargo was damaged at sea, again very likely the responsibility of the carrier.

It follows that great care must be exercised by Ship's Masters and by Port Agents alike to ensure that Bills of Lading contain only accurate statements as to cargo condition, despite pressures and inducements from shippers and from certain port authorities.

On the other hand, remarks contained should not be of a trivial nature covering some insignificant defect normally acceptable in the trade concerned, as this might have the effect of interfering with a letter of credit transaction for no reason.

It can be seen that a shipper or seller presented with "unclean" Bills of Lading for a transaction where "clean" bills are needed, is in a difficult position. The problem need not be insurmountable however. The consignee or buyer can be informed of the difficulty, given a copy of a relevant survey report, perhaps renegotiate the purchase price, and still give instructions to his bankers to accept the "qualified" bills. Alternatively, and very occasionally, the issue of clean bills against a letter of indemnity may be justified where the buyer is fully aware of the actual condition of the cargo, and where the goods will not be resold prior to the delivery at the port(s) of discharge. However it should again be noted that such an indemnity is not legally enforceable.

Bills of Lading at the Discharging Port

Cargo should only be delivered to a party (a consignee) who can produce an original Bill of Lading covering the item of cargo claimed. The Port Agent should examine the Bill of Lading thus presented so as to ensure its good order and, once he is satisfied that all is correct, he will release the cargo, or issue a *"delivery order"* in exchange for the Bill of Lading.

The consignee thereafter presents the delivery order to the dock authority/terminal operator or the stevedores and claims release of the item/cargo concerned.

In the meantime, the original Bill of Lading presented should be stamped, signed and dated by the Port Agent, and in doing this he is said to have *"sighted" the Bill of Lading* on the

Master's behalf. Should the Agent return the Bill of Lading to the consignee where this is the custom instead of issuing a delivery order, he must keep a careful record, as it is essential that not more than one "original" be "sighted", or more than one "delivery order" be prepared for every set of bills. As an aid to record keeping in this regard, a copy of the "cargo manifest" may be utilised, on which to record "sighted" bills.

Where the consignee claims an original bill from the "ship's bag", the Master and/or Port Agent must, of course, satisfy themselves of the correct identity of the claimant.

It is customary in certain trades for a consignee to endorse the reverse sides of Bills of Lading with confirmation of receipt of cargo, and such bills are said to be *"accomplished"*. Occasionally it is necessary for a Shipowner to obtain an "accomplished" Bill of Lading as a prerequisite for all or part of his freight.

Where Bills of Lading arrive at a discharge port unreasonably late (for example, after a ship's arrival) they may be said to be *"stale"*, the same term being used to describe bills presented to a bank for freight collection later than the terms set by a letter of credit.

Delivery of Goods Without Production of a Bill of Lading

Perhaps the most serious difficulty arising at a discharging port in relation to Bills of Lading is where for some reason the bills are unavailable. Normally such difficulty can be overcome providing the consignee issues a suitable **letter of indemnity,** fully guaranteed by a reputable bank. This indemnity is held by the port agent on the Shipowner's behalf, and eventually exchanged for the original Bill of Lading, which latter document can then be attended to in the normal way.

Agents should not delay in exchanging a Letter of Indemnity for the properly presented Bill of Lading because banks charge quite steeply on a time basis for their counter-signature on such documents, (**Appendix 32** is an example of such a Letter of Indemnity.)

Such letters of indemnity must not contain any value or time limitation clauses because delivery of cargo to a person not entitled to receive it is a fundamental breach of the Bill of Lading contract and places the carrier outside the terms of that contract, opening the door to an action in 'tort' where the damages are not limited by the Bill of Lading clauses.

8.3   TYPES OF BILLS OF LADING

A Clean Bill of Lading

As already discussed, this is a Bill which is **unclaused** and is therefore a fully negotiable document.

A Foul (or Dirty) Bill of Lading

Is a Bill of Lading which is in some way **claused** or **dirty.** This implies that the cargo loaded on board is not perfect in every condition and the Shipowner is therefore protecting himself against a cargo claim for bad delivery at the discharge port with an appropriate endorsement.

Received for Shipment Bill of Lading

Whilst most Bills of Lading are issued when the cargo is actually shipped on board the vessel, in the liner trades there is the alternative where cargo is actually received into the custody of the Shipowner or his Agent, such as a wharfinger or dock authority, and is not actually on board the vessel at that particular time. It is also sometimes called a **Custody Bill of Lading.** If such a Bill of Lading is issued, the shipper is entitled to demand from the carrier an endorsement on the Bill of Lading. Under UCP 500 this endorsement must identify the date of shipment and reconfirm the name of the carrier and the carrying vessel:

e.g. "Shipped onboard *M.V. Pigeon* at Hamburg 27th July 1999.

Signed ....

Liner Agencies Co as agent for the Carrier Bulk Shipping Ltd"

Received for shipment Bills of Lading are common in the container trade where containers or cargo are often taken into the carrier's custody at an inland depot.

Shipped Bills of Lading

As the name implies, this is the Bill of Lading which is normally issued, especially for bulk cargo, and confirms that the cargo described is actually on board the vessel. Needless to say, if the Shipowner has previously issued a *"Received for Shipment Bill of Lading"*, this must be surrendered when he issues the actual *"Shipped Bill of Lading"* itself. Alternatively he can merely endorse the *"Received Bill of Lading"* as above. A Shipped Bill of Lading is often (especially in letters of credit) tautologically described as a **"Shipped on Board"** Bill of Lading.

Direct Bill of Lading

This is a bill covering the carriage of goods in one vessel direct from one port to another.

Through Bill of Lading

Such Bills of Lading are issued where the cargo will only be carried for part of the voyage by the carrier signing the Bill of Lading. The remainder may be overland transport or it may be transhipment into another vessel. The essence of a Through Bill of Lading as opposed to a Combined Transport Bill of Lading (q.v.) is that with a through Bill of Lading the carrier signing it is only responsible as a Principal for his part of the carriage and acts as an Agent for the shipper for the other part(s).

Combined Transport Bill of Lading

As the name implies, such a Bill of Lading is for cargo carried by more means than the ship itself. It is particulary used in the container trade when the different 'modes' of carriage can, in an extreme case, be quite complicated. For example, the carrier could take delivery of a container at the shipper's premises, truck it to a railway terminal, rail to the port, ship it on board a feeder vessel, tranship it on to the ocean vessel and then repeat all that in reverse at the discharging end. With a Combined Transport Bill of Lading the carrier signing it takes responsibility as a Principal from start to finish but includes limitations of liability for the different sections according to the appropriate international conventions (e.g. Hague-Visby for the sea transport, C.I.M. convention for rail, C.M.R. for road etc.).

Order Bill of Lading

This is not to be confused with an "open" Bill of Lading which shows no consignee at all; this would be a most unsatisfactory document as it would be like a blank cheque.

An Order Bill of Lading is very common indeed because of its value in letter of credit transactions. It can best be compared with a cheque drawn to "cash" and once it is endorsed by the shipper it becomes in effect a "bearer" document. This sounds a very dangerous procedure as, theoretically, if someone dropped it in the street, the person picking it up could claim the cargo; in fact the system works very well.

You will recall earlier in the chapter it was mentioned that the banks in a Letter of Credit transaction do not want to assume the liabilities and responsibilities of a consignee but simply want to hold the original Bills of Lading as security. Therefore, instead of the bank being named as the consignee and then endorsing it over to the actual importer, the bank insists on the section of the Bill of Lading marked 'Consignee' having just the words "To Order" written in, and the shipper's endorsement on the back. When all is in order the Bill of Lading is handed to the importer who can claim the cargo from the carrier. Most Order Bills of Lading have a space for a 'notify Party' to be inserted. This is usually the actual importer and putting his name there ensures that he knows when to contact the bank. Incidentally, there is no actual legal obligation on a line to pass information to the notify party.

Liner Bill of Lading

Whilst a Liner Bill of Lading is still only *evidence* of a contract it carries far more detail than a charter party Bill of Lading because the reverse of a Liner Bill of Lading contains the full text of the contract of carriage. With a charter party Bill of Lading such masses of wording are not necessary as the contract is, of course, the charter party itself and it is only, therefore, necessary to devote a sentence or two to incorporate it (and the arbitration clause) into the Bill of Lading. Appendix 8:4 shows the front and back of a typical liner Bill of Lading (The 'Conline' Bill of Lading, reproduced by kind permission of the Baltic and International Maritime Council). Study the various clauses, comparing and contrasting them with the wording of a charter party.

Waybills

Using a Sea Waybill instead of a Bill of Lading is becoming more prevalent, especially in the liner trades. There is nothing new about a Waybill as a document, as it has been in use for air freight almost since the beginning of carrying merchandise by air. A Waybill looks very similar to a Bill of Lading and indeed has to cover two of its uses, as a receipt for cargo and evidence of a contract. What it does not have is any negotiability; it is not a document of title. This means that the goods can only be delivered by the carrier to the named consignee.

That is no disadvantage at all if the consignee has no intention of 'selling the cargo on' and/ or if Letters of Credit are not involved, such as trading with a branch office or with a tried and trusted trading partner who will settle the invoice for the goods at the right time. A Waybill's very lack of negotiability is one of its advantages because there can be no doubt and therefore no room for error when it comes to delivering the cargo to the consignee. Not being proof of title, it does not matter if the ship arrives before the documents. You will readily see that a Waybill lends itself admirably to electronic transmission. There were some problems to be overcome before Waybills could become more widespread; these were mainly due to their not being thought of when most Bill of Lading Acts were written into statute books. In the UK the Carriage of Goods by Sea Act 1992 has replaced the Bill of Lading Act 1855 and included Seaway bills in its provision.

Bills of Lading and Time Charters

Under a voyage charter, the contract of carriage is quite clearly between the shipper and the Shipowner. However under a Time Charter the shipper will not necessarily be aware of the relationship between the Shipowner and the disponent or Time Charter Owner. Consequently the law recognises that in certain cases the contract entered into between the shipper and the Time Charterer will also involve the Shipowner.

How this affects matters when cargo claims are involved is addressed later in this Chapter but there are other matters that need to be considered. Almost always the time charterer has the same liberties as the Shipowner to make contract terms with shippers and this means that "prepaid", "freight payable" or "received for shipment" bills may be issued as well as through bills of lading that impose more liabilities on the issuer and the Shipowner.

While relationships between the charterer and the Shipowner are good, very few problems will arise but in cases where the Owner has contracted with an unsubstantial or unethical charterer there are many potential pitfalls for the Owner. The worst scenario is if the charterer defaults on paying hire money. Then the Shipowner will most probably withdraw the vessel from the charter and take over the running of it himself.

If the vessel has cargo on board at such a time the Owner will need to determine what types of Bills of Lading have been issued. He will also need to establish what payments, if any, the shipper has paid over to the charterer. If "freight payable at destination" bills have been issued, then the Shipowner can demand the freight from the shipper before delivering the cargo.

Where the bills are "freight payable as per charter party" or call for payment within a certain period after loading, the Owner may be fortunate enough to discover that payment had not yet been made, in which case he can demand the freight, or unfortunate to find that the shipper had sent the money to the Time Charterer.

When "freight prepaid" bills have been issued the Owner will be unlikely to recover any of the freight for the cargo. However he is legally obliged to continue the voyage and deliver the cargo to a Bill of Lading holder at the port of discharge, even if this involves a voyage of thousands of miles, expensive port costs and the bunkers necessary to make the voyage. He can claim these costs back from the Time Charterer but of course if the charterer was not in a position to pay hire, he will hardly be able to settle the Owners claim.

If the cargo in question belongs to the defaulting Time Charterer, the Owner will be able to exercise a lien for unpaid daily hire and any associated costs in completing the voyage.

8.4 CARGO CLAIMS

8.4.1 Insurance

This chapter does not attempt to deal with Marine Insurance in depth. In essence, however, a Shipowner's insurance will fall under three main categories:

(a) Hull and Machinery

(b) War Risk

(c) Protection and Indemnity

The first two major types are self-explanatory and are normally covered through Lloyd's of London or major insurance companies, or a combination of the two.

The third type, Protection and Indemnity can best be thought of as insurance against third party risks and is almost invariably covered through a mutual association or 'Club' as they are usually called. Such Clubs, as their name implies are not profit making companies or individuals as in the case of other, insurers, but are associations run by groups of Shipowners for their mutual benefit. The operation of their day-to-day business is entrusted to firms of professional managers.

The risks covered with the P&I Clubs include such things as claims for damage to other people's property (e.g. hitting a quay wall) injury to individuals (e.g. a crew member or a stevedore falling into a hold) and cargo claims (e.g. claims made by consignees for damage done to (or loss of) their cargo whilst in transit).

8.4.2 Cargo Damage

Even the best run ship may eventually be involved in damage to cargo. There are also certain commodities that are notorious in that Shipowners may be held responsible for damage when the damage occurred either before loading or following discharge - steel products being the better known example, and where it is essential to conduct "pre-loading" and "after-discharge" surveys to verify the condition of every item carried so as to avoid potential claims at a later date.

Most voyage charter parties incorporate by means of a Clause Paramount either the international 'Hague Rules' or the later, updated version, the 'Hague-Visby Rules', which set out the responsibilities of carrier and Owner of goods at sea. In fact the whole subject of cargo damage is very important to be understood by those trading in ships and commodities and it would help to understand it better if we took the opportunity in this chapter of briefly plotting the progress of the law relating to cargo carriage during the past century, before examining the Rules in greater detail. Since much international sea-trading is conducted under the terms of English Law, we will examine the 'Hague Rules' and the 'Hague-Visby Rules' under the English equivalents, the 'Carriage of Goods by Sea Acts, 1924 and 1971'.

We shall also look more briefly at the 'Hamburg Rules' established under a UN convention in 1978 and ratified in 1992. While these are still of only minor impact in international shipping terms they will become increasingly relevant in the future.

8.4.3   Brief Background to the Hague Rules and the Hague-Visby Rules

During the 19th century there was a great deal of general dissatisfaction and unrest with the conditions upon which goods were carried by sea. This unrest came about due to many elaborate 'negligence clauses' which were introduced into bills of lading. These Clauses were designed to defeat completely the effect of legal decisions against Shipowners in the Courts. Many of these clauses were produced in an extremely ambiguous fashion and were quite impossible to interpret. As a consequence of this the position of many shippers, bankers and cargo underwriters became ludicrous as they were quite unable to understand and interpret the extent of their rights against a carrier in the area of carriage of cargo by sea.

The liner companies at this time found themselves in a most monopolistic position because, being relatively few in number, they could combine together to agree various terms of carriage whereas shippers, for example, found that they were quite unable to combine effectively in order to negotiate with Shipowners on equal terms. The general effect of this was to produce a feeling within the industry of general dissatisfaction and growing agitation for Governments to introduce legislation to remedy the situation that had developed for the necessary protection of shippers, bankers and underwriters alike.

In 1893, the United States passed the Harter Act which laid down many conditions upon which goods were to be carried by sea. This, of course, affected only the carriage of goods being shipped to and from the United States of America. Following this, however, similar legislation was introduced by other Governments in an effort to correct the unfair situation and, among the leaders in this respect, were Australia (who developed their Sea Carriage of Goods Act, 1904), Canada (The Water-Carriage of Goods Act, 1910) and also New Zealand, where a series of new Acts was passed.

In 1921 the Imperial Shipping Committee made recommendations to the Government that there should be some uniform legislation throughout the British Empire to standardise the Law regarding the carriage of goods by sea. However, the shipping community itself favoured more the idea of adopting a set of uniform rules for voluntary adoption rather than to introduce legislation.

The Maritime Law Committee of the International Law Association, therefore, held a meeting to discuss the conflicting views of Shipowners and cargo interests and did, in effect, draw up a set of rules subsequently to be known as the **Hague Rules, 1921.**

Nevertheless, the voluntary adoption of these rules did not materialise and there was further agitation for legislation on this issue. This in turn led to the Conference on Maritime Law at Brussels in 1922 where the "Hague Rules" were adopted as the basis of a "draft convention for the unification of certain Rules relating to Bills of Lading". The International Convention was signed by many participating countries at Brussels on 25th August, 1924, and was subsequently given force of Law in the United Kingdom by the **"Carriage of Goods by Sea Act, 1924"**. This legislation remained in existence until 1971 when further legislation was introduced following amendments to the "Hague Rules" by a set of modified Rules known as the **"Hague-Visby Rules"**, which were given the force of Law in the United Kingdom by the **"Carriage of Goods by Sea Act 1971"**. The original "Hague Rules", as embodied in the "Carriage of Goods by Sea Act, 1924" were modified and extended to a certain degree. This means that the 1924 Act has now been repealed and replaced by "The Carriage of Goods by Sea Act 1971". One of the main reasons for the 1971 amendments was, of course, to take account of the effect of containerisation. Most other major Maritime nations subsequently enacted the Hague Rules and in most cases also Hague-Visby.

8.5   THE CARRIAGE OF GOODS BY SEA ACTS

The effect of the 1971 UK Act, like its predecessor in 1924, was to place the Hague-Visby Rules into Britain's statute book making it a "contracting state". The majority of countries in the world did something similar.

The Rules apply to any Bill of Lading or similar document of title relating to the carriage of goods by sea providing:

1.   The Bill of Lading is issued in a contracting State, OR

2.   The carriage is from a port in a contracting State, OR

3.   The Contract contained in or evidenced by the Bill of Lading provides that the rules or the legislation of any State giving effect to them are to govern the Contract, whatever may be the nationality of the ship, the carrier, the shipper, the consignee or any other interested person.

Those three sub-paragraphs are part of Article X of the Hague-Visby Rules and you will see that the third way for the rules to take effect is if "The Contract...provides that the Rules...are to govern the Contract..." The way in which you ensure the Bill of Lading makes that provision is by including a **Clause Paramount** (you will see this in the Conline Bill of Lading **Appendix 33).** The word 'Paramount' is used because the effect of such a clause is to make it clear that if there is anything in the Bill of Lading which would place the shipper in a worse position than provided for in the Rules then the Rules take precedence over the wording of the Bill of Lading in that regard.

The Hague/Hague-Visby Rules do not apply to charter parties but it is common practice to insert a clause in a charter party stipulating that any Bills of Lading issued under that charter shall contain a Clause Paramount.

8.6   SOME IMPORTANT ELEMENTS OF THE ACTS

Coasting Trade

Under the 1924 Act, owing to strong representation made by parties interested in the Coasting Trade, the Act allowed such parties freedom of Contract so long as the Contract was not embodied in a Bill of Lading but was contained in a receipt which had to be marked clearly as a "non-negotiable document". Under the 1971 Act, however, this exemption has disappeared and even Coasting Shipments if carried under a Bill of Lading will be subject to the Rules even though strict application of the Rules does not demand this.

Live Animals

Under the 1924 Act the parties concerned in the carriage of live animals were free to contract on any agreed terms; in other words, the Act had no application to the carriage of live animals. However, where the contract is contained in or evidenced by a Bill of Lading or receipt which expressly provides that the 1971 Act will apply, then this shall include contracts for the carriage of live animals. In this respect the 1971 Act in fact goes beyond the demands of the Rules.

Deck Cargo

Here again, if a contract is contained in or evidenced by a Bill of Lading or receipt which expressly provides that the Rules shall apply, then this shall include contracts for the carriage of deck cargo. However, as was the position under the 1924 Act, deck cargo means cargo which, by the Contract of Carriage, is stated as being carried on deck, and is so carried. If in such circumstances the Bill of Lading is clearly claused to the effect that cargo is carried on deck "at shipper's risk and liability" then, in those circumstances, a Shipowner would be exempt from liability if loss or damage occurred to the cargo.

Voyages Covered

Under the 1924 Act, voyages covered by the Rules were from ports in the United Kingdom and Northern Ireland only. However, this has been amended by the Hague-Visby Rules to the effect that the Rules will apply to every Bill of Lading relating to the carriage of goods between ports in two different States, as follows:

1. Providing the Bill of Lading is issued in a Contracting State, OR

2. The carriage is from a port in a Contracting State, OR

3. The Contract contained in or evidenced by the Bill of Lading provides that the Rules or legislation of any State giving effect to them are to govern the Contract, whatever may be the nationality of the ship, the carrier, the shipper, the consignee or any other interested person.

Seaworthiness

Before the Hague Rules (Carriage of Goods by Sea Act, 1924) were introduced, the Common Law position was that there was implied in every contract of carriage of goods by sea an *absolute warranty* that the vessel was seaworthy at the "commencement of the voyage" and also at the commencement of each "subsequent stage" of the voyage. Only the most clear and unambiguous language in a Bill of Lading could exclude this implied warranty. The reference to the commencement of each "subsequent stage" of the voyage brought into consideration what was termed as the "Doctrine of Stages" which meant in effect that a ship had to be seaworthy at the commencement of each particular stage of the voyage. For example, a vessel proceeding in ballast as opposed to having cargo on board or a voyage which necessitated the vessel having a long down-river passage prior to setting off across the open sea. Different seaworthiness considerations would apply depending on the section of the voyage contemplated.

The 1924 Act and subsequently the 1971 Act categorically abolished the absolute warranty of seaworthiness in all Contracts to which it applied. Shipowners, however, are still under a legal obligation to exercise *due diligence* to make a vessel seaworthy in all respects and to make cargo compartments fit for the reception of cargo. But a Shipowner will not be liable for losses due to unseaworthiness, unless due to want of due diligence.

Obligation to Issue a Bill of Lading

When cargo is delivered into the custody of a Shipowner, that Shipowner is obligated to issue a Bill of Lading, on demand, to the shipper, giving full particulars of the goods accepted and, of course, their apparent order and condition. It is apparent that once cargo has been accepted into the custody of the Shipowner and the Bill of Lading issued, then the particulars of that bill constitute *"prima facie"* evidence that the cargo has in fact been received by the carrier. This obligation to issue the Bill of Lading does not indeed depend on the goods having been loaded on board the vessel. As we have seen, bills can, in fact, be issued prior to actual shipment on board a vessel and this is done by carriers issuing a received for **Shipment Bill of Lading.** But when goods are finally loaded on board, a shipper may demand a **Shipped Bill of Lading** to replace this.

The Obligations of the Shipper

It is important that in the preparation of a Bill of Lading, a shipper furnishes full particulars of cargo to be shipped, by ensuring that all details noted thereon are accurate. The shipper must fulfil an obligation by which he will indemnify the carrier in the event that there is any loss or damage arising from any inaccuracy in the particulars provided by him. This especially applies to dangerous cargo. To ensure that the shipper is liable, the carrier must show that, in the event of subsequent loss or damage, this loss or damage was indeed caused through the actual fault or neglect of the shipper, or his servants.

From Loading to Discharge

A Shipowner has certain obligations also towards the cargo prior to loading it on board the vessel, and also following its discharge from the vessel. However, the Act leaves the Shipowner free to contract on any agreed terms in respect of the transit of the goods prior to loading and subsequent to discharge. It is only for the actual period of the voyage itself that the "Hague-Visby Rules" will apply.

General Average

The "Carriage of Goods by Sea Act, 1971" states expressly that the parties to the Contract are free to make any reasonable arrangements with regard to the application of General Average, normally stated in charter parties, for example, as **"General Average to be adjusted in London in accordance with the York-Antwerp Rules, 1990"** In effect, the Rules have no application to General Average.

Deviation

In every contract it is implied that a vessel shall proceed on her voyage without departure from her proper course as described in the contract, and, if she does, she will, in effect, deviate from contractual terms unless such deviation is fully justifiable.

Under **Common Law,** deviation from a contracted voyage will only be allowed when saving or attempting to save human life.

This position was changed by the introduction of the Hague and Hague-Visby Rules, whereby any deviation in saving or attempting to save life or property at sea, or indeed any reasonable deviation, would not be deemed to be an infringement or breach of the Rules or of the contract of carriage. The carrier would not be liable for any loss or damage resulting from that situation. Whether a deviation is said to be "reasonable" is in every particular case a question of fact and must be considered in accordance with the particular circumstances in every case.

Limitation of Liability

In the Carriage of Goods by Sea Act 1924 (Hague Rules), the **Limitation of Liability** provisions available to a Shipowner were that, unless the value and nature of the goods were declared and inserted in the Bill of Lading before the goods were actually shipped on board, liability was limited to £100 per package or unit. The parties to a contract were, however, free to insert a higher limit if they so wished, but a Shipowner was unable to restrict his liability to any amount less than £100. This limitation had been effective since 1924 and since that time great steps forward had been taken within the shipping industry with regard to the methods of carrying cargo by sea. These new and modern methods included such concepts as containerisation, palletisation and roll-on/roll-off methods of loading and discharge.

In the light of this modernisation it was decided that as well as the limitation of liability itself being too low, the limitation of liability provisions were outdated and need amending. These amendments took place following the introduction of the Hague-Visby Rules and were brought into English Law by the Carriage of Goods by Sea Act, 1971. These amendments provided for the following:

1.	In any event there shall be no liability in respect of loss or damage to goods unless legal action is **commenced within one year of their delivery or of the date when they should have been delivered.** It being permissible to extend this period should the parties so agree.

2.	Recourse actions may be brought by the plaintiff after the expiration of the one-year time limit, within the time limit allowed by the Law of the Court seized of the case.

	This meant, of course, that, depending upon the Law of the Country under which the claim was being brought then, if that jurisdiction provided for a time limitation period in excess of the one year time limit laid down in the Hague-Visby Rules, such time limit, as defined by the Law of the Country would prevail.

3. Under the Hague Rules and therefore the 1924 Act, the limitation of liability was £100 per package or unit. Inflation overtook this small level of compensation to such an extent that the British Maritime Law Association produced a voluntary agreement in 1950 called the 'Gold Clause Agreement' which doubled the limit of compensation to £200. (This agreement naturally ceased to exist when UK Ratified the Hague-Visby Rules).

Under Hague-Visby, the aim was to protect the limitation from inflation by relating it to a 'manufactured' currency called the Gold (or Poincare) franc and the Rules stipulated the exact weight and degree of fineness of the gold. The new rate was 10,000 of these gold francs. Subsequently (started in 1981 but not internationally accepted until 1984) a protocol was agreed to replace the gold francs with what it calls 'units of account' but which are more familiarly known as Special Drawing Rights (SDR's) which are another 'manufactured' currency by the International Monetary Fund and for which a rate of exchange is published each day in the financial press.

Therefore, if we look specifically at how these special drawing rights affect the Hague-Visby Rules the alteration can be explained as follows:

(a) for the equivalent of 10,000 Poincare Francs substitute "666.67 units of account".

(b) for the words, "30 Poincare Francs per kilo" substitute "2 units of account per kilo".

The Merchant Shipping Act, 1981 which gave effect to this change, specifies for the purposes of the schedule to the Carriage of Goods by Sea Act, 1971, as amended the value, on a particular day, of one "special drawing right" shall be treated as equal to such a sum in Sterling as the International Monetary Fund have fixed as being the equivalent for that particular day.

The limitation of liability provisions have been added to by the introduction of an alternative limit to the package of unit using weight per kilo as a basis for limitation. It must be pointed out that the basis of limitation giving the higher result shall be adopted for application to claims.

It is deemed under the Rules that the total amount recoverable in respect of any claim is to be calculated by reference to the value of the goods at the time and place at which the goods are discharged from the vessel.

When deciding, in situations where the method of consolidating cargo is by container, pallet or other similar article of transport, whether the limitation of liability is to be based on **"per package"** or **"unit"** or indeed on **"weight"**, this is to be decided by referring to the Bill of Lading itself. If the packages or units are actually enumerated in the Bill of Lading as being packed inside the container, then the **"unit"** basis of limitation will be adopted, otherwise the container itself will be the basis of limitation.

Dangerous Cargo

The provisions of the Hague-Visby Rules relative to the carriage of **dangerous cargo** are very similar to the conditions contained in the "Merchant Shipping Act, 1984". If any dangerous cargo is shipped on board a vessel without the knowledge or consent of the Master or the carrier then the Act would allow the carrier to take appropriate action to have the cargo landed or indeed destroyed at the shippers' expense should any loss or damage be sustained to those goods.

Similarly if, during the course of a voyage, dangerous cargo becomes a danger to the ship and the crew, even in circumstances where the cargo has been shipped on board in a proper and legal fashion, then the Master of the vessel is entitled to take action to destroy or dispose of such cargo as he deems fit and the carrier shall not incur any liability whatsoever other than an obligation to contribute in General Average, if any.

"Himalaya Clause"

The Hague-Visby Rules have introduced a completely new Article and the intention of this was to add to the Rules, provisions in order that any servants or agents of the carrier would be entitled to benefit from the definitions and limits of liability presently available to the carriers. Such servants or agents of the carrier would not, however, be able to avail themselves of these provisions if it were to be proved that any loss or damage resulted from an act or omission of the servant, or agent, done with intent to cause damage or with knowledge that damage would probably result.

The clause gets its name "Himalaya" as this was the ship involved in the case of *Adler v Dickson (1955)* when a passenger injured herself on a badly secured ladder but found that the conditions on the passenger ticket prevented her from taking action against the Shipowner under their contractual agreement so instead she successfully sued the captain under tort. The "Himalaya" clause expressly prevents this by stipulating that servants of the owner have the same limitation of liability protection as the Shipowner under the Bill of Lading. Prior to the Hague-Visby Rules, this clause had to be specifically written into the contract of carriage.

Rights and Immunities

There are considerable rights available to a Shipowner with exemptions or immunities from liability. A number of these including unseaworthiness, deviation and limitation of liability provisions have already been examined in some detail. However, there are many other exemptions:

(a) "Act, neglect or default of the Master, Mariner, Pilot of servant to the Carrier in the navigation or in the management of the ship".

This exemption from liability must be considered very carefully and a comparison made between faults or errors in the **navigation** of the vessel as opposed to faults or errors in the **management** of the vessel. Obviously, related to navigation, such errors would refer to navigational errors possibly resulting in collision or in grounding and may result in the Shipowner being able to avoid liability by pleading the referred exception. With regard to the exception related to act, neglect or default of the Master, etc. in the management of the ship, then this is somewhat complicated in that it must be decided what situation would result in an error in the management of the ship as opposed to act, neglect or default of the Master, Mariner, etc. in the management of the cargo itself. A distinction must be made, therefore, between "want of due care of the cargo" and "want of due care of the vessel by itself indirectly affecting cargo".

(b) "Fire, unless caused by the actual fault or privity of the Carrier".

This exception is an unqualified exemption for loss or damage arising out of fire. It is however, subject to the fact that the fire had not been caused by the actual fault or privity of the carrier and the burden of proof is on the carrier in this respect.

(c) "Perils, dangers and accidents of the sea or other navigable waters".

This is a somewhat difficult exception for a Shipowner to take advantage of, particularly as he must produce evidence that the damage was caused by such a peril of the sea and was without the Shipowner's negligence or fault. It would also have to be proved that the vessel had encountered abnormally bad weather caused by freak conditions in respect of which there would probably be structural damage to the vessel as well. Of course the vessel is expected to meet the normal hazards and weather conditions at sea in any case so that any evidence would have to substantiate extremely abnormal conditions.

(d)   "Act of God".

With regard to this exception, a Shipowner would have to prove that the loss or damage arose without human intervention. It is a situation whereby an occurrence may take place without human intervention and one which could not have been prevented by any amount of human foresight or care of a reasonable nature.

(e)   "Act of War".

This would appear to be self-explanatory and can be defined as to mean losses due to war or hostile situations. It would include the phrase "Queen's Enemies".

(f)   "Acts of Public Enemies".

It may be suggested that this covers enemies of the Queen, or of the State to which the carrier belongs.

(g)   "Arrest or restraint of Princes, Rulers or People, or seizure under legal process".

This exception would include forcible interference by a State and they include such things as blockage of discharge, embargo or arrest of ships by the action of a State.

(h)   "Quarantine Restrictions".

Under this section the Shipowner may expect to avoid liability for loss or damage to cargo caused through quarantine of the vessel.

(i)   "Act or omission of the Shipper or Owner of the goods, his Agent or Representative".

If it can be proved under this exception that any act or omission on the part of a shipper was directly responsible for the loss or damage to the cargo then the carrier can be relieved from liability.

(j)   "Strikes, or lock-outs or stoppage or restraint of labour from whatever cause, whether partial or general".

Most of this statement is self-explanatory but it would also include any "boycott".

(k)   "Riots and Civil Commotions".

This particular exception would include any local disturbance in respect of which is included lawlessness and/or violence.

(l)   "Saving or attempting to save life or property at sea".

As has already been discussed in this chapter, with regard to the effects of deviation, this exception gives the Shipowner the right to deviate from the terms of the contract for the said purposes.

(m)   "Wastage in bulk or weight or any other loss or damage arising from inherent defect, quality, or vice of the goods".

(n)   "Insufficiency of packing or inadequacy of marks".

The above exceptions all relate to defences available to the Shipowner for the quoted losses and need little further comment.

(o)   "Latent defects not discoverable by due diligence".

This exception may be best explained by referring to the case of *Brown & Company v Nitrate Producers Steamship Company (1937)*. In this case cargo was damaged due to leakage through rivets, used in the construction of the vessel, which was latent in nature. Despite careful investigations such leaks could not be discovered by the Shipowner in the exercise of due diligence and consequently were not liable for the damage sustained to the cargo.

(p)   "Any other cause arising without the actual fault or privity of the Carrier, or without the fault or neglect of the Agents or servants of the Carrier, but the burden of proof shall be on the person claiming the benefit of this exception to show that neither the actual fault or privity of the Carrier nor the fault or neglect of the Agents or servants of the Carrier contributed to the loss or damage".

This exception can be referred to as the "Catch-All Clause" and is there to protect the Carrier from responsibility for loss or damage, of whatever nature that may be, which has not already been specifically covered by the Rules, providing, of course, that such loss or damage did not arise with the fault or privity of the Carrier or with the fault or neglect of the agents or other servants of the Carrier.

The Hamburg Rules

The object of the Hague and Hague-Visby Rules was to spell out the responsibilities and liabilities of the parties, particularly the Carrier, in an internationally acceptable way. In the process, the liabilities of the Carrier have been limited and in so doing they are in effect saying to the shipper "This is the point where my insurance of your goods ends so this must be the point where yours must start".

This is not so onerous as it might at first sound because it is a fact of life that the premium charged to a shipper for his goods and trade, which would be well known to his insurer, will inevitably be lower than the premium insurers would have to demand from the carrier to cover all the different types of goods that a ship *might* carry. As the cost of insurance, like any other expense, eventually has to be passed on to the shipper, it is bound to be cheaper for the shipper to do his own insurance. The Rules help all concerned because they know the point at which their risks begin and end.

The United Nations Council for Trade and Development (UNCTAD) which is unashamedly on the side of the less developed nations of the world, felt that the Hague-Visby Rules were weighted too much in favour of the carriers most of whom, it seemed to UNCTAD, were operated by the developed nations.

In 1978, therefore, the UN published a draft convention entitled the Hamburg Rules which required 20 Nations to ratify them before they became an International Convention. It took 14 years for the requisite number of signatories to be found. None of the ratifying countries are significant maritime nations; indeed several of them are landlocked.

Not surprisingly there is, in the Hamburg Rules, a clear shift of liability to the Carrier as well as increased levels of compensation for the merchant. The fear generally expressed is that, firstly, the exporters and importers will be no better off because the carriers will have to pass on their increased costs. Secondly, and more importantly, the clauses in the Hague Rules have stood the test of time in the law courts throughout the world and the Hague-Visby Rules did not alter the fundamentals. The Hamburg Rules, however, introduce vast untried areas of potential legal dispute.

In point of fact the Hamburg Rules have already come in, as several countries, notably Morocco, Algeria and Egypt, have incorporated them into national law.

Over time the rules will be tested and depending upon the outcome of legal cases and the commercial strength of negotiating parties, they will doubtless find their way into some shipping contracts. While the potential changes in liability that will follow the introduction of the Hamburg Rules should not be dismissed out of hand and must be closely monitored, it is a fact that for the time being it is the Hague-Visby Rules that apply to most contracts.

A new set of rules known as the Rotterdam Rules has been developed by the UN and is currently (2011) available for ratification. Although aimed at simplifying the current situation, the presence of a third set of rules may actually make matters more complicated particularly as the Rotterdam Rules have been developed mostly for the liner sector and with door-to-door transport foremost in mind. Most cargoes carried under dry cargo charter parties are carried port to port with the landside transport most commonly not the concern of the ship operator.

Time Charter Cargo Claims

The rights and responsibilities enumerated in the notes about the Hague Rules and the Hague-Visby Rules apply to Carriers and Cargo Owners/shippers whether or not the vessel is employed on voyage or on time charter terms and conditions. However, where time charter applies, there is a complication because the "carrier" can be defined as either the time charterers in the role of "disponent Owner", or the actual Owners themselves. Indeed some claims can arise due to default by the time charterers whilst others may be entirely the ship's fault.

Accordingly, and in order to avoid any misunderstanding where simultaneous dual negotiations might be carried out between an aggrieved cargo owner and both the actual and the disponent Owners, a code of practice has grown up around the New York Produce Time Charter Party, into which it is common to incorporate the 'Inter Club New York Produce Exchange Agreement', a copy of which is included as **Appendix 34.**

The 'Inter Club Agreement' was last amended in 1984 and sets out what is to happen in the event that cargo claims are lodged against the Carrier. It also sets out the responsibilities and liabilities in the relationship between the time charterer and the Shipowner.

It is important to take the time to read and understand the Inter-Club Agreement, especially if becoming involved with time chartering, and particularly to realise the significance of the inclusion or absence of the words "and responsibility" in Clause 8 of the NYPE Charter Party and/or the words "cargo claims" in the second sentence of Clause 26.

Time Bars

Under English law there is a one year time limit for charterers and/or cargo owners to bring claims against carriers or shipowners. This may, however, be exceeded in certain circumstances under the terms of the 'Arbitration Act, 1950', if an English arbitration applies and if the claimant can show the court that 'undue hardship' might otherwise occur. Generally though, one year time limitations means what it says for charterers, although many feel it to be unfair that shipowners are not prevented from bringing claims against charterers in similar circumstances.

However, in regard to the 'Inter Club Agreement', there is a provision in respect of a time-bar in which claims are subject to a time-bar of two years, no matter whether they are made by owners or by charterers.

8.7   SELF-ASSESSMENT AND TEST QUESTIONS

Attempt the following and check your answers from the text or appendices:

1.   What is a clean Bill of Lading?

2.   Why do many Bills of Lading show the words "To Order" instead of named consignee?

3.   Who signs the Letter of Indemnity presented in lieu of a Bill of Lading at port of discharge and what points need to be treated with caution?

4.   What are the Bills of Lading three basic functions?

5.   Why was it necessary to amend the Hague Rules and introduce the Hague-Visby Rules?

6.   What voyages are covered by the Hague-Visby Rules?

7.   How is the limit of compensation calculated under the Hague-Visby Rules?

8.   What is the purpose of a "Himalaya" Clause?

Having completed Chapter Eight, attempt the following and submit your essays to your Tutor.

1.   A shipment of steel coils has been fixed on a voyage charter that calls for Clean Bills of Lading marked "freight prepaid". What instructions should the Owner give and to whom, to ensure that in complying with the charter party he does not jeopardise his interests?

2.   Suggest a situation (imaginary) where the "Himalaya" clause could provide protection and another situation where it would not help at all.

Chapter 9

WORLD TRADES

9.1 INTRODUCTION

It is essential that those engaged in dry cargo chartering have a good working knowledge of relevant world trades and the maritime environment in which they operate. Already in this book, we have touched upon numerous aspects of the subject but readers should actively seek out other sources of information to expand their knowledge.

This chapter aims to set out essentials, although daily working efficiency in this important commercial shipping activity will be greatly enhanced by the use of:

(a) A Maritime Atlas (such as *"Lloyd's Maritime Atlas"* or *"The Ship's Atlas"*).

(b) A set of Maritime Distance Tables (such as "Reed's").

(c) A book on Maritime Geography.

(d) A Load-line Map (sometimes contained in Maritime Atlases).

(e) An Institute Navigational Limits Map (published by Witherby Seamanship International Ltd. ISBN 1 85609 316 6).

(f) A book on Port Information (Fairplay and Lloyd's each publish such a book, whilst there is also a similar publication by "Shipping Guides", the publishers of *"The Ship's Atlas"*).

(g) A good Shipping Dictionary/*(Dictionary of Shipping International Business Trade Terms and Abbreviations,* published by Witherby Seamanship International Ltd. ISBN 1 85609 236 4).

(h) Shipping magazines and newspapers, also your daily newspaper. Have an enquiring mind and seek out the location and activities of a strange port, the use of an unfamiliar commodity, its carriage requirements, etc.

9.2 THE DRY CARGO TRAMP TRADES

There are many dry-cargo tramp trades, some international, some local. Because of the diversity of the background of this book (where, for example local trades affecting those in the Eastern Mediterranean will not particularly affect or interest those involved in local trades around Japan and Korea and *vice versa*) the intention of the following pages is to concentrate on internationally important trades routes and commodities. This will be tackled in two stages. First from the aspect of a commodity (perhaps of most interest to a charterer or trader in that commodity), and secondly from the aspect of type/size of vessel (ie. from the Shipowner's, Ship Operator's viewpoint).

You should set yourself the task of reading fixture and market reports that appear in shipping publications and, from these, you will learn of some of the major ports involved in the shipment and delivery of any particular commodity, as well as the speed of cargo handling at ports involved and the preferred size of vessel.

9.3   CARGOES FOR SHIPS

The three major seaborne trade dry-cargo commodities (in terms of volume) are iron ore, coal and grains, in that order. You will have learned about the ships that carry such cargoes earlier in this book. It is now necessary to complete that data with consideration of the actual trades arranged around these three major commodities. **(See Appendices 35, 36, 37, 38 and 39).**

The information that follows is largely historic and will be affected from time to time by political and natural events. China's membership of the WTO (World Trade Organisation) together with a simultaneous relaxation of its internal political system, saw it become an aggressive importer of raw materials and exporter of manufactured goods.

There was a surge in world demand for steel products that saw steel prices double in the period 2004/2005. Consequently demand for coal and iron ore also increased. In many cases demand from one country could not be satisfied by its nearby trading partners, and new suppliers were sought from further abroad.

This led to a need for more ships because the longer voyages involved means that each ship makes fewer voyages in a year and so overall carries less cargo than used to be the case. An increase in tonne/miles is the driving force behind the rising freight rates that were witnessed since 2003 and before the recent slump.

Iron Ore: Ore in its various forms comes mainly from developing nations, such as Brazil, Venezuela, West and South-east Africa and India, also from advanced nations such as Australia and Canada and, to a lesser extent, from Scandinavia. The receiving end of such voyages is almost always one of the major industrialised countries, such as in Europe, the United States of America, China or Japan.

However, raw, unrefined ores are frequently partly processed into commodities such as sinter, pig iron, pellets or concentrates, often at processing plants in developing nations, before being carried onwards in other ships to their eventual destinations.

The advantages of this first processing stage taking place in the country of origin are therefore threefold. The exporting country earns vital foreign exchange as a result of the added value, the importing country saves the cost of this processing stage and the iron content of the cargo is considerably increased saving freighting costs.

In the modern port of shipment for iron ore, cargoes are loaded at great speed, usually by a chute fed by conveyors, with the ore dropped from a great height. Trimming is rarely required in modern bulk carriers as installations are usually flexible enough to distribute the cargo fairly evenly in cargo holds during loading. You will often find the stipulation in chartering negotiations that the cargo has to be 'spout trimmed' at loading port. Because of the speed at which large bulkers are loaded, they require the facility to change trim rapidly to preserve their safety, and high capacity ballast pumps are usually fitted for this purpose. Also frequent draft checks may be required as the vessel nears full cargo, and allowance should ideally be made for the time taken on such surveys in the charter party laytime clauses.

Discharge of iron ore in all except the smallest ports is handled by sophisticated equipment, although the one common element is the grab. Having said that, it is not possible to describe the many systems available, which vary from the common slewing crane to highly specialised transporters. To some extent, the method used will depend on the type of inland transport being used, but the appetite of the steel industry is voracious, and speed of turn-around is essential. Consequently, it is not unusual for cargoes in excess of 200,000 tonnes of iron ore to be loaded and discharged within a few days, perhaps at rates approaching 50,000 tonnes daily.

The system utilised for weighing cargo during discharge is equally variable, although a large proportion goes through hoppers where it can be weighed in transit.

Major sources of iron ore exports are:

Brazil:	Ponta do Ubu, Tubarao, Sebetiba Bay
Venezuela:	Orinoco ports
Mauretania:	Nouadhibou
Liberia:	Monrovia
South Africa:	Saldanha Bay
India:	New Mangalore, Mormugoa
Australia:	Dampier, Cape Lambert
Canada:	Seven Islands
Sweden:	Luleâ
Norway:	Narvik

It is difficult to predict future development in the iron ore trades, because a number of nations possess very large reserves that have yet to be exploited. This is largely due to the cost and the inaccessibility of the deposits but, as the more easily tapped resources decline, the incentive will increase to develop new supplies. Much will then depend on the political will of the countries concerned as to whether they wish to take advantage of the high technology available internationally.

Coal: Coal is not one simple substance but arises with many different chemical and physical properties which, in turn, make the different types and grades suitable for a wide variation of uses.

The two most important consumers of coal from the chartering aspect are those intending to use it as a primary fuel and the electricity industry is naturally the biggest in this group. The other is the steel industry which converts the coal into coke for use in blast furnaces.

Coal is found in varying quantities on all continents and in many countries. The areas which produce an exportable surplus, however, are led by the United States of America, Australia, South Africa, Canada, Russia and China. Exports from the United Kingdom (once a major exporter) have dwindled almost to extinction, and Polish exports are far less than a decade ago. However, new sources are being exploited, with Venezuela, Colombia and Indonesia seeming set to become major players in this market arena.

The patterns of shipment are dictated by the consumption of the main industrial centres of the world, with Japan and the EU nations predominant in this respect. However, the volume of imports does not necessarily bear any relation to the overall consumption of coal because, in Western Europe, for example, a large portion of requirements is obtained from indigenous sources. Japan is far less fortunate in this respect, needing to import much coal and iron ore to serve its industrial requirements.

Geographical and economic factors also play their part, with the result that Europe receives its major imports from the United States, with Japan and the Far East relying more on sources in Australia, Western Canada, China and Eastern Russia and, to a certain extent, South Africa.

When considering the demand for coking coal and iron ore, it will become obvious how the health of the tramp market depends on the success or failures of the steel industry. In theory, therefore, a recession in steel making would automatically have a knock-on effect on the demand for bulk carrier space. But, as always, the situation is not necessarily so simple. Often at such times, it is found that a counterbalance is provided by, say, an increase in demand for grain.

The main ports of loading for coal in the **United States** are in the area known as Hampton Roads, particularly the ports of Norfolk and Newport News, as well as nearby Baltimore and Philadelphia. Significant quantities also originate in the huge Mississippi River basin, being exported via New Orleans and Mobile, in the United States Gulf, also via Long Beach and Los Angeles from the United States West Coast.

The traditional **Australian** coal exporting ports are in New South Wales, comprising Newcastle, Port Kembla and Gladstone. However, during the past decade hugh deposits have been exploited in Queensland, and ports such as Hay Point and Abbots Point have been established, trading to and from these ports being facilitated by the discovery of deep-water navigation channels (e.g. Hydrographers Passage) through the Great Barrier Reef.

South Africa has greatly enhanced its exportation potential by the opening of the specialised Richards Bay terminal near Durban, whilst Canada now has the Port of Robertsbank, near Vancouver.

Russia exports from the Black Sea but importantly, as part of an expanding trade, via the Far Eastern port of Vostochny (near Vladivostock), handily placed to meet the demands of Japan and Korea. China is also developing its coal exports, mainly from northern Chinese ports, such as Qinghauangdao (Chinwangtao), but coal exports are set to become increasingly important from Asian nations with Indonesia gearing up its production and export facilities and coal is occasionally exported also from Vietnam.

India, once an important exporter through its eastern port of Calcutta, now requires internally all the coal it can produce and is an important customer for Australian coal, which is usually transported to India in ships fitted with self-discharging capabilities to overcome inadequate port facilities on the sub-continent.

The future of coal is reasonably bright despite its main disadvantage when compared with oil as a primary fuel in that the transportation of coal from source to consumer is more complex. To this must be added the need for more sophisticated appliances for burning it (many power stations have to grind coal to fine dust before putting it into the furnace) and then there is an ash disposal problem. Nevertheless, coal is obtainable from so many different areas that it cannot be used as a political weapon as we have seen happen with oil.

Coal is usually brought to the loading port in rail wagons then loaded via a chute or conveyor. Discharging is normally by shore cranes equipped with grabs. Much thought is devoted to speeding up the handling process and self-unloading carriers may be one answer but they are, by their very nature, of higher capital value and thus we are back again to cost. It may well be that experiments with transportation in slurry form, or other methods of liquifying coal may be successful and permit tankers to carry coal, although there are many problems to be overcome before this will be commonplace, if ever.

It is not possible to generalise on methods of inland transportation of coal either prior to shipment or after delivery although, in view of the large quantities handled, probably rail or canal transport will be utilised. Like so many bulk commodities, one major problem is that of storage space and, since land in industrial areas tends to be expensive, it is usually vital that such space is kept to a minimum. This necessitates an efficient system of co-operation between the mines, inland transport, loading facilities and the Shipowner, perhaps being more vital in respect of coal industry than any other. It is, in fact, generally supposed that the expression "subject stem" originates from the coal trade, when it became necessary first to secure a ship on this "subject" before finalising the whole operation to provide that vessel with her cargo.

Petroleum Coke tends to be considered as part of the coal 'market' but, as the name implies, it is in fact a by-product of oil refining. It is exported from those areas where major refineries exist in particular from both coasts of the USA including the US Gulf; Europe and Japan are the major importers.

It is produced in various grades depending upon the design of the refinery and is not the most popular of cargoes with owners. Some types are granular (up to about 5mm) and are rather oily whilst others are very fine and cause a dust problem.

It has several uses because it is a source of almost pure carbon and one of its principal applications is in the manufacture of electrodes for use in the refining of aluminium.

Grain. As it applies to ocean transport, grain includes wheat, rye, corn, sorghums, barley, oats, rice and oil seeds (the latter although not technically 'grain' is considered such from a chartering point of view).

A pattern of grain trading has emerged during the 20th century, main producers being China, Russia, India, The United States, Canada, France and Argentina. Much of this production is needed close to home, however, and major exporters are the United States, Canada, Australia, Argentina and France. Major importers at present are Japan, China, the EU, North African countries and the Middle East, Brazil and, above all, Russia. In addition, there are specific emergency trades developed to areas of the world where local famines and disasters occur, often organised by the World Food Agency, part of the United Nations.

The largest phenomenon of the post-war decades, however, has been an ever-growing trend in former developing nations, as their prosperity has increased, to refuse to be content with eating bread, rice or maize as a staple diet and to seek instead meat, or meat products, poultry and eggs. This evolution, translated into transportation and grain logistics, has created fundamental changes in trade.

Cattle and poultry feeds are mainly supplied by corn, sorghum, barley and other coarse grains, in addition to soya beans and other oil seeds, and a combination of them all by way of derivatives such as meals, expellers and oil cakes. The main exporters of these products are the United States, Argentina, Brazil and Thailand. Among the heaviest importers: Russia, the EU, Japan, China and Taiwan.

In the main grain loading ports of the world, the cargo is brought to seaboard terminals by rail, road or barge. The sophisticated and developed nations have an internal network of country elevators, which are in effect collecting points for local harvesting centres. These are linked to the seaboard with an intensive bulk grain transport infrastructure, rail sidings, specialised grain hopper railcars, bulk grain road transport or special grain barges where river transport is appropriate.

Where storage is inadequate, surplus stocks are held in a variety of alternative facilities, temporarily modified and pressed into service eg. redundant factories.

Terminals at sea ports are mostly modern and use high-speed elevators, equipped to unload inland transport and transfer the commodity into ships.

Any port congestion, which seems a recurring problem in grain, is due to greater demands being placed on the internal and seaboard elevator capacities than can possibly be accommodated, due often to commercial pressures or to grain price structures. When you realises that an average loading rate in North American ports, for example, is between 10,000 and 20,000 daily, it can be seen that the major cause for congestion is not within the capacity of the shore equipment.

As far as discharging is concerned, methods vary considerably. In locations such as the EU and Japan, discharge may be performed by static or travelling suction unloaders. Some, however, may be bucket elevator type. Conveyor belts are used to tranship the grain from ocean-going vessel coasters or to inland transport to store in associated grain silos.

In Venezuela and parts of South Korea, discharge of grain may be effected by the use of portable Buhlers (SKT machines) held vertically into the vessel's holds by the ship's gear, and discharged direct to road transport.

The usual method that is employed by many countries is that of discharging by crane and clamshell grabs into hoppers on the decks, feeding direct to road transport, or from hoppers to sacking machines, with the bags being stacked in adjoining warehouses. There are also portable suckers (Vacuvatortype), small pneumatic vacuum cleaner type machines on wheels, lifted onto a vessel by shore cranes or ship's gear, and moved on deck from hold to hold. In some ports using this method, the grain can either be bagged by hand on the dock side and stacked in a warehouse or stored there in bulk. Vacuvators are powered either by internal combustion engines or electricity.

In some of the more primitive ports, clamshell grabs are fitted to ship's gear and grain discharged in bulk, as already described when using shore cranes. There are still some ports where grain is sacked in the holds and discharged by sling (either by shore cranes or ship's gear), as is often the case with aid cargoes to famine-affected areas.

Ports through which grain is exported include:

United States:	Mississippi River delta, Houston, Baltimore, Norfolk, Seattle, Portland (Oregon).
Canada:	Thunder Bay (Great Lakes), Churchill (Hudson Bay) Montreal, Quebec Sorel (Upper St Lawrence River), Seven Islands, Baie Comeau (Lower St. Lawrence River).
Australia:	Fremantle, Bunbury, Esperance, Adelaide, Portland, Geelong.
Argentina:	Rosario, Buenos Aires, Bahia Blanca.
Brazil:	Santos, Rio Grando do Sul.
France:	Rouen, Le Havre.

Where nations with poor inland facilities are involved, and this is usually the case with aid cargoes, bags are frequently the only practicable method of moving grain about. Consequently, the grain may be loaded in bulk and bagged later at the destination port, or bagged at the start of the journey, in the loading port itself. These bags are usually of the size that can be conveniently moved by manpower alone, eg. 50 kilos each.

Charter parties will often include a clause that extra bags are to be carried (usually free of charge) in case of damage or splitting of bags when they are moved, as well as in some cases, the carriage of needles and twine, so that bags can be filled and fastened, to prevent spillage of their contents.

It is unusual these days for more than one grade of grain to be carried in the same cargo compartment but, where this is required, separations will have to be employed, usually tarpaulins, or some similar material, great care being taken to avoid a mixture of separate commodities. Responsibility for the risk and cost of this exercise (cost of labour as well as cost of material) should be considered, negotiated, and entered in the contract.

Agricultural Products

These are many and varied but from a volume point of view the most important is probably sugar.

Sugar is carried in sea-going vessels in either its raw bulk state, usually cane sugar but very occasionally beet sugar, from an area of production to a refining site (eg. Tate & Lyle cane sugar from Mauritius or Fiji to the Silvertown Refinery on the River Thames, London); or refined, usually bagged sugar, from a refinery to a consuming nation. Many exporting nations of bulk raw sugar employ mechanical installations where the product is carried on a moving band before dropping through a spout into a vessel's holds. Sometimes spreaders are used to distribute the sugar in those holds, thereby improving the trimming and obtaining a better stow.

Discharge of bulk raw sugar is effected by grabs, the contents being dropped into hoppers that empty onto a moving band via a weigh tower into the refinery, storage area, or onward transportation vehicle.

Many tropical areas produce and export bulk sugar, eg. from the Caribbean and the North Coast of the South American Continent (eg. Barbados and Georgetown, Guyana); from the islands of the Indian Ocean (Mauritius and Reunion); from Southern Africa (eg. Swaziland) via ports such as Durban; from Bangkok, Thailand; from Fiji; from the Philippines; from Queensland (Australia); and from Brazil (eg. Santos or Recife). Major importers include the United Kingdom, France and the United States of America.

Cassava (tapioca) is another prolific tropical plant, although for seaborne purposes, by far the largest exporter is Thailand; exports being through the port of Bangkok (to 26 feet fresh depth of water) or, more frequently given the size of vessels engaged in this trade, via Kohsichang, downriver of Bangkok, where large ships can load. Thailand ranks only seventh in terms of world production but, from an exporting point of view, has 80 percent of the market, much of its exports destined for EU animal feed purposes. With constant world-wide pressure to reduce or eliminate altogether grants and subsidies to farmers, this trade may change dramatically, but whilst the EU is geared to maintaining grain prices at high levels to protect domestic producers, it will remain economically attractive for European animal feed compounders to substitute cheap imports of protein and energy feedstock such as cassava for eventual food for pigs and cattle, rather than use the more expensive locally grown grain.

Whereas large vessels, commonly panamax or capesize bulk carriers, are used for the transportation of cassava from Thailand to the EU, other nations in the area, eg. Malaysia and Indonesia, commonly use handy-sized bulk carriers of around 20/40,000 dwt. to carry a variety of agricultural products in each shipment (usually separated "naturally" hold by hold) for such as copra derivatives, cassava, etc;) the reasons being twofold. First, the shore-based industry is not so mechanised as in Thailand and, secondly, the ports are not so deep-drafted and well-equipped with loading equipment as is Kohsichang. In fact, a vessel engaged in the carriage of "agri-prods" from Indonesia may need to load at several ports to obtain a full cargo.

Forest Products

This is the name given generally to any wood derived product. Just like the other trades, forest products can be divided into those appertaining to raw materials and processed goods.

Raw Materials: In trading terms, raw forest products can be sub-divided between roundwood (logs), sawn timber, pulpwood, and woodchips. The main receivers of these diverse materials are Europe, the Far East and North America, with around half the world's requirements being met from North American and Scandinavian origins; although there is a thriving log trade from the West Coast of South America, where Chile is a major exporter.

Those areas supply principally softwood and we have to turn to tropical and sub-tropical areas, such as Central America, Guyana, Brazil, West Africa, India, Burma, Malaysia and Indonesia for hardwood sources. There is no set pattern for hardwoods as, unlike softwoods which are fast growing and so can be produced as a crop in readily accessible areas, hardwood trees are dotted around various forests, are more difficult to locate, having to be individually felled and transported to an exporting location. Consequently, hardwoods tend to be shipped as liner parcels, although there are full cargoes in this commodity, principally from West Africa and from the River Amazon basin.

Softwoods are frequently sawn before shipment and an increasing amount moves in sawn condition direct to a convenient distribution place in an importing area, rather than to sawmills located in those receiving regions.

Nothing is wasted and the sawdust and general remains from sawmills, termed "woodchips", are also in demand for various wood products, eg. paper, chipboard, linerboard, etc. and a major trade exists in this commodity from the West Coast of North America to Japan.

Incidentally, the expressions 'hardwood' and 'softwood' relate more to the type of tree rather than strictly to the actual hardness or otherwise of the wood. For example, Balsa wood which is the softest and lightest of all woods is technically a 'hardwood'. Conversely, Columbian pine which is a favourite material for the part of a quay that has to take the shock of a ship coming alongside, is actually a 'softwood'.

The future of the hardwood trade is not clear because there is enormous pressure from conservationists to reduce its use. Most hardwoods take many decades to grow to maturity so that much of such timber being exploited is, to all intents and purposes, a non-renewable resource and such trees are a vital element in reducing the 'greenhouse' effect.

On the other hand, softwoods, which are the firs, larches and pines, tend to be 'farmed' under strictly controlled conditions so that in most producing areas the total amount is being increased rather than the reverse.

There is a considerable trade in illegal hardwoods in most areas where they grow. In some instances illegal goods from one country are often shipped from a neighbouring state and described as originating from there. Once this trade was 'overlooked' by officials but there has been a noticeable trend to crack down on this practice in parts of Asia. As a result, intended cargoes from some of the more suspect exporters might not actually materialise when shipment is due and so some care should be exercised in ascertaining the legality of cargoes before committing ships to carry them.

Processed Material: Here there is a very wide variety, ranging from plywood through to newsprint.

This latter product is especially valuable and susceptible to mishandling damage and so much of the trade is conducted in specially designed vessels engaged in long-term contracts. The main exporting areas are Canada (both East and West) and Finland. Naturally, winter conditions can cause disruption, particularly when ice affects the St. Lawrence River and the Gulf of Bothnia. As a result, those vessel's engaged in this trade need to be ice-strengthened.

Although unaffected by the ice difficulty, Western Canadian exporting terminals are frequently beset by heavy rainfall and newsprint has to be kept dry at all costs.

Linerboard: A product in heavy demand for the packaging and carton manufacturing industries, is supplied mainly from North America, especially the US Gulf and the West Coast, also from Scandinavia.

Fertilisers

There can be little doubt of the importance of the various raw materials and finished products covered under this heading when you realises that twenty-five years ago India, with its massive population, was heavily reliant on the outside world for supplies of grain. It is now quite rare to see grains being imported into that nation, a circumstance brought about almost solely by the use of fertilisers. Similar improvements in agriculture through the use of fertilisers may be found in most developing countries.

The three main chemicals required for plant growth are *nitrogen, phosphate* and *potash*. All three occur naturally, but nitrogen is usually manufactured today as a by-process of the oil and chemical industries. Chile is the main source of nitrates and this natural commodity is still in demand because of its other constituents, such as iodine.

Sulphate of Ammonia and Ammonium Nitrate are examples of manufactured nitrates, and a valuable agent in their production is sulphuric acid, a product which also finds a use in a large number of other manufacturing processes. Although there are specialised molten-sulphur carriers and tankers capable of transporting sulphuric acid, by far the majority of sulphur is moved in dry-bulk state and converted into sulphuric acid "on-site".

Sulphur is obtained naturally in many parts of the world, particularly from Sicily (Gela) and from Western France (Bayonne), whilst the US Gulf was once a major exporter. Now, however, much sulphur is obtained as a by-product of the oil and gas industries and forms a major export from Western Canada, from Poland and Northern Germany, from Libya and Syria in the Mediterranean, and from the nations of the Arabian Gulf.

Some importers use it to up-grade their own products. For example, Morocco enhances the quality of its exploitation of vast natural phosphate deposits by using imported sulphur to manufacture stronger and more valuable Di-Ammonium (DAP) and Triple-Super Phosphate (TSP).

Phosphate is found all around the African coastal nations from Togo (Kpeme) in West Africa northwards via Senegal (Dakar) and Morocco (Casablanca, Jorf Lasfar, Safi), to Tunisia (Sfax and Gabes), the latter national also being engaged in the manufacture and export of Ammonium Nitrate.

Other prolific exporters of phosphate and its derivatives are Jordan (via Aqaba) and Egypt (El Hamrawein), certain of the Pacific Islands (eg. Christmas Island) and also the South Eastern United States (from the port of Tampa) which also exports upgraded material such as DAP and TSP. The USSR is also an exporter, via Murmansk (where it may be called apatite) and overland through Finland (where Russian mono-ammonium phosphate (MAP) may be exported via the port of Kokkola).

Potash can be shipped naturally (especially from Israel, Jordan and from Canada), or as manufactured potassium chloride.

All these fertilisers, whether natural or manufactured, need care in handling, although most can be carried in safety whether bagged or in bulk, giving rise to the oft-encountered expression "BHF" - "Bulk Harmless Fertilisers".

Part of the reassurance of the word 'harmless' dates back to the early days of transporting ammonium nitrate in bulk before such processes as 'calcining' this material had been perfected. Without this treatment, a large quantity of ammonium nitrate in bulk can, under certain conditions, become spontaneously explosive which was tragically proved when a US Gulf port was almost destroyed many years ago.

This problem is now so well understood that very many fertilisers are completely 'harmless' from the dangerous cargo point of view. However, the IMDG Code should always be referred to especially if more than one type is to be loaded because some otherwise harmless fertilisers are incompatible one with another.

Of course, Shipowners need to be aware of the non-dangerous harm that certain fertilisers can do. Some can have a damaging effect on the paintwork in the holds whilst others can cause severe corrosion to unprotected steel.

Steels

Under this heading is a considerable variety of cargoes, ranging from material such as bars, rods and beams, through to plate, coils and pipes.

As may seem obvious, steel products emanate mainly from the major industrialised nations both for cross-trading to others and for the developing nations. However, there is a major trade around semi-processed materials such as *pig-iron, concentrates, direct-reduced iron,* etc. wherein developing nations (eg. Brazil, Chile and Peru) have a role to play.

From the other end of manufacturing processes come scrap metals which also form an important seaborne commodity, the scrap being recycled in the steel industry and form relatively inexpensive ready material around which some steel industries have been developed.

The main scrap trade used to be concentrated on the US, Japan, Korea and Taiwan routes where electric furnaces for steel making were fed with scrap rather than ore. However the world demand for steel is such that in recent years many more countries are buying scrap steel for recycling.

The trade is not restricted to any particular vessel size and ships used range from small coasters to handy and handymax size vessels.

Minerals

Other than iron-ore and natural fertilisers, there are very many other minerals carried at sea, some forming an important volume trade. One such is bauxite, the staple constituent of the aluminium industry, the raw materials being exported in large quantities from West Africa (Guinea) and from Brazil in particular, to various aluminium smelters world-wide, eg. in Canada, Venezuela and the UK/Eire.

9.4   SHIPS FOR CARGOES

Dry-cargo vessels can be divided into various size and type categories, of which those of major importance are:

Capesize: These vessels (of around 100,000/200,000 tonnes dwt) are, of course, limited very much by port restrictions and they concentrate on cargoes of iron-ore or coal on long-haul runs, operating principally from loading areas in Australia, South Africa, Brazil, West Africa and the United States and Canada, discharging mainly in the Far East and Europe.

Not all vessels operating in this size category are pure dry-cargo vessels; many combination carriers, principally "VLOOs" (Very Large Ore-Oilers) transferring into the oil trades when the opportunity arises or out of the oil trade when freight levels are uninviting.

Panamax: These ships of around 60,000/80,000 dwt are arguably the new "workhorses" of the dry-cargo trades and many port facilities have been upgraded in recent years to accommodate ships of these dimensions.

This process is continuing (eg. Iraq's deepening of the channels to and from the ports of Khor Al Zubair and Umm Qasr to around 12 metres) and as it develops, so the range of commodities these vessels regularly engage in carrying can widen still further. Most Panamaxes are pure bulk carriers, although they have to compete with OBOs in the Atlantic when economic circumstances dictate, and the availability or otherwise of these "invaders" from the oil industry can have a profound effect upon the state of the dry-cargo market.

The main trades for Panamaxes are the "big three" of bulk coal, iron ore and grain, although Panamaxes may be found carrying other commodities, notably bulk phosphate, cassava from Thailand (along with capesize vessels), and bauxite. Thus these vessels will be found world-wide, although their market divides into various regions:

(a) The Atlantic Basin
(b) The Pacific/Indian Ocean Basin
(c) From Atlantic to Pacific/Indian
(d) From Pacific/Indian to Atlantic.

Of these it is usual to find the highest returns being paid for cargoes from the Atlantic to the Pacific/Indian Oceans with the lowest in the reverse direction, this imbalance created by normally higher freight levels for trans-Atlantic trades over trans-Pacific trades.

A major trade route comprises that of grain from the US Gulf to Japan and this rate is a major contributor to the freight futures market operated by BIFFEX (The Baltic International Freight Futures Exchange) and a ready barometer of the health of the dry-cargo market. In recent years freight rates have fluctuated from as low as US$10.00 up to US$73.00 per ton for this particular trade and this alone serves as a ready indicator of the volatility of the dry-cargo freight market, and for Panamax rates in particular.

Handy-Size: These are really two categories of "handy-sized" bulk carriers, those around 20/30,000 dwt and those between 30/55,000 dwt. The larger category emulates the trading pattern of Panamax bulkers, but adds to its list of carriageable commodities the major trade of steels and scrap, and forest products. As a result, many of these vessels are relatively sophisticated, with a variety of deck gear of up to around 25 tonne cranes, etc. The smaller vessels have an even wider range of commodities and are in especial demand for regions of the world with restricted dimensions, eg. the Great Lakes. There is no regular pattern for these smaller bulk carriers as can be identified for their larger competitors, and they tend to be found in all parts of the world engaged in the carriage of any number of commodities.

Around handy-sized bulk carriers what is termed "parcelling" has developed, and frequently operators will hire ships of this type and size to load various commodities in adjacent holds from a variety of nearby ports to another, general destination, eg. Australian minerals to Europe.

Tweendeckers: Most modern deep-sea tweendeckers range in size around 20,000 deadweight, although there are still very many vessels in this market of around 12/18,000 tonnes dwt. This latter fleet is generally ageing, however, and their modern counterparts are frequently better described as "multi-purpose" having the ability to fold tweendecks to convert to and compete with smaller bulk carriers. The modern versions of this category are in demand for liner traffic from the Far East and for the more sophisticated trades ex Europe, whilst the older versions are the true "tramps" of today's dry-cargo market, scouring the world's oceans for whatever profitable cargo is around, frequently engaged in the carriage of bagged fertilisers, grains and agricultural products and occasional bulk commodities, eg. sugar.

However, just as tweendeckers compete for the cargoes that might otherwise be the exclusive domain of smaller bulk carriers, so those bulkcarriers can be used for what were once considered exclusive tweendeck "liner" trades, as more and more of the liner trades that remain after the deprivations associated with containerisation develop more of a "parcelling" attitude to the services they advertise, for which bulk carriers are perfectly suitable.

Short Sea: Enterprising modern short sea owners are not necessarily restricting themselves to coastal trades, and it is not uncommon to find small vessels of less than 10,000 tonnes trading far afield from their normal operating area. In fact they provide a valuable alternative shipment means to parcelling for those shippers and traders seeking a more personal involvement in the carriage of their commodities. This process has been aided by a general move to ship smaller commodity parcels and by the removal of crewing restrictions by various governments. There is no reason why it should not become more common in the years ahead for smaller vessels to be found around the world in a purely "tramp" capacity, having been enticed away form their normal waters by an attractive freight.

9.5   TRADING RESTRICTIONS

Quite apart from the commercial aspects of marrying ship and cargo, those engaged in the dry cargo chartering market must bear in mind certain other factors which affect trade, namely:

(a)   Navigational
(b)   Political
(c)   Labour
(d)   Ports

Navigational Restrictions: Obviously, climatic influences affect trade and a clear example is that ice will interrupt voyages at certain times and seasons of the year. Thus seaborne trading to and from the Great Lakes of North America is not possible between January and March. Trading to the Northern Baltic is at the very least difficult during that period and voyages to and from the Hudson Bay are possible only between July and October each year.

There are many other hazards to be borne in mind, however, eg. Monsoons in certain areas at certain times, Hurricanes or Typhoons at others.

Close attention must also be paid to the route between loading and discharging port(s). Does it entail the crossing of load-line zones? Will these affect cargo intake? Does it entail expensive pilotage? Passing round an obstacle such as the Magellan Straits or Cape Horn, or navigating via a Canal? Has the cost and risk of this element in the voyage been calculated?

Major canals and waterways affecting dry cargo trades will be found to be:

Suez Canal
Panama Canal
St Lawrence Seaway/Great Lakes System
Magellan Straits/Cape Horn
Cape of Good Hope
Malacca/Lombok/Sunda Straits
Straits of Hormuz
Red Sea/Gulf of Aqaba-Eilat
Torres Straits/Great Barrier Reef
Kiel Canal/Skaw
Pentland Firth
Dover Straits/English Channel
Straits of Gibraltar
Dardanelles/Bosphorous

Consult your maritime atlas to familiarise yourself with the location of these places.

At the same time, locate the following landmarks used in dry cargo trading, particularly as delivery/redelivery positions in time charters:

Cape Passero (Sicily)
Cape Finisterre (N.W. Spain)
Ushant (France)
Dakar/Douala (West Africa)
Baton Rouge (River Mississippi)
Rosario, Santa Fe (Argentine)
Muscat (The Gulf)
Dondra Head (Sri Lanka)

Reference to the Port Information books will provide details of canal and waterway size restrictions also the equipment that needs to be fitted on a vessel before transit. Certainly vessels time chartered for either trip or period charters involving any of these canals or waterways should include clauses in which the Shipowners/operators confirm that the vessels reasonably conform to local requirements and have appropriate fittings. In the case of the

Panama and Suez Canal, include the Canal Gross and Nett Registered Tonnages which differ from the usual NRT and GRT and upon which transit tolls are based.

Political Restrictions: Most shipping people tend to have an "international" and a "commercial" view of the world and its events rather than a political one. Nevertheless, the ports of certain nations are not popular calling places, because of future repercussions affecting vessels and their owners/operators as a result of trading there. It is, therefore, common practice to list certain political exclusions in time charter parties and those engaged in voyage trading should also be especially careful in fixing cargoes to or from those nations.

Examples of areas that have been sensitive in recent years are:

Israel: Because of likely black-listing by Arab nations for future trading. As a result it is common practice for time charterers and for those engaged in voyage business involving Arab nations, to negotiate and to insert in charter parties an "Arab boycott clause", under which the Shipowner confirms that his vessel is not boycotted (blacklisted) by Arab nations as a result of previous visits to Israel.

Libya: Under Libyan law, all documents appertaining to ships and or cargoes must be translated into Arabic. Trading with Libya involves heavy extra costs for translations. Additionally, Libyan customs are likely to search vessels for any sign of goods or equipment involving nations (eg. Israel) of which they disapprove and, if such are discovered, impose heavy fines against the vessel. Consequently, Libya is not a popular calling place.

Cyprus ports under Turkish control: Greek flag ships have been prohibited by their Government from trading to those ports since the Turkish invasion of Cyprus some years ago. Similarly, the Greek Government is not willing to permit other nations' vessels to call at Greek ports after trading to Turkish-controlled Cyprus. As a direct consequence, Greek-flag ships are not always welcome to trade to Turkey itself and, although little official ruling is declared over this by the Turkish Government, it will be found that some Turkish-bound cargoes are not fixable in Greek tonnage. However, with Cyprus now a member of the EU and Turkey invited to enter negotiations for membership, it might be expected that this situation will soon change.

Cuba: The USA has relaxed its ban on vessels trading to Cuba, although Cuba is still mentioned in some charter parties as an exclusion "for vessels that have traded to Cuba since 1962....". The restriction is gradually being lifted since it is a relic of a bygone age, but it can still cause occasional problems.

North Korea: There are few signs remaining of countries actually boycotting North Korea but some owners are still reluctant to have their ships ordered there.

There are other ports where local problems of a political nature occur. In certain cases it may not be wise to have on board crew members of particular nationalities. Even the nationality of the eventual owners of a vessel may create problems despite the actual flag the vessel flies being acceptable. For example, Liberian flag ships and vessels owned by Liberian corporations are not welcome in Syria.

It is vital that those engaged in international trading keep abreast of the news and especially international news. There is little that is read about in daily newspapers that will not have at least an indirect effect on international shipping. This is especially so in political and in economic matters.

Also try to avoid being inadvertently impolite. If a nation renames a port, for example, it would be good manners to address communications to the new name. Hence "Saigon" is now known as "Ho Chi Minh City". Polish people prefer "Swinoujscie" to be so-named rather than the Germanic "Swinemunde". "Hamburg" and "Rostock" are now part of "Germany" not "West Germany" or "East Germany". Iranian people prefer the Gulf to be called the "Persian Gulf" rather than the "Arabian Gulf", whilst citizens of Bahrain would prefer the latter.

Labour restrictions: Also contained in the "trading exclusions clause" will be nations entered because of labour rather than political restrictive factors. Prominent among these are Australia and New Zealand (usually collectively termed as "Australasia") and "Scandinavia". (Be careful with this latter expression as some people consider that the term "Scandinavia" includes "Finland" and others (especially Finns) do not.

The reason for these exclusions is that the nations involved in these two areas (including Finland) are strongholds of the International Transport Workers' Federation, known as the "ITF". This is an international organisation set up to assist seamen to maintain wages and conditions at certain levels. The ITF demands that Shipowners internationally should comply with these restrictions but, in general, the ITF is concerned mainly with vessels flying so-called "flags of convenience" (eg. Panamanian or Liberian), as they allege that the conditions of the crews aboard such vessels is frequently below those standards set by the ITF.

In those nations listed above, the ITF (supported by local unions) may have the power to hold vessels until the wages and conditions are brought up to their requirements, including back-pay to which the crew may become entitled. For vessels flying some flags of convenience, Australasia, Scandinavia and Finland may be excluded.

Another stringent union requirement in Australasia and Finland, and in certain parts of Scandinavia, is that dry cargo vessels must be fitted with hold-ladders conforming to a certain style and dimensions, as defined by the Waterside Workers' Federation. These require that, for every six-metre drop in the ladder, a resting platform must be constructed. It is not always necessary providing that cargo compartments are completely clean and when loading bulk cargoes that can be "poured" into those compartments, for vessels to have ladders of that design.

However, if there is any problem with cargo holds and the workers are required to descend into the compartments, they will do so only if the ladders conform to the established design.

Port Restrictions: Once again reference to Port Information books is essential to gauge just what is involved in a prospective voyage. Many ports have "hidden" restrictions that are only discovered by appropriate reference. Douala (Cameroon) for example, is what is termed a "neap port", where tidal levels change dramatically every week or so, meaning that at certain times a vessel may be prevented from berthing for some days due to insufficient water. Safi (Morocco) has a harbour bar which, at times when Atlantic Ocean roller waves are predominant, means extreme difficulty for ships of certain drafts in entering the port. Particular berths in Genoa (Italy) have an air-draft restriction, not a physical restriction, but one nonetheless rigorously imposed by the port authorities because of the danger to aircraft overflying the port area to and from Genoa airport. Many ports on the west coast of South America are badly affected from time to time by steep waves causing wide ranging damage to ship and/or berth. In Butterworth (Malaysia) berthing priority is given to gas tankers, so much so that a partly discharged or loaded vessel may have to leave the berth to the gas tanker, returning only after the tanker has completed its cargo operations.

Port restrictions are not necessarily only dimensional. The hours that ships are "worked" by port labour, holidays, etc. all need consideration. BIMCO (The Baltic and International Maritime Council) publish an annual "Holiday Calendar" listing world-wide national and local holidays and port working hours, a valuable tool in any shipping office.

Port costs also vary widely. The charges in some ports are subsidised in order to attract business, whilst others have to be self-supporting and profitable. The costs vary enormously, often not only between adjacent countries, but between ports in the same country.

Let us take as an example a Panamax bulk carrier that might trade to various European countries and the approximate port charges that might be imposed assuming, or course, that exactly the same ship, flag and crew is involved:

	US$
Rotterdam	60,000
Hamburg	65,000
Bordeaux	80,000
Helsinki	170,000
Liverpool	160,000
Southampton	160,000
Port Talbot	65,000
Lisbon	15,000
Genoa	35,000

As can be seen there is quite a disparity. The secret, of course, of avoiding unpleasant surprises is to check before fixing. One means is from reference books, such as produced by BIMCO and others. Alternatively, and the means favoured by many in the industry, via a local port agent.

Apart from port costs, another charge that might be encountered is that of freight taxes. These can be extremely high, Syria imposes something like 13% of freight, Turkey not far behind at over 10%. These are imposed on the recipient of the freight, not the organisation paying, although it may be deducted at source by local law. To complicate matters, there are bilateral agreements between nations over the imposition of freight taxes so that not all Shipowners/operators are required to pay, or need to pay only a part of the total cost to the ships of "non-approved nations".

Most freight taxes are imposed against the vessel's flag, but some against the nation of the recipient of the freight, ie. perhaps a disponent owner in the case of a time chartered vessel.

As for port costs, forewarned is forearmed and allowance for this deduction can be included in the costing of the exercise when considering the business. BIMCO again publish a useful aid, an annual book on world-wide freight taxes and exemptions. Otherwise it is another message to the local port agent.

9.6   TIME

Time is vital to the work of a dry cargo shipbroker, whether working under time-constraints when negotiating charters; maintaining contact with, for example, principals, brokers or ship's Masters; calculating time charter duration; or establishing estimated dates of arrival of ships.

However, it is important to understand how time is "calculated".

On a global basis, "Time" can be said to start at the Greenwich Meridian, which passes close to central London and which is taken to be zero degrees or 0°. From this starting point, imaginary lines of longitude are drawn, westwards and eastwards, for 180° each making a total of 360° for a complete circumference of the globe. Therefore, if three hundred and sixty meridians (or lines of longitude) are drawn from pole to pole at equal intervals, they will be 1° of longitude apart. Starting from the Greenwich Meridian and travelling eastwards (towards India), time "advances" one hour for every 15° of longitude. A complete circle of the Earth coming back to the starting point of the Greenwich Meridian, will take 24 hours (i.e. 360 ÷ 15) and time will have "advanced" by 24 hours, or by one day. Westwards from Greenwich (towards the United States) will have the reverse effect. One hour will be lost for every 15° and upon returning to the Greenwich Meridian, one day will have been "lost".

Where those tracing eastwards and westwards passages meet "half way round" at the 180° meridian (in the central Pacific Ocean) is located the imaginary International Date Line (or "IDL") for short, which is not completely straight, taking minor deviations so as not to bisect small islands or affect land masses.

By travelling eastwards across the "eastern hemisphere" from the Greenwich Meridian, local time advances hour by hour until 180° East or the "IDL" is reached, at which stage one is 12 hours ahead of "Greenwich Mean Time" (GMT for short). Moving in the opposite direction from the Greenwich Meridian across the "western hemisphere", one "loses" 12 hours in reaching 180° west.

Consequently, the date is one day earlier to the east of the "IDL" than to the west and this, of course, affects vessels trading trans-Pacific. A ship proceeding eastwards from Japan towards the North American Continent will therefore "gain" one day upon crossing the IDL. A ship transmitting in the opposite direction will "lose" one day. It is important to take this into consideration when calculating estimated dates or arrival and cancelling dates involving voyages across the Pacific Ocean.

But wherever ships are in the world, if travelling generally eastwards or westwards, small time differences are eliminated by adjusting clocks and watches by one hour, either forwards or backwards, when passing from one time "zone" to another, these time zones being identified in the world map of any good atlas.

Most meridians are straight, but some, like the IDL are "bent" here and there so as to make all one country (or state in the USA) in the same zone.

So exactly how is dry cargo chartering affected by "time"?

Perhaps most importantly during chartering negotiations. Ignoring daylight saving schemes (such as the UK's "summer time", when time is advanced by one hour from GMT) when it is 1200 hours in London it is 0700 hours in New York and 2100 hours in Tokyo. In any of these centres a dry-cargo executive is in the middle of the working day when one of his counterparts is between breakfast and the office and another is thinking of going to bed.

There is, therefore, little point in making firm offers with reply times where there is little chance of principals being contactable. Cases of emergency are another matter and all shipping people tend to be prepared to sacrifice sleep and convenience at one time or another.

It is, of course, vital to state in firm offers not only what the offer expiry time is, but in whose time it is to be expressed. "Reply 1200 hours" could be misinterpreted. "Reply 1200 hours London time" is clear.

More easily overlooked can be the time factor affecting time charter deliveries and redeliveries. Let us assume that a vessel delivers on time charter in London for a trip to Bombay, where she will redeliver. Let us also assume that the voyage will take exactly 30 days (720 hours) and the daily hire rate of the vessel is US$9,000.

If the time charter party stipulates that delivery and redelivery are to be calculated in 'local' time, the effect would be that the vessel will remain 'on hire' for some five hours in excess of the actual time taken and this can be of benefit to a vessel's owners, who will undoubtedly claim extra hire of US$1,875 for those five hours. On the other hand, a vessel proceeding on the same terms in the reverse direction will 'lose' five hours of hire, an advantage, therefore, to her time charterers.

Those interested in equity will doubtless ask why a time charterer should pay more hire than for the period a ship actually spends on time charter, or a Shipowner receive less than the time a ship is hired out. In this they would echo current English Law on the subject, which has established the principle of "elapsed time" perhaps more easily understood by most of us as "stop-watch time".

To understand elapsed time, it has to be assumed that a stop-watch is started the moment a ship delivers and time runs continuously (less any off-hire periods) until it is halted upon redelivery. The time that has accumulated is the 'elapsed time' and is the legal period on hire, unless the parties have specifically agreed in their contract to be bound by local times for delivery and/or re-delivery.

Another way of achieving a time charter period based on elapsed or stop-watch time is to apply a 'standard' to delivery and re-delivery, such as GMT. The important thing is to specify in a time charter party whether local time or GMT is to apply to delivery and redelivery times. If the charter party remains silent on this aspect, in the event of a legal dispute the result depends on the legal code which applies to the contract, and there can be varying results. A recent American arbitrator, for example, found that in the event of silence in the charter party, local time would be deemed to apply. English Law, as explained above, would specify actual 'elapsed' time, or time established by a common standard such as GMT at both ends of a time charter.

9.7 SALINITY

Shipping executives should be able to understand how salinity calculations are performed as they may expect to encounter ports where the cargo intake needs to be calculated, and where the prevailing water may be salt, fresh or brackish (a mixture of both). As you know, a vessel in fresh water will be deeper drafted than if she were in more buoyant salt water. Salinity affects many trades, for example the Panama Canal is a freshwater canal, and the available draft so expressed.

Fortunately, the calculation is relatively simple, given the "freshwater allowance" (FWA) of a vessel, usually shown on the ship's capacity plan and the density of the prevailing water in the port or canal (obtainable from port information books or from the local port agent).

Assuming, for example, that the vessel's FWA is 200 mm and the brackish water density is 1015 kg/m³, the application of the following formula provides:

$$\frac{FWA \times (\text{Density of Sea Water} - \text{Density of Brackish Water})}{\text{Density of Sea Water} - \text{Density of Fresh Water}}$$

$$\text{Therefore: Increased Draft} = \frac{200 \text{ mm} \times (1025 - 1015)}{1025 - 1000}$$

$$\text{Therefore: Increased Draft} = \frac{200 \text{ mm} \times 10}{25}$$

$$\text{Therefore: Increased Draft} = \frac{2000}{25}$$

$$= 80 \text{ mm}$$

9.8 SELF-ASSESSMENT AND TEST QUESTIONS

Attempt the following and check your answers from the text:

1. Using your atlas, locate:

    i)   Cape Passero,
    ii)   Skaw,
    iii)   Torres Straits,
    iv)   Dardanelles

2. The following ports all have certain restrictions which should be taken into account when contemplating fixing vessels to them. What are they?

    Buenaventura
    Toledo
    Calcutta
    Bangkok
    Churchill

3. What is the maximum draft in the St. Lawrence Seaway?

4. What is the "new" Chinese name for the Port of Whampoa?

5. What is the "new" Burmese name for the port of Rangoon?

6. What is the "old" name for the port of Ho Chi Minh City?

7. If it is Monday noon in Tokyo what day/time is it in New York?

8. How many degrees of longitude represent one hour gained (or lost)?

Having completed Chapter Nine attempt the following and submit your essay to your Tutor:

The m.v. *"Whimbrel"*, a Lakes fitted, geared bulk carrier, performs the following loaded voyages:

HOLLAND	–	GREAT LAKES
GREAT LAKES	–	VENEZUELA
U.S. GULF	–	W.C. MEXICO
U.S. WEST COAST	–	JAPAN
JAPAN	–	GERMANY

State the number of days the vessel would reasonably take to perform each laden voyage and ballast leg; give the name of one loading and one discharging port in each area; state a probable cargo and cargo size, (each cargo must be different) that the vessel could load on each voyage and suggest suitable bunkering ports.

Chapter 10

DISPUTES AND PROFESSIONAL INDEMNITY

10.1 INTRODUCTION

It is inevitable that there will be disagreements between contracting partners from time-to-time, although most differences will be settled amicably and with a minimum of trouble and expense. A few disputes, though, will cause much more difficulty and it may be that outsiders well versed in commercial law will need to be called in to provide independent settlement.

In such cases it is important to establish the legal code that will apply, since laws vary from place-to-place, and different decisions might be reached on the same set of circumstances depending on the jurisdiction that is to apply. We have seen from earlier Chapter material how the place of residence of the contracting parties, the place where the contract was "made", or specific reference to a particular place or applicable law may each have a bearing on where a dispute should be considered, debated and settled.

Consequently, it is advisable to specify in a charter party or other shipping contract the legal code that is applicable for the reference of any disputes that may arise, e.g: "English Law to apply", and to spell out the format of any legal hearing, i.e. whether disputes are to be referred to Court or, as it almost always the preference of those engaged in shipping contracts, to Maritime Arbitration.

Much of international shipping is conducted in the English language and, given the long history of deep sea trading during the formulative years of commercial shipping over recent centuries by the British nation, it follows that a wide ranging and adaptable commercial legal code has evolved which many citizens of the world of non-British background select in time of dispute. Thus it is quite common to find, for example, a Greek Shipowner and a Japanese Charterer resolving a dry cargo charter party dispute before a London Arbitration based, of course, on English law. Equally, might a South American Cargo Receiver and a Scandinavian Ship Operator have a dispute heard before a judge in the English Commercial Court.

That is not to say that other codes do not find international favour, and there are important arbitration centres in New York (The Society of Marine Arbitrators) and in Paris (the arbitration facilities of the International Chamber of Commerce), although by far the largest number of shipping disputes are conducted in London under the terms of English law.

Accordingly, there have grown up in London the Head Offices of numerous P&I Clubs; the London Maritime Arbitrators Association, and a large number of lawyers specialising in shipping disputes. Consequently, companies and individuals from the world over look to London and to English law for guidance on the drafting of shipping contracts and for resolving disputes thereunder.

Mention should be made of two specific documents that have been drafted to help interpret some of the more common causes of disputes under charter parties. The VOYLAY rules have already been mentioned in Chapter Six as an aid in cutting through the confusion that surrounds the perennial problem of laytime calculating.

FONASBA has produced the Time Charter Interpretation Code 2000 **(Appendix 41)** which is a similar attempt to remove the mystery of some common areas of dispute in time charters. Unlike the Voylay rules, it does not concern itself with one topic but covers a number of different areas.

The English Courts. A shipping dispute that is to be resolved in the English Courts would be referred to a judge in the Commercial Court in the first instance, the Commercial Court being part of the Queen's Bench Division of the High Court, in London. Many times the dispute will end with judgement at that stage, although it may be possible to appeal against the verdict to the decision of a panel of judges sitting in the Court of Appeal and, similarly, against their judgement, to the highest Court in England, the House of Lords. All this is expensive and likely to be time consuming however, as a consequence of which, most parties selecting English law opt in their contract for any disputes to be referred to Maritime Arbitration in London.

English Maritime Arbitration. Although the practice of shipping arbitration is not restricted to its members, most active London-based maritime arbitrators are full members of the London Maritime Arbitrators Association, an association presently numbering around fifty maritime arbitrators. Their backgrounds are extremely diverse and, to place the significance of this organisation into perspective, its members between them publish around 500 "awards" annually, receiving around 4000 "appointments" each year, probably more than all other maritime arbitration centres added together. These disputes cover a wide range of subjects, including charter party, Bill of Lading, sale and purchase, ship operation, shipbuilding, commodity and oil trading contracts.

Whereas in some jurisdictions arbitrators may in effect be able substantially to disregard any system of law, LMAA members (and other English arbitrators) are bound to and consistently apply English commercial and maritime law. As we have seen, this code of law is now so highly developed as to be widely regarded and applied as if it were the international law of commerce and shipping. It continues to develop in order to meet changing needs largely due to the possibility of appealing from decisions, "awards", of arbitrators, mainly in those cases where commercial public interest is involved. Under the English Arbitration Act, 1950, as amended by the Arbitration Act, 1979, appeals are restricted, but those that are granted are heard in the Commercial Court (see above) whose judges have great experience in commercial and maritime arbitration, a factor that often facilitates equitable compromise in disputes of this nature.

The idea of *"arbitration"* was originally conceived as a distinctly non-legal method of solving disputes and the arbitrators preferred and chosen were men with a commercial background rather than with legal qualifications. It was thought that they would lend a fairer and less 'straight-laced' mind to the disputes on hand and interpret the provisions of the relevant charter party or other commercial agreement without being strictly concerned with the legal niceties and sheer accuracy or non-accuracy of the language used in the charter party wording. One of the best known of all arbitration clauses, the Centrocon Arbitration Clause, requires the appointment of men "engaged in the shipping and/or grain trades" and who are "Members of the Baltic Exchange", and, of course, where the charter party is peculiar to a particular trade, this is a most reasonable and logical stipulation. Nevertheless, over the years, some might say inevitably, the procedure of arbitration has gradually assumed a legal flavour.

When a charter party calls for each party to appoint their own arbitrator (and if they are unable to agree, an *"umpire"* to be mutually appointed), it might be thought that there is a tendency towards the arbitrators being advocates for their appointers. This, however, is a misconceived idea since an arbitrator is a private judge ruling impartially between the parties whether sitting as sole arbitrator or as member of a larger tribunal.

However, the formality of the concept of arbitration must not be underestimated. Though it may have been intended originally to have a non-legal flavour, it must nevertheless retain something of the judicial since it is after all an alternative, in fact the only alternative in the absence of an amicable solution between the parties themselves, to court proceedings. Although the agreement to arbitrate any dispute may originally be an oral agreement between the contracting parties it is usual and advisable for the agreement to be contained in writing either as an express clause in the charter party contract (see Multiform Clause 30 and NYPE Clause 17) though it is unlikely that a court of law would grant a stay of proceedings in favour of arbitration.

Such arbitration clauses can, and frequently do, contain a time limit within which appointments of arbitrators should be made and the leading case of the 'Ion' (1971 1 Lloyds 541) provides a court ruling as to what happens when an arbitration clause provision of three months time limit (Centrocon) conflicts with the twelve month (Clause Paramount - Hague Rules) provisions which applied to the same contract. The Hague Rules limitation period prevailed.

Whether an arbitration clause in a charter party can be binding upon the innocent holder of a bill of lading issued pursuant to a charter party is dependent entirely upon the incorporating words in the Bill of Lading, which, if sufficiently comprehensive, could entitle a shipowner/carrier to compel a Bill of Lading holder to arbitration under an arbitration agreement (or *vice versa).*

An arbitration agreement to be binding and to have the protection afforded by the United Kingdom's Arbitration Acts, 1950 and 1979, must be in writing and should be explicit in its terms. So a charter party clause with wording such as "Arbitration, if any, to be held in New York" is not a binding agreement to arbitrate. It merely agrees to arbitrate in a certain named place if there is agreement to arbitrate at all, a very different thing. An agreement to arbitrate, being contractual in nature, must for this reason be precise, unambiguous and clear in its terms and wording. The United Kingdom Act gives a definition of an arbitration agreement as a "written agreement to submit present or future differences to arbitration, whether an arbitrator is named or not". How wide in scope the agreement to arbitrate is, depends again on the actual wording of the clause. If it contains such words as "all matters in difference" the scope is of course extremely comprehensive, but the more commonly used wording in maritime contracts, "disputes arising out of the contract", would by its 'face value' sense exclude a dispute as to whether the contract was ever entered into in the first place.

The inclusion of an arbitration agreement in a charter party does not automatically exclude the jurisdiction of a Court of Law to try disputes. Despite being a party to an arbitration agreement an aggrieved party in a charter party agreement is not barred from taking legal action through the machinery of the law. What occurs in such a situation is that the Court has a discretionary power to decide whether it will "stay" proceedings in favour of arbitration or whether it will try the issue.

It should be remembered that even if the Court stays proceedings in favour of arbitration, their intervention may become inevitable as a means of enforcing any arbitration award that may eventually be made, or alternatively to set aside an award when there may have been misconduct of an arbitrator or umpire or the award has been for some reason "improperly secured", or simply there has been an "error on the face of the award". To elaborate on this last phrase an error of *law* on the face of the award has been described as some legal proposition contained in the award, or documents incorporated into it, which is the basis of the award and which can be said to be erroneous. The error, however, must appear on the face of the award otherwise the Courts have no discretionary power to set aside.

Who may be appointed an arbitrator? Certainly not a madman, an idiot, an infant or an outlaw. These are recognised disabilities. An 'able' arbitrator is a person of 'sufficient skill' in the matter under dispute and is not impeded 'legally or naturally' from giving good sound judgement. The category of persons may be limited and defined as indeed it is in the Centrocon Arbitration clause where the idea is to appoint persons versed in the shipping and/or grain trades. It is important, naturally to be impartial and have no bias, interest or leaning towards one or the other party. This is a ground for disqualification. If, of necessity, an arbitrator becomes a witness in the arbitration, this is also ground for disqualification.

The procedure to be followed in arbitration proceedings in chronological order is as follows. First, the arbitrator(s) must be appointed by the parties to the dispute and accept the appointment. Secondly the arbitrator(s) may wish to meet with the parties to the dispute informally prior to an official hearing. Thirdly, the matter goes to a hearing, the time and place being the choice of the arbitrator(s) unless otherwise specified. Alternatively, if the parties choose, the matter may be resolved on **'documents alone'.**

Each party's counsel may be present at a hearing, at their option, provided sufficient notice is given to the opposing party. All evidence must be fully heard and the arbitrators have absolute right to decide whether evidence is admissible or not. Great care should be exercised since the wrong admission of evidence could be such a fundamental mistake as to lead eventually to the setting aside of the arbitration award. After conclusion of the hearing the arbitrators must prepare the 'Award' which is the document containing their decision. The award is final and for this reason must be clear, unambiguous and decisive.

The referring of a dispute to arbitrators is known technically as the **'reference'.** Distinction should be made between the **'costs'** of the reference and the **'costs'** of the award. Basically, these are in the discretion of the arbitrators. The costs of the reference include all those general and special expenses incurred in the course of enquiries either by the parties or by their legal advisers. The costs of the award are the remuneration and expenses due to the arbitrator and which he has a right to demand as a condition precedent to his delivering his award. The usual rule regarding costs is that they 'follow the event'. That is to say that the party which is unsuccessful bears all the costs. The arbitrator may, however, in his discretion vary this and may, for example, direct that each party bears his own costs (i.e. his own costs of the reference) and half the costs of the award.

The 1979 Act abolished the 'case stated' procedure originally introduced by Section 21 of the 1950 Act. In sweeping away this procedure the new Act also removed the right to have an arbitration award set aside because of an error of fact or of law on the face of the award. This was a long standing right under the Common Law. It was due to the strength of this right that Maritime Arbitrators have traditionally given the **'reasons'** for their award in a separate document for the information of the parties, not to be considered as an official part of the award itself.

The new Act introduced a new procedure of Appeal exclusively concerned with an error in law. To some extent also there is still limited latitude given to an Arbitrator or either of the parties, if, during the course of the arbitration proceeding a difficult question of law arises, to apply to the High Court for an answer. The question, however, must be of real importance substantially affecting the rights of one or both parties and one which "might potentially mean substantial saving on the parties' costs".

When the Act first became effective it was thought generally that an appeal from an award would be the exception rather than the rule but it soon became apparent that it was the other way round. Losing parties rushed to appeal. The result of this was that it has now become difficult to get leave to appeal. The vast majority of applications have been turned down. It is important, therefore, to regard the Arbitrators as the final arbiters (particularly so if the parties jointly expressed their wishes to that effect in the wording of the arbitration agreement), unless the findings were so obviously wrong that, in the interests of justice they have to be corrected. For a judge to reverse the decision of an arbitrator on purely technical points of little significance to the real issues, was not what the drafters of the legislation had in mind. One guideline suggested was that if, for example, the charter party clause in dispute was a 'one-off contract which was unlikely to arise again, leave to appeal should be denied unless the arbitrator was so obviously wrong in his decision that it would be inequitable not to disturb his award.

One section of the 1950 Act which has remained unaffected by the 1979 Act, allows relief in certain circumstances when one party has strictly raised against the other the time bar, due to the failure by the other party to appoint his arbitrator within the time allowed (perhaps this is a feature of what Lord Denning meant when he said the law was about justice and not strictness). If to stand firm on the time bar would cause the other party undue hardship, then the Court is empowered to extend the time at its discretion. In the VIRGO case (1978 2 Lloyds) the Court of Appeal said that it would be quite wrong if shipowner/his P&I Club, could profit from their own laxness/inactivity during investigation of a claim, by 'leaping in and screaming time bar'. The time bar cannot be applied absolutely and strictly if to do so would result in undue hardship, whether the time bar itself is regarded as totally extinguishing the claim or as merely barring the remedy.

Can an Arbitrator award *interest?* Yes, he is cloaked with the same authority as any commercial judge and is given ample discretion, provided that it is just and equitable to do so.

Interest is in effect compensation for a person who is being kept from his money. What should be the interest rate? Should it be the lending or the borrowing rate? i.e. should the party be compensated because he has had to borrow money to meet a commitment which he would not have had to borrow had he been timely paid the capital sum due to him or because he has been robbed of the opportunity to timely invest the capital sum due to him and thus earn interest? One view has been that a suitable rate of interest should be the minimum lending rate plus 1% to arrive at a reasonable borrowing rate *(Wallersteiner v Moir- 1975 IQB 373)*.

Note particularly the *Tehno Impex* case (1981 1 Lloyds) which confirms that the Arbitrator's discretionary power in relation to awarding interest includes even situations where the principal sum has actually been paid before or after the arbitration has been commenced or before or after the award has been made. I seems that Arbitrators have power to award interest where, for example the respondent has paid up only at the 'eleventh hour' before the award was made.

Any doubt as to the correct rate of interest should be resolved in the light of any factors relevant to the currency in which the award itself is made.

In many ways, arbitrators are even more qualified than judges to award interest, since arbitrators are commercially minded men and what is more commercially orientated than the concept of interest?

The practice and procedures for maritime arbitration in London have become highly developed and have been codified into the "LMAA Terms", the latest version in 1987 particularly encouraging speed and early hearings, the power of arbitrators to order the provision of security for costs, and to order rectification of a contract in certain circumstances.

There is now also a codified *small claims procedure* to simplify smaller cases, and which limits costs to a fixed, modest sum, whilst conciliation and mediation procedures are also possible.

It may also be useful to note that the LMAA recommends a particular arbitration clause for insertion into contracts, and this is reproduced in **Appendix 40**.

The LMAA Clause does not refer to the small claims procedure, but parties to shipping contracts are not precluded from adding an extra sentence to their arbitration clause, such as:

> "Notwithstanding the above conditions, all disputes up to a value of $25,000 are to be dealt with under the terms and conditions of the LMAA Small Claims procedure, 1989",

10.2 PROTECTION AND INDEMNITY ASSOCIATIONS (P&I CLUBS)

Much has been mentioned about P&I Clubs in various chapters in this text, and the activities of these organisations permeate almost every section of the dry cargo shipping industry. But what exactly are they?

There are several types of Club, although by far the largest and financially strongest sector are Shipowners' Protection and Indemnity Associations, mutual and non-profit making organisations which provide insurance cover for shipowners and operators which is complementary to the insurance cover placed on the insurance market, and which was discussed briefly in Chapter Eight. Although there is no precise dividing line between the cover afforded by insurance companies and that provided by P&I Clubs (in fact pandi insurance [pandi = P&I] is also available to a limited degree from the insurance market, whilst Clubs traditionally provide one quarter of a Shipowner's collision insurance liability), in general terms it might be said that Lloyds underwriters and insurance companies insure ships and cargoes, whilst shipowners P&I Clubs insure their liabilities.

For the most part, P&I clubs are mutual associations where the members are both the insured and the insurer. This means that the members must each contribute to a level sufficient to ensure that all claims against all members can be satisfied. Clubs are run on a non-profit basis. There are also some commercial companies that offer P&I cover on a fixed premium basis.

Two of the factors which contributed to the formation of Shipowners' P&I Clubs were the additional risks which Shipowners had to assume following the almost universal acceptance of the Hague Rules (which we also learned about in Chapter Eight), and the reluctance of underwriters to accept more than three-quarters of an Owner's liability for damage done to another ship in a collision (British). In other parts of the world, there has not been this reluctance and so the P&I clubs in those areas – Scandinavia is a good example – do not offer the extra hull insurance as it is not needed. Accordingly Owners associated together on a mutual basis, forming the directing boards of the Clubs, whose managers are mostly professional legal partnerships with legal experience. Subscriptions (or 'calls') are made annually based on the tonnage entered and on the record of the party involved. A high claims record should mean that the calls will be levied at a higher rate than for an entered owner with a low claims record. If forecasted claims are higher than expected, supplementary calls will need to be levied to enable the Club to pay its way.

'Protection' would deal with matters such as: one quarter of Owner's collision liability, personal injury, crew liabilities, damage to piers, and removal of wrecks.

'Indemnity' would involve: loss of or damage to cargo; a ship's proportion of General Average; and customs' fines.

A third section of cover: 'Freight, Demurrage and Defence', would be concerned with the enforcement of legal proceedings for collection of freight and hire; conduct of actions and arbitrations, and general legal advice to members.

Some Shipowners' Clubs seek to attract Charterers and Operators as members whilst specialised Charterers P&I Clubs exist to provide a range of services for charterers such as cover for costs and expenses incurred in asserting or defending court actions or arbitrations (i.e. Defence cover) and indemnity for liabilities towards Shipowners, disponent Owners and cargo Owners under voyage and time charter parties (i.e. Liability cover).

The third Club type: Professional Indemnity Insurance, exists for the benefit of Shipbrokers and Agents, providing services for members acting in the exercise of their profession as Agents in chartering, sale and purchase of ships, port agency, freight forwarding, liner agency, travel agency, airbroking, bunker broking and ship management. This cover is available from one specialist club, based in London, the International Transport Intermediaries Club (ITIC), brought about by the merger of the Transport Intermediaries Mutual (TIM) and Chartered and International Ship Brokers and Agents Club (CISBA).

The cover is designed to assist in the recovery of brokerages and port disbursements, and indemnifies members against errors, omissions and negligence, including breach of warranty of authority, a subject discussed in detail earlier in this publication. Somewhat similar cover may be obtained on the Lloyds market and from a few insurance companies.

In their 'Non Mandatory Rules for Shipping Agents' UNCTAD require an appropriate level of liability insurance whilst it is mandatory for Members of the Baltic Exchange and for Company Members of the Institute of Chartered Shipbrokers to have satisfactory "professional indemnity" insurance cover.

10.3 UNKNOWN CHARTERERS AND OWNERS

By far the majority of Charterers, Operators, Shipowners, Brokers and Agents are honest, although in most cases shrewd and keen to take the maximum advantage of trading opportunities. In fact, the functioning of this most complex of markets depends to a great extent upon mutual trust.

Consequently, an unscrupulous trader or Shipowner does have the opportunity to exploit the trust of others (albeit briefly). It is therefore imperative that Shipowners encountering previously unknown Charterers and Charterers uncertain about the credentials of a new Shipowner, should investigate the others' background.

Can the newcomer provide a bank reference and/or guarantee before completing business? Are others who have conducted business with them before prepared to offer a recommendation?

Have they come to the notice of bodies such as BIMCO, The Baltic Exchange, or the International Maritime Bureau (the branch of the International Chamber of Commerce, dealing with unscrupulous activities)? What has 'market gossip' to say about them?

10.4 PROFESSIONAL SURVIVAL

Shipping can be a lot of fun and an entertaining career. But it can also be commercially dangerous. It is essential to learn from experience, to arm yourself with knowledge, and to develop guile and ability, at the same time gaining a reputation for integrity. If all this can be allied to obtaining a professional qualification, such as that offered by the Institute of Chartered Shipbrokers, so much the better.

All this may seem a tall order. But like any other objective it needs to be analysed and a means of achieving these aims planned out; that done, it will not appear an unattainable goal.

Firstly you need to acquire knowledge, not only of day-to-day market events but also of more basic data. A good start in this direction will be membership of various bodies, either individually or as an employee of a corporate entity. Valuable shipping organisations involved in dry cargo shipping include:

1. The Baltic Exchange (open now to "associates" who do not necessarily attend daily and who may be resident outside the UK).

2. Institute of Chartered Shipbrokers – both individual and corporate, the former through examination and leading to fellowship status which qualifies the individual to be termed a "Chartered Shipbroker".

3. The Baltic International Maritime Council – open to shipping organisations and providing valuable expertise and facilities to the international shipping community.

4. International Maritime Bureau – one of shipping's 'police' forces, there to protect its members from dealing with less desirable corporations and individuals.

5. P&I Clubs – an essential for Owners and Charterers alike, although it is surprising how many Charterers still carry on without the protection of a P&I Club behind them.

6. Professional Indemnity Club – becoming more and more essential for such as Brokers and ship Managers.

Secondly, despite a possibly busy work schedule, time should always be found to be as wide read as possible. Apart from reading your local shipping press (such as Lloyd's List in the UK), it is important also to keep up-to-date with both industrial and international news in order to be prepared for its impact upon the shipping world.

In addition, build up a personal and/or a corporate library of such textbooks that are directly relevant to your business activities, always keeping alert for new books or new editions of existing ones.

Some of the organisations listed above (e.g. BIMCO) publish regular magazines as part of their membership whilst others (e.g. Lloyd's of London Press) issue periodical reports on maritime affairs such as current law cases.

All of this, however, is of little protection if great care is not exercised in daily trading and especially in the drafting of contracts. Here the charter party library referred to earlier in this text will assist but there is little substitute for experience and for having the ability to incorporate what has been learned from knowledge, experience and wide reading into adapted contract clauses.

Finally, it helps greatly to operate in an efficient, encouraging environment, bringing us to the important topic of office organisation.

10.5 OFFICE ORGANISATION

There are some offices with low overheads which regularly produce a high income and turnover with limited staff numbers. On the other hand, there are over-staffed organisations, which perform badly. It is not that staff in either group work particularly harder than in the other, although personal motivation is an important factor. The main difference comes down to 'organisation'.

In the dry cargo market with its variety of 'players' ranging from Shipowners to Charterers, from Traders to Operators, and from Brokers to Agents, different sectors require different organisation techniques. Consequently, it is difficult here to do more than to generalise, except to mention that with computerisation, many of the labour and time demanding tasks can now be tackled far more effectively. It should therefore be an essential duty of anyone given the responsibility for office administration to consider carefully and regularly how essential activities may be better performed, at the same time giving staff an interesting and responsible opportunity to contribute to the overall aims of the company.

For Shipowners, office personnel numbers can be related to the number of vessel units at sea in order to assess whether or not administration staff is being kept to reasonable proportions. Obviously, with a small fleet of, say, less than five ships, office personnel per vessel will probably be at a higher ratio than is necessary for a larger fleet.

With a large fleet it is possible that effective control from the very top of the organisation may be weakened unless stringent reporting procedures are laid down and adhered to. One way of exercising effective control is to create teams of administrators operating individual "fleets" within the whole, thereby doing away with departmentalisation that would otherwise be required and which tends to create unnecessary rivalries, rather than to build up a more healthy, competition amongst internal "fleets", which is to be encouraged.

Whether departmentalised or divided into fleet units the activities which need adequate coverage mirror ship-management duties, such as operations, chartering, port captaincy, technical, insurance, storing and provisioning, and accountancy.

The size of a *shipbroker's* organisation depends on the number of clients they service, be they Charterers, Operators or Shipowners. The more clients, the more Brokers. The more Brokers the more back-up staff such as those engaged in post-fixture and accountancy roles.

The introduction of desktop personal computers in shipbroking has largely eliminated secretarial assistance in the more technically advanced Shipbrokers' offices but there are still two major areas of difficulty tending to prevent a truly thorough computerised system. The first is the difficulty of preparing charter parties, nearly all forms being based on paper of odd dimensions and in old-fashioned printed text that is frequently amended during negotiations, calling for accuracy of precise deletions and insertions when drafting.

Secondly, although the facsimile machine and efficient courier services have reduced if not entirely eliminated the necessity for junior staff to spend much time running errands outside Shipbrokers' offices, those office juniors still employed find more and more of their time spent "feeding" computers with tonnage position data, including ship characteristics, whereabouts and availability, all designed to speed the identification of potentially suitable vessels for Charterers seeking tonnage.

It would seem that a central bureau to whom Shipowners could pass details of available tonnage and from whom enlisting Shipbrokers could extract appropriate data would be the answer to this problem. This, however, overlooks the demand for secrecy, both from Owners who wish to disguise from the general market the availability of some or all of their ships, and secondly from the more efficient Brokers who do not wish to give away their advantage. In fact, the last thing that any Shipbroker wants is for Charterers and Owners to communicate directly, as this will reduce demand for Shipbroking services.

The administration of a *Charterer's* office depends very much on the size and type of Charterer. What many shipping personnel tend to overlook, however, is that a ship chartering department of a Charterer may be a very small and perhaps insignificant part of the organisation as a whole. In many such organisations the major role is in marketing their products. With steel works, for example, the supply of a power source such as coal, important though it may be to the well being of the company, may rank very low in order of corporate priority. Similarly with traders, where the lion's share of profits is to be made in successful buying and selling of products rather than in shipment activities.

Some such companies recognise the need to be efficient in chartering as in all other corporate activities and hire talented and effective staff to perform these duties. Others, however, rely heavily on outside Shipbroking expertise. The former will obviously tend to be more highly staffed than the latter.

10.6 PUTTING YOUR KNOWLEDGE INTO EFFECT

It is continually surprising that for such a professional and long established activity as international shipping, contract clauses are frequently poorly drafted and open to various interpretations.

1.   The time charter example:

"This time charter is for eighteen months, with Charterers' option of a further twelve months, to be declared minimum three months prior expiration of first period. Plus or minus one month in Charterers' option on final period".

It is clear that no later than fifteen months into the charter party period the Charterer has to declare whether the option to extend the charter by a further twelve months is to be exercised or not. It is also clear that, having declared that option, the Charterer can redeliver the vessel somewhere between 29 and 31 months after delivery onto time charter.

What is not clear is what happens if the Charterers do not declare the extension option. It is almost impossible to redeliver a vessel after exactly eighteen months, unless the vessel is kept idle for some time following completion of her discharge immediately previous to the expiration of eighteen months. This might mean leaving the vessel idle for some days, if not weeks. Yet on the face of it that is what the clause requires the Charterers to do. There is no 'one month more or less' to be applied to the straight eighteen months period. This may be legally implied. Equally it may not. It is an example of a poorly drafted clause.

2.   The voyage charter example:

"The cargo to be loaded at Pusan (South Korea) and discharged at Bangkok and Port Kelang".

The Charterers ordered the vessel first to Port Kelang and then to Bangkok to discharge, lightening at Port Kelang down to Bangkok draft. The Owners insisted on discharging first at Bangkok (lightening locally at Kohsichang) and then completing at Port Kelang, because this would save them extra steaming and bunker consumption.

Study the atlas and you will see what the argument was all about.

No mention was made in the charter party of discharging in geographic rotation, nor was there any clause making discharge port rotation in Charterers' or in Owner' option.

There is apparently no legal precedent in English Law which indicates who was right or wrong, but advice ranged from discharging in the order as shown in the charter party (but if this was so what would the Owner say if discharge was to be at Bangkok and Bombay, and Bombay was first mentioned?) to reference to standard textbooks which refer to the "reasonable, direct route". Is it "reasonable" to allow for lightening at Bangkok or to disregard this?
Another example of a poorly worded clause!

Wrong contract choice

With so many forms and contract choices available it is not surprising that sometimes ill-advised marriages of terms and clauses arise as well as attempts to mix items from totally different types of contracts.

In February 2003 an interesting case referred to as the *Jordan II* was heard in the UK Court of Appeal and decided in the Owner's favour. Since there is the possibility that this case may go to the House of Lords the final outcome may yet be changed.

The case revolves around some damage caused to a steel cargo because of poor stowage. The Bill of Lading incorporated the **Hague-Visby Rules, which, according to Article III Rule 2 states:** "The carrier shall properly and carefully load, handle, stow, carry, keep, care for, and discharge the goods carried".

Rule 8: "Any ... agreement in a contract of carriage relieving the carrier or ship from liability for loss or damage ... arising from negligence, fault or failure in the ... obligations provided in this Article... shall be null and void..."

Although the cargo was steel products the parties had chosen to use the **Stemmor 1983 form of voyage charter:** which stated:

Clause 3. Freight to be paid at ... $3.3 per metric ton. F.I.O.S.T. – lashed/secured/ dunnaged..."

Clause 17. Shippers/Charterers/receivers to put the cargo onboard, trim and discharge cargo free of expense to vessel..."

Last year a deputy High Court Judge, Nigel Teare QC, held that neither the Shipper or Receiver of a steel cargo, nor the voyage Charterer, were entitled to sue the *Jordan II's* Owner for alleged damage due to poor stowing and handling. Applying the 1954 precedent of *Pyrene v Scindia,* he ruled that Article III rule 2 of the Hague-Visby (formerly Hague) Rules which requires 'proper performance' of loading, stowing and carriage by the carrier, only applies if he had agreed to undertake those functions. The appeal court unanimously upheld that decision.

The Courts were asked for a preliminary ruling in principle, in advance of the main claim. If the parties had agreed the Charterer would pay for the services, was the Shipowner still liable for 'defective loading, stowage, lashing, securing, dunnaging, separation and discharge', and responsible for 'proper performance' of the operations?

They had to decide what the parties had actually agreed in the charter and Bills of Lading, and whether Hague-Visby still applied.

In December 1997 Islamic Solidarity Shipping voyage chartered the Jordan II to TCI Trans Commodities to carry 5,500 tonnes of galvanised steel coils from India to Spain, freight to be paid (clause 3) 'per metric ton FIOST [free in and out, stowed and trimmed] –

lashed/secured/dunnaged'. Clause 7 was modified to read: 'Charterers to have full use of all vessel's gear to assist in loading and discharging', but only 'supplementary to the shore gear'. Shore winchmen and cranemen were 'to be used at all times'.

The charter was on a Stemmor 1983 form, designed for the carriage of bulk ore. Clause 17 retained its original wording: the 'shipper / charterer / receiver' were to load, 'trim' and discharge the cargo 'free of expense to the vessel'.

"Trimming" is defined as "levelling off the top of the pile", appropriate to ore in bulk, but how was it supposed to apply to steel coils? The charter was subject to English law, and incorporated the Hague-Visby Rules.

The shipper, Jindal Iron; the Receiver, Hiansa; and Charterer TCI Trans Commodities, subsequently started proceedings against Islamic, alleging damage in transit. TCI sued under the charter party. Jindal and Hiansa sued as Bills of Lading holders. Islamic argued it was not liable for the cargo operations, either under the charter or the Bills of Lading, which were on the Congenbill form and incorporated the charter terms.

According to the claimants, clause 3 was inconsistent with Hague-Visby Art III r 8 and so did not transfer the 'proper performance' obligations from the Owner to the cargo interests. Islamic responded that clauses 3 and 17, taken together, transferred both obligations, to pay, and to ensure the operations were properly carried out.

The judge decided that if clause 3 (with the FIOST requirements) was read with clause 17, the wording clearly showed the parties intended to transfer to the Charterer the Owner's common law responsibility for performance. "The obligation to 'trim'", he said, was intended to mean responsibility for lashing, stowing and dunnage. These were transferred to TCI, as Charterer, so it could not sue under the charter, while Jindal and Hiansa could not claim compensation under the Bills of Lading so long as the damage was not caused by the carrier. The parties had agreed to be governed by English law, under which (according to *Pyrene v Scindia*) Art III r 2 only applied to the carrier if he had agreed to carry out the specified functions relating to the cargo.

Jindal, Hiansa and TCI appealed against the judge's interpretation of the charter party and the effect of Art III on the Bills of Lading. They contended that although in the case of bulk ore, clause 17 would have transferred all cargo work obligations to the Charterer, the word 'trim' could not be taken to apply to manufactured steel.

The appeal judges rejected this argument. They agreed with the judge that while FIOST was only a 'who is to pay' provision, the word "free" simply meaning "at no cost to the Shipowner", it must be read with clause 17, which determined the transfer of responsibility. Although 'trim' was inappropriate, the rest of the clause showed the Charterer was to load and discharge the cargo.

The parties had "clearly put their minds to what is required to stow the steel coils," said the Judge namely the obligation to 'lash, secure and dunnage'. They intended to transfer the obligation to the Charterer, and there was no other wording to suggest they did not mean this to happen.

As to Hague-Visby Art III, he confirmed that *Pyrene v Scindia* (later confirmed by the House of Lords in *Renton v Palmyra)* was binding in English law. So the effect of the Bills of Lading was not invalidated by Rule 8. "Article III rule 2," does not compel the Shipowner to be responsible for the loading and unloading or for the way other parties carried out the work. "It simply compels the Shipowner to load and unload properly if he undertakes those functions" and he could contract out of them.

None of us should believe that we are not capable of drawing up clauses that are equally potentially difficult to interpret. We are all liable to do so. But we must all guard against this to the best of our ability unless we wish to end up in arbitration or a court of law!

10.7   SELF-ASSESSMENT AND TEST QUESTIONS

Attempt the following and check your answers from the text:

1.   Where are the main Maritime Arbitration centres?

2.   What are names of the arbitration associations in London and in New York?

3.   In London, to where would you appeal following an Arbitration Award and on what grounds?

4.   What is the date of England's latest Arbitration Act?

5.   What types of dry cargo would an Owner try to avoid even though they are not actually classified as "Dangerous" and why?

6.   The Owner of a general cargo vessel negotiates with a Line Operator to permit the carriage of any IMO Dangerous Goods up to a maximum of 1000 tonnes, excepting Classes 1,2,6,7 and 9. What type of dangerous goods are permitted for carriage?

Having completed Chapter Ten attempt the following and submit your essay to your Tutor:

1.   The relevant clauses of a voyage charter party read as follows:

Clause 7:   "Cargo to be discharged at the average rate of ...tonnes per weather working day of 24 running hours. Time from noon Saturday, or a day preceding a holiday, through to 08.00 hours Monday, or the day following a holiday excepted, unless used (when actual time used to count)".

Clause 9:   "Time at discharging port to commence at 08.00 hours on the working day following the day Master has tendered vessel's Notice of Readiness to discharge to Receivers during business hours, whether in berth or not, whether in free pratique or not, whether customs cleared or not. Business hours are 08.00 hours to 17.00 hours on weekdays, and 08.00 hours to noon on Saturdays".

The vessel arrived off the discharge port on a Saturday at 13.45 hours and the Master tendered notice immediately. The vessel berthed at 14.15 hours and commenced discharge at 15.00 hours. Thereafter discharge progressed more or less continuously (except for meal breaks, shifting along the berth, and occasional shore crane repairs) through to completion of discharge on the following Friday.

The Statement of Facts shows that the Port Agents accepted the notice of readiness on Saturday at 13.45 hours.

Owners maintain that, in accordance with Clause 7, laytime commences with commencement of discharge and that time actually used during the weekend counts as laytime. Charterers maintain that, as per Clause 9, no time counts as laytime before Tuesday 08.00 hours, whether the vessel was discharging or not.

Prepare a written submission of either (A) Owner's or (B) Charterer's case for presentation to the arbitrator (your Tutor) appointed to resolve the dispute. Explain (1) why you believe your Principal's point of view is correct and (2) why, in your opinion, the other side is wrong.

(**NB.** You will not lose any marks if your Tutor disagrees with your opinion. We merely want to give you the opportunity and practice of thinking about a typical dispute, providing a logical and well reasoned argument and expressing it clearly in writing, the type of activity shipping people engaged in dry cargo chartering have to do in their everyday work).

2. Toxic Wastes have been much in the news in recent months. What are the problems associated with the carriage of toxic wastes, and to whom should Shipowners look for advice before contracting to carry such a cargo?

APPENDICES

DRY CARGO SHIP TYPES AND THEIR INTER-RELATIONSHIP

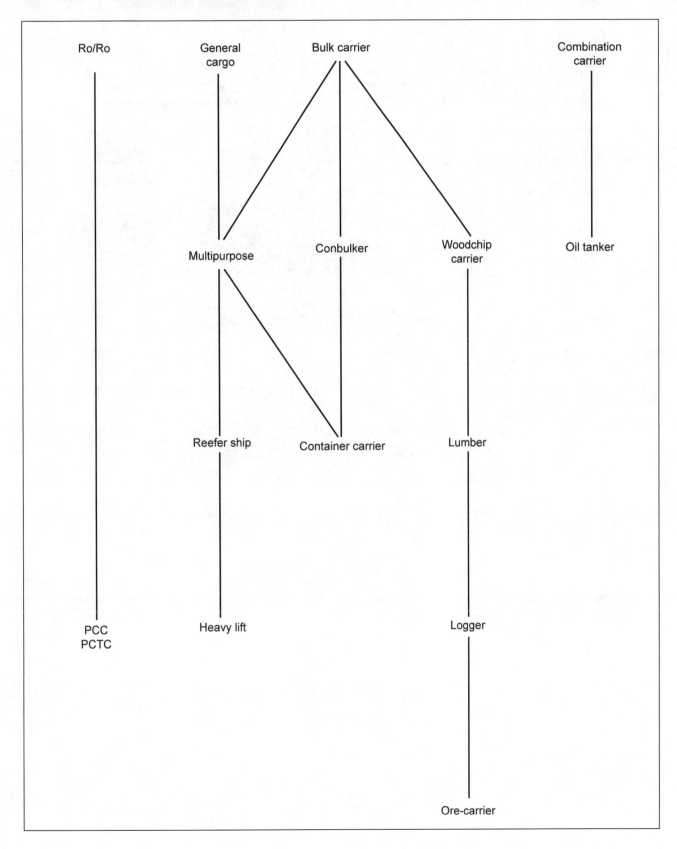

Appendix 2

DERRICKS

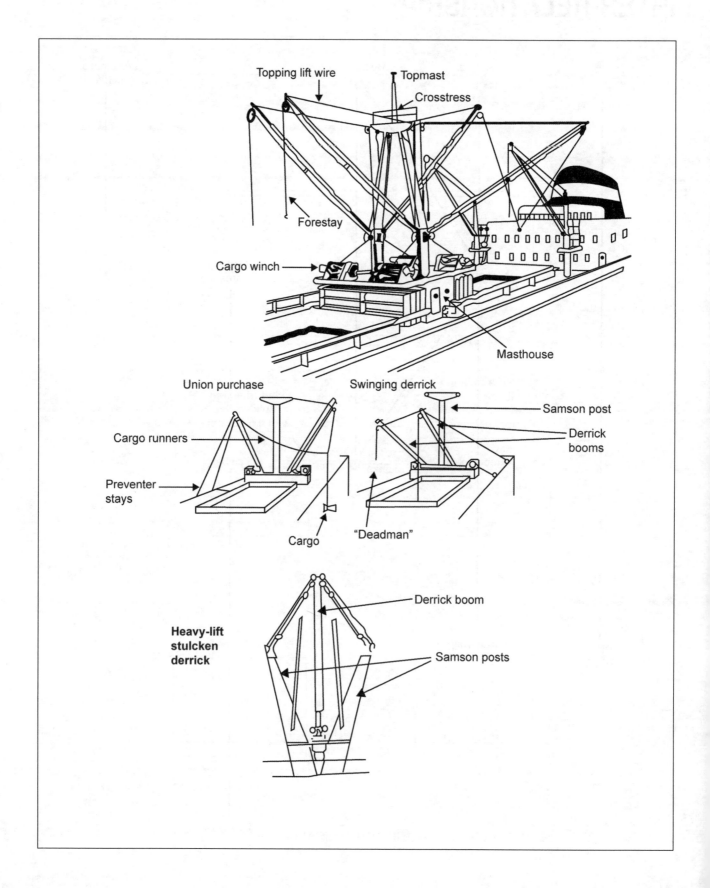

MIDSHIP SECTIONS

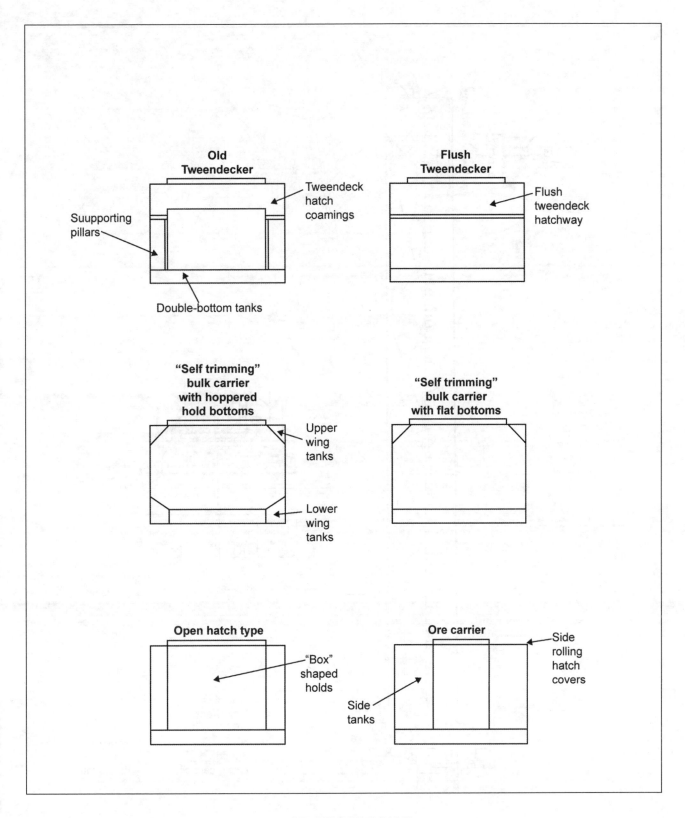

Old Tweendecker — Tweendeck hatch coamings — Suupporting pillars — Double-bottom tanks

Flush Tweendecker — Flush tweendeck hatchway

"Self trimming" bulk carrier with hoppered hold bottoms — Upper wing tanks — Lower wing tanks

"Self trimming" bulk carrier with flat bottoms

Open hatch type — "Box" shaped holds

Ore carrier — Side rolling hatch covers — Side tanks

(NB: NOT TO SCALE)

Appendix 4

SEMI-SUBMERSIBLE HEAVY-LIFT VESSEL

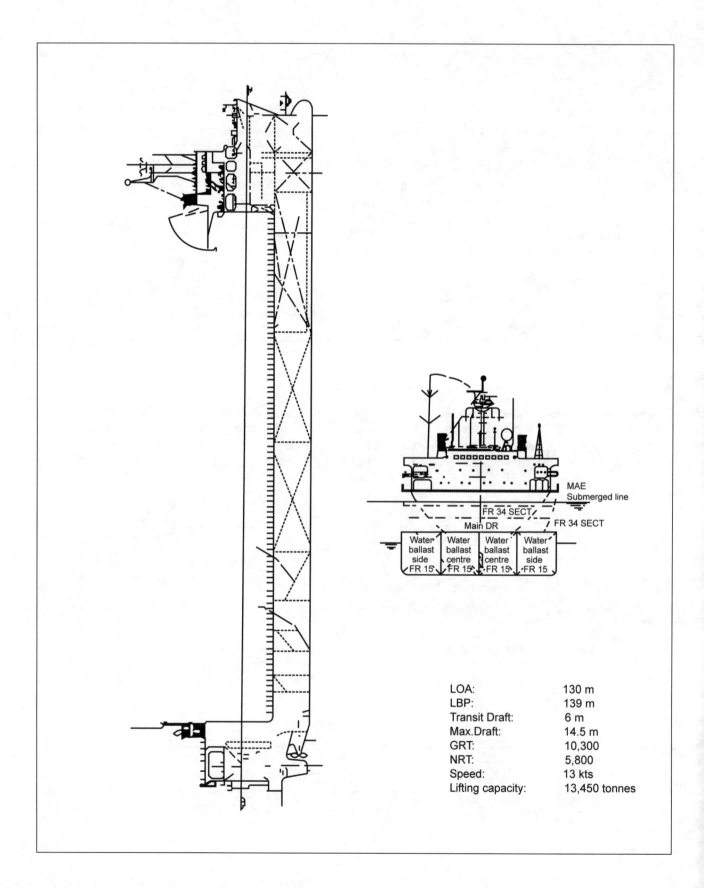

LOA:	130 m
LBP:	139 m
Transit Draft:	6 m
Max.Draft:	14.5 m
GRT:	10,300
NRT:	5,800
Speed:	13 kts
Lifting capacity:	13,450 tonnes

CATTLE CARRIER (PURPOSE BUILT)

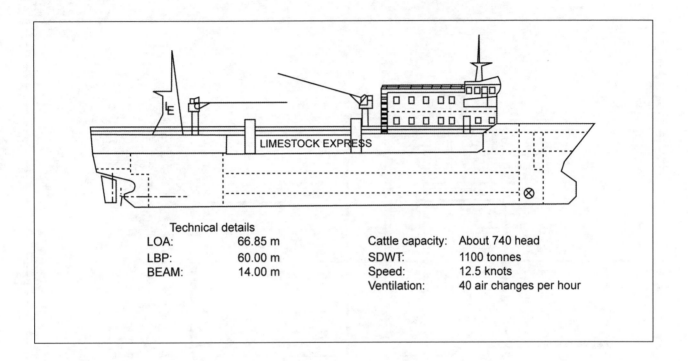

Technical details

LOA:	66.85 m	Cattle capacity:	About 740 head
LBP:	60.00 m	SDWT:	1100 tonnes
BEAM:	14.00 m	Speed:	12.5 knots
		Ventilation:	40 air changes per hour

SHEEP CARRIER (CONVERSION)

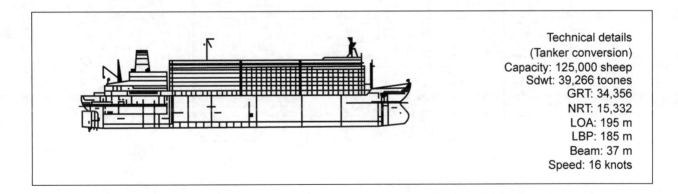

Technical details
(Tanker conversion)
Capacity: 125,000 sheep
Sdwt: 39,266 toones
GRT: 34,356
NRT: 15,332
LOA: 195 m
LBP: 185 m
Beam: 37 m
Speed: 16 knots

Appendix 6

OBO

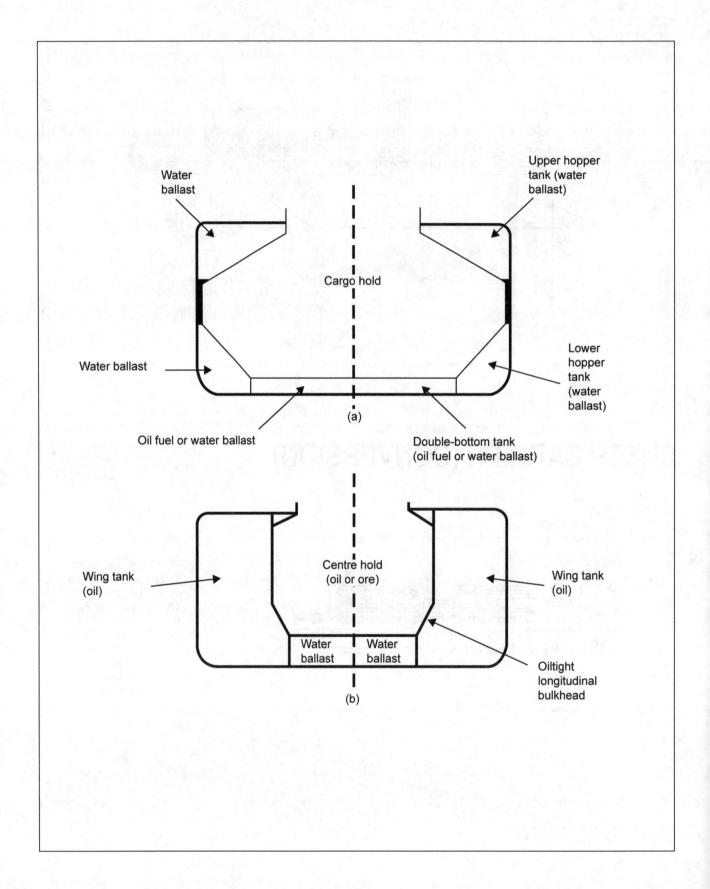

BOX SHAPED HOLD

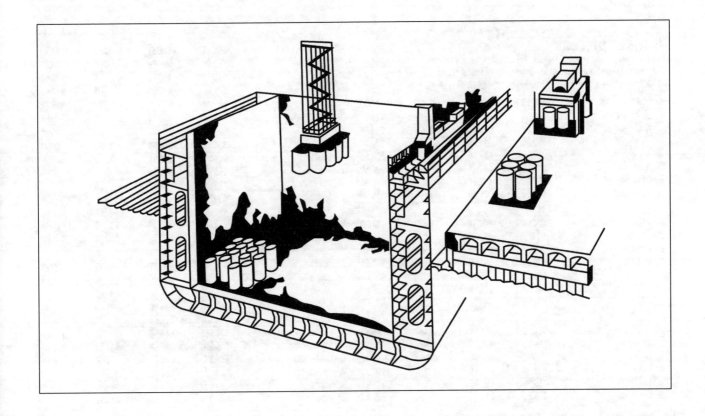

Appendix 8

MARKET FIXTURES AND REPORTS

Bunker prices
[Source: Cockett Marine Oil Ltd. Tel: +44 1689 883400]

Latest mid-range prices listed in $ as at Monday 28 February 2011.
D=delivered, W=ex-wharf. Ports listed regionally clockwise from NE.

EUROPE	380CST	180CST	MDO	MGO
D St Petersburg	422.50	432.50	700.00	780.00
D Great Belt	641.00	666.00	924.00	969.00
D Hamburg	628.00	648.00	970.00	970.00
D Rotterdam	597.50	621.00	936.00	936.00
D Antwerp	604.50	631.50	885.00	930.50
D Le Havre	456.00	475.00	N/A	722.50
D Falmouth	673.00	706.00	986.00	986.00

MEDITERRANEAN	380CST	180CST	MDO	MGO
D Istanbul	647.50	662.50	N/A	980.00
D Piraeus	601.50	635.50	N/A	933.50
D Valletta	576.50	599.50	N/A	890.00
D Augusta	591.50	625.50	N/A	916.00
D Fos/Lavera	601.50	622.50	N/A	935.00
D Gibraltar	614.50	647.50	952.50	967.50

AFRICA	380CST	180CST	MDO	MGO
D Arzew	506.00	526.00	N/A	772.00
D Durban	N/A	663.00	978.00	988.00
D Lagos	633.50	658.50	N/A	955.00
D Dakar	710.00	765.00	N/A	972.50
D Las Palmas	626.00	643.00	965.00	975.00

MIDDLE EAST	380CST	180CST	MDO	MGO
D Khor Fakkan	662.50	700.50	N/A	997.50
D Aden	690.00	705.00	N/A	975.00
D Jeddah	645.00	655.00	N/A	940.00
D Suez	642.50	665.00	N/A	960.00
D Dammam	645.00	660.00	N/A	970.00

ASIA	380CST	180CST	MDO	MGO
D Tokyo	705.00	712.50	935.00	N/A
D Sydney	553.50	553.50	736.50	736.50
D Colombo	610.00	632.50	N/A	905.00
D Singapore	637.50	647.50	932.50	937.50
D Hong Kong	652.50	667.50	947.50	955.00
D Kaohsiung	713.00	725.00	995.00	1,010.00
D South Korea	666.00	680.00	962.50	970.00

AMERICAS	380CST	180CST	MDO	MGO
W New York	641.00	661.00	952.50	N/A
W Houston	630.00	660.00	967.50	N/A
W Cristobal	646.00	676.00	995.00	N/A
W Venezuelan ports	646.50	676.50	N/A	988.00
D Rio de Janeiro	621.00	644.50	N/A	970.00
D Buenos Aires	575.50	586.50	942.50	942.50
D La Libertad	636.00	684.00	N/A	1,348.00
W Los Angeles	640.00	660.00	857.50	N/A
W Seattle	669.00	689.00	883.00	N/A
W Vancouver BC	672.00	692.00	887.50	N/A

For online bunker information: www.fairplay.co.uk/markets or visit or www.cockettgroup.com

Bunkerworld Indices

BW380: $635 ▲ $37   BW180: $657.50 ▲ $36   BWDI: $935.50 ▲ $48

Outlook: Bunker prices last week surged – the BW380 index increasing by $37/tonne to $635/tonne. At some ports, prices tailed off toward the end of the week as bunker buyers seemed to be adopting a 'wait-and-see' policy, expecting bunker prices to slide. Crude oil futures prices saw the largest weekly gain for 127 weeks (up by $11.68/barrel). WTI front-month crude oil contracts on the New York Mercantile Exchange (NYMEX) reached $97.88/barrel, edging closer to the $100 psychological barrier that Brent has already smashed (trading at $112.14/barrel last week).

Stock availability was a major factor reported to have influenced the price of residual bunker fuel in Singapore. Stocks were reported to be adequate by the end of the week. Prices of IFO380 centistoke (cSt) fell to $646.50/tonne,

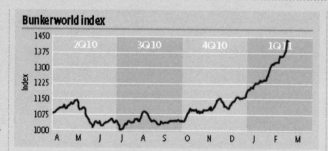

Bunkerworld index

softening by $24/tonne overnight.

Meanwhile, bunker prices at Fujairah followed suit, closing the week at $646/tonne for IFO380 cSt, a rise of $14.50/tonne through the week. Prices from key suppliers at the port showed some divergence, but the average price spread between Singapore and Fujairah narrowed to just $0.50/tonne – this compared with a premium of $22.50/

tonne a week prior to this at Fujairah.

Similar price gains were seen in Rotterdam. IFO380 cSt reached $606.50/tonne, an aggregate increment of $42.50/tonne over the week. Delivered marine gasoil at Rotterdam also gained, by about 7%, to reach $869/tonne, a level not seen since September 2008.

The average price of delivered IFO380 cSt at Houston hit $633/tonne. Although

prices have reached exceptional levels, demand has renewed as the crack spread between IFO380 sold at Houston and WTI crude oil reached $113/tonne, compared with $82/tonne a week earlier, making it relatively good value, in comparison with the price of crude oil.

Continued tension in Libya has affected crude oil exports from the country's ports. According to Reuters, more than two-thirds of crude oil exports have been halted from the country (approximately 1.07M bpd). Commentators have noted a danger that instability could spread to the wider Middle East region. Typically, Libyan crude oil assays are light and sweet, suited to clean petroleum product.

bunkerworld

For online bunker information: www.fairplay.co.uk/markets or visit www.bunkerworld.com/prices   BW380, BW180 in centi Stoke **BWDI** for distillate fuels

Appendix 8

MARKET FIXTURES AND REPORTS (continued)

Baltic dry indices

BDI: 1,245 ▼ -56 (-4.3%)

Outlook: Cyclones in Western Australia and increased bunker prices have held Capesize rates in stasis. To China, rates were $6.50/tonne for mid-March. Brazil-China fixtures were about $18/tonne, firming for late March to $19. Panamax markets saw grain trips fixed at about $52/tonne from Gulf of Mexico for March; in southern Brazil it is $47/tonne for April. Handysizes made $10,000/day for trips within the Asia/Pacific region. Indian iron ore shipments have been strong, with Handymaxes at $16,000/day. Short period rates for Handymaxes and Supramaxes in Gulf of Mexico firmed to $20,000/day with charterers seeking $17,000-18,000/day.

Capesize Index		
This week: 1,315	3 MH:	3,233
Last week: 1,442	3 ML:	1,281

Panamax Index		
This week: 1,812	3 MH:	2,386
Last week: 2,004	3 ML:	1,296

Supramax Index		
This week: 1,385	3 MH:	1,678
Last week: 1,267	3 ML:	1,086

Handy Index		
This week: 688	3 MH:	839
Last week: 670	3 ML:	634

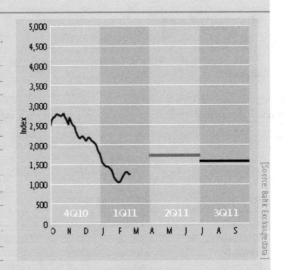

[Source: Baltic Exchange data]

Baltic tanker indices

BDTI: 872 ▲ 92 (11.8%)   BCTI: 709 ▲ 74 (11.7%)

Outlook: Despite bunker price surges, VLCC and Suezmax rates softened across the board. Ice-class Aframaxes saw rates from Primorsk-UK/Continent rise 61 points in a week to W175 on a shortage of suitable tonnage. Softening of rates is possible as charterers are able to withhold cargoes to redirect the market. Uncertainties about loading in Libya saw rates rise by 61 points to W155.6. Braemar Seascope says a two-tier market is possible – one for Libya-Mediterranean cargoes, the other for non-Libya business. The effects are felt in Black Sea markets, where "charters have had to steer clear of any ships that are or will be ex-Libya due to the uncertainty of what will happen".

VLCC TCE	
This week:	$2,737/day
Last week:	$23,924/day

Suezmax TCE	
This week:	$20,748/day
Last week:	$21,318/day

Aframax TCE	
This week:	$21,599/day
Last week:	$10,003/day

MR-TCE	
This week:	$7,717/day
Last week:	$7,508/day

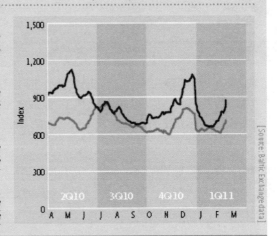

[Source: Baltic Exchange data]

Container indices

ConTex: 662 ▲ 18 (2.8%)

Outlook: The market keeps rising amid strong demand and short supply of tonnage. Brokers put Panamax benchmark rates for 12-month periods at about $30,000/day. This trend could see rates in all sectors "back at their long term average in four weeks", said Paul Dowell of London broker Howe Robinson. In the post-Panamax segment, APL has reportedly secured two 8,500 teu units for delivery in the second half at a rate in the high $40,000s. The 2,000-3,000 teu sectors saw 12-month rates for gearless 2,800 teu vessels top $16,000/day.

Container ship Timecharter Assessment

Type	17 Feb	24 Feb
1,100 teu	$9,176	$9,298
1,700 teu	$10,329	$10,532
2,500 teu	$14,842	$15,249
2,700 teu	$15,948	$16,456
3,500 teu	$18,875	$19,500
4,250 teu	$25,624	$26,814

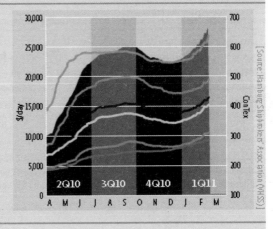

[Source: Hamburg Shipbrokers' Association (VHSS)]

Appendix 8

MARKET FIXTURES AND REPORTS (continued)

Newbuildings

[Source: IHS Fairplay]

SELECTED NEWBUILDING ORDERS REPORTED WEEK ENDING 25 FEBRUARY 2011

Shipbuilder	No	Owner/Operator	Delivery	Type	Capacity
Daewoo	10	AP Møller-Maersk	2012/12	Container ship	18,000teu
Shanhaiguan Industry	4	Greathorse Shipping	2012/8	Bulk carrier	76,000dwt
STX Shipbuilding Jinhae	4	Mitsubishi	2013/8	Bulk carrier	82,000dwt

SELECTED DELIVERIES REPORTED WEEK ENDING 25 FEBRUARY 2011

Vessel	Shipbuilder	Owner/Operator	Delivery	Type	Capacity
Agios Dimitrios	Hanjin HI	Technomar	2011/2	Container ship	6,572teu
Captain V Livanos	STX Dalian	Trojan Maritime	2011/2	Bulk carrier	57,700dwt
Charles Darwin	Construcciones Navales del Norte	Jan De Nul	2011/2	Hopper dredger	53,036dwt
CMB Boris	Samjin Industries	CMB	2011/2	Bulk carrier	33,500dwt
Cosco Shengshi	COSCO Zhoushan	COSCO	2011/2	Vehicles carrier	5,000cars
Eastern Frontier	Jong Shyn	Mitsui	2011/2	General cargo ship	8,969dwt
Erika Schulte	Jiangzhou Union	Schulte Group	2011/2	Chemical/oil prods tanker	16,500dwt
Hanjin Pioneer	Shinan HI	Hanjin	2011/2	General cargo ship	12,180dwt
Iver Balance	Hyundai Mipo	Vroon	2011/2	Bitumen tanker	6,050dwt
KWK Legacy	Daewoo	Tai Chong Cheang	2011/2	Bulk carrier	180,000dwt
Maersk Edmonton	Hyundai HI	Polaris Shipmanagement	2011/2	Container ship	13,092teu
Mega Star	COSCO Dalian	Fleet Management	2011/2	Bulk carrier	79,500dwt
MOL Modern	Mitsubishi HI	Mitsui OSK	2011/2	Container ship	6,724teu
Nighthawk	Yangzhou Dayang	Eagle Bulk	2011/2	Bulk carrier	58,000dwt
Orange Star	Brodosplit - Brodogradiliste	Atlanship	2011/2	Fruit juice tanker	35,750dwt
Osttank Norway	Yangfan Group	Zacchello Group	2011/2	Chemical/oil prods tanker	16,500dwt
Samskip Endeavour	Damen Galati	Samskip	2011/2	Container ship	812teu
SKS Darent	Hyundai Samho HI	Kristian Gerhard Jebsen Skipsrederi	2011/2	Oil products tanker	119,456dwt
Torm Amalie	Guangzhou Shipyard	TORM	2011/2	Chemical/oil prods tanker	50,500dwt

For full listings of newbuilding orders and deliveries: see www.fairplay.co.uk/markets

Sale & purchase

All details given in good faith but without guarantee

CONTAINER & MULTI-PURPOSE

KOTA MAWAR (container ship) ex-Ibuki: sold by Schlussel Reederei, Germany, to undisclosed interests, United States of America, $9.5M. 1994. 22,494dwt, 16,266gt, 1,684teu. Built Stocznia Szczecinska, Sulzer/19kt.

ROTHORN & WEISSHORN (container ships): sold en bloc by Contal Shipping, Switzerland, to undisclosed interests, Greece, $18M. Rothorn ex-MOL Amazonas: 1996. 14,587dwt, 12,029gt, 1,122teu. Built Volkswerft Stralsund, Sulzer/18kt. Weisshorn ex-MSC Ghana: 1996. 14,643dwt, 12,029gt, 1,122teu. Built Volkswerft Stralsund, Sulzer/20kt.

BULKERS

CLIPPER LANCASTER ex-Paclogger: sold by Clipper Group, Denmark, to undisclosed interests, Vietnam, $14M. Last sale: $13.45M (1999). 1996. 28,249dwt, 17,209gt.

Built KK Kanasashi, Mitsubishi, 7,200bhp/14kt.

FAVIOLA ex-Ever Champion: sold by Grecomar Shipping Agency, Greece, to undisclosed interests, $6.5M. Last sale: $4.5M (1999). 1982. 62,343dwt, 35,319gt. Built Namura, Sulzer/15kt.

IRON YANDI: sold by Teekay, Canada, to undisclosed interests, $24M. 1996. 169,963dwt, 82,306gt. Built Daewoo HI, B&W, 17,261bhp/14kt.

SOUL OF LUCK (wood chips carrier) ex-Forest King: sold by Victoria Oceanway, Greece, to Pasifik Lojistik Grubu ve Denizcili, Turkey, $11M. Last sale: $6.5M (2009). 1991.

TANKERS

FIDELITY (crude oil tanker): sold by Dynacom Tankers Management, Greece, to undisclosed interests, China, $34.50M. 2005. 71,049dwt, 38,842gt.

Built Onomichi, B&W/16kt.

KENDAL & KESWICK sold en bloc by MC Shipping, Monaco, to Petredec, Bermuda, $45M. Kendal (LPG tanker): 2003. 8,709dwt, 7,893gt. Built Asakawa. B&W/15kt. Keswick (LPG tanker): 2003. 8,692dwt, 7,884gt. Built Asakawa. B&W/15kt.

TAUNUS (chemical/oil products tanker): sold by Engineering Srl to undisclosed interests, Italy, $25M. 2004. 38,140dwt, 25,487gt. Built STX, MAN-B&W/14kt.

NEWBUILDING RESALES

PACIFIC IVY & PACIFIC POPPY (crude oil tanker) sold en bloc by Cido Shipping, Hong Kong, to Polembros Shipping, Greece, $97M. Pacific Ivy: 2011. 104,280dwt. Built Sumitomo HI Marine, MAN-B&W, 15,671bhp/15kt. Sumitomo 1364 (TBN Pacific Poppy): 2011. 104,280dwt, 56,300gt. Built Sumitomo, MAN-B&W, 15,671bhp/15kt.

For full listings of sale and purchase deals: see www.fairplay.co.uk/markets

Source: Maritime Research Inc
www.fairplay.co.uk

3 March 2011

Appendix 8

MARKET FIXTURES AND REPORTS (continued)

Fixtures
[Source: Maritime Research Inc / www.maritime-research.com]

DRY FIXTURES

Cargo	Vessel	From	To	Tonnes	Date	$/tonne	Chart	Terms
Coal	Steamer, (Noblechart)	ECUS	China	140,000-10%	Mar 5/15	30.25	Winsway	FIO;30,000tShinc/30,000tShinc
Coal	Aristides NP, 93	New Orleans	Rotterdam	70,000-10%	Mar 5/10	21.00	J Aron	FIO;20,000tShinc/25,000tShinc
Corn	Steamer, (Clipper)	R Plate	Casablanca	25,000-5%	28 Feb/Mar 8	37.25	Gavilon	FIO;7,000t/5,000t
Iron ore	Kanaris, 10	Guaita	Taranto	170,000-10%	Mar 14/23	9.50	Ilva	FIO;30,000t/30,000t
Iron ore	Steamer	Tubarao	Qingdao	160,000-10%	Apr/Jun	20.75	CTC	FIO;ScLd/30,000t;2ndCargo-Jul
Iron ore	Steamer, (Cargill)	Tubarao	Qingdao	160,000-10%	Mar 1/10	18.40	PanOcean	FIO;ScLd/30,000t
Iron ore	Fu Yuan, 92	Marmagoa	Xingang	140,000-10%	Mar 1/10	10.30	Plutus	FIO;25,000t/25,000t
Iron ore	North Friendship, 99	Maputo Or Rich Bay	Qingdao	70,000-10%	Mar 1/15	28.00	Rio Tinto	FIO;ScLd/30,000t

TIMECHARTERS

Consumption	Vessel	From	To	Dwt	Date	$/day	Chart	Terms
14k/52t	Athenian Phoenix, 09	Del Pass Muscat	Redel ChinaViaMarmagoa	179,223	Feb 21/24	13,800	Oldendorff	Trip out
14k/36t	Okinawa, 09	Del Singapore	Redel Sing/Japan	81,397	Feb 25/Mar 5	19,600	Cargill	EC SoAmRd
14k/35t	Alessandro Volta, 05	Del Hazira	Redel China Via WC India	76,806	Feb 26/Mar 2	22,000	Oldendorff	Trip out
14k/34t	Nord Neptune, 06	Del Off EC US	Redel UK/Continent	75,726	Mar 10/15	16,000	SwissMarin	Trip out $350,000 bonus
14.8k/32t	Nirefs, 01	Del San Ciprian	Redel San Ciprian	75,311	Feb 25/28	18,500	Cargill	PtlGamsarRd,DC
14k/33t	Ocean Favour, 98	Del Lake Charles	Redel Sing/Japan	72,400	Mar 6/11	24,500	PanOcean	Trip out $600,000 bonus
Unrptd	Heroic Striker, 10	Del USGulf	Redel WC Cent America	57,000	Mar 1/5	24,000	Navision	Trip out
Unrptd	Avocet, 10	Del Brake	Redel India Via Baltic	53,500	Feb 21/24	24,000	CNR	Trip out, fertilisers
14k/32t	Florence D, 07	Del Sail Lagos	Redel Spain Via Owendo	53,460	Feb 20/24	13,150	Oldendorff	Trip out, manganese ore
Unrptd	Amber Alena, 10	Del Continent	Redel E Mediterranean	53,193	Feb 24/27	15,000	U-SeaBulk	Trip out, scrap
Unrptd	ID Nord, 99	Del Off Santos	Redel Nigeria	46,640	Feb 25/28	12,500	Oldendorff	Trip out $275,000 BB
13k/25t	Union Ranger, 95	Del Mejillones	Redel Skaw/CapePassero	45,621	Feb 25/28	14,000	SwissMarin	Trip out

WET FIXTURES

Cargo	Vessel	From	To	Tonnes	Date	Rate	Chart	Terms
Oil dirty	Cosmerry Lake, 06	ME Gulf	US Gulf	280,000	Mar 09	W40	Vela	
Oil dirty	Hawtah, 96	Caribbeans	Jamnagar	270,000	Mar 21	$4,250,000	Reliance	PtC;Lump sum
Oil dirty	Asian Progress III, 04	ME Gulf	Japan	265,000	Mar 07	W79	Shell	Part cargo
Oil dirty	Raphael, 00	W Africa	WC India	260,000	Mar 05	$5,500,000	IOC	PtC;lump sum
Oil dirty	Kimolos, 98	Qua Iboe	EC India	260,000	Mar 19	$4,860,000	IOC	PtC;lump sum
Oil dirty	Aegean Horizon, 07	Ceyhan Terminal	UK/Continent Med	135,000	Mar 03	W92	BP	
Oil dirty	Four Smile, 01	Libya	China	130,000	Mar 12	$3,800,000	Unipec	Lump sum; Hi heat
Oil dirty	Olympysky Prospect	Primorsk	UK/Continent	100,000	Mar 03	W100	Unipec	
Oil dirty	Adele Marina Rizzo, 10	Kozmino	WC US	100,000	Mar 21	W108	Vitol	
Oil dirty	Torm Marina, 07	Black Sea	Mediterranean	80,000	Mar 08	W100	Clearlake	Part cargo
Oil dirty	Bahamas Spirit, 98	ME Gulf	Far East	80,000	Mar 13	W95	Shell	Part cargo
Oil dirty	Desh Gaurav, 03	Bushire	Far East	80,000	Mar 13	W117	PDI	Part cargo
Oil dirty	Montiron, 03	EC Mexico	US Gulf	70,000	Feb 25	W107.5	Shell	Part cargo
Oil clean	Desh Suraksha, 11	Sikka	UK/Continent	90,000	Mar 10	$1,850,000	CNR	Lump sum
Oil clean	Pink Stars, 10	ME Gulf	Far East	75,000	Mar 06	W97	Shell	Part cargo
Oil clean	Yang Li Hu, 10	Mohammedia	Japan	75,000	Feb 27	$1,950,000	Vitol	Lump sum
Oil clean	Delight Victoria, 07	ME Gulf	Japan	55,000	Mar 05	W110	Daelim	Part cargo
Oil clean	Pro Jade, 03	So Korea	Singapore	40,000	Mar 03	$390,000	BP	Lump sum
Oil clean	Torm Platte, 06	USGulf	UK/Continent Med	38,000	Feb 17	W75	CNR	
Oil clean	High Efficiency, 09	UK/Continent	US Atlantic	37,000	Feb 28	W162.5	CNR	
Fuel oil	Minerva Libra, 07	Tallinn	US Gulf	100,000	Mar 02	W110	BP	
Fuel oil	Prem Divya, 98	Mangalore	Singapore	80,000	Mar 08	W100	Itochu	Part cargo

For more information on fixtures see: www.fairplay.co.uk/markets

MARKET REPORT – GALBRAITH'S LIMITED

Comparative Bunker Prices:

Ports	380 Cst	180 Cst	MDO
Rotterdam	84 (–3)	90 (–2)	152 (+2)
Fujairah	98 (0)	104 (–1)	210 (+1)
Singapore	99 (+3)	103 (+1)	185 (0)
New Orleans	98 (0)	102 (–1)	180 (–1)

GALBRAITH'S LIMITED

Whilst every care has been taken in the preparation of this report no liability can be accepted for any persons relying on the information contained herein.

Appendix 9

MARKET REPORT – GALBRAITH'S LIMITED (cont)

PANAMAX FIXTURES

SEA UNION 50000 MT TAMPA / CHINA 22 - 28 MAY 25 DAYS SHINC USD 20.50 (GRAND)

VESSEL TBN 62000 MT HSS MISS RIV / LISBON PROMPT 10 DAYS USD 10.00 (TOEPPER)

VESSEL TBN 52500 MT BARLEY ST LAN / SAUDI ARABIA 01 MAY - 30 JUN 6000 / 3000 USD 21.50 (GLENCORE)

KAPITAN STANKOV 50000 MT COAL NORFOLK / BOURGAS 10-20 JUN 25,000 SC / 10,000 SC USD 10.95 (VANOMM)

NAVARINO 50000 MT HSS UP R PLATE / IRAN 25 - 31 MAY 5000 / 4000 USD 28.50 (SEABONI)

MILITOS 54000 MT HSS USG / JAPAN 09 - 16 JUN 11 DAYS USD 21.20 (MSK)

SILVER STAR 69235 DWT 14K L/ 14.5 B 31.8 (380 CET) NO MDO AT SE DELY RIZHAO 01 - 10 JUN TCT JAPAN USD 9750 PLUS USD 15000 (DAIICHI)

AVALON 73200 DWT DELY NAGOYA 27 - 31 MAY NTH PAC LB R / V USD 9000 (HALLA)

C FILYOS 72136 DWT DELY USG 02- 10 JUN TCT JAPAN USD 12000 PLUS USD 200,000 (CHO YANG)

STAMOS 63865 DWT 14 ON 33 MT (1500) NO MDO / 13.5 ON 30 / 13 DELY USWC 29 MAY - 05 JUN TCT CONTINENT USD 7000 PLUS USD 10000 (AIMCOR)

CAPTAIN GEORGE TSANGARIS 61349 DWT DELY TAICHUNG PROMPT VIA PHILIPPINES REDEL JAPAN USD 9000 (NAVIX)

MANIFEST PKWN 60969 DWT 12.5 ON 34 + 1 DELY SHIBUSHI 20 - 31 MAY 3 - 5 MTHS REDEL FAR EAST USD 8500 (GLENCORE)

COSCO VESSEL 69000 DWT DELY CONTINENT 25 - 31 MAY VIA BRAZIL REDEL JAPAN USD 12000 (SANKO)

CAPESIZE FIXTURES

CAPE CATHAY 140000 MT COAL RICH BAY / 2 PTS DENMARK 01 - 31 JUL SCALE LD / 30,000 - 20,000 USD 7.50 (PANDO)

COMANESTI 140000 MT COAL USWC/CNZA 01 JUN - 31 JUL SCALE LD/ 15,M000 SX USD 11.50 (NOVA COAL)

THALASSINI AXIA 150000 MT POTY CARTIER / ROTTERDAM 25 - 30 JUN 6 DAYS SHINC USD 4.85 (ROHSTOFF)

CHO YANG VESSEL 132000 MT RICHARDS BAY / KOREA 01 - 10 JUL USD 7.70 (KEPCO)

HYDRA 150000 MT CAPE LAMBERT / ROTTERDAM 6 DAYS SHINC USD 7.25 (ROBE RIVER)

AMBER 150000 MT TUBARAO / IJMUIDEN 20 - 30 JUN USD 5.97 (HOOGOVENS)

MARSHAL GOVOROV 100000 MT COAL RICH BAY / WILHELMSHAVN 05 - 20 JUL SCALE LD / 20,000 SC USD 7.90 (PREAG)

MARKET REPORT – GALBRAITH'S LIMITED (cont)

HANDYSIZE FIXTURES

J SUDA 45150 DWT 14K ON 28.5 IFO NO DAS DEY JAKARTA 25 - 30 MAY REDEL JAPAN USD 9500 (NYK)

OCEAN TRADER 42053 DWT 13.5K ON 25.5L / 24.2B (380) + 1.1 MDO DELY VANCOUVER PROMPT 4 - 6 MTHS USD 8300 ≠ USD 125000 BB (PAN OCEAN)

ADRIANA 38973 DWT 12. K ON 29.5B / 27L (180) + MT GASOIL DELY SPORE 25 - 30 MAY VIA KRABI REDEL JAPAN USD 8000 (DAIICHI)

SEA RAINBOW 38325 DWT 13K ON 23 (L) / 20 (B) (180) + 0.2 MDO DELY USG SPOT REDEL MOROCCO USD 10000 (AIMCOR)

KAPITAN BETKHER 36663 DWT 14K ON 28 (180) + NO MDO DELY VANCOUVER 25 - 30 MAY 5 - 7 MTHS USD 8200 + USD 177500 BB (WESTBULK)

IOLCOS LEGEND 35100 DWT 13K ON 30 (1500) + 2.5 DO DELY USG 20 - 1 MAY REDEL MOROCCO USD 8500 (DREYFUS)

VARVA 33041 DWT 13K ON 29 (180) + 2 MDO DELY NOPAC 26 - 30 MAY REDEL W AFRICA USD 6750 + USD 100000 BB (LALEMENT)

OLYMPIC MENTOR 29693 DWT 13K ON 18 (3500) + 1.5 MDO DELY WC CANADA 21 - 27 MAY REDEL SPORE JPN RG USD 7900 + USD 150000 BB (MEDMAR)

REGINA OLDENDORFF 28031 DWT 14.5K ON 31L I4K ON 30B (180) + 3 MDO DELY GIBRALTAR 25 - 31 MAY 5 - 7 MTHS REDEL ATLANTIC USD 7500 (BRODIN)

GALBRAITH'S LIMITED

BALTIC FREIGHT INDEX (continued)

Baltic Exchange Daily Fixture/Index List 03/03/2011

BDI 1317 (UP 36) BCI 1390 (UP 53) BPI 1929 (UP 71) BSI 1454 (UP 19) BHSI 703 (No change) Last published BDTI 1000 (UP 35) BCTI 760 (UP 11)

TIME CHARTER

'GCL Argentina' 2010 177000 dwt dely Qingdao 9/11 Mar trip via Esperance redel China $4000 daily - 'K' Line

'Cape Spencer' 2010 169092 dwt dely aps Ponta Da Madeira 1/15 Mar trip redel Skaw-Cape Passero rge $4850 daily + $500000 bb - Classic Maritime - <fixed earlier this week>

'Yiannis B' 2008 83000 dwt dely Hong Kong 2/6 Mar trip via Indonesia redel India $12750 daily - British Marine

'Angelo Della Gatta 1' 2006 82500 dwt dely aps Richards Bay 5 Mar trip redel China $28000 daily + $400000 bb - Norden

'YM Rightness' 2004 77684 dwt dely Mundra 7/10 Mar trip via India redel China $22000 daily - NCS

'Nord Fortune' 2008 76896 dwt dely Immingham ely Mar trip via Continent and Sudan redel Cape Passero $17500 daily - Mina Shipping - <recent>

'Lowlands Camellia' STX Pan Ocean relet 2006 76807 dwt dely Civitavecchia 4/6 Mar trip via EC South America redel Singapore-Japan rge $24000 daily - Bunge

'Red Lily' 2004 76606 dwt dely retro Paradip 20 Feb trip via EC South America redel Singapore-Japan rge $18500 daily - cnr

'Coral Diamond' 2007 76596 dwt dely psg Taiwan 8/12 Mar trip via Indonesia redel India $13000 daily - Libra

'Mulberry Wilton' 2004 76300 dwt dely Rotterdam in d/c 5/7 Mar trip via Baltic redel UKC $15250 daily - Swiss Marine

'Milagro' 2009 75205 dwt dely Recalada 5/15 Mar trip via EC South America redel Singapore-Japan rge $26250 daily + $650000 bb - cnr - <recent>

'Dream Seas' Michele Bottiglieri relet 2009 75151 dwt dely US Gulf 20/30 Mar trip redel Singapore-Japan rge $26000 daily + $600000 bb - Alfred C.Toepfer

'Angelic Power' 2002 74750 dwt dely retro CJK 28 Feb trip via Australia redel India $16000 daily - BHP Billiton

'Merian' Deiulemar relet 2000 74500 dwt dely Santos 10/15 Mar trip redel Singapore-Japan rge $26500 daily + $690000 bb - Beibu

'Great Wisdom' 2000 74293 dwt dely Rotterdam 4/8 Mar trip via Norfolk redel Gijon $15000 daily - STX Pan Ocean UK

'Georgios S' 2001 74249 dwt dely retro Cape Passero 21/24 Feb trip via US Gulf & Syria redel Cape Passero $15250 daily - Cargill

'Tian Yang Feng' 2000 74027 dwt dely psg Gibraltar 4 Mar trip via EC South America redel Singapore-Japan rge $27000 daily - cnr

'Angela Star' 1998 73798 dwt dely Santos 20/24 Mar trip redel Singapore-Japan rge $26000 daily + $650000 bb - Cargill

'Elinakos' 1997 73751 dwt dely Recalada 1/10 Apr trip via EC South America redel Singapore-Japan rge $26500 daily + $750000 bb - Glencore

'Jian Hua' 2000 73747 dwt dely Cape Passero 9 Mar 2 laden legs redel Skaw-Cape Passero $16500 daily - Practica

'Corona' 2007 73593 dwt dely SW Pass 7/9 Mar trip redel Singapore-Japan rge $24000 daily + $600000 bb - Suisse Atlantique

'Cape' 1997 73409 dwt dely Lanshan in d/c 7/10 Mar trip via EC Australia redel Singapore-Japan rge $12000 daily - BHP BIlliton

'Aenaos' Transgrain relet 1998 72413 dwt dely Recalada 4/10 Mar trip via Upriver & PG redel PMO $24000 daily $500000 bb - GIEX

'Joyous World' 1995 69286 dwt dely Xingang 4/6 Mar trip via NoPac redel Singapore-Japan rge $12250 daily - cnr

BALTIC FREIGHT INDEX (continued)

'Okialos' 1994 69149 dwt dely Mobile 12/20 Mar trip via US Gulf redel Cape Passero $15000 daily + $500000 bb - Bunge

'Silver Mei' 1989 68676 dwt dely Inchon 5/8 Mar trip via NoPac redel Singapore-Japan rge $13500 daily - Cargill

'Ozgur Aksoy' 2011 58929 dwt dely Inchon spot trip via Vancouver redel UKCont intention woodchip pellets $9500 daily - Greig Star

'Doric Viking' 2010 58000 dwt dely Portland Oregon 15/25 March trip redel SE Asia $17000 daily + $500000 bb - cnr

'Belstar' 2009 57970 dwt   - <charterers of fixture reported 02/03 were IVS>

'Trident Challenger' 2010 57000 dwt dely Magdalla 9/11 March trip redel China $17750 daily - cnr

'SITC Taishan' 2010 57000 dwt dely Lianyungang 6/8 March trip via SE Asia redel China intention Nickel ore $17000 daily - Intermarine

'K.Opal' 2010 56000 dwt dely USGulf 10/15 March trip redel Spain $34000 daily - STX Pan Ocean

'Dubai Energy' 2004 55389 dwt dely retro Kakinada 28 February trip via South Africa redel Singapore-Japan $17500 daily - Noble

'Port Menier' 2007 53808 dwt dely Jintang 5/7 March trip via Indonesia redel India $13000 daily - cnr

'Vela' 2007 53565 dwt dely Kohsichang spot trip via Indonesia redel India $16000 daily - Oldendorff

'Kang Fu' 2002 51069 dwt dely Tuticorin 4/6 March trip via South Africa redel Singapore-Japan intention grain $17000 daily - cnr

'Great Reward' 2010 32000 dwt dely Longview 20/25 Mar trip via Nopac redel Singapore-Japan rge $11000 daily + $380000 bb - STX Pan Ocean

'Kent Tenacious' 2007 29300 dwt dely Japan prompt trip intention pipes redel north Continent-Dunkirk $6000 daily - cnr - <fixed abt 10 days ago>

PERIOD

'Prabhu Sakhawat' 2005 75944 dwt dely Sakaide 4/7 Mar 4/6 months trading redel worldwide $17500 daily - Cargill

'Parnon' 2011 56000 dwt dely ex yard China March 2011 1 years trading redel worldwide $14950 daily - Hudson - <corrects name of vessel reported 02/03>

ORE

'Nord Power' 2005 170000/10 Port Hedland/Qingdao 14/20 Mar $6.70 fio scale/30000sc - FMG - <corrects the 02/03 report of the ship fixing to Rio Tinto, although Rio did fix a 2nd ship from Dampier to Qingdao>

'Maltida' 1993 70000/10 Pointe Noire/Piombino & Trieste 16/23 Mar $24.75 fio 2 days shinc/3 days shinc-3 days shinc - Lucchini

'Happy Day' 1997 70000/10 Tubarao/Qingdao 5/8 Mar $37.00 fio scale/25000sc - Vale

Appendix 11

DRY CARGO CHARTER PARTIES OF MAJOR IMPORTANCE

1: Voyage Forms

General Purpose

Title	Date	Codename	PUBLISHER
Uniform General	As revised 1922 (l966 layout)	GENCON	BIMCO
Uniform General (Boxtype)	As revised 1944 (1994 layout)	GENCON	BIMCO
General	1982 (revised 1986)	MULTIFORM	FONASBA
Grain:			
Approved Baltimore Berth	1913	BALTIMORE	
Grain C/P – Steamer	(adapted 1971)	FORMC	
North American Grain	1973 (amended 1989)	NORGRAIN 89	ASBA
Grain Voyage	1966 (revised 1974)	GRAINVOY	
Continent Grain	1957 (amended 1990)	SYNACOMEX 90	Syndicat National du Commerce Exterieur des Cereales
Australian Wheat	1990 (amended 1991)	AUSTWHEAT	Australian Wheat Board
Australian Barley	1975 (revised 1980)	AUSBAR	Australian Barley Board
River Plate of Shipping	1914	CENTROCON	UK Chamber

DRY CARGO CHARTER PARTIES OF MAJOR IMPORTANCE (continued)

Feritiliser:			
Fertilisers Charter	1942 (amended 1974)	FERTICON	UK Chamber of Shipping
North American Fertiliser	1978 (revised 1988	FERTIVOY 88	Canpotex Shipping Services, Vancouver
Phosphate C?P	1950	AFRICANPHOS	
Coal:			
South African Anthracite	1974	SAFANCHART	S. African No. 2 Anthracite Producers Assn, Johannesburg
Americanised Welsh Coal	1953 (revised 1993)	AMWELSH	ASBA
Australian Coal Charter		AUSCOAL	
Ore:			
Mediterranean Iron Ore		C(ORE)7	
Iron Ore	1973	NIPPONORE	The Japan Shg Exchange Inc
Standard Ore	1980	OREVOY	BIMCO
Sugar:			
Sugar C?P	1969 (revised 1977)	-	
Bulk Sugar Charter – USA	1962 (revised 1968)	-	
Cuban Sugar	1973	CUBASUGAR	
Australia/Japan – Bulk Raw Sugar	1975		
Fiji Sugar	1977	-	
Mauritius Bulk Sugar	-		MSS Form
Timber:			
Baltic Wood	1964	NUBALTWOOD	UK Chamber of Shipping
C/P for Logs	1967	NANYOZAI	The Japan Shg Exchange Inc

Appendix 11

DRY CARGO CHARTER PARTIES OF MAJOR IMPORTANCE (continued)

2: Period Forms

Timecharter			
Uniform Time Charter	1939 (amended 1974)	BALTIME	B1MCO
Uniform Time Charter	1968 (amended 1974)	LINERTIME	B1MCO
New York Produce Exchange T/C	1981	ASBATIME	ASBA
New York Produce Exchange T/C	1993	NYPE 93	ASBA
Uniform Time Charter for container vessels	1990	BOXTIME	BIMCO
Bareboat:			
Standard Bareboat Charter	1989	BARECON	BIMCO

Appendix 12

FONASBA

Codename: "Multiform 1982"

This Charter Party is not designed for use in the Container trade.

The Federation of National Associations of Ship Brokers and Agents

F O N A S B A

MULTI-PURPOSE CHARTER PARTY 1982

	Place. 19	
1.	IT IS THIS DAY MUTUALLY AGREED between..	1
	....of..	2
	the Owners/disponent Owners, hereinafter called the Owners, of the vessel	3
	(as described hereunder), now	4
	and expected ready to load under this Charter Party about .... on her present position,	5
	and	6
	of .... the Charterers.	7

Vessel's Description

The Owners describe the vessel as: Built 19.............. Flag .... Classed	8
Callsign .... GRT .... NRT .... Summer deadweight all told of about	9
.... metric/long tons on a draft of ....in salt water.	10
Number of decks .... Number of holds .... Number of hatches	11
Type of hatch covers in main and tweendecks (and sizes if required)	12
....	13
Cubic feet grain/bale in main holds and tweendecks	14
....	15
....	16
Cubic feet grain/bale in other compartments available for cargo	17
....	18
Engines placed .... Bridge placed .... Length overall .... Extreme breadth	19
Type, number and capacity of cargo lifting gear	20
.... metric/long tons S.W.L.	21
	22

Loading Place and Cargo

2.	That the said vessel, being tight, staunch and strong and in every way fit for the voyage, shall with all convenient speed proceed to	23
	....	24
		25
	as ordered by Charterers, or so near thereto as she may safely get and there load at one or two safe berths, as ordered by Charterers, always afloat, a full	26
	and complete/part cargo of minimum .... tons of 1000 kilos and maximum	27
	....tons of 1000 kilos, ... quantity in the	28
	Master's option, of	29
		30

Orders for Loading Ports(s)

The loading port(s) shall be declared by Charterers not later than	31
....	32

Rotation

If the vessel loads at more than one port, the rotation shall be	33
....	34

Discharging Place

3.	Being so loaded, the vessel shall proceed to	35
	....	36
		37
	as ordered by Charterers, or so near thereto as she may safely get and there deliver the cargo at one or two safe berths, as ordered by	38
	Charterers, always afloat. Owners guarantee the vessel's deepest draft in saltwater on arrival at first or sole discharging port shall not	39
	exceed	40

Orders for Discharging Ports(s)

The discharging port(s) shall be declared by Charterers not later than	41
....	42

Rotation

If the vessel discharges at more than one port, the rotation shall be	43
....	44
	45

Laydays and Cancelling

4.	Laytime for loading shall not commence before 0800 hours on .... and should the vessel's notice	46
	of readiness not be given before 1700 hours on .... in accordance with Clause 7, the Charterers shall, at	47
	any time thereafter, but not later than the time when such notice has been delivered, have the option of cancelling this Charter Party.	48
	If, prior to tendering notice under this Charter Party, the vessel's cancelling date has already passed or, which ever first occurs, the vessel has begun her approach	49
	voyage and in the ordinary course of events would be unable to tender notice before the cancelling date, the Owners, having given a revised expected readiness to	50
	load date, may require the Charterers to declare whether they elect to cancel the Charter Party and Charterers shall be given up to 48 running hours to make this	51
	declaration Should the Charterers not elect	

Appendix 12

FONASBA (continued)

to cancel, the cancelling date shall be extended by three running days, Sundays (or their equivalents) and holidays excluded, from the vessel's revised expected readiness to load date. This provision shall be without prejudice to any claim the Charterers may have as to Owners' possible misrepresentation of the vessel's expected readiness date and/or laydays/canceling dates contained herein.

Freight   5.   The freight is to be paid at the rate of .... per ton of 1000 kilos on gross Bill of Lading weight and is to be paid in the following manner:-

....

....

The freight shall be deemed earned as cargo is loaded on board and shall be discountless and non-returnable, vessel and/or cargo lost or not lost.

Cost of Loading and Discharging Stevedores   6.   The cargo shall be loaded, stowed/trimmed and discharged, to the Master's satisfaction in respect of seaworthiness, free of expense to the vessel.

Stevedores at loading and discharging ports are to be appointed and paid by Charterers. The stevedores shall be deemed to be the servants of the Owners and shall work under the supervision of the Master.

Notice of Readiness/Time Counting   7.   Notification of the vessel's readiness to load/discharge at the first or sole loading/discharging port shall be delivered in writing at the office of the Shippers/Receivers or their agents between 0900 hours and 1700 hours on any day except Sunday (or its local equivalent) and holidays, and between 0900 hours and 1200 hours on Saturday (or its local equivalent). Such notice of readiness shall be delivered when the vessel is in the loading/discharging berth and is in all respects ready to load/discharge. However, if the loading/discharging berth is unavailable, the Master may give notice of readiness on the vessel's arrival within the port or at a customary waiting place outside the port limits, whether or not in free pratique and whether or not cleared by Customs. At the first or sole loading/discharging port laytime shall commence at 1300 hours if notice of readiness is given before noon and at 0800 hours on the next working day that is not excepted from laytime, if notice is given after noon, unless sooner commenced, in which case only time actually used shall count against laytime. At any other loading/discharging port laytime shall commence on vessel's arrival as above. However time shifting from the waiting place(s) to the loading/discharging berth shall not count even if the vessel is already on demurrage.

If the vessel is found not to be ready to load or discharge, the time taken to make the vessel ready is not to count as laytime or time on demurrage and all expenses to make the vessel ready shall be for Owners' account.

Provided Charterers consent to loading before lay days (as shown in Line 45) commences, any such time actually used shall count against laytime.

Rate of Loading and Discharging and Excepted Time   8.   The cargo shall be: - (a) loaded and stowed/trimmed at the average rate of .... tons of 1000 kilos and discharged at the average rate of .... tons of 1000 kilos, both per working day of 24 consecutive hours, weather permitting, Sundays (or their local equivalents) and Holidays excepted unless used when only time actually used shall count.

OR (b) loaded, stowed/trimmed and discharged within .... working days of 24 consecutive hours, weather permitting, Sundays (or their local equivalents) and Holidays excepted, unless used when only time actually used shall count.

Demurrage and Despatch   9.   If the vessel is longer detained in loading/discharging, demurrage is to be paid by Charterers to Owners at the rate of .... per day or pro rata.

For laytime saved in loading/discharging, Owners are to pay Charterers despatch money at the rate of half the demurrage rate per day or pro rata.

Notices   10.   (a) The Owners shall give .... days' approximate and .... days' definite notice of the vessel's readiness to load date and shall confirm her ETA at the first loading port 48 and 24 hours in advance, to ....

....

(b) Upon the vessel's sailing from the (last) loading port, the Master shall radio to ....

....

giving the sailing time, the quantity of cargo loaded and the vessel's ETA at first or sole discharging port and shall thereafter radio .... hours' and .... hours' notice of her ETA to ....

Opening and Closing of Hatches   11.   At each loading and discharging port, provided local regulations permit, the first opening and last closing of hatches including removal and replacing of beams, if any, shall be effected by the vessel's crew at Owners' expense. If local regulations do not so permit, then these operations shall be effected by shore labour at Charterers' expense. In either event, time so used shall not count as laytime. Any other such operations shall be effected by shore labour at Charterers' expense and time so used shall count as laytime.

Gear and Lights   12.   The vessel shall give, free of expense to Charterers, full use of vessel's lighting on deck and in the cargo compartments, also full and free use of her tackle, derricks and winches and/or cranes, with the necessary power to work all gear simultaneously at all times, as may be required by Charterers. Shore winchmen/crane drivers shall be for Charterers' account.

The vessel's cargo gear and runners shall be in good working order, the vessel having a valid gear certificate on board. Owners warrant that the vessel's gear complies with Clause 1.

In the event of a breakdown of a winch or winches or crane(s), not caused by Charterers, their Agents or contractors, the period of delay thereby caused to the vessel is not to count as laytime or time on demurrage and the cost of any stevedore stand-by time and all other expenses thereby directly incurred shall be for Owners' account.

Separations

Grab Discharge   13.   Any separations required by Charterers between parcels within the vessel's compartments shall be at their risk and expense and to the 108 Master's satisfaction.

14.   The vessel is to be suitable for grab discharge. No cargo shall be loaded in any cargo compartments not readily accessible for grab discharge. However, should any cargo be loaded in any inaccessible spaces, all extra expenses so incurred shall be for Owners' account and any time lost to the vessel shall not count as laytime or time on demurrage.

Stevedore Damage   15.   Stevedore damage to the vessel shall be for Charterers' account, subject to the following conditions:—

At the time of the occurrence the Master is to notify the Charterers by telecommunication the details of the stevedore damage in the case of damage discoverable by the exercise of due diligence and otherwise on discovery thereof, but in no case later than completion of discharge of the cargo, failing which any claim shall be deemed to be waived.

Furthermore, immediately visible damage occurs the Master shall place the stevedores on notice in writing holding them responsible, and endeavour to obtain their acknowledgement of liability therefor.

Stevedore damage affecting the seaworthiness of the vessel shall be repaired by the Charterers at their expense in the port where the damage occurs and they are to compensate Owners at the demurrage rate for any time so used, over and above that required for cargo handling purposes.

Damage not affecting vessel's seaworthiness shall be for Charterers' account when actually repaired, but no compensation is to be paid to Owners for any time so used.

52
53
54
55
56
57
58
59
60
61
62
63
64
65
66
67
68
69
70
71
72
73
74
75
76
77
78
79
80
81
82
83
84
85
86
87
88
89
90
91
92
93
94
95
96
97
98
99
100
101
102
103
104
105
106
107
108
109
110
111
112
113
114
115
116
117
118
119
120
121
122
123

FONASBA (continued)

Packaged Cargo Tallying Cargo Battens	16. Tallying, if ordered by Owners, shall be arranged and paid for by the Owners. If tallying is ordered by any other party, it shall be paid for by Charterers.	124 125
	If cargo in units/packages is loaded, the vessel shall be fully net or wooden cargo batten fitted. Any missing battens shall be replaced by any suitable material to protect the cargo from the ship's steel plating at Owners' expense and in their time. Any other dunnage required shall be provided, laid and paid for by Charterers.	126 127 128
Overtime	17. All overtime expenses at loading and discharging port(s) shall be for account of the party ordering same. If overtime is ordered by port authorities or the party controlling the loading and/or discharging terminal or facility, all such expenses shall be for Charterers' account.	129 130 131
	Overtime expenses for the vessel's officers and crew shall always be for Owners' account.	132
Seaworthy Trim	18. If ordered to load or discharge at two berths and/or ports, the vessel is to be left in seaworthy trim to the Master's satisfaction for the passage between such berths and/or ports at Charterers' expense. Time used for placing the vessel in seaworthy trim shall count as laytime or time on demurrage.	133 134 135
Shifting	19. If two loading/discharging berths are used, the cost of shifting between berths shall be for Charterers' account and time so used shall count.	136 137
Dues and Taxes Any other Taxes	20. Any dues and/or wharfage and/or taxes on the vessel shall be for Owners' account and any on the cargo shall be for Charterers' account	138 139 140
Agents	21. Owners shall appoint their own agents at loading port(s) and their own agents at discharging port(s).	141
Bills of Lading	22. The Master shall sign Bills of Lading as presented (but in accordance with Mate's receipts) without prejudice to the terms, conditions and exceptions of this Charter Party. Should it be impracticable for the Master to sign Bills of Lading, he may authorise in writing the port agents to sign them on his behalf in accordance with Mate's receipts. See also Clause 34.	142 143 144
Lightening	23. Provided the vessel has complied with the draft provision in Clause 3, any lightening necessary at port(s) of discharge to enable the vessel to reach her discharging berth(s) shall be at Charterers' risk and expense, time counting as laytime or time on demurrage but time shifting from the place of lightening to the discharging berth(s) is not to count.	145 146 147
Lien and Cesser	24. The Owners shall have a lien on the cargo for freight, deadfreight, demurrage and average contributions due to them under this Charter Party. Charterers' liability under this Charter Party shall cease on the cargo being shipped except for payment of freight, deadfreight and demurrage and except for all other matters provided for in this Charter Party where the Charterers' responsibility is specified.	148 149 150
Deviation	25. Any deviation in saving or attempting to save life and/or property at sea shall not be deemed to be an infringement or breach of this Charter Party and the Owners shall not be liable for any loss or damage resulting therefrom.	151 152
	Should the vessel put into unscheduled port(s) whilst on the voyage, the Owners are to inform Charterers and agents at discharging port(s) thereof immediately.	153 154
General average	26. General Average shall be settled according to the York/Antwerp Rules 1974 and shall be adjusted in .... and paid in	155 156
New Jason Clause	Where the adjustment is made in accordance with the law and practice of the United States of America, the foil owing clause shall apply :- "In the event of accident, danger, damage or disaster before or after the commencement of the voyage, resulting from any cause whatsoever, whether due to negligence or not, for which, or for the consequences of which, the carrier is not responsible, by Statute, contract or otherwise, the goods, shippers, consignees or owners of the goods shall contribute with the carrier in general average to the payment of any sacrifices, losses, or expenses of a general average nature that may be made or incurred and shall pay salvage and special charges incurred in respect of the goods.	157 158 159 160 161 162
	If a salving vessel is owned or operated by the carrier, salvage shall be paid for as fully as if the said salving vessel or vessels belonged to strangers. Such deposit as the carrier or his agents may deem sufficient to cover the estimated contribution of the goods and any salvage and special charges thereon shall, if required, be made by the goods, shippers, consignees, or owners of the goods to the carrier before delivery."	163 164 165 166
	The Charterers shall procure that all Bills of Lading issued under this Charter Party shall contain this clause.	167
Strikes	27. Neither Charterers nor Owners shall be responsible for the consequences of any strikes or lock-outs preventing or delaying the fulfilment of any obligations under this contract. If there is a strike or lock-out affecting the loading of the cargo, or any part of it, when the vessel is ready to proceed from her last port or at any time during the voyage to the port or ports of loading or after her arrival there, the Master or Owners may ask Charterers to declare that they agree to reckon the laytime as if there were no strike or lock-out.	168 169 170 171
	Unless Charterers have given such declaration in writing (by telecommunication, if necessary) within 24 hours. Owners shall have the option of cancelling this contract. If part cargo has already been loaded, the vessel must proceed with same and the freight shall be payable only on the quantity loaded, the Owners having the liberty to complete with other cargo on the way for their own account.	172 173 174
	If there is a strike or lock-out affecting the discharge of the cargo on or after the vessel's arrival at or off port of discharge and same has not been settled within 48 hours, Charterers shall have the option of keeping vessel waiting until such strike or lock-out is at an end against paying half demurrage after expiration of the time provided for discharging or of ordering the vessel to a safe port where she can safely discharge without risk of being detained by strike or lock-out. Such orders shall be given within 48 hours after Captain or Owners have given notice to Charterers of the strike or lock-out affecting the discharge. On delivery of the cargo at the substituted port, all conditions of this Charter Party and the Bill of Lading shall apply and the vessel shall receive the same freight as if she had discharged at the original port of destination, except that if the distance of the substituted port exceeds 100 nautical miles the freight on the cargo delivered at the substituted port shall be increased in proportion.	175 176 177 178 179 180 181 182
Exceptions	28. The vessel, her Master, the Owners and the Charterers shall not, unless otherwise expressly provided for in this Charter Party, be responsible for loss of or damage to or delay to or failure to supply, load, discharge or deliver the cargo arising or resulting from:	183 184
	Act of God, act of war, act of public enemies, pirates or assailing thieves; arrest or restraints of princes,rulers or people; seizure under legal process provided a bond is promptly furnished to release the vessel or cargo, floods, fires; blockades; riots; insurrections; Civil Commotions; earthquakes; explosions.	185 186 187
	No exceptions afforded the Charterers or Receivers under this clause shall relieve the Charterers or Receivers of or diminish their obligations for payment of any sums due to the Owners under the provisions of this Charter Party.	188 189
Relet	29. Charterers have the privilege of reletting all or part of this Charter Party to others, subject to Owners' approval, which shall not be unreasonably withheld, Charterers guaranteeing to the Owners the due fulfilment of this Charter Party.	190 191

...ued)

192
193
194
195
196
197
198
199

...under this Charter Party are to be referred to arbitration in .... and subject to the law applicable to Charter
... e city of the arbitral forum.

... the general practice in the selected arbitral forum for such disputes to be arbitrated by a tripartite tribunal, one arbitrator is to be appointed
... parties, and in the case the arbitrators shall not agree, the issues in contention shall be submitted to an umpire selected by the two arbitrators.
... the second or tripartite basis, one arbitrator is to be appointed by each of the parties, and a third by the two so chosen.

... on of the arbitrators or umpire in the first case and that of the tripartite tribunal or a majority of it in the second case shall be binding on the parties,
... the applicable law.

A... Com... ...dress commission of .... % on gross freight, deadfreight and demurrage is due to Charterers at the time that freight, respectively
...urrage, is paid, vessel lost or not lost.

...arterers have The right to deduct such commissions from payment of freight, respectively demurrage.

Brokerage	A brokerage of	.... % to ....
		.... % to ....
		.... % to ....

on gross freight, deadfreight and demurrage is payable by Owners at the time of receiving freight, respectively demurrage, vessel lost or not lost.

Protecting Clauses

33. The following clauses are fully incorporated in, and are to form part of, this Charter Party:

P. & I. Bunkering clause:

The vessel shall have the liberty as part of the contract voyage to proceed to any port or ports at which bunker fuel is available for the purpose of bunkering at any stage of the voyage whatsoever and whether such ports are on or off the direct and/or customary route or routes between any of the ports of loading or discharge named in this Charter Party and may there take bunkers in any quantity in the discretion of Owners even to the full capacity of fuel tanks and deep tanks and any other compartment in which fuel can be carried, whether such amount is or is not required for the chartered voyage.

Both to Blame Collision clause:

If the liability for any collision in which the vessel is involved while performing this Charter Party falls to be determined in accordance with the laws of the United States of America, the following clause shall apply:

"If the vessel comes into collision with another vessel as a result of the negligence of the other vessel and any act, neglect or default of the master, mariner, pilot or the servants of the Carrier in the navigation or in the management of the vessel, the owners of the goods carried hereunder will indemnify the Carrier against all loss or liability to the other or noncarrying vessel or her Owners in so far as such loss or liability represents loss of or damage to or any claim whatsoever of the owners d the said goods, paid or payable by the other or non-carrying vessel or her owners to the owners of the said goods and set off, recouped or recovered by the other or non-carrying vessel or her owners as part of their claim against the carrying vessel or carrier.

The foregoing provisions shall also apply where the Owners, operators or those in charge of any vessel or vessels or objects other than, or in addition to, the colliding vessels or objects are at fault in respect to a collision or contact"

The Charterers shall procure that all Bills of Lading issued under this Charter Party shall contain the same clause.

Ice clause:
Port of loading
(a) In the event of the loading port being inaccessible by reason of ice when vessel is ready to proceed from her last port or at any time during the voyage or on vessel's arrival or m case frost sets in after vessel's arrival, the Captain for fear of being frozen m is at liberty to leave without cargo, and this Charter shall be null and void.
(b) If during loading the Captain, for fear of vessel being frozen in, deems it advisable to leave, he has liberty to do so with what cargo he has on board and to proceed to any other port or ports with option of completing cargo for Owners' benefit for any port or ports including port of discharge. Any part of cargo thus loaded under this Charter shall be forwarded to destination at vessel's expense but against payment of freight, provided that no extra expenses be thereby caused to the Receivers, freight being paid on quantity delivered (in proportion if lumpsum), all other conditions as per this Charter Party.

(c) In case of more than one loading port, and if one or more of the ports are closed by ice, the Captain or Owners shall be at liberty either to load the part cargo at the open port and fill up elsewhere for their own account as under section (b) or to declare the Charter null and void unless Charterers agree to load full cargo at the open port.
(d) This Ice Clause is not to apply in the Spring.

Port of discharge.
(a) Should ice (except m the Spring) prevent vessel from reaching port of discharge Receivers shall have the option of keeping vessel waiting until the re-opening of navigation and paying demurrage, or of ordering the vessel to a safe and immediately accessible port where she can safely discharge without risk of detention by ice Such orders shall be given within 48 hours after Captain or Owners have given notice to Charterers of the impossibility of reaching port of destination.
(b) If during discharging the Captain for fear of vessel being frozen in deems it advisable to leave, he has liberty to do so with what cargo he has on board and to proceed to the nearest accessible port where she can safely discharge.
(c) On delivery of the cargo at such port, all conditions of the Bill of Lading shall applly and vessel shall receive the same freight as if she had discharged at the original port of destination, except that if the distance of the substituted port exceeds 100 nautical miles, the freight on the cargo delivered at the substituted port shall be increased m proportion.

War Risks clause:
(1) In these Clauses "War Risks" shall include any blockade or any action which is announced as a blockade by any Government or by any belligerent or by any organized body, sabotage, curacy, and any actual or threatened war, hostilities, warlike operations, civil war, civil commotion, or revolution.
(2) If at any time before the Vessel commences loading, it appears That performance of the contract will subject the Vessel or her Master and crew or her cargo to war risks at any stage of the adventure, the Owners shall be entitled by letter or telegram despatched to the Charterers, to cancel this Charter.
(3) The Master shad not be required to load cargo or to continue loading or to proceed on or to sign Bill(s) of Lading for any adventure on which or any port at which it appears that the Vessel, her Master and crew or her cargo will be subjected to war risks. In the event of the exercise by the Master of his right under this Clause after part or full cargo has been loaded, the Master shall be at liberty either to discharge such cargo at the loading port or to proceed therewith. In the latter case the Vessel shall have liberty to carry other cargo for Owners' benefit and accordingly to proceed to and load or discharge such other cargo at any other port c ports whatsoever, backwards or forwards, although in a contrary direction to or out of or beyond the ordinary route. In the event of the Master electing to proceed with part cargo under this Clause freight shall in any case be payable on the quantity delivered.
(4) If at the time the Master elects to proceed with part or full cargo under Clause 3, or after the Vessel has left the loading port, or the last of the loading ports, if more than one, it appears that further performance of the contract will subject the Vessel, her Master and crew or her cargo, to war risks, the cargo shall be discharged, or if the discharge has been commenced shall be completed, at any safe port in vicinity of the port of discharge as may be ordered by the Charterers If no such orders shall be received from the Charterers within 48 hours after the Owners have despatched a request by telegram to the Charterers for the nomination of a substitute discharging port, the Owners shall be at liberty to discharge the cargo at any safe port which they may in their discretion, decide on and such discharge shall be deemed to be due fulfilment of the contract of affreightment. In the event of cargo being discharged at any such other port, the Owners shall be entitled to freight as if the discharge had been effected at the port or ports named in the BiN(s) of Lading or to which the Vessel may have been ordered pursuant thereto.
(5) (a) The Vessel shall have liberty to comply with any directions or recommendations as to loading, departure, arrival, routes, ports of call, stoppages, destination, ;ones, waters, discharge, delivery or m any other wise whatsoever (including any direction or recommendation not to go to the port of destination or to delay proceeding thereto or to proceed to some other port) given by any Government or by any belligerent or by any organized body engaged in civil war, hostilities or warlike operations or by any person or body acting or belligerent or of any such organized body or by any committee or person having under the terms of the war risks insurance on the Vessel, the right to give any such directions or recommendations. If by reason of or in compliance with any such direction or recommendation, anything is done or is not done, such shall not be deemed a deviation.
(b) If, by reason of or »n compliance with any such directions or recommendations, the Vessel does not proceed to the port or ports named in the Bill(s) of Lading or to which she may have been ordered pursuant thereto, the Vessel may proceed to any port as directed or recommended or to any safe port which the Owners in their discretion may decide on and there discharge the cargo Such discharge shall be deemed to be due fulfilment of the contract of affreightment and the Owners shall be entitled to freight as if discharge had been effected at the oort or oorts named in the Bill(s) of Lading or to which the Vessel may have been ordered pursuant thereto.
(6) All extra expenses (including insurance costs) involved in discharging cargo at the loading port or in reaching or discharging the cargo at any port as provided in Clauses 4 and 5 (b) hereof shall be paid by the Charterers and/or cargo owners, and the Owners shall have a lien on the cargo for all moneys due under these Clauses

Clauses Paramount

34. The Hague Rules as Amended by the Brussels Protocol 1968 shall apply to this Charter Party and to any Bills of Lading issued hereunder. The Charterers shall procure that all Bills of Lading issued under this Charter Party shall contain a clause to include these rules.

200
201
202
203
204
205
206
207
208
209
210
211
212
213
214
215
216
217
218
219
220
221
222
223
224
225
226
227
228
229
230
231
232
233
234
235
236
237
238
239
240
241
242
243
244
245
246
247
248
249
250
251
252
253
254
255
256
257
258
259
260
261
262
263
264
265
266
267
268
269
270
271
272
273
274
275
276
277
278
279
280
281
252

Appendix 13

AMWELSH 93

Code Name: **"AMWELSH 93"**
Recommended by
The Baltic and International Maritime Council (BIMCO)
The Federation of National Associations of
Ship Brokers and Agents (FONASBA)

AMERICANIZED WELSH COAL CHARTER©

Issued by the Association of Ship Brokers and Agents (U.S.A), Inc.
New York - 1953; Amended 1979; Revised 1993

THIS CHARTER PARTY, made and concluded in ....
this .... day of ....19 ....

Between ....
....

<u>Owners</u> of the .... (flag) Vessel ....
of...built....................................... (year) at...(where)
of... tons of 1000 kilos total deadweight on summer freeboard, inclusive of bunkers,
classed..in..and registered
at..under No .... The Vessel's length overall is
.... and beam is .... The Vessel's fully laden draft on summer
freeboard is...................... now ....and
....

<u>Charterers</u>...
of the city of ....

1.   <u>Loading Port(s)/Discharging Port(s)</u>

That the said Vessel being tight, staunch and strong, and in every way fit for the voyage, shall, with all convenient speed,
proceed to ....
....
....and there load, always afloat, and in the
customary manner from the Charterers, in such safe berth as they shall direct, a full and complete cargo of coal ....
.... tons of 2240 lbs/1000 kilos* .... % more or less in the
Owners' option; and being so loaded, shall therefrom proceed, with all convenient speed, to ....
.... or so near thereunto as she can safely get,
and there deliver her cargo, as ordered by the Charterers, where she can safely deliver it, always afloat, on having been
paid freight at the rate of .. US $ per ton of 2240 lbs/1000 kilos* on bill of lading quantity.

*) Delete as appropriate

2.   <u>Freight Payment</u>

The FREIGHT shall be paid in...
....
....

Appendix 13

AMWELSH 93 (continued)

3. Notices & Loading Port Orders

The Master shall give the Charterers (telegraphic address " .... " , Telex No .... Fax No ....) and .... days notice of the date of the Vessel's expected readiness to load, and approximate quantity of cargo required with the .... day notice. The Charterers shall be kept advised by any form of telecommunication of any alterations in that date, as and when known. The Charterers shall declare first or sole loading port on receipt of the Master's .... day notice, unless declared earlier.

4. Discharging Port Orders

The Master shall apply to the Charterers by any form of telecommunication for declaration of the first or sole discharging port 96 hours before the Vessel is due off/at .... and they are to declare same to the Master not later than 48 hours following receipt of the Master's application.

5. Laydays/Cancelling

Laytime for loading shall not commence before 0800 on the .... day of .... Should the Vessel's notice of readiness not have been tendered in accordance with Clause 6, before 1700 on the .... day of .... the Charterers shall have the option of cancelling this Charter Party, not later than one hour after the said notice has been tendered. The said cancelling date shall be extended by as many days (rounded to the nearest day) as the Charterers shall have failed to give loading port orders as provided in Clause 3 hereabove, without prejudice to the Owners' claim for detention.

If the Owners warrant that, despite the exercise of due diligence by the Owners, the Vessel will not be ready to tender notice of readiness by the cancelling date, and provided the Owners are able to state with reasonable certainty the date on which the Vessel will be ready, they may, at the earliest seven days before the Vessel is expected to sail for the port or place of loading, require the Charterers to declare whether or not they will cancel the Charter. Should the Charterers elect not to cancel, or should they fail to reply within seven days or by the cancelling date, whichever shall first occur, then the seventh day after the expected date of readiness for loading as notified by the Owners shall replace the original cancelling date. Should the Vessel be further delayed, the Owners shall be entitled to require further declarations of the Charterers in accordance with this Clause.

6. Time Counting

(a)   Notice of the Vessel's readiness to load and discharge at the first or sole port shall be tendered in writing to the Charterers between 0800 and 1700 on Mondays to Fridays and between 0800 and 1200 on Saturdays. Following tender of notice of readiness, laytime shall commence 12 hours thereafter, unless the Vessel's loading or discharging has sooner commenced.

Such notice of readiness shall be tendered when the Vessel is in the loading or discharging berth, if available, and is in all respects ready to load or discharge the cargo, unless the berth is not available on the Vessel's arrival, whereupon the Master may tender the said notice from a lay berth or anchorage within the port limits.

AMWELSH 93 (continued)

(b)   If the Vessel is prevented from entering the port limits because the first or sole loading or discharging berth, or a lay berth or anchorage is not available, or on the order of the Charterers or any competent official body or authority, and the Master warrants that the Vessel is physically ready in all respects to load or discharge, he may tender notice, by radio, if desired, from the usual anchorage outside the port limits, whether in free pratique or not, and/or whether customs cleared or not. If after entering the port limits the Vessel is found not to be ready, the time lost from the discovery thereof, until she is ready, shall not count as laytime, or time on demurrage.

(c)   Once the loading or discharging berth becomes available laytime or time on demurrage shall cease until the Vessel is in the berth, and shifting expenses shall be for the Owners' account.

(d)   *Subsequent Ports* - At second or subsequent ports of loading and/or discharging, laytime or time on demurrage shall resume counting from the Vessel's arrival in loading or discharging berth, if available, or if unavailable, from the arrival time within or outside the port limits, as provided in paragraph (a) supra.

7.   <u>Laytime</u>

(a)   The Vessel shall be loaded at the average rate of .... tons of 1000 kilos per day, or pro-rata for any part of a day, or within .... running days, both of twenty-four consecutive hours, weather permitting, Sundays and Holidays excepted/included*, and discharged at the average rate of... tons   of 1000 kilos per day, or pro-rata for any part of a day, or within.. r u n n i n g days, both of twenty four consecutive hours, weather permitting, Sundays and Holidays excepted/included*.

Days Purposes

(b)   Vessel shall be loaded and discharged within .... days of twenty-four consecutive hours, weather permitting, Sundays and Holidays excepted/included* at loading, and excepted/included* at discharge.

(c)   Time used in loading and discharging during excepted periods, if any, shall count as laytime.

Non-reversible laytime

(d)   In cases of separate laytime for loading and discharging, laytime shall be non-reversible.

*) Delete as appropriate

8.   <u>Exceptions</u>

The Owners shall be bound before and at the beginning of the voyage to exercise due diligence to make the Vessel seaworthy, and to have her properly manned, equipped and supplied, and neither the Vessel, nor the Master, or Owners shall be, or shall be held liable for any loss of, or damage, or delay to the cargo for causes excepted by the Hague Rules, or the Hague-Visby Rules, where applicable.

Appendix 13

AMWELSH 93 (continued)

Neither the Vessel, her Master or Owners, nor the Charterers shall, unless otherwise expressly provided in this Charter Party, be responsible for loss or damage to, or failure to supply, load, discharge or deliver the cargo resulting from: Act of God, act of war, act of public enemies, pirates or assailing thieves; arrest or restraint of princes, rulers or people; embargoes; seizure under legal process, provided bond is promptly furnished to release vessel or cargo; floods; frosts; fogs; fires; blockades; riots; insurrections; civil commotions; earthquakes; explosions; collisions; strandings and accidents of navigation; accidents at the mines or to machinery or to loading equipment; or any other causes beyond the Owners' or the Charterers' control; always provided that such events directly affect the loading and/or discharging process of the Vessel, and its performance under this Charter Party.

9.   Strikes

In the event of loss of time to the Vessel directly affecting the loading or discharging of this cargo, caused by a strike or lockout of any personnel connected with the production, mining, or any essential inland transport of the cargo to be loaded or discharged into/from this Vessel from point of origin, up to, and including the actual loading and discharging operations, or by any personnel essential to the actual loading and discharging of the cargo, half the laytime shall count during such periods, provided always that none of the aforementioned events did exist at the date of the charter party. If at any time during the continuance of such strikes or lockouts the Vessel goes on demurrage, said demurrage shall be paid at half the rate specified in Clause 10, hereunder, until such time as the strike or lockout terminates; thence full demurrage unless the Vessel was already on demurrage before the strike broke out, in which case full demurrage shall be paid for its entire period.

10.   Demurrage/Despatch

Demurrage, if incurred, at loading and/or discharging port(s), shall be paid by the Charterers to the Owners at the rate of .... per day, or pro-rata for part of a day. Despatch money shall be paid by the Owners to the Charterers at half the demurrage rate for all laytime saved.

11.   Cost of Loading and Discharging

The cargo shall be loaded, dumped, spout trimmed, and discharged by Charterers'*/Receivers'* stevedores free of risk and expense to the Vessel, under the supervision of the Master. Should the stevedores refuse to follow his instructions, the Master shall protest to them in writing and shall advise the Charterers immediately thereof.

12.   Overtime

(a)   *Expenses*

    (i)   All overtime expenses at loading and discharging ports shall be for account of the party ordering same.

    (ii)   If overtime is ordered by port authorities or the party controlling the loading and/or discharging terminal or facility all overtime expenses shall be equally shared between the Owners and the Charterers*/Receivers*.

AMWELSH 93 (continued)

(iii) Overtime expenses for the Vessel's officers and crew shall always be for the Owners' account.

(b) *Time Counting*

If overtime work ordered by the Owners be performed during periods excepted from laytime the actual time used shall count; if ordered by the Charterers/Receivers, the actual time used shall not count; if ordered by port authorities or the party controlling the loading and/or discharging terminal or facility half the actual time used shall count.

) Delete as appropriate

13. **Opening & Closing Hatches**

Opening and closing of hatches at commencement and completion of loading and discharging shall be for the Owners' account and time so used is not to count. All other opening and closing of hatches shall be for the Charterers' account and time so used shall count.

14. **Seaworthy Trim**

Charterers shall leave the Vessel in seaworthy trim and with cargo on board safely stowed to Master's satisfaction between loading berths/ports and between discharging berths/ports, respectively; any expenses resulting therefrom shall be for Charterers' account and any time used shall count.

15. **Shifting**

If more than one berth of loading and discharging has been agreed, and used, costs of shifting, including cost of bunkers used, shall be for the Charterers' account, time counting.

16. **Lighterage**

Should the Vessel be ordered to discharge at a place where there is insufficient water for the Vessel to reach it in the first tide after her arrival there, without lightening and lie always afloat, laytime shall count as per Clause 6 at a safe anchorage or lightening place for similar size vessels bound for such a place, and any lighterage expenses incurred to enable her to reach the place of discharge shall be for the Charterers' account, any custom of the port to the contrary notwithstanding. Time occupied in proceeding from the lightening place to the discharging berth shall not count as laytime or time on demurrage.

17. **Agents**

The Vessel shall be consigned to .... agents at port(s) of loading, and to ....agents at port(s) of discharge.

Appendix 13

AMWELSH 93 (continued)

18. Extra Insurance on Cargo

Any extra insurance on cargo, incurred owing to Vessel's age, class, flag, or ownership to be for Owners' account up to a maximum of .... and may be deducted from the freight in the Charterers' option. The Charterers shall furnish evidence of payment supporting such deduction.

19. Stevedore Damage

(a)   Any damage caused by stevedores shall be settled directly between the Owners and the stevedores.

(b)   * In case the Owners are unsuccessful in obtaining compensation from the stevedores for damage for which they are legally liable, then the Charterers shall indemnify the Owners for any sums so due and unpaid.

*) Sub-clause (b) is optional and shall apply unless deleted.

20. Deviation

Should the Vessel deviate to save or attempt to save life or property at sea, or make any reasonable deviation, the said deviation shall not be deemed to be an infringement or breach of this Charter Party, and the Owners shall not be liable for any loss or damage resulting therefrom provided, however, that if the deviation is for the purpose of loading or unloading cargo or passengers, it shall "prima facie", be regarded as unreasonable.

21. Lien and Cesser

The Charterers' liability under this Charter Party shall cease on cargo being shipped, except for payment of freight, deadfreight and demurrage, and except for all other matters provided for in this Charter Party where the Charterers' responsibility is specified. The Owners shall have a lien on the cargo for freight, deadfreight, demurrage and general average contribution due to them under this Charter Party.

22. Bills of Lading

The bills of lading shall be prepared in accordance with the dock or railway weight and shall be endorsed by the Master, agent or Owners, weight unknown, freight and all conditions as per this Charter, such bills of lading to be signed at the Charterers' or shippers' office within twenty four hours after the Vessel is loaded. The Master shall sign a certificate stating that the weight of the cargo loaded is in accordance with railway weight certificate. The Charterers are to hold the Owners harmless should any shortage occur.

23. Grab Discharge

No cargo shall be loaded in any cargo compartment inaccessible to reach by grabs.

AMWELSH 93 (continued)

24. Protective Clauses

This Charter Party is subject to the following clauses all of which are also to be included in all bills of lading issued hereunder:

(a)   "CLAUSE PARAMOUNT: This bill of lading shall have effect subject to the provisions of the Carriage of Goods by Sea Act of the United States, the Hague Rules, or the Hague-Visby Rules, as applicable, or such other similar national legislation as may mandatorily apply by virtue of origin or destination of the bills of lading, which shall be deemed to be incorporated herein and nothing herein contained shall be deemed a surrender by the carrier of any of its rights or immunities or an increase of any of its responsibilities or liabilities under said applicable Act. If any term of this bill of lading be repugnant to said applicable Act to any extent, such term shall be void to that extent, but no further."

and

(b)   "NEW BOTH-TO-BLAME COLLISION CLAUSE: If the ship comes into collision with another ship as a result of the negligence of the other ship and any act, neglect or default of the master, mariner, pilot or the servants of the carrier in the navigation or in the management of the ship, the owners of the goods carried hereunder will indemnify the carrier against all loss or liability to the other or non-carrying ship or her owners in so far as such loss or liability represents loss of, or damage to, or any claim whatsoever of the owners of said goods, paid or payable by the other or non-carrying ship or her owners to the owners of said goods and set off, recouped or recovered by the other or non-carrying ship or her owners as part of their claim against the carrying ship or carrier.

The foregoing provisions shall also apply where the owners, operators or those in charge of any ship or ships or objects other than, or in addition to, the colliding ships or objects are at fault in respect to a collision or contact."

and

(c)   "NEW JASON CLAUSE: In the event of accident, danger, damage or disaster before or after commencement of the voyage, resulting from any cause whatsoever, whether due to negligence or not, for which, or for the consequences of which, the carrier is not responsible, by statute, contract or otherwise, the goods, shippers, consignees or owners of the goods shall contribute with the carrier in general average to the payment of any sacrifices, losses or expenses of a general average nature that may be made or incurred, and shall pay salvage and special charges incurred in respect of the goods.

If a salving ship is owned or operated by the carrier, salvage shall be paid for as fully as if such salving ship or ships belonged to strangers. Such deposit as the carrier or his agents may deem sufficient to cover the estimated contribution of the goods, and any salvage and special charges thereon shall, if required, be made by the goods, shippers, consignees or owners of the goods to the carrier before delivery."

and

Appendix 13

AMWELSH 93 (continued)

(d)   "PROTECTION AND INDEMNITY BUNKERING CLAUSE: The Vessel in addition to all other liberties shall have liberty as part of the contract voyage and at any stage thereof to proceed to any port or ports whatsoever whether such ports are on or off the direct and/or customary route or routes to the ports of loading or discharge named in this Charter and there take oil bunkers in any quantity in the discretion of the Owners even to the full capacity of fuel tanks, deep tanks and any other compartment in which oil can be carried whether such amount is or is not required for the chartered voyage."

25.   Ice Clause

Loading Port

(a)   If the Vessel cannot reach the loading port by reason of ice when she is ready to proceed from her last port, or at any time during the voyage, or on her arrival, or if frost sets in after her arrival, the Master - for fear of the Vessel being frozen in - is at liberty to leave without cargo; in such cases this Charter Party shall be null and void.

(b)   If during loading, the Master, for fear of the Vessel being frozen in, deems it advisable to leave, he has the liberty to do so with what cargo he has on board and to proceed to any other port with option of completing cargo for the Owners' own account to any port or ports including the port of discharge. Any part cargo thus loaded under this Charter Party to be forwarded to destination at the Vessel's expense against payment of the agreed freight, provided that no extra expenses be thereby caused to the Consignees, freight being paid on quantity delivered (in proportion if lump sum), all other conditions as per Charter Party.

(c)   In case of more than one loading port, and if one or more of the ports are closed by ice, the Master or Owners to be at liberty either to load the pan cargo at the open port and fill up elsewhere for the Owners' own account as under sub-clause (b) or to declare the Charter Party null and void unless the Charterers agree to load full cargo at the open port.

Voyage and Discharging Port

(d)   Should ice prevent the Vessel from reaching the port of discharge, the Charterers/Receivers shall have the option of keeping the Vessel waiting until the re-opening of navigation and paying demurrage or of ordering the Vessel to a safe and immediately accessible port where she can safely discharge without risk of detention by ice. Such orders to be given within 48 hours after the Owners or Master have given notice to the Charterers/Receivers of impossibility of reaching port of destination.

(e)   If during discharging, the Master, for fear of the Vessel being frozen in, deems it advisable to leave, he has liberty to do so with what cargo he has on board and to proceed to the nearest safe and accessible port. Such port to be nominated by the Charterers/Receivers as soon as possible, but not later than 24 running hours, Sundays and holidays excluded, of receipt of the Owners' request for nomination of a substitute discharging port, failing which the Master will himself choose such port.

AMWELSH 93 (continued)

(f)   On delivery of the cargo at such port, all conditions of the Bill of Lading shall apply and the Owners shall receive the same freight as if the Vessel had discharged at the original port of destination, except that if the distance to the substitute port exceeds 100 nautical miles the freight on the cargo delivered at that port to be increased in proportion.

26.   General Average

General average shall be adjusted according to York-Antwerp Rules 1974, as amended 1990, or any subsequent modification thereof, in .... and settled in .... currency.

27.   War Risks

1.   The Master shall not be required or bound to sign Bills of Lading for any blockaded port or for any port which the Master or Owners in his or their discretion consider dangerous or impossible to enter or reach.

2.   (A) If any port of loading or of discharge named in this Charter Party or to which the Vessel may properly be ordered pursuant to the terms of the Bills of Lading be blockaded, or

(B) If owing to any war, hostilities, warlike operations, civil war, civil commotions, revolutions, or the operation of international law (a) entry to any such port of loading or of discharge or the loading or discharge of cargo at any such port be considered by the Master or Owners in his or their discretion dangerous or (b) it be considered by the Master or Owners in his or their discretion dangerous or impossible for the Vessel to reach any such port of loading or of discharge - the Charterers shall have the right to order the cargo or such part of it as may be affected to be loaded or discharged at any other safe port of loading or of discharge within the range of loading or discharging ports respectively established under the provisions of the Charter Party (provided such other port is not blockaded or that entry thereto or loading or discharge of cargo thereat is not in the Master's or Owners' discretion dangerous or prohibited). If in respect of a port of discharge no orders be received from the Charterers within 48 hours after they or their agents have received from the Owners a request for the nomination of a substitute port, the Owners shall then be at liberty to discharge the cargo at any safe port which they or the Master may in their or his discretion decide on (whether within the range of discharging ports established under the provisions of the Charter Party or not) and such discharge shall be deemed to be due fulfilment of the contract or contracts of affreightment so far as cargo so discharged is concerned. In the event of the cargo being loaded or discharged at any such other port within the respective range of loading or discharging ports established under the provisions of the Charter Party, the Charter Party shall be read in respect of the freight and all other conditions whatsoever as if the voyage performed were that originally designated. In the event, however, that the Vessel discharges the cargo at a port outside the range of discharging ports established under the provisions of the Charter Party, freight shall be paid for as for the voyage originally designated and all extra expenses involved in reaching the actual port of discharge and/or discharging the cargo thereat shall be paid by the Charterers or cargo owners. In this latter event the Owners shall have a lien on the cargo for all such extra expenses.

Appendix 13

AMWELSH 93 (continued)

3.   The Vessel shall have liberty to comply with any directions or recommendations as to departure, arrival, routes, ports of call, stoppages, destinations, zones, waters, delivery or in any other wise whatsoever given by the government of the nation under whose flag the Vessel sails or any other government or local authority including any de facto government or local authority or by any person or body acting or purporting to act as or with the authority of any such government or authority or by any committee or person having under the terms of the war risks insurance on the Vessel the right to give any such directions or recommendations. If by reason of or in compliance with any such directions or recommendations, anything is done or is not done such shall not be deemed a deviation.

If by reason of or in compliance with any such directions or recommendations the Vessel does not proceed to the port or ports of discharge originally designated or to which she may have been ordered pursuant to the terms of the Bills of Lading, the Vessel may proceed to any safe port of discharge which the Master or Owners in his or their discretion may decide on and there discharge the cargo. Such discharge shall be deemed to be due fulfilment of the contract or contracts of affreightment and the Owners shall be entitled to freight as if discharge has been effected at the port or ports originally designated or to which the Vessel may have been ordered pursuant to the terms of the Bill of Lading. All extra expenses involved in reaching and discharging the cargo at any such other port of discharge shall be paid by the Charterers and/or cargo owners and the Owners shall have a lien on the cargo for freight and all such expenses.

28.   **Dues and/or Taxes**

....

....

....

29.   **Transfer**

The Charterers shall have the privilege of transferring part or whole of the Charter Party to others, guaranteeing to the Owners due fulfillment of this Charter Party.

30.   **Address Commission**

An address commission of .... % on gross freight, deadfreight, and demurrage is due to the Charterers at the time these are paid, Vessel lost or not lost. The Charterers shall have the right to deduct such commissions from such payments.

31.   **Brokerage Commission**

A brokerage commission of .... % on gross freight, deadfreight and demurrage is payable by the Owners to ....
....
.... at the time of the Owners receiving these payments.

AMWELSH 93 (continued)

32. <u>Arbitration</u>

(a)   *NEW YORK

All disputes arising out of this contract shall be arbitrated at New York in the following manner, and subject to U.S. Law:

One Arbitrator is to be appointed by each of the parties hereto and a third by the two so chosen. Their decision or that of any two of them shall be final, and for the purpose of enforcing any award, this agreement may be made a rule of court. The Arbitrators shall be commercial men, conversant with shipping matters. Such Arbitration is to be conducted in accordance with the rules of the Society of Maritime Arbitrators Inc.

For disputes where the total amount claimed by either party does not exceed US $ ....
................** the arbitration shall be conducted in accordance with the Shortened Arbitration Procedure of the Society of Maritime Arbitrators Inc.

(b)   *LONDON

All disputes arising out of this contract shall be arbitrated at London and, unless the parties agree forthwith on a single Arbitrator, be referred to the final arbitrament of two Arbitrators carrying on business in London who shall be members of the Baltic Mercantile & Shipping Exchange and engaged in Shipping, one to be appointed by each of the parties, with power to such Arbitrators to appoint an Umpire. No award shall be questioned or invalidated on the ground that any of the Arbitrators is not qualified as above, unless objection to his action be taken before the award is made. Any dispute arising hereunder shall be governed by English Law.

For disputes where the total amount claimed by either party does not exceed US $ ....
................** the arbitration shall be conducted in accordance with the Small Claims Procedure of the London Maritime Arbitrators Association.

* Delete (a) or (b) as appropriate

** Where no figure is supplied in the blank space this provision only shall be void but the other provisions of this clause shall have full force and remain in effect.

Appendix 14

ASBATIME – ASBA

TIME CHARTER
New York Produce Exchange Form

November 6th, 1913 — Amended October 20th, 1921; August 6th, 1931; October 3rd, 1946; June 12th, 1981

THIS CHARTER PARTY, made and concluded in ....

.... day of .... 19 ....

Owners between ....

.... Owners of

Steamship

the good .... Motorship ....

Description of Vessel of .... of .... tons gross register, and

...............................tons net register, having engines of ....

horsepower and with hull, machinery and equipment in a thoroughly efficient state, and

classed .... of about

.... cubic feet grain/bale capacity ....

.... and about

.... long/metric tons deadweight capacity (cargo and

bunkers, including fresh water and stores not exceeding ....

long/metric tons) on a salt water draft of .... on summer

freeboard, inclusive of permanent bunkers, which are of the capacity of about

.... long/metric tons of

.... fuel oil and ....

long/metric tons of ...., and

capable of steaming, fully laden, under good weather conditions about

.... knots on a consumption of about ....

long/metric tons of ....

....

now ....

Charterers .... and

.... Charterers of the City of ....

Duration The Owners agree to let and the Charterers agree to hire the vessel from the

time of delivery for about ....

....

.... within below mentioned trading limits.

Sublet Charterers shall have liberty to sublet the vessel for all or any part of the time covered

by this Charter, but Charterers shall remain responsible for the fulfillment of this Charter.

Delivery Vessel shall be placed at the disposal of the Charterers ....

....

....

....

in such dock or at such berth or place (where she may safely lie, always afloat, at all

times of tide, except as otherwise provided in Clause 6) as the Charterers may direct.

If such dock, berth or place be not available, time shall count as provided in Clause

5. Vessel on her delivery shall be ready to receive cargo with clean-swept holds and tight,

staunch, strong and in every way fitted for ordinary cargo service, having water ballast

and with sufficient power to operate all cargo-handling gear simultaneously (and with

full complement of officers and crew for a vessel of her tonnage), to be employed in

carrying lawful merchandise excluding any goods of a dangerous, injurious, flammable or

Dangerous Cargo corrosive nature unless carried in accordance with the requirements or recommendations

of the proper authorities of the state of the vessel's registry and of the states of ports of

shipment and discharge and of any intermediate states or ports through whose waters

the vessel must pass. Without prejudice to the generality of the foregoing, in addition

Cargo Exclusions the following are specifically excluded: livestock of any description, arms, ammunition,

explosives ....

....

....

....

Trading Limits The vessel shall be employed in such lawful trades between safe ports and

places within ....

.... excluding ....

....

....

....

as the Charterers or their agents shall direct, on the following conditions:

Owners to Provide 1. The Owners shall provide and pay for the insurance of the vessel and for all

provisions, cabin, deck, engine-room and other necessary stores, including boiler water;

shall pay for wages, consular shipping and discharging fees of the crew and charges

for port services pertaining to the crew; shall maintain vessel's class and keep her in a

thoroughly efficient state in hull, machinery and equipment for and during the service.

[handwritten notes in margin: "Provide only Pay for insurance and for all provisions for wages fees and charges for port services"]

Appendix 14

ASBATIME – ASBA (continued)

Charterers to Provide

2. The Charterers, while the vessel is on hire, shall provide and pay for all the fuel except as otherwise agreed, port charges, pilotages, towages, agencies, commissions, consular charges (except those pertaining to individual crew members or flag of the vessel), and all other usual expenses except those stated in Clause 1, but when the vessel puts into a port for causes for which vessel is responsible, then all such charges incurred shall be paid by the Owners. Fumigations ordered because of illness of the crew shall be for Owners' account. Fumigations ordered because of cargoes carried or ports visited while vessel is employed under this Charter shall be for Charterers' account. All other fumigations shall be for Charterers' account after vessel has been on charter for a continuous period of six months or more.

Charterers shall provide necessary dunnage and shifting boards, also any extra fittings requisite for a special trade or unusual cargo, but Owners shall allow them the use of any dunnage and shifting boards already aboard vessel.

Bunkers on Delivery and Redelivery

3. The Charterers on delivery, and the Owners on redelivery, shall take over and pay for all fuel and diesel oil remaining on board the vessel as hereunder. The vessel shall be delivered with: ....
long/metric* tons of fuel oil at the price of .... per ton; .... tons of diesel oil at the price of ....
per ton. The vessel shall be redelivered with ....
tons of fuel oil at the price of .... per ton; ....
.... tons of diesel oil at the price of .... per ton
(*Same tons apply throughout this clause)

Rate of Hire

4. The Charterers shall pay for the use and hire of the said vessel at the rate of ....
.... daily, or
.... United States Currency
per ton on vessel's total deadweight carrying capacity, including bunkers and stores, on .... summer freeboard, per calendar month, commencing on and from the day of her delivery, as aforesaid, and at and after the same rate for any part of a month; hire shall continue until the hour of the day of her redelivery in like good order and condition, ordinary wear and tear

Redelivery Areas and Notices

excepted, to the Owners (unless vessel lost) at ....
....
....
.... unless otherwise mutually agreed.
Charterers shall give Owners not less than .... days notice
of vessel's expected date of redelivery and probable port. ....
....

Hire Payment and Commencement

5. Payment of hire shall be made so as to be received by Owners or their designated payee in New York, i.e. ....
....
....
.... in United States Currency, in funds available to the Owners on the due date, semi-monthly in advance, and for the last half month or part of same the approximate amount of hire, and should same not cover the actual time, hire shall be paid for the balance day by day as it becomes due, if so required by Owners. Failing the punctual and regular payment of the hire, or on any breach of this Charter, the Owners shall be at liberty to withdraw the vessel from the service of the Charterers without prejudice to any claims they (the Owners) may otherwise have on the Charterers.

Time shall count from 7 A.M. on the working day following that on which written notice of readiness has been given to Charterers or their agents before 4 P.M., but if required by Charterers, they shall have the privilege of using vessel at once, in which case the vessel will be on hire from the commencement of work.

Cash Advance

Cash for vessel's ordinary disbursements at any port may be advanced, as required by the Captain, by the Charterers or their agents, subject to 2½ percent commission and such advances shall be deducted from the hire. The Charterers, however, shall in no way be responsible for the application of such advances.

Berths

6. Vessel shall be loaded and discharged in any dock or at any berth or place that Charterers or their agents may direct, provided the vessel can safely lie always afloat at any time of tide, except at such places where it is customary for similar size vessels to safely lie aground.

Spaces Available

7. The whole reach of the vessel's holds, decks, and usual places of loading (not more than she can reasonably and safely stow and carry), also accommodations for supercargo, if carried, shall be at the Charterers' disposal, reserving only proper and sufficient space for ship's officers, crew, tackle, apparel, furniture, provisions, stores and fuel.

Prosecution of Voyages

8. The Captain shall prosecute his voyages with due despatch, and shall render all customary assistance with ship's crew and boats. The Captain (although appointed by the Owners) shall be under the orders and directions of the Charterers as regards employment and agency; and Charterers are to perform all cargo handling at their expense under the supervision of the Captain, who is to sign the bills of lading for

Appendix 14

ASBATIME – ASBA (continued)

S.S./M.S .... Charter Dated ....

Bills of Lading	cargo as presented in conformity with mate's or tally clerk's receipts. However, at Charterers' option, the Charterers or their agents may sign bills of lading on behalf of the Captain always in conformity with mate's or tally clerks receipts. All bills of lading shall be without prejudice to this Charter and the Charterers shall indemnify the Owners against all consequences or liabilities which may arise from any inconsistency between this Charter and any bills of lading or waybills signed by the Charterers or their agents or by the Captain at their request.
Conduct of Captain	9. If the Charterers shall have reason to be dissatisfied with the conduct of the Captain or officers, the Owners shall, on receiving particulars of the complaint, investigate the same, and, if necessary, make a change in the appointments.
Supercargo and Meals	10. The Charterers are entitled to appoint a supercargo, who shall accompany the vessel and see that voyages are prosecuted with due despatch. He is to be furnished with free accommodation and same fare as provided for Captain's table, Charterers paying at the rate of .... per day. Owners shall victual pilots and customs officers, and also, when authorized by Charterers or their agents, shall victual tally clerks, stevedore's foreman, etc., Charterers paying at the rate of .... per meal for all such victualling.
Sailing Orders and Logs	11. The Charterers shall furnish the Captain from time to time with all requisite instructions and sailing directions, in writing, and the Captain shall keep full and correct deck and engine logs of the voyage or voyages, which are to be patent to the Charterers or their agents, and furnish the Charterers, their agents or supercargo, when required, with a true copy of such deck and engine logs, showing the course of the vessel, distance run and the consumption of fuel.
Ventilation	12. The Captain shall use diligence in caring for the ventilation of the cargo.
Continuation	13. The Charterers shall have the option of continuing this Charter for a further period of ....
Laydays/ Cancelling	14. If required by Charterers, time shall not commence before .... and should vessel not have given written notice of readiness on or before .... but not later than 4 P.M. Charterers or their agents shall have the option of cancelling this Charter at any time not later than the day of vessel's readiness.
Off Hire	15. In the event of the loss of time from deficiency and/or default of officers or crew or deficiency of stores, fire, breakdown of, or damages to, hull, machinery or equipment, grounding, detention by average accidents to ship or cargo unless resulting from inherent vice, quality or defect of the cargo, drydock in for the purpose of examination or painting bottom, or by any other similar cause preventing the full working of the vessel, the payment of hire and overtime, if any, shall cease for the time thereby lost. Should the vessel deviate or put back during a voyage, contrary to the orders or directions of the Charterers, for any reason other than accident to the cargo, the hire is to be suspended from the time of her deviating or putting back until she is again in the same or equidistant position from the destination and the voyage resumed therefrom. All fuel used by the vessel while off hire shall be for Owners' account. In the event of the vessel being driven into port or to anchorage through stress of weather, trading to shallow harbors or to rivers or ports with bars, any detention of the vessel and/or expenses resulting from such detention shall be for the Charterers account. If upon the voyage the speed be reduced by defect in, or breakdown of, any part of her hull, machinery or equipment, the time so lost, and the cost of any extra fuel consumed in consequence thereof, and all extra expenses shall be deducted from the hire.
Total Loss	16. Should the vessel be lost, money paid in advance and not earned (reckoning from the date of loss or being last heard of) shall be returned to the Charterers at once.
Exceptions	The act of God, enemies, fire, restraint of princes, rulers and people, and all dangers and accidents of the seas, rivers, machinery, boilers and steam navigation, and errors of navigation throughout this Charter, always mutually excepted.
Liberties	The vessel shall have the liberty to sail with or without pilots, to tow and to be towed, to assist vessels in distress, and to deviate for the purpose of saving life and property.
Arbitration	17. Should any dispute arise between Owners and the Charterers, the matter in dispute shall be referred to three persons at New York, one to be appointed by each of the parties hereto, and the third by the two so chosen; their decision, or that of any two of them, shall be final and for the purpose of enforcing any award this agreement may be made a rule of the Court. The arbitrators shall be commercial men conversant with shipping matters.
Liens	18. The Owners shall have a lien upon all cargoes and all sub-freights for any amounts due under this Charter, including general average contributions, and the Charterers shall have a lien on the ship for all monies paid in advance and not earned, and any overpaid hire or excess deposit to be returned at once.

ASBATIME – ASBA (continued)

Charterers will not suffer, nor permit to be continued, any lien or encumbrance incurred by them or their agents, which might have priority over the title and interest of the Owners in the vessel.

Salvage

19. All derelicts and salvage shall be for Owners' and Charterers' equal benefit after deducting Owners' and Charterers' expenses and crew's proportion.

General Average

General average shall be adjusted, according to York-Antwerp Rules 1974, at such port or place in the United States as may be selected by the Owners and as to matters not provided for by these Rules, according to the laws and usage at the port of New York. In such adjustment disbursements in foreign currencies shall be exchanged into United States money at the rate prevailing on the dates made and allowances for damage to cargo claimed in foreign currency shall be converted at the rate prevailing on the last day of discharge at the port or place of final discharge of such damaged cargo from the ship. Average agreement or bond and such additional security, as may be required by the Owners, must be furnished before delivery of the goods. Such cash deposit as the Owners or their agents may deem sufficient as additional security for the contribution of the goods and for any salvage and special charges thereon, shall, if required, be made by the goods, shippers, consignees or owners of the goods to the Owners before delivery. Such deposit shall, at the option of the Owners, be payable in United States money and remitted to the adjuster. When so remitted the deposit shall be held in a special account at the place of adjustment in the name of the adjuster pending settlement of the general average and refunds or credit balances, if any, shall be paid in United States money.

York-Antwerp Rules

Charterers shall procure that all bills of lading issued during the currency of the Charter will contain a provision to the effect that general average shall be adjusted according to York-Antwerp Rules 1974 and will include the "New Jason Clause" as per Clause 23.

Drydocking

20. The vessel was last drydocked .... The Owners shall have the option to place the vessel in drydock during the currency of this Charter at a convenient time and place, to be mutually agreed upon between Owners and Charterers, for bottom cleaning and painting and/or repair as required by class or dictated by circumstances. Payment of hire shall be suspended upon deviation from Charterers service until vessel is again placed at Charterers' disposal at a point not less favorable to Charterers than when the hire was suspended. ....
....
....

Cargo Gear

21 Owners shall maintain the cargo-handling gear of the ship which is as follows' ....
....
providing gear (for all derricks or cranes) capable of lifting capacity as described Owners shall also provide on the vessel for night work lights as on board, but all additional lights over those on board shall be at Charterers' expense The Charterers shall have the use of any gear on board the vessel. If required by Charterers, the vessel shall work night and day and all cargo-handling gear shall beat Charterers' disposal during loading and discharging.

Stevedore Stand-by

In the event of disabled cargo-handling gear, or insufficient power to operate the same, the vessel is to be considered to be off hire to the extent that time is actually lost to the Charterers and Owners to pay stevedore stand-by charges occasioned thereby. If required by the Charterers, the Owners are to bear the cost of hiring shore gear in lieu thereof.

Crew Overtime

22. In lieu of any overtime payments to officers and crew for work ordered by Charterers or their agents, Charterers shall pay Owners $ ....
per month or pro rata.

Clauses Paramount

23. The following clause is to be included in all bills of lading issued hereunder:

This bill of lading shall have effect subject to the provisions of the Carriage of Goods by Sea Act of the United States, the Hague Rules, or the Hague-Visby Rules, as applicable, or such other similar national legislation as may mandatorily apply by virtue of origin or destination of the bills of lading, which shall be deemed to be incorporated herein and nothing herein contained shall be deemed a surrender by the carrier of any of its rights or immunities or an increase of any of its responsibilities or liabilities under said applicable Act. If any term of this bill of lading be repugnant to said applicable Act to any extent, such term shall be void to that extent, but no further.

This Charter is subject to the following clauses all of which are to be included in all bills of lading issued hereunder:

New Both-to-Blame Collision Clause

If the ship comes into collision with another ship as a result of the negligence of the other ship and any act, neglect or default of the master, mariner, pilot or the servants of the carrier in the navigation or in the management of the ship, the owners of the goods carried hereunder will indemnify the carrier against all loss or liability to the other or non-carrying ship or her owners insofar as such loss or liability represents loss of, or damage to, or any claim whatsoever of the owners of said goods, paid or payable by the other or non-carrying ship or her owners to the owners of said goods and set off,

Appendix 14

ASBATIME – ASBA (continued)

S.S./M.S .... Charter Dated ....

recouped or recovered by the other or non-carrying ship or her owners as part of their claim against the carrying ship or carrier.

The foregoing provisions shall also apply where the owners, operators or those in charge of any ships or objects other than, or in addition to, the colliding ships or objects are at fault in respect to a collision or contact.

New Jason Clause

In the event of accident, danger, damage or disaster before or after commencement of the voyage resulting from any cause whatsoever, whether due to negligence or not, for which, or for the consequences of which, the carrier is not responsible, by statute, contract, or otherwise, the goods, shippers, consignees, or owners of the goods shall contribute with the carrier in general average to the payment of any sacrifices, losses, or expenses of a general average nature that may be made or incurred, and shall pay salvage and special charges incurred in respect of the goods.

If a salving ship is owned or operated by the carrier, salvage shall be paid for as fully as if salving ship or ships belonged to strangers. Such deposit as the carrier or his agents may deem sufficient to cover the estimated contribution of the goods and any salvage and special charges thereon shall, if required, be made by the goods, shippers, consignees or owners of the goods to the carrier before delivery.

War Clauses

(a) No contraband of war shall be shipped. Vessel shall not be required, without the consent of Owners, which shall not be unreasonably withheld, to enter any port or zone which is involved in a state of war, warlike operations, or hostilities, civil strife, insurrection or piracy whether there be a declaration of war or not, where vessel, cargo or crew might reasonably be expected to be subject to capture, seizure or arrest, or to a hostile act by a belligerent power (the term "power" meaning any de jure or de facto authority or any purported governmental organization maintaining naval, military or air forces).

(b) If such consent is given by Owners, Charterers will pay the provable additional cost of insuring vessel against hull war risks in an amount equal to the value under her ordinary hull policy but not exceeding a valuation of ....
.... In addition, Owners may purchase and Charterers will pay for war risk insurance on ancillary risks such as loss of hire, freight disbursements, total loss, blocking and trapping, etc. If such insurance is not obtainable commercially or through a government program, vessel shall not be required to enter or remain at any such port or zone.

(c) In the event of the existence of the conditions described in (a) subsequent to the date of this Charter, or while vessel is on hire under this Charter, Charterers shall, in respect of voyages to any such port or zone assume the provable additional cost of wages and insurance properly incurred in connection with master, officers and crew as a consequence of such war, warlike operations or hostilities.

Ice

24. The vessel shall not be required to enter or remain in any icebound port or area, nor any port or area where lights or lightships have been or are about to be withdrawn by reason of ice, nor where there is risk that in the ordinary course of things the vessel will not be able on account of ice to safely enter and remain in the port or area or to get out after having completed loading or discharging.

Navigation

25. Nothing herein stated is to be construed as a demise of the vessel to the Time Charterers. The Owners shall remain responsible for the navigation of the vessel, acts of pilots and tug boats, insurance, crew, and all other similar matters, same as when trading for their own account.

Commissions

26. A commission of .... percent is payable by the vessel and Owners to ....
....
on hire earned and paid under this Charter, and also upon any continuation or extension of this Charter.

Address

27. An address commission of .... percent is payable to ....
....
on hire earned and paid under this Charter.

Rider

Rider Clauses ....
as attached hereto are incorporated in this Charter.

Appendix 14

ASBATIME – ASBA (continued)

Rider of Suggested Additional Clauses

(None of these Clauses apply unless expressly agreed during the negotiations and enumerated in line 362)

Extension of Cancelling

28. If it clearly appears that, despite the exercise of due diligence by Owners, the vessel will not be ready for delivery by the cancelling date, and provided Owners are able to state with reasonable certainty the date on which the vessel will be ready, they may, at the earliest seven days before the vessel is expected to sail for the port or place of delivery, require Charterers to declare whether or not they will cancel the Charter. Should Charterers elect not to cancel, or should they fail to reply within seven days or by the cancelling date, whichever shall first occur, then the seventh day after the expected date of readiness for delivery as notified by Owners shall replace the original cancelling date. Should the vessel be further delayed, Owners shall be entitled to require further declarations of Charterers in accordance with this Clause.

Grace Period

29. Where there is failure to make "punctual and regular payment" of hire, Charterers shall be given by Owners two clear banking days (as recognized at the agreed place of payment) written notice to rectify the failure, and when so rectified within those two days following Owners' notice, the payment shall stand as regular and punctual. Payment received by Owners' bank after the original due date will bear interest at the rate of 0.1 percent per day which shall be payable immediately by Charterers in addition to hire.

At any time while hire is outstanding the Owners shall be absolutely entitled to withhold the performance of any and all of their obligations hereunder and shall have no responsibility whatsoever for any consequences thereof in respect of which the Charterers hereby indemnify the Owners and hire shall continue to accrue and any extra expenses resulting from such withholding shall be for the Charterers' account.

Cargo Claims

30. Damage to and claims on cargo shall be for Owners' account if caused by unseaworthiness of the vessel, but shall be for Charterers' account if caused by handling and stowage, including slackage. Claims for shortage ex ship shall be shared equally between Owners and Charterers.

War Cancellation

31. In the event of the outbreak of war (whether there be a declaration of war or not) between any two or more of the following countries: The United States of America, the United Kingdom, France, the Union of Soviet Socialist Republics, the People's Republic of China, ...

....

....

or in the event of the nation under whose flag the vessel sails becoming involved in war (whether there be a declaration of war or not), either the Owners or the Charterers may cancel this Charter. Whereupon the Charterers shall redeliver the vessel to the Owners in accordance with Clause 4; if she has cargo on board, after discharge thereof at destination, or, if debarred under this Clause from reaching or entering it, at a near open and safe port as directed by the Owners, or, if she has no cargo on board, at the port at which she then is; or, if at sea. at a near open and safe port as directed by the Owners. In all cases hire shall continue to be paid in accordance with Clause 4 and except as aforesaid all other provisions of this Charter shall apply until redelivery.

War Bonus

32. Any war bonus to officers and crew due to vessel's trading or cargo carried shall be for Charterers' account.

Requisition

33. Should the vessel be requisitioned by the government of the vessel's flag during the period of this Charter, the vessel shall be deemed to be off hire during the period of such requisition, and any hire paid by the said government in respect of such requisition period shall be retained by Owners. The period during which the vessel is on requisition to the said government shall count as part of the period provided for in this Charter.

If the period of requisition exceeds .... months, either party shall have the option of cancelling this Charter and no consequential claim may be made by either party.

On/Off-hire Survey

34. Prior to delivery and redelivery the parties shall each appoint surveyors, for their respective accounts, who shall conduct joint on-hire/off-hire surveys. A single report shall be prepared on each occasion and signed by each surveyor, without prejudice to his right to file a separate report setting forth items upon which the surveyors cannot agree. If either party fails to have a representative attend the survey and sign the joint survey report, such party shall nevertheless be bound for all purposes by the findings in any report prepared by the other party. On-hire survey shall be on Charterers' time and off-hire survey on Owners' time.

Stevedore Damage

35. Any damage caused by stevedores during the currency of this Charter shall be reported by Captain to Charterers or their agents, in writing, within 24 hours of the occurrence or as soon as possible thereafter. The Captain shall use his best efforts to obtain written acknowledgement by responsible parties causing damage unless damage should have been made good in the meantime.

Appendix 14

ASBATIME – ASBA (continued)

Stevedore damages involving seaworthiness shall be repaired without delay to the vessel after each occurrence in Charterers' time and shall be paid for by the Charterers. Other minor repairs shall be done at the same time, but if this is not possible, same shall be repaired while vessel is in drydock in Owners time, provided this does not interfere with Owners' repair work, or by vessel's crew at Owners' convenience. All costs of such repairs shall be for Charterers' account. Any time spent in repairing stevedore damage shall be for Charterers' account.

Charterers' Colors
Charterers shall pay for stevedore damages whether or not payment has been made by stevedores to Charterers.

36. Charterers shall have the privilege of flying their own house flag and painting the vessel with their own markings. The vessel shall be repainted in Owners' colors before termination of the Charter. Cost and time of painting, maintaining and repainting those changes effected by Charterers shall be for Charterers' account.

Return Premium
37. Charterers shall have the benefit of any return insurance premium receivable by Owners from their underwriters as and when received from underwriters by reason of vessel being in port for a minimum period of 30 days if on full hire for this period or pro rata for the time actually on hire.

Water Pollution
38. The vessel shall be off hire during anytime lost on account of vessel's non-compliance with government and/or state and/or provincial regulations pertaining to water pollution. In cases where vessel calls at a U.S. port, Owners warrant to have secured and carry on board the vessel a Certificate of Financial Responsibility as required under U.S. law.

NYPE 93 – New York Produce

Code Name: "**NYPE 93**"

Recommended by:
The Baltic and International Maritime Council (BIMCO)
The Federation of National Associations of
Ship Brokers and Agents (FONASBA)

TIME CHARTER©

New York Produce Exchange Form
Issued by the Association of Ship Brokers and Agents (U.S.A.) Inc.

November 6th, 1913 - Amended October 20th, 1921; August 6th, 1931; October 3rd, 1946;
Revised June 12th, 1981; September 14th 1993.

THIS CHARTER PARTY, made and concluded in	1
this day of 19	2
Between	3
	4
Owners of the Vessel described below, and	5
	6
	7
Charteres.	8
Description of Vessel	9
Name Flag Built (year).	10
Port and number of Registry	11
Classed in	12
Deadweight long*/metric* tons (cargo and bunkers, including freshwater and	13
stores not exceeding long*/metric* tons) on a salt water draft of	14
on summer freeboard.	15
Capacity cubic feet grain cubic feet bale space.	16
Tonnage GT/GRT.	17
Speed about knots, fully laden, in good weather conditions up to and including maximum	18
Force on the Beaufort wind scale, on a consumption of about long*/metric*	19
tons of	20
* Delete as appropriate.	21
For further description see Appendix "A" (if applicable)	22

1.   Duration   23

The Owners agree to let and the Chaarterers agree to hire the Vessel from the time of delivery for a period   24
of   25
                                                                                                              26
                                                                                                              27
                                                                       within below mentioned trading limits.   28

2.   Delivery   29

The Vessel shall be placed at the disposal of the Charterers at   30
                                                                                                              31
                                                      The Vessel on her delivery   32
shall be ready to receive cargo with clean-swept holds and tight, staunch, strong and in every way fitted for   33
ordinary cargo service, having water ballast and with sufficient power to operate all cargo-handling gear   34
simultaneously.   35
                                                                                                              36
The Owners shall give the Charterers not less than   days notice of expected date of   37
delivery.   38

Appendix 15

NYPE 93 – New York Produce (continued)

3.   On-Off Hire Survey   39

Prior to delivery and redelivery the parties shall, unless otherwise agreed, each appoint surveyors, for their   40
respective accounts, who shall not later than at first loading port/last discharging port respectively, conduct joint on-   41
hire/off-hire surveys, for the purpose of ascertaining quantity of bunkers on board and the condition of the Vessel.   42
A single report shall be prepared on each occasion and signed by each surveyor, without prejudice to his right to   43
file a separate report setting forth items upon which the surveyors cannot agree.   44
If either party fails to have a representative attend the survey and sign the joint survey report, such party shall   45
nevertheless be bound for all purposes by the findings in any report prepared by the other party.   46
On-hire survey shall be on Charterers' time and off-hire survey on Owners' time.   47

4.   Dangerous Cargo/Cargo Exclusions   48

(a)   The Vessel shall be employed in carrying lawful merchandise excluding any goods of a dangerous, injurious,   49
flammable or corrosive nature unless carried in accordance with the requirements or recommendations of the   50
competent authorities of the country of the Vessel's registry and of ports of shipment and discharge and of any   51
intermediate countries or ports through whose waters the Vessel must pass. Without prejudice to the generality   52
of the foregoing, in addition the following are specifically excluded: livestock of any description, arms, ammunition,   53
explosives, nuclear and radioactive materials,   54
                                                                                        55
                                                                                        56
                                                                                        57
                                                                                        58
                                                                                        59
                                                                                        60
                                                                                        61
                                                                                        62
                                                                                        63
                                                                                        64

(b)   If IMO-classified cargo is agreed to be carried, the amount of such cargo shall be limited to   65
                        tons and the Charterers shall provide the Master with any evidence he   66
may reasonably require to show that the cargo is packaged, labelled, loaded and stowed in accordance with IMO   67
regulations, failing which the Master is entitled to refuse such cargo or, if already loaded, to unload it at the Charterers'   68
risk and expense.   69

5.   Trading Limits   70

The   Vessel   shall   be   employed   in   such   lawful   trades   between   safe   ports   and   safe   places   71
within   72
                                                                            excluding   73
                                                                                        74
                                                                                        75
                                                                    as the Charterers shall direct.   76

6.   Owners to Provide   77

The Owners shall provide and pay for the insurance of the Vessel, except as otherwise provided, and for all provisions,   78
cabin, deck, engine-room and other necessary stores, including boiler water; shall pay for wages, consular shipping   79
and discharging fees of the crew and charges for port services pertaining to the crew; shall maintain the Vessel's class   80
and keep her in a thoroughly efficient state in hull, machinery and equipment for and during the service, and have a   81
full complement of officers and crew.   82

7.   Charterers to Provide   83

The Charterers, while the Vessel is on hire, shall provide and pay for all the bunkers except as otherwise   84
agreed; shall pay for port charges (including compulsory watchmen and cargo watchmen and compulsory   85
garbage disposal), all communication expenses pertaining to the Charterers' business at cost, pilotages,   86

NYPE 93 – New York Produce (continued)

towages, agencies, commissions, consular charges (except those pertaining to individual crew members	87
or flag of the Vessel), and all other usual expenses except those stated in Clause 6, but when the Vessel	88
puts into a port for causes for which the Vessel is responsible (other than by stress of weather), then all	89
such charges incurred shall be paid by the Owners. Fumigations ordered because of illness of the crew	90
shall be for the Owners' account. Fumigations ordered because of cargoes carried or ports visited while	91
the Vessel is employed under this Charter Party shall be for the Charterers' account. All other fumigations	92
shall be for the Charterers' account after the Vessel has been on charter for a continuous period of six	93
months or more.	94

The Charterers shall provide and pay for necessary dunnage and also any extra fittings requisite for a special trade or unusual cargo, but the Owners shall allow them the use of any dunnage already aboard the Vessel. Prior to redelivery the Charterers shall remove their dunnage and fittings at their cost and in their time.

95
96
97
98

8.   Performance of Voyages   99

(a)   The Master shall perform the voyages with due despatch, and shall render all customary assistance with the Vessel's crew. The Master shall be conversant with the English language and (although appointed by the Owners) shall be under the orders and directions of the Charterers as regards employment and agency; and the Charterers shall perform all cargo handling, including but not limited to loading, stowing, trimming, lashing, securing, dunnaging, unlashing, discharging, and tallying, at their risk and expense, under the supervision of the Master.

100
101
102
103
104
105

(b)   If the Charterers shall have reasonable cause to be dissatisfied with the conduct of the Master or officers, the Owners shall, on receiving particulars of the complaint, investigate the same, and, if necessary, make a change in the appointments.

106
107
108

9.   Bunkers   109

(a)   The Charterers on delivery, and the Owners on redelivery, shall take over and pay for all fuel and diesel oil remaining on board the Vessel as hereunder. The Vessel shall be delivered with: long*/metric* tons of fuel oil at the price of   per ton; tons of diesel oil at the price of   per ton. The vessel shall be redelivered with: tons of fuel oil at the price of   per ton; tons of diesel oil at the price of   per ton.

110
111
112
113
114
115

* Same tons apply throughout this clause.   116

(b)   The Charterers shall supply bunkers of a quality suitable for burning in the Vessel's engines and auxiliaries and which conform to the specification(s) as set out in Appendix A.

117
118

The Owners reserve their right to make a claim against the Charterers for any damage to the main engines or the auxiliaries caused by the use of unsuitable fuels or fuels not complying with the agreed specification(s). Additionally, if bunker fuels supplied do not conform with the mutually agreed specification(s) or otherwise prove unsuitable for burning in the Vessel's engines or auxiliaries, the Owners shall not be held responsible for any reduction in the Vessel's speed performance and/or increased bunker consumption, nor for any time lost and any other consequences.

119
120
121
122
123
124

10.   Rate of Hire/Redelivery Areas and Notices   125

The Charterers shall pay for the use and hire of the said Vessel at the rate of $ 126
U.S. currency, daily, or $ U.S. currency per ton on the Vessel's total deadweight   127
carrying capacity, including bunkers and stores, on   summer freeboard, per 30 days,   128
commencing on and from the day of her delivery, as aforesaid, and at and after the same rate for any part   129
of a month; hire shall continue until the hour of the day of her redelivery in like good order and condition, 130
ordinary wear and tear excepted, to the Owners (unless Vessel lost) at   131
132
133
unless otherwise mutually agreed.   134

Appendix 15

NYPE 93 – New York Produce (continued)

The Charterers shall give the Owners not less than   days notice of the Vessel's 135
expected date and probable port of redelivery. 136

For the purpose of hire calculations, the times of delivery, redelivery or termination of charter shall be 137
adjusted to GMT. 138

11.   Hire Payment 139

(a)   Payment 140

Payment of Hire shall be made so as to be received by the Owners or their designated payee in 141
                     ,viz 142
 143
 144
in 145
currency, or in United States Currency, in funds available to the 146
Owners on the due date, 15 days in advance, and for the last month or part of same the approximate 147
amount of hire, and should same not cover the actual time, hire shall be paid for the balance day by day 148
as it becomes due, if so required by the Owners. Failing the punctual and regular payment of the hire, 149
or on any fundamental breach whatsoever of this Charter Party, the Owners shall be at liberty to 150
withdraw the Vessel from the service of the Charterers without prejudice to any claims they (the Owners) 151
may otherwise have on the Charterers. 152

At any time after the expiry of the grace period provided in Sub-clause 11 (b) hereunder and while the 153
hire is outstanding, the Owners shall, without prejudice to the liberty to withdraw, be entitled to withhold 154
the performance of any and all of their obligations hereunder and shall have no responsibility whatsoever 155
for any consequences thereof, in respect of which the Charterers hereby indemnify the Owners, and hire 156
shall continue to accrue and any extra expenses resulting from such withholding shall be for the 157
Charterers' account. 158

(b)   Grace Period 159

Where there is failure to make punctual and regular payment of hire due to oversight, negligence, errors 160
or omissions on the part of the Charterers or their bankers, the Charterers shall be given by the Owners 161
               clear banking days (as recognized at the agreed place of payment) written notice to rectify the 162
failure, and when so rectified within those   days following the Owners' notice, the payment shall 163
stand as regular and punctual. 164

Failure by the Charterers to pay the hire within   days of their receiving the Owners' notice as 165
provided herein, shall entitle the Owners to withdraw as set forth in Sub-clause 11 (a) above. 166

(c)   Last Hire Payment 167

Should the Vessel be on her voyage towards port of redelivery at the time the last and/or the penultimate 168
payment of hire is/are due, said payment(s) is/are to be made for such length of time as the Owners and 169
the Charterers may agree upon as being the estimated time necessary to complete the voyage, and taking 170
into account bunkers actually on board, to be taken over by the Owners and estimated disbursements for 171
the Owners' account before redelivery. Should same not cover the actual time, hire is to be paid for the 172
balance, day by day, as it becomes due. When the Vessel has been redelivered, any difference is to be 173
refunded by the Owners or paid by the Charterers, as the case may be. 174

(d)   Cash Advances 175

Cash for the Vessel's ordinary disbursements at any port may be advanced by the Charterers, as required 176
by the Owners, subject to 2$\frac{1}{2}$ percent commission and such advances shall be deducted from the hire. 177
The Charterers, however, shall in no way be responsible for the application of such advances. 178

Appendix 15

NYPE 93 – New York Produce (continued)

| 12. Berths | 179 |

The Vessel shall be loaded and discharged in any safe dock or at any safe berth or safe place that 180
Charterers or their agents may direct, provided the Vessel can safely enter, lie and depart always afloat 181
at any time of tide. 182

13. Spaces Available   183

(a) The whole reach of the Vessel's holds, decks, and other cargo spaces (not more than she can 184
reasonably and safely stow and carry), also accommodations for supercargo, if carried, shall be at the 185
Charterers' disposal, reserving only proper and sufficient space for the Vessel's officers, crew, tackle, 186
apparel, furniture, provisions, stores and fuel. 187

(b) In the event of deck cargo being carried, the Owners are to be and are hereby indemnified by the 188
Charterers for any loss and/or damage and/or liability of whatsoever nature caused to the Vessel as a 189
result of the carriage of deck cargo and which would not have arisen had deck cargo not been loaded. 190

14. Supercargo and Meals   191

The Charterers are entitled to appoint a supercargo, who shall accompany the Vessel at the Charterers' 192
risk and see that voyages are performed with due despatch. He is to be furnished with free 193
accommodation and same fare as provided for the Master's table, the Charterers paying at the rate of 194
    per day. The Owners shall victual pilots and customs officers, and also, when 195
authorized by the Charterers or their agents, shall victual tally clerks, stevedore's foreman, etc., 196
Charterers paying at the rate of per meal for all such victualling. 197

15. Sailing Orders and Logs   198

The Charterers shall furnish the Master from time to time with all requisite instructions and sailing 199
directions, in writing, in the English language, and the Master shall keep full and correct deck and engine 200
logs of the voyage or voyages, which are to be patent to the Charterers or their agents, and furnish the 201
Charterers, their agents or supercargo, when required, with a true copy of such deck and engine logs, 202
showing the course of the Vessel, distance run and the consumption of bunkers. Any log extracts 203
required by the Charterers shall be in the English language. 204

16. Delivery/Cancelling   205

If required by the Charterers, time shall not commence before   and should the 206
Vessel not be ready for delivery on or before   but not later than   hours, 207
the Charterers shall have the option of cancelling this Charter Party. 208

Extension of Cancelling   209

If the Owners warrant that, despite the exercise of due diligence by them, the Vessel will not be ready 210
for delivery by the cancelling date, and provided the Owners are able to state with reasonable certainty 211
the date on which the Vessel will be ready, they may, at the earliest seven days before the Vessel is 212
expected to sail for the port or place of delivery, require the Charterers to declare whether or not they will 213
cancel the Charter Party. Should the Charterers elect not to cancel, or should they fail to reply within two 214
days or by the cancelling date, whichever shall first occur, then the seventh day after the expected date 215
of readiness for delivery as notified by the Owners shall replace the original cancelling date. Should the 216
Vessel be further delayed, the Owners shall be entitled to require further declarations of the Charterers in 217
accordance with this Clause. 218

17. Off Hire   219

In the event of loss of time from deficiency and/or default and/or strike of officers or crew, or deficiency 220
of stores, fire, breakdown of, or damages to hull, machinery or equipment, grounding, detention by the 221
arrest of the Vessel, (unless such arrest is caused by events for which the Charterers, their servants, 222
agents or subcontractors are responsible), or detention by average accidents to the Vessel or cargo unless 223
resulting from inherent vice, quality or defect of the cargo, drydocking for the purpose of examination or 224
painting bottom, or by any other similar cause preventing the full working of the Vessel, the payment of 225

Appendix 15

NYPE 93 – New York Produce (continued)

hire and overtime, if any, shall cease for the time thereby lost. Should the Vessel deviate or put back 226
during a voyage, contrary to the orders or directions of the Charterers, for any reason other than accident 227
to the cargo or where permitted in lines 257 to 258 hereunder, the hire is to be suspended from the time 228
of her deviating or putting back until she is again in the same or equidistant position from the destination 229
and the voyage resumed therefrom. All bunkers used by the Vessel while off hire shall be for the Owners' 230
account. In the event of the Vessel being driven into port or to anchorage through stress of weather, 231
trading to shallow harbors or to rivers or ports with bars, any detention of the Vessel and/or expenses 232
resulting from such detention shall be for the Charterers' account. If upon the voyage the speed be 233
reduced by defect in, or breakdown of, any part of her hull, machinery or equipment, the time so lost, and 234
the cost of any extra bunkers consumed in consequence thereof, and all extra proven expenses may be 235
deducted from the hire. 236

18. Sublet 237

Unless otherwise agreed, the Charterers shall have the liberty to sublet the Vessel for all or any part of 238
the time covered by this Charter Party, but the Charterers remain responsible for the fulfillment of this 239
Charter Party. 240

19. Drvdocking 241

The Vessel was last drydocked 242

*(a) The Owners shall have the option to place the Vessel in drydock during the currency of this Charter 243
at a convenient time and place, to be mutually agreed upon between the Owners and the Charterers, for 244
bottom cleaning and painting and/or repair as required by class or dictated by circumstances. 245

*(b) Except in case of emergency no drydocking shall take place during the currency of this Charter 246
Party. 247

* Delete as appropriate 248

20. Total Loss 249

Should the Vessel be lost, money paid in advance and not earned (reckoning from the date of loss or 250
being last heard of) shall be returned to the Charterers at once. 251

21. Exceptions 252

The act of God, enemies, fire, restraint of princes, rulers and people, and all dangers and accidents of the 253
seas, rivers, machinery, boilers, and navigation, and errors of navigation throughout this Charter, always 254
mutually excepted. 255

22. Liberties 256

The Vessel shall have the liberty to sail with or without pilots, to tow and to be towed, to assist vessels 257
in distress, and to deviate for the purpose of saving life and property. 258

23. Liens 259

The Owners shall have a lien upon all cargoes and all sub-freights and/or sub-hire for any amounts due 260
under this Charter Party, including general average contributions, and the Charterers shall have a lien on 261
the Vessel for all monies paid in advance and not earned, and any overpaid hire or excess deposit to be 262
returned at once. 263

The Charterers will not directly or indirectly suffer, nor permit to be continued, any lien or encumbrance, 264
which might have priority over the title and interest of the Owners in the Vessel. The Charterers 265
undertake that during the period of this Charter Party, they will not procure any supplies or necessaries 266
or services, including any port expenses and bunkers, on the credit of the Owners or in the Owners' time. 267

Appendix 15

NYPE 93 – New York Produce (continued)

24. <u>Salvage</u>   268

All derelicts and salvage shall be for the Owners' and the Charterers' equal benefit after deducting 269
Owners' and Charterers' expenses and crew's proportion.   270

25. <u>General Average</u>   271

General average shall be adjusted according to York-Antwerp Rules 1974, as amended 1990, or any 272
subsequent modification thereof, in   and settled in   273
currency.   274

The Charterers shall procure that all bills of lading issued during the currency of the Charter Party will 275
contain a provision to the effect that general average shall be adjusted according to York-Antwerp Rules 276
1974, as amended 1990, or any subsequent modification thereof and will include the "New Jason 277
Clause" as per Clause 31.   278

Time charter hire shall not contribute to general average.   279

26. <u>Navigation</u>   280

Nothing herein stated is to be construed as a demise of the Vessel to the Time Charterers. The Owners 281
shall remain responsible for the navigation of the Vessel, acts of pilots and tug boats, insurance, crew, 282
and all other matters, same as when trading for their own account.   283

27. <u>Cargo Claims</u>   284

Cargo claims as between the Owners and the Charterers shall be settled in accordance with the Inter-Club 285
New York Produce Exchange Agreement of February 1970, as amended May, 1984, or any subsequent 286
modification or replacement thereof.   287

28. <u>Cargo Gear and Lights</u>   288

The Owners shall maintain the cargo handling gear of the Vessel which is as follows: 289
    290
    291
    292

providing gear (for all derricks or cranes) capable of lifting capacity as described. The Owners shall also 293
provide on the Vessel for night work lights as on board, but all additional lights over those on board shall 294
be at the Charterers' expense. The Charterers shall have the use of any gear on board the Vessel. If 295
required by the Charterers, the Vessel shall work night and day and all cargo handling gear shall be at the 296
Charterers' disposal during loading and discharging. In the event of disabled cargo handling gear, or 297
insufficient power to operate the same, the Vessel is to be considered to be off hire to the extent that 298
time is actually lost to the Charterers and the Owners to pay stevedore stand-by charges occasioned 299
thereby, unless such disablement or insufficiency of power is caused by the Charterers' stevedores. If 300
required by the Charterers, the Owners shall bear the cost of hiring shore gear in lieu thereof, in which 301
case the Vessel shall remain on hire.   302

29. <u>Crew Overtime</u>   303

In lieu of any overtime payments to officers and crew for work ordered by the Charterers or their agents, 304
the Charterers shall pay the Owners, concurrently with the hire   per month 305
or pro rata.   306

30. <u>Bills of Lading</u>   307

(a) The Master shall sign the bills of lading or waybills for cargo as presented in conformity with mates 308
or tally clerk's receipts. However, the Charterers may sign bills of lading or waybills on behalf of the 309
Master, with the Owner's prior written authority, always in conformity with mates or tally clerk's receipts. 310

Appendix 15

NYPE 93 – New York Produce (continued)

(b)   All bills of lading or waybills shall be without prejudice to this Charter Party and the Charterers shall 311
indemnify the Owners against all consequences or liabilities which may arise from any inconsistency 312
between this Charter Party and any bills of lading or waybills signed by the Charterers or by the Master 313
at their request. 314

(c)   Bills of lading covering deck cargo shall be claused: "Shipped on deck at Charterers', Shippers' and 315
Receivers' risk, expense and responsibility, without liability on the part of the Vessel, or her Owners for 316
any loss, damage, expense or delay howsoever caused." 317

31. Protective Clauses 318

This Charter Party is subject to the following clauses all of which are also to be included in all bills of lading 319
or waybills issued hereunder: 320

(a)   CLAUSE PARAMOUNT 321
"This bill of lading shall have effect subject to the provisions of the Carriage of Goods by Sea Act of the 322
United States, the Hague Rules, or the Hague-Visby Rules, as applicable, or such other similar national 323
legislation as may mandatorily apply by virtue of origin or destination of the bills of lading, which shall 324
be deemed to be incorporated herein and nothing herein contained shall be deemed a surrender by the 325
carrier of any of its rights or immunities or an increase of any of its responsibilities or liabilities under said 326
applicable Act. If any term of this bill of lading be repugnant to said applicable Act to any extent, such 327
term shall be void to that extent, but no further." 328

and 329

(b)   BOTH-TO-BLAME COLLISION CLAUSE 330
"If the ship comes into collision with another ship as a result of the negligence of the other ship and any 331
act, neglect or default of the master, manner, pilot or the servants of the carrier in the navigation or in 332
the management of the ship, the owners of the goods carried hereunder will indemnify the carrier against 333
all loss or liability to the other or non-carrying ship or her owners insofar as such loss or liability represents 334
loss of, or damage to, or any claim whatsoever of the owners of said goods, paid or payable by the other 335
or non-carrying ship or her owners to the owners of said goods and set off, recouped or recovered by the 336
other or non-carrying ship or her owners as part of their claim against the carrying ship or carrier. 337

The foregoing provisions shall also apply where the owners, operators or those in charge of any ships or 338
objects other than, or in addition to, the colliding ships or objects are at fault in respect to a collision or 339
contact." 340

and 341

(c)   NEW JASON CLAUSE 342
"In the event of accident, danger, damage or disaster before or after the commencement of the voyage 343
resulting from any cause whatsoever, whether due to negligence or not, for which, or for the 344
consequences of which, the carrier is not responsible, by statute, contract, or otherwise, the goods, 345
shippers, consignees, or owners of the goods shall contribute with the carrier in general average to the 346
payment of any sacrifices, losses, or expenses of a general average nature that may be made or incurred, 347
and shall pay salvage and special charges incurred in respect of the goods. 348

If a salving ship is owned or operated by the carrier, salvage shall be paid for as fully as if salving ship 349
or ships belonged to strangers. Such deposit as the carrier or his agents may deem sufficient to cover 350
the estimated contribution of the goods and any salvage and special charges thereon shall, if required, 351
be made by the goods, shippers, consignees or owners of the goods to the carrier before delivery." 352

and 353

(d)   U.S. TRADE - DRUG CLAUSE 354
"In pursuance of the provisions of the U.S. Anti Drug Abuse Act 1986 or any re-enactment thereof, the 355
Charterers warrant to exercise the highest degree of care and diligence in preventing unmanifested 356
narcotic drugs and marijuana to be loaded or concealed on board the Vessel. 357

Appendix 15

NYPE 93 – New York Produce (continued)

Non-compliance with the provisions of this clause shall amount to breach of warranty for consequences 358
of which the Charterers shall be liable and shall hold the Owners, the Master and the crew of the Vessel 359
harmless and shall keep them indemnified against all claims whatsoever which may arise and be made 360
against them individually or jointly. Furthermore, all time lost and all expenses incurred, including fines, 361
as a result of the Charterers' breach of the provisions of this clause shall be for the Charterer's account 362
and the Vessel shall remain on hire. 363

Should the Vessel be arrested as a result of the Charterers' non-compliance with the provisions of this 364
clause, the Charterers shall at their expense take all reasonable steps to secure that within a reasonable 365
time the Vessel is released and at their expense put up the bails to secure release of the Vessel. 366

The Owners shall remain responsible for all time lost and all expenses incurred, including fines, in the 367
event that unmanifested narcotic drugs and marijuana are found in the possession or effects of the 368
Vessel's personnel." 369

and 370

(e)   WAR CLAUSES 371
"(i)   No contraband of war shall be shipped. The Vessel shall not be required, without the consent of the 372
Owners, which shall not be unreasonably withheld, to enter any port or zone which is involved in a state 373
of war, warlike operations, or hostilities, civil strife, insurrection or piracy whether there be a declaration 374
of war or not, where the Vessel, cargo or crew might reasonably be expected to be subject to capture, 375
seizure or arrest, or to a hostile act by a belligerent power (the term "power" meaning any de jure or de 376
facto authority or any purported governmental organization maintaining naval, military or air forces). 377

(ii)   If such consent is given by the Owners, the Charterers will pay the provable additional cost of insuring 378
the Vessel against hull war risks in an amount equal to the value under her ordinary hull policy but not 379
exceeding a valuation of   In addition, the Owners may purchase and the 380
Charterers will pay for war risk insurance on ancillary risks such as loss of hire, freight disbursements, 381
total loss, blocking and trapping, etc. If such insurance is not obtainable commercially or through a 382
government program, the Vessel shall not be required to enter or remain at any such port or zone. 383

(iii)   In the event of the existence of the conditions described in (i) subsequent to the date of this Charter, 384
or while the Vessel is on hire under this Charter, the Charterers shall, in respect of voyages to any such 385
port or zone assume the provable additional cost of wages and insurance properly incurred in connection 386
with master, officers and crew as a consequence of such war, warlike operations or hostilities. 387

(iv)   Any war bonus to officers and crew due to the Vessel's trading or cargo carried shall be for the 388
Charterers' account." 389

32.   War Cancellation 390

In the event of the outbreak of war (whether there be a declaration of war or not) between any two or 391
more of the following countries: 392
393
394
395
either the Owners or the Charterers may cancel this Charter Party. Whereupon, the Charterers shall 396
redeliver the Vessel to the Owners in accordance with Clause 10; if she has cargo on board, after 397
discharge thereof at destination, or, if debarred under this Clause from reaching or entering it, at a near 398
open and safe port as directed by the Owners; or, if she has no cargo on board, at the port at which she 399
then is; or, if at sea, at a near open and safe port as directed by the Owners. In all cases hire shall 400
continue to be paid in accordance with Clause 11 and except as aforesaid all other provisions of this 401
Charter Party shall apply until redelivery. 402

33.   Ice 403

The Vessel shall not be required to enter or remain in any icebound port or area, nor any port or area 404

Appendix 15

NYPE 93 – New York Produce (continued)

where lights or lightships have been or are about to be withdrawn by reason of ice, nor where there is 405
risk that in the ordinary course of things the Vessel will not be able on account of ice to safely enter and 406
remain in the port or area or to get out after having completed loading or discharging. Subject to the 407
Owners' prior approval the Vessel is to follow ice-breakers when reasonably required with regard to her 408
size, construction and ice class. 409

34. Requisition 410

Should the Vessel be requisitioned by the government of the Vessel's flag during the period of this Charter 411
Party, the Vessel shall be deemed to be off hire during the period of such requisition, and any hire paid 412
by the said government in respect of such requisition period shall be retained by the Owners. The period 413
during which the Vessel is on requisition to the said government shall count as part of the period provided 414
for in this Charter Party. 415
If the period of requisition exceeds   months, either party shall have the option 416
of cancelling this Charter Party and no consequential claim may be made by either party. 417

35. Stevedore Damage 418

Notwithstanding anything contained herein to the contrary, the Charterers shall pay for any and all 419
damage to the Vessel caused by stevedores provided the Master has notified the Charterers and/or their 420
agents in writing as soon as practical but not later than 48 hours after any damage is discovered. Such 421
notice to specify the damage in detail and to invite Charterers to appoint a surveyor to assess the extent 422
of such damage. 423

(a)   In case of any and all damage(s) affecting the Vessel's seaworthiness and/or the safety of the crew 424
and/or affecting the trading capabilities of the Vessel, the Charterers shall immediately arrange for repairs 425
of such damage(s) at their expense and the Vessel is to remain on hire until such repairs are completed 426
and if required passed by the Vessel's classification society. 427

(b)   Any and all damage(s) not described under point (a) above shall be repaired at the Charterers' option, 428
before or after redelivery concurrently with the Owners' work. In such case no hire and/or expenses will 429
be paid to the Owners except and insofar as the time and/or the expenses required for the repairs for 430
which the Charterers are responsible, exceed the time and/or expenses necessary to carry out the 431
Owners' work. 432

36. Cleaning of Holds 433

The Charterers shall provide and pay extra for sweeping and/or washing and/or cleaning of holds between 434
voyages and/or between cargoes provided such work can be undertaken by the crew and is permitted by 435
local regulations, at the rate of   per hold. 436

In connection with any such operation, the Owners shall not be responsible if the Vessel's holds are not 437
accepted or passed by the port or any other authority. The Charterers shall have the option to re-deliver 438
the Vessel with unclean/upswept holds against a lumpsum payment of   in lieu of cleaning. 439

37. Taxes 440

Charterers to pay all local, State, National taxes and/or dues assessed on the Vessel or the Owners 441
resulting from the Charterers' orders herein, whether assessed during or after the currency of this Charter 442
Party including any taxes and/or dues on cargo and/or freights and/or sub-freights and/or hire (excluding 443
taxes levied by the country of the flag of the Vessel or the Owners). 444

38. Charterers' Colors 445

The Charterers shall have the privilege of flying their own house flag and painting the Vessel with their 446
own markings. The Vessel shall be repainted in the Owners' colors before termination of the Charter 447
Party. Cost and time of painting, maintaining and repainting those changes effected by the Charterers 448
shall be for the Charterers' account. 449

NYPE 93 – New York Produce (continued)

39. <u>Laid up Returns</u>   450

The Charterers shall have the benefit of any return insurance premium receivable by the Owners from their   451
underwriters as and when received from underwriters by reason of the Vessel being in port for a minimum   452
period of 30 days if on full hire for this period or pro rata for the time actually on hire.   453

40. <u>Documentation</u>   454

The Owners shall provide any documentation relating to the Vessel that may be required to permit the   455
Vessel to trade within the agreed trade limits, including, but not limited to certificates of financial   456
responsibility for oil pollution, provided such oil pollution certificates are obtainable from the Owners'   457
P & I club, valid international tonnage certificate, Suez and Panama tonnage certificates, valid certificate 458
of registry and certificates relating to the strength and/or serviceability of the Vessel's gear.   459

41. <u>Stowaways</u>   460

(a) (i)   The Charterers warrant to exercise due care and diligence in preventing stowaways in gaining   461
           access to the Vessel by means of secreting away in the goods and/or containers shipped by the   462
           Charterers.   463

     (ii) If, despite the exercise of due care and diligence by the Charterers, stowaways have gained   464
           access to the Vessel by means of secreting away in the goods and/or containers shipped by the   465
           Charterers, this shall amount to breach of charter for the consequences of which the Charterers   466
           shall be liable and shall hold the Owners harmless and shall keep them indemnified against all   467
           claims whatsoever which may arise and be made against them. Furthermore, all time lost and all   468
           expenses whatsoever and howsoever incurred, including fines, shall be for the Charterers' account 469
           and the Vessel shall remain on hire.   470

     (iii) Should the Vessel be arrested as a result of the Charterers' breach of charter according to   471
           sub-clause (a)(ii) above, the Charterers shall take all reasonable steps to secure that, within a 472
           reasonable time, the Vessel is released and at their expense put up bail to secure release of the 473
           Vessel.   474

(b) (i)   If, despite the exercise of due care and diligence by the Owners, stowaways have gained   475
           access to the Vessel by means other than secreting away in the goods and/or containers shipped   476
           by the Charterers, all time lost and all expenses whatsoever and howsoever incurred, including   477
           fines, shall be for the Owners' account and the Vessel shall be off hire.   478

     (ii) Should the Vessel be arrested as a result of stowaways having gained access to the Vessel   479
           by means other than secreting away in the goods and/or containers shipped by the Charterers,   480
           the Owners shall take all reasonable steps to secure that, within a reasonable time, the Vessel   481
           is released and at their expense put up bail to secure release of the Vessel.   482

42. <u>Smuggling</u>   483

In the event of smuggling by the Master, Officers and/or crew, the Owners shall bear the cost of any   484
fines, taxes, or imposts levied and the Vessel shall be off hire for any time lost as a result thereof.   485

43. <u>Commissions</u>   486

A commission of   percent is payable by the Vessel and the Owners to   487
                                                                                                             488
                                                                                                             489
                                                                                                             490
on hire earned and paid under this Charter, and also upon any continuation or extension of this Charter.   491

44. <u>Address Commission</u>   492

An address commission of   percent is payable to   493

Appendix 15

NYPE 93 – New York Produce (continued)

	494
	495
on hire earned and paid under this Charter.	496

45. Arbitration   497

(a)   NEW YORK   498
All disputes arising out of this contract shall be arbitrated at New York in the following manner, and   499
subject to U.S. Law: 500

One Arbitrator is to be appointed by each of the parties hereto and a third by the two so chosen. Their   501
decision or that of any two of them shall be final, and for the purpose of enforcing any award, this   502
agreement may be made a rule of the court. The Arbitrators shall be commercial men, conversant with   503
shipping matters. Such Arbitration is to be conducted in accordance with the rules of the Society of   504
Maritime Arbitrators Inc.   505

For disputes where the total amount claimed by either party does not exceed US $ ** 506
the arbitration shall be conducted in accordance with the Shortened Arbitration Procedure of the Society   507
of Maritime Arbitrators Inc.   508

(b)   LONDON   509
All disputes arising out of this contract shall be arbitrated at London and, unless the parties agree   510
forthwith on a single Arbitrator, be referred to the final arbitrament of two Arbitrators carrying on business   511
in London who shall be members of the Baltic Mercantile & Shipping Exchange and engaged in Shipping,   512
one to be appointed by each of the parties, with power to such Arbitrators to appoint an Umpire. No   513
award shall be questioned or invalidated on the ground that any of the Arbitrators is not qualified as   514
above, unless objection to his action be taken before the award is made. Any dispute arising hereunder   515
shall be governed by English Law.   516

For disputes where the total amount claimed by either party does not exceed US $ ** 517
the arbitration shall be conducted in accordance with the Small Claims Procedure of the London Maritime   518
Arbitrators Association.   519

* Delete para (a) or (b) as appropriate   520

** Where no figure is supplied in the blank space this provision only shall be void but the other provisions   521
of this clause shall have full force and remain in effect.   522

If mutually agreed, clauses   to   , both inclusive, as attached hereto are fully   523
incorporated in this Charter Party.   524

Draft Copy

APPENDIX "A"	525

To Charter Party dated		526
Between	Owners	527
and	Charterers	528
		529
Further details of the Vessel:		530

Appendix 16

BARECON 89

1. Shipbroker	THE BALTIC AND INTERNATIONAL MARITIME COUNCIL (BIMCO) STANDARD BAREBOAT CHARTER CODE NAME: "BARECON 89"	PART 1
	2. Place and date	
3. Owners/Place of business	4. Bareboat charterers (Charterers)/Place of business	

5. Vessel's name, Call Sign and Flag (Cl. 9(c))		
6. Type of Vessel	7. GRT/NRT	
8. When/Where built	9. Total DWT (abt.) in metric tons on summer freeboard	
10. Class (Cl. 9)	11. Date of last special survey by the Vessel's classification society	

12. Further particulars of Vessel (also indicate minimum number of months' validity of class certificates agreed ace. to Cl. 14)

13. Port or Race of delivery (Cl. 2)	14. Time for delivery (Cl. 3)	15. Cancelling date (Cl. 4)
	16. Port or Race of redelivery (Cl. 14)	
17. Running days' notice if other than stated in Cl. 3	18. Frequency of dry-docking if other than stated in Cl. 9(f)	

19. Trading Limits (Cl. 5)

20. Charter period	21. Charter hire (Cl. 10)
22. Rate of interest payable acc. to Cl. 10(f) and, if applicable, acc. to PART IV	23. Currency and method of payment (Cl. 10)

Appendix 16

BARECON 89 (continued)

24. Race of payment; also state beneficiary and bank account (Cl. 10)	25. Bank guarantee/bond (sum and place) (Cl. 22) (optional)
26. Mortgage(s), if any, (state whether Cl. 11(a) or (b) applies; if 11(b) applies state date of Deed(s) of Covenant and name of Mortgagee(s)/Place of business) (Cl. 11)	27. Insurance (marine and war risks) (state value acc. to Cl. 12(f) or, If applicable, acc. to Cl. 13(k)) (also state if Cl. 13 applies)
28. Additional insurance cover, if any, for Owners' account limited to (Cl. 12(b)) or, if applicable, (Cl. 13(g))	29. Additional insurance cover, if any, for Charterers' account limited to (Cl. 12(b)) or, if applicable, (Cl. 13(g))
30. Latent defects (only to be filled in if period other than stated in Cl. 2)	31. War cancellation (indicate countries agreed) (Cl. 24)
32. Brokerage commission and to whom payable (Cl. 25)	
33. Law and arbitration (state 26.1., 26.2. or 26.3. of Cl. 26 as agreed; if 26.3. agreed, also state place of arbitration) (Cl. 26)	34. Number of additional clauses covering special provisions, if agreed
35. Newbuilding-Vessel (indicate with "yes" or "no" whether Part III applies) (optional)	36. Name and place of Builders (only to be filled in if Part III applies)
37. Vessel's Yard Building No. (only to be filled in if Part III applies)	38. Date of Building Contract (only to be filled in if Part III applies)
39. Hire/Purchase agreement (indicate with "yes" or "no" whether Part IV applies) (optional)	40. Bareboat Charter Registry (indicate with "yes" or "no" whether Part V applies) (optional)
41. Flag and Country of the Bareboat Charter Registry (only to be filled in if Part V applies)	42. Country of the Underlying Registry (only to be filled in if Part V applies)

PREAMBLE. – It is mutually agreed that this Contract shall be performed subject to the conditions contained in this Charter which shall include PART I and PART II. In the event of a conflict of conditions, the provisions of PART I shall prevail over those of PART II to the extent of such conflict but no further. It is further mutually agreed that PART III and/or PART IV and/or PART V shall only apply and shall only form part of this Charter if expressly agreed and stated in the Boxes 35, 39 and 40. If PART III and/or PART IV and/or PART V apply, it is further mutually agreed that in the event of a conflict of conditions, the provisions of PART I and PART II shall prevail over those of PART III and/or PART IV and/or PART V to the extent of such conflict but no further.

Signature (Owners)	Signature (Charterers)

Appendix 16

BARECON 89 (continued)

"BARECON 89" STANDARD BAREBOAT CHARTER

"Japanese Terms"

(In case when "Tokyo" is stated in Box 33, the provisions regarding arbitration procedures in Clause 26.3. shall be considered deleted and substituted by the following provisions.)

Law and Arbitration

This Charter shall be governed by Japanese law. Any dispute arising from this Charter shall be referred to arbitration held in Tokyo by the Tokyo Maritime Arbitration Commission (TOMAC) of The Japan Shipping Exchange, inc. in accordance with the Rules of TOMAC and any amendment thereto, and the award given by the arbitrators shall be final and binding on both parties.

Appendix 16

BARECON 89 (continued)

PART II
"BARECON 89" Standard Bareboat Charter

1. Definitions

In this Charter, the following terms shall have the meanings hereby assigned to them:

"The Owners" shall mean the person or company registered as Owners of the Vessel.

"The Charterers" shall mean the Bareboat charterers and shall not be construed to mean a time charterer or a voyage charterer

2. Delivery (*not* applicable to newbuilding vessels)

The Vessel shall be delivered and taken over by the Charterers at the port or place indicated in Box 13, in such ready berth as the Charterers may direct The Owners shall before and at the time of delivery exercise due diligence to make the Vessel seaworthy and in every respect ready in hull, machinery and equipment for service under this Charter The Vessel shall be properly documented at time of delivery.

The delivery to the Charterers of the Vessel and the taking over of the Vessel by the Charterers shall constitute a full performance by the Owners of all the Owners' obligations under Clause 2, and thereafter the Charterers shall not be entitled to make or assert any claim against the Owners on account of any conditions, representations or warranties expressed or implied with respect to the Vessel but the Owners shall be responsible for repairs or renewals occasioned by latent defects in the Vessel, her machinery or appurtenances, existing at the time of delivery under the Charter, provided such defects have manifested themselves within 18 months after delivery unless otherwise provided in Box 30.

3. Time for Delivery (*not* applicable to newbuilding vessels)

The Vessel to be delivered not before the date indicated in Box 14 unless with the Charterers' consent

Unless otherwise agreed in Box 17, the Owners to give the Charterers not less than 30 running days' preliminary and not less than 14 days' definite notice of the date on which the Vessel is expected to be ready for delivery.

The Owners to keep the Charterers closely advised of possible changes in the Vessel's position.

4. Cancelling (*not* applicable to newbuilding vessels)

Should the Vessel not be delivered latest by the cancelling date indicated in Box 15. the Charterers to have the option of cancelling this Charter without prejudice to any claim the Charterers may otherwise have on the Owners under the Charter.

If it appears that the Vessel will be delayed beyond the cancelling date, the Owners shall, as soon as they are in a position to state with reasonable certainty the day on which the Vessel should be ready, give notice thereof to the Charterers asking whether they will exercise their option of cancelling, and the option must then be declared within one hundred and sixty-eight (168) hours of the receipt by the Charterers of such notice If the Charterers do not then exercise their option of cancelling, the seventh day after the readiness date stated in the Owners' notice shall be regarded as a new cancelling date for the purpose of this Clause.

5. Trading Limits

The Vessel shall be employed m lawful trades for the carnage of suitable lawful merchandise within the trading limits indicated in Box 19.

The Charterers undertake not to employ the Vessel or suffer the Vessel to be employed otherwise than in conformity with the terms of the instruments of insurance (including any warranties expressed or implied therein) without first obtaining the consent to such employment of the Insurers and complying with such requirements as to extra premium or otherwise as the Insurers may prescribe If required, the Charterers shall keep the Owners and the Mortgagees advised of the intended employment of the Vessel.

The Charterers also undertake not to employ the Vessel or suffer her employment in any trade or business which is forbidden by the law of any country to which the Vessel may sail or is otherwise illicit or in carrying illicit or prohibited goods or in any manner whatsoever which may render her liable to condemnation, destruction, seizure or confiscation.

Notwithstanding any other provisions contained in this Charter it is agreed that nuclear fuels or radioactive products or waste are specifically excluded from the cargo permitted to be loaded or carried under this Charter This exclusion does not apply to radio-isotopes used or intended to be used for any industrial, commercial, agricultural, medical or scientific purposes provided the Owners' prior approval has been obtained to loading thereof.

6. Surveys (*not* applicable to newbuilding vessels)

Survey on Delivery and Redelivery – The Owners and Charterers shall each appoint surveyors for the purpose of determining and agreeing in writing the condition of the Vessel at the time of delivery and redelivery hereunder The Owners shall bear all expenses of the On-Survey including loss of time, if any and the Charterers shall bear all expenses of the Off- Survey including loss of time, if any, at the rate of hire per day or pro rata, also including in each case the cost of any docking and undocking, if required, in connection herewith.

7. Inspection

Inspection. – The Owners shall have the right at any time to inspect or survey the Vessel or instruct a duly authorised surveyor to carry out such survey on their behalf to ascertain the condition of the Vessel and satisfy themselves that the Vessel is being properly repaired and maintained. Inspection or survey in dry-dock shall be made only when the Vessel shall be in dry-dock for the Charterers' purpose However, the Owners shall have the right to require the Vessel to be dry-docked for inspection if the Charterers are not docking her at normal classification intervals The fees for such inspection or survey shall in the event of the Vessel being found to be in the condition provided in Clause 9 of this Charter be payable by the Owners and shall be paid by the Charterers only in the event of the Vessel being found to require repairs or maintenance in order to achieve the condition so provided. All time taken in respect of inspection, survey or repairs shall count as time on hire and shall form part of the Charter period.

The Charterers shall also permit the Owners to inspect the Vessel's log books whenever requested and shall whenever required by the Owners furnish them with full information regarding any casualties or other accidents or damage to the Vessel. For the purpose of this Clause, the Charterers shall keep the Owners advised of the intended employment of the Vessel.

8. Inventories and Consumable Oil and Stores

A complete inventory of the Vessel's entire equipment, outfit, appliances and of all consumable stores on board the Vessel shall be made by the Charterers in conjunction with the Owners on delivery and again on redelivery of the Vessel. The Charterers and the Owners, respectively, shall at the time of delivery and redelivery take over and pay for all bunkers, lubricating oil, water and unbroached provisions, paints, oils, ropes and other consumable stores in the said Vessel at the then current market prices at the ports of delivery and redelivery, respectively.

9. Maintenance and Operation

(a) The Vessel shall during the Charter period be in the full possession and at the absolute disposal for all purposes of the Charterers and under their complete control in every respect The Charterers shall maintain the Vessel, her machinery, boilers, appurtenances and spare parts in a good state of repair, in efficient operating condition and in accordance with good commercial maintenance practice and except as provided for in Clause 13 (I), they shall keep the Vessel with unexpired classification of the class indicated in Box 10 and with other required certificates in force at all times.

The Charterers to take immediate steps to have the necessary repairs done within a reasonable time failing which the Owners shall have the right of withdrawing the Vessel from the service of the Charterers without noting any protest and without prejudice to any claim the Owners may otherwise have against the Charterers under the Charter.

Unless otherwise agreed, in the event of any improvement, structural changes or expensive new equipment becoming necessary for the continued operation of the Vessel by reason of new class requirements or by compulsory legislation costing more than 5 per cent of the Vessel's marine insurance value as stated in Box 27, then the extent, if any, to which the rate of hire shall be varied and the ratio in which the cost of compliance shall be shared between the parties concerned in order to achieve a reasonable distribution thereof as between the Owners and the Charterers having regard inter alia, to the length of the period remaining under the Charter, shall in the absence of agreement, be referred to arbitration according to Clause 26.

The Charterers are required to establish and maintain financial security or responsibility in respect of oil or other pollution damage as required by any government, including Federal, state or municipal or other division or authority thereof, to enable the Vessel, without penalty or charge, lawfully to enter, remain at or leave any port, place, territorial or contiguous waters of any country, state or municipality in performance of this Charter without any delay This obligation shall apply whether or not such requirements have been lawfully imposed by such government or division or authority thereof. The Charterers shall make and maintain all arrangements by bond or otherwise as may be necessary to satisfy such requirements at the Charterers' sole expense and the Charterers shall indemnify the Owners against all consequences whatsoever (including loss of time) for any failure or inability to do so.

TOVALOP SCHEME. (*Applicable to oil tank vessels only*) - The Charterers are required to enter the Vessel under the **TOVALOP SCHEME** or under any similar compulsory scheme upon delivery under this Charter and to maintain her so during the currency of this Charter.

(b) The Charterers shall at their own expense and by their own procurement man, victual, navigate, operate, supply, fuel and repair the Vessel whenever required during the Charter period and they shall pay all charges and expenses of every kind and nature whatsoever incidental to their use and operation of the Vessel under this Charter, including any foreign general municipality and/or state taxes The Master, officers and crew of the Vessel shall be the servants of the Charterers for all purposes whatsoever, even if for any reason appointed by the Owners.

Charterers shall comply with the regulations regarding officers and crew in force in the country of the Vessel's flag or any other applicable law.

(c) During the currency of this Charter, the Vessel shall retain her present name as indicated in Box 5 and shall remain under and fly the flag as indicated in Box 5. Provided, however, that the Charterers shall have the liberty to paint the Vessel in their own colours, install and display their funnel insignia and fly their own house flag Painting and re-painting, instalment and re-instalment to be for the Charterers' account and time used thereby to count as time on hire.

(d) The Charterers shall make no structural changes in the Vessel or changes in the machinery, boilers, appurtenances or spare parts thereof without in each instance first securing the Owners' approval thereof. If the Owners so agree, the Charterers shall, if the Owners so require, restore the Vessel to its former condition before the termination of the Charter.

(e) The Charterers shall have the use of all outfit, equipment, and appliances on board the Vessel at the time of delivery, provided the same or their substantial equivalent shall be returned to the Owners on redelivery in the same good order and condition as when received, ordinary wear and tear excepted The Charterers shall from time to time during the Charter period replace such items of equipment as shall be so damaged or worn as to be unfit for use The Charterers are to procure that all repairs to or replacement of any damaged, worn or lost parts or equipment be effected in such manner (both as regards workmanship and quality of materials) as not to diminish the value of the Vessel The Charterers have the right to fit additional equipment at their expense and risk but the Charterers shall remove such equipment at the end of the period if requested by the Owners.

Any equipment including radio equipment on hire on the Vessel at time of delivery shall be kept and maintained by the Charterers and the Charterers shall assume the obligations and liabilities of the Owners under any lease contracts in connection therewith and shall reimburse the Owners for all expenses incurred in connection therewith, also for any new equipment required in order to comply with radio regulations.

(f) The Charterers shall dry-dock the Vessel and clean and paint her underwater parts whenever the same may be necessary, but not less than once in every eighteen calendar months after delivery unless otherwise agreed in Box 18.

10. Hire

(a) The Charterers shall pay to the Owners for the hire of the Vessel at the lump sum per calendar month as indicated in Box 21 commencing on and from the date and hour of her delivery to the Charterers and at and after the agreed lump sum for any part of a month. Hire to continue until the date and hour when the Vessel is redelivered by the Charterers to her Owners.

(b) Payment of Hire, except for the first and last month's Hire, if sub-clause (c) of this Clause is applicable, shall be made in cash without discount every month in advance

246

on the first day of each month in the currency and in the manner indicated in Box 23 and at the place mentioned in Box 24.

Appendix 16

BARECON 89 (continued)

PART II

"BARECON 89" Standard Bareboat Charter

(c) Payment of Hire for the first and last month's Hire if less than a full month shall be calculated proportionally according to the number of days in the particular calendar month and advance payment to be effected accordingly.

(d) Should the Vessel be lost or missing, Hire to cease from the date and time when she was lost or last heard of. Any Hire paid in advance to be adjusted accordingly.

(e) Time shall be of the essence in relation to payment of Hire hereunder. In default of payment beyond a period of seven running days, the Owners shall have the right to withdraw the Vessel from the service of the Charterers without noting any protest and without interference by any court or any other formality whatsoever, and shall, without prejudice to any other claim the Owners may otherwise have against the Charterers under the Charter, be entitled to damages in respect of all costs and losses incurred as a result of the Charterers' default and the ensuing withdrawal of the Vessel.

(f) Any delay in payment of Hire shall entitle the Owners to an interest at the rate per annum as agreed in Box 22. If Box 22 has not been filled in the current market rate in the country where the Owners have their Principal Place of Business shall apply.

11. Mortgage

*) (a) Owners warrant that they have not effected any mortgage of the Vessel.

*) (b) The Vessel chartered under this Charter is financed by a mortgage according to the Deed(s) of Covenant annexed to this Charter and as stated in Box 26. By their counter-signature on the Deed(s) of Covenant, the Charterers undertake to have acquainted themselves with all terms. conditions and provisions of the said Deed(s) of Covenant The Charterers undertake that they will comply with at such instructions or directions in regard to the employment, insurances, repairs and maintenance of the Vessel, etc., as laid down in the Deed(s) of Covenant or as may be directed from time to time during the currency of the Charter by the Mortgagee(s) in conformity with the Deed(s) of Covenant.

(c) The Owners warrant that they have not effected any mortgage(s) other than stated in Box 26 and that they will not effect any other mortgage(s) without the prior consent of the Charterers.

*) *(Oolional, Clauses 11 (a) and 11 (b) are alternatives, indicate alternative agreed in Box 26).*

12. Insurance and Repairs

(a) During the Charter period the Vessel shall be kept insured by the Charterers at their expense against marine, war and Protection and Indemnity risks in such form as the Owners shall in writing approve, which approval shall not be unreasonably withheld Such marine, war and P. and I. insurances shall be arranged by the Charterers to protect the interests of both the Owners and the Charterers and mortgagees (if any), and the Charterers shall be at liberty to protect under such insurances the interests of any managers they may appoint AM insurance policies shall be m the joint names of the Owners and the Charterers as their interests may appear.

If the Charterers fail to arrange and keep any of the the insurances provided for under the provisions of sub-clause (a) above in the manner described therein, the Owners shall notify the Charterers whereupon the Charterers shall rectify the position within seven running days, failing which Owners shall have the right to withdraw the Vessel from the service of the Charterers without prejudice to any claim the Owners may otherwise have against the Charterers.

The Charterers shall, subject to the approval of the Owners and the Underwriters, effect all insured repairs and shall undertake settlement of all costs in connection with such repairs as well as insured charges, expenses and liabilities (reimbursement to be secured by the Charterers from the Underwriters) to the extent of coverage under the insurances herein provided for.

The Charterers also to remain responsible for and to effect repairs and settlement of costs and expenses incurred thereby in respect of all other repairs not covered by the insurances and/or not exceeding any possible franchise(s) or deductibles provided for in the insurances.

All time used for repairs under the provisions of sub-clause (a) of this Clause and for repairs of latent defects according to Clause 2 above including any deviation shall count as time on hire and shall form part of the Charter period.

(b) If the conditions of the above insurances permit additional insurance to be placed by the parties, such cover shall be limited to the amount for each party set out in Box 28 and Box 29, respectively The Owners or the Charterers as the case may be shall immediately furnish the other party with particulars of any additional insurance effected, including copies of any cover notes or policies and the written consent of the insurers of any such required insurance in any case where the consent of such insurers is necessary.

(c) Should the Vessel become an actual, constructive, compromised or agreed total loss under the insurances required under sub-clause (a) of Clause 12, all insurance payments for such loss shall De paid to the Mortgagee, if any, in the manner described in the Deed(s) of Covenant, who shall distribute the moneys between themselves, the Owners and the Charterers according to their respective interests The Charterers undertake to notify the Owners and the Mortgagee, if any, of any occurrences in consequence of which the Vessel is likely to become a Total Loss as defined in this Clause.

(d) H the Vessel becomes an actual, constructive, compromised or agreed total loss under the insurances arranged by the Charterers in accordance with sub-clause (a) of this Clause, this Charter shall terminate as of the date o' such loss.

(e) The Owners shall upon the request of the Charterers, promptly execute such documents as may be required to enable the Charterers to abandon the Vessel to insurers and claim a constructive total loss.

(f) For the purpose of insurance coverage against marine and war risks under the provisions of sub-clause (a) of this Clause, the value of the Vessel is the sum indicated in Box 27.

13. Insurance, Repairs and Classification

(Optional, only to apply if expressly agreed and stated in Box 27 in which event Clause 12 shall be considered deleted).

(a) During the Charter period the Vessel shall be kept insured by the Owners at their expense against marine and war risks under the form of policy or policies attached hereto. The Owners and/or insurers shall not have any right of recovery or subrogation against the Charterers on account of loss of or any damage to the Vessel or her machinery or appurtenances covered by such insurance, or on account of payments made to discharge claims against or liabilities of the Vessel or the Owners covered by such insurance. All insurance policies shall be in the joint names of the Owners and the Charterers as their interests may appear.

(b) During the Charter period the Vessel shall be kept insured by the Charterers at their expense against Protection and Indemnity risks in such form as the Owners shall in writing approve which approval shall not be unreasonably withheld If the Charterers fail to arrange and keep any of the insurances provided for under the provisions of sub-clause (b) in the manner described therein, the Owners shall notify the Charterers whereupon the Charterers shall rectify the position within seven running days, failing which the Owners shall have the right to withdraw the Vessel from the service of the Charterers without prejudice to any claim the Owners may otherwise have against the Charterers.

(c) In the event that any act or negligence of the Charterers shall vitiate any of the insurance herein provided, the Charterers shall pay to the Owners all losses and indemnify the Owners against all claims and demands which would otherwise have been covered by such insurance.

(d) The Charterers shall, subject to the approval of the Owners or Owners' Underwriters, effect all insured repairs, and the Charterers shall undertake settlement of all miscellaneous expenses in connection with such repairs as welt as all insured charges, expenses and liabilities, to the extent of coverage under the insurances provided for under the provisions of sub-clause (at of this Clause. The Charterers to be secured reimbursement through the Owners' Underwriters for such expenditures upon presentation of accounts.

(e) The Charterers to remain responsible for and to effect repairs and settlement of costs and expenses incurred thereby in respect of all other repairs not covered by the insurances and/or not exceeding any possible franchise(s) or deductibles provided for in the insurances.

(f) All time used for repairs under the provisions of sub-clause (d) and (e) of this Clause and for repairs of latent defects according to Clause 2 above, including any deviation, shall count as lime on hire and shall form part of the Charter period.

The Owners shall not be responsible for any expenses as are incident to the use and operation of the Vessel for such time as may be required to make such repairs.

(g) If the conditions o' the above insurances permit additional insurance to be placed by the parties such cover shall be limited to the amount for each party set out in Box 28 and Box 29, respectively The Owners or the Charterers as the case may be shall immediately furnish the other party with particulars of any additional insurance effected, including copies of any cover notes or policies and the written consent of the insurers of any such required insurance in any case where the consent of such Insurers is necessary.

(h) Should the Vessel become an actual, constructive, compromised or agreed total loss under the insurances required under sub-clause (a) of this Clause, all insurance payments for such loss shall be paid to the Owners, who shall distribute the moneys between themselves and the Charterers according to their respective interests.

(i) If the Vessel becomes an actual, constructive, compromised or agreed total loss under the insurances arranged by the Owners in accordance with sub-clause (a) of this Clause, this Charter shall terminate as of the date of such loss.

(j) The Charterers shall upon the request of the Owners promptly execute such documents as may be required to enable the Owners to abandon the Vessel to Insurers and claim a constructive total loss.

(k) For the purpose of insurance coverage against marine and war risks under the provisions of sub-clause (a) of this Clause, the value of the Vessel is the sum indicated in Box 27.

(l) Notwithstanding anything contained in Clause 9 (a) it is agreed that under the provisions of Clause 13, if applicable. The Owners shall keep the Vessel with unexpired classification in farce at all times during the Charter period.

14. Redelivery

The Charterers shall at the expiration of the Charter period redeliver the Vessel at a safe and ice-free port or place as indicated in Box 16. The Charterers shall give the Owners not less than 30 running days' preliminary and not less than 14 days' definite notice of expected date, range of ports of redelivery or port or place of redelivery. Any changes thereafter in Vessel's position shall be notified immediately to the Owners.

Should the Vessel be ordered on a voyage by which the Charter period may be exceeded the Charterers to have the use of the Vessel to enable them to complete the voyage, provided it could be reasonably calculated that the voyage would allow redelivery about the time fixed for the termination of the Charter.

The Vessel shall be redelivered to the Owners in the same or as good structure, stale, condition and class as that in which she was delivered, fair wear and tear not affecting class excepted.

The Vessel upon redelivery shall have her survey cycles up to date and class certificates valid for at least the number of months agreed in Box 12.

15. Non-Lien and Indemnity

The Charterers will not suffer, nor permit to be continued, any lien or encumbrance incurred by them or their agents, which might have priority over the title and interest of the Owners in the Vessel.

The Charterers further agree to fasten to the Vessel in a conspicuous place and to keep so fastened during the Charter period a notice reading as follows:-

"This Vessel is the property of (name of Owners) It is under charter to (name of Charterers) and by the terms of the Charter Party neither the Charterers nor the Master have any right, power or authority to create, incur or permit to be imposed on the Vessel any lien whatsoever".

The Charterers shall indemnify and hold the Owners harmless against any lien of whatsoever nature arising upon the Vessel during the Charter period while she is under the control of the Charterers, and against any claims against the Owners arising out of or in relation to the operation of the Vessel by the Charterers. Should the Vessel be arrested by reason of claims or liens arising out of her operation hereunder by the Charterers, the Charterers shall at their own expense take all reasonable steps to secure that within a reasonable time the Vessel is released and at their own expense put up bail to secure release of the Vessel.

16. Lien

The Owners to have a lien upon all cargoes and sub-freights belonging to the Charterers and any Bill of Lading freight for all claims under this Charter, and the

Charterers to have a lien on the Vessel for all moneys paid in advance and not earned.

17. Salvage

All salvage and towage performed by the Vessel shall be for the Charterers' benefit and the cost of repairing damage occasioned thereby shall be borne by the Charterers.

Appendix 16

BARECON 89 (continued)

PART II
"BARECON 89" Standard Bareboat Charter

18. Wrack Removal

In the event of the Vessel becoming a wreck or obstruction to navigation the Charterers shall indemnify the Owners against any sums whatsoever which the Owners shall became liable to pay and shall pay in consequence of the Vessel becoming a wreck or obstruction to navigation.

19. General Average

General Average, if any, shall be adjusted according to the York-Antwerp Rules 1974 or any subsequent modification thereof current at the time of the casualty.
The Charter Hire not to contribute to General Average.

20. Assignment and Sub-Demise

The Charterers shall not assign this Charter nor sub-demise the Vessel except with the prior consent in writing of the Owners which shall not be unreasonably withheld and subject to such terms and conditions as the Owners shall approve.

21. Bills of Lading

The Charterers are to procure that all Bills of Lading issued for carriage of goods under this Charter shall contain a Paramount Clause incorporating any legislation relating to Carrier's liability for cargo compulsorily applicable in the trade; if no such legislation exists, the Bills of Lading shall incorporate the British Carriage of Goods by Sea Act. The Bills of Lading shall also contain the amended New Jason Clause and the Both-to-Blame Collision Clause The Charterers agree to indemnify the Owners against all consequences or liabilities arising from the Master, officers or agents signing Bills of Lading or other documents.

22. Bank Guarantee

The Charterers undertake to furnish, before delivery of the Vessel, a first class bank guarantee or bond in the sum and at the place as indicated in Box 25 as guarantee for full performance of their obligations under this Charter. *(Optional, only to apply it Sox 25 filled in).*

23. Requisition/Acquisition

(a) In the event of the Requisition for Hire of the Vessel by any governmental or other competent authority (hereinafter referred to as "Requisition for Hire") irrespective of the date during the Charter period when "Requisition far Hire" may occur and irrespective of the length thereof and whether or not it be for *an* indefinite or a limited period of time, and irrespective of whether it may or will remain in force for the remainder of the Charter period, this Charter shall not be deemed thereby or thereupon to be frustrated or otherwise terminated and the Charterers shall continue to pay the stipulated hire in the manner provided by this Charter until the time when the Charter would have terminated pursuant to any of the provisions hereof always provided however that in the event of "Requisition for Hire" any Requisition Hire or compensation received or receivable by the Owners shall be payable to the Charterers during the remainder of the Charter period or the period of the "Requisition for Hire" whichever be the shorter.

The Hire under this Charter shall be payable to the Owners from the same time as the Requisition Hire is payable to the Charterers.

(b) In the event of the Owners being deprived of their ownership in the Vessel by any Compulsory Acquisition of the Vessel or requisition for title by any governmental or other competent authority (hereinafter referred to as "Compulsory Acquisition"), then, Irrespective of the date during the Charter period when "Compulsory Acquisition" may occur, this Charter shall be deemed terminated as of the date of such "Compulsory Acquisition" In such event Charter Hire to be considered as earned and to be paid up to the date and tir..e of such "Compulsory Acquisition".

24. War

(a) The Vessel unless the consent of the Owners be first obtained not to be ordered nor continue to any place or on any voyage nor be used on any service which will bring her within a zone which is dangerous as the result of any actual or threatened act of war, war, hostilities, warlike operations, acts of piracy or of hostility or malicious damage against this or any other vessel or its cargo by any person, body or State whatsoever, revolution, civil war, civil commotion or the operation of international law, nor be exposed in any way to any risks or penalties whatsoever consequent upon the imposition of Sanctions, nor carry any goods that may in any way expose her to any risks of seizure, capture, penalties or any other interference of any kind whatsoever by the belligerent or fighting powers or parties or by any Government or Ruler.

(b) The Vessel to have liberty to comply with any orders or directions as to departure, arrival, routes, ports of call, stoppages, destination, delivery or in any other wise whatsoever given by the Government of the nation under whose flag the Vessel sails or any other Government or any person (or body) acting or purporting to act with the authority of such Government or by any committee or person having under the terms of the war risks insurance on the Vessel the right to give any such orders or directions.

(c) In the event of outbreak of war (whether there be a declaration of war or not) between any two or more of the countries as stated in Box 31, both the Owners and the Charterers shall have the right to cancel this Charter, whereupon the Charterers shall redeliver the Vessel to the Owners in accordance with Clause 14, if she has cargo on board after discharge thereof at destination, or if debarred under this Clause from reaching or entering it at a near open and safe port as directed by the Owners, or if she has no cargo on board, at the port at which she then is or it at sea at a near open and safe port as directed by the Owners. In all cases hire shall continue to be paid in accordance with Clause 10 and except as aforesaid all other provisions of this Charter shall apply until redelivery.

25. Commission

The Owners to pay a commission at the rate indicated in Box 32 to the Brokers named in Box 32 on any Hire paid under the Charter but in no case less than is necessary to cover the actual expenses of the Brokers and a reasonable fee for their work if the full Hire is not paid owing to breach of Charter by either of the parties the party liable therefor to indemnify the Brokers against their loss of commission.

Should the parties agree to cancel the Charter, the Owners to indemnify the Brokers against any loss of commission but in such case the commission not to exceed the brokerage on one year's Hire.

26. Law and Arbitration

*) 26.1. This Charter shall be governed by English law and any dispute arising out of this Charter shall be referred to arbitration in London, one arbitrator being appointed by each party, in accordance with the Arbitration Acts 1950 and 1979 or any statutory modification or re-enactment thereof for the time being in force. On the receipt by one party of the nomination in writing of the other party's arbitrator, that party shall appoint their arbitrator within fourteen days, failing which the decision of the single Arbitrator appointed shall apply If two Arbitrators properly appointed shall not agree they shall appoint an umpire whose decision shall be final.

*) 26.2. Should any dispute arise out of this Charter, the matter in dispute shall be referred to three persons at New York, one to be appointed by each of the parties hereto, and the third by the two so chosen, their decision or that of any two of them shall be final, and for purpose of enforcing any award, this agreement may be made a rule of the Court.

The arbitrators shall be members of the Society of Maritime Arbitrators. Inc. of New York and the proceedings shall be conducted in accordance with the rules of the Society.

*) 26.3. Any dispute arising out of this Charter shall be referred to arbitration at the place indicated in Box 33, subject to the law and procedures applicable there.

26.4 If Box 33 in Part I is not filled in. sub-clause 26.1. of this Clause shall apply.

*) 26.1., 26.2. and 26.3. are alternatives; indicate alternative agreed in Box 33.

Appendix 16

BARECON 89 (continued)

"BARECON 89" Standard Bareboat Charter

PART III
PROVISIONS TO APPLY FOR NEWBUILDING VESSELS ONLY
(Optional, only to apply if expressly agreed and stated in Box 35)

Specifications and Building Contract

(a) The Vessel shall be constructed in accordance with the Building Contract (hereafter called "the Building Contract") as annexed to this Charter, made between the Builders and the Owners and in accordance with the specifications and plans annexed thereto, such Building Contract, specifications and plans having been counter-signed as approved by the Charterers.

(b) No change shall be made in the Building Contract or in the specifications or plans of the Vessel as approved by the Charterers as aforesaid, without the Charterers' consent.

(c) The Charterers shall have the right to send their representative to the Builders' Yard to inspect the Vessel during the course of her construction to satisfy themselves that construction is in accordance with such approved specifications and plans as referred to under sub-clause (a) of this Clause.

(d) The Vessel shall be built in accordance with the Building Contract and shall be of the description set out therein provided nevertheless that the Charterers shall be bound to accept the Vessel from the Owners on the date of delivery by the Builders as having been completed and constructed in accordance with the Building Contract and the Charterers undertake that after having so accepted the Vessel they will not thereafter raise any claims against the Owners in respect of the Vessel's performance or specification or defects if any except that in respect of any repair or replacement of any defects which appear within the first 12 months from delivery the Owners shall use their best endeavours to recover any expenditure incurred in remedying such defects from the Builders, but shall only be liable to the Charterers to the extent the Owners have a valid claim against the Builders under the guarantee clause of the Building Contract (a copy whereof has been supplied to the Charterers) provided that the Charterers shall be bound to accept such sums as the Owners are able to recover under this clause and shall make no claim upon the Owners for any difference between the amounts so recovered and the actual expenditure incurred on repairs or replacements or for any loss of time incurred thereby.

Time and Place of Delivery

(a) Subject to the Vessel having completed her acceptance trials including trials of cargo equipment in accordance with the Building Contract and specifications to the satisfaction of the Charterers, the Owners shall give and the Charterers shall take delivery of the Vessel afloat when ready for delivery at the Builders' Yard or some other safe and readil/accessible dock, wharf or place as may be agreed between the parties hereto and the Builders. Under the Building Contract the Builders have estimated that the Vessel will be ready for delivery to the Owners as therein provided but the delivery date for the purpose of this Charter shall be the date when the Vessel is in fact ready for delivery by the Builders after completion of trials whether that be before or after as indicated in the Building Contract. Notwithstanding the foregoing, the Charterers shall not be obliged to take delivery of the Vessel until she has been classed and documented as provided in this Charter and free for transfer to the flag she has to fly. Subject as aforesaid the Charterers shall not be entitled to refuse acceptance of delivery of the Vessel and upon and after such acceptance the Charterers shall not be entitled to make any claim against the Owners in respect of any conditions, representations or warranties, whether express or implied, as to the seaworthiness of the Vessel or in respect of delay in delivery or otherwise howsoever.

(b) If for any reason other than a default by the Owners under the Building Contract, the Builders become entitled under that Contract not to deliver the Vessel to the Owners, the Owners shall upon giving to the Charterers written notice of Builders becoming so entitled, be excused from giving delivery of the Vessel to the Charterers and upon receipt of such notice by the Charterers this Charter shall cease to have effect.

(c) If for any reason the Owners become entitled under the Building Contract to reject the Vessel the Owners shall, before exercising such right of rejection, consult the Charterers and thereupon

i) it the Charterers do not wish to take delivery of the Vessel they shall inform the Owners within seven (7) days by notice in writing and upon receipt by the Owners of such notice this Charter shall cease to have effect; or

ii) if the Charterers wish to take delivery of the Vessel they may by notice in writing within seven (7) days require the Owners to negotiate with the Builders as to the terms on which delivery should be taken and/or refrain from exercising their right to rejection and upon receipt of such notice the Owners shall commence such negotiations and/or take delivery of the Vessel from the Builders and deliver her to the Charterers;

iii) in no circumstances shall the Charterers be entitled to reject the Vessel unless the Owners are able to reject the Vessel from the Builders;

iv) if this Charter terminates under sub-clause (b) or (c) of this Clause, the Owners shall thereafter not be liable to the Charterers for any claim under or arising out of this Charter or its termination.

Guarantee Works

If not otherwise agreed, the Owners authorize the Charterers to arrange for the guarantee works to be performed in accordance with the budding contract terms, and hire to continue during the period of guarantee works. The Charterers have to advise the Owners about the performance to the extent the Owners may request.

Name of Vessel

The name of the Vessel shall be mutually agreed between the Owners and the Charterers and the Vessel shall be painted in the colours, display the funnel insignia and fly the house flag as required by the Charterers.

Survey on Redelivery

The Owners and the Charterers shall appoint surveyors (or the purpose of determining and agreeing in writing the condition of the Vessel at the time of redelivery.

Without prejudice to Clause 14 (Part II), the Charterers shall bear all survey expenses and all other costs, if any, including the cost of docking andundocking, if required, as well as all repair costs incurred.

The Charterers shall also bear all loss of time spent in connection with any docking and undocking as well as repairs, which shall be paid at the rate of Hire per day or pro rata.

PART IV
HIRE/PURCHASE AGREEMENT
(Optional, only to apply if expressly agreed and stated in Box 39)

On expiration of this Charter and provided the Charterers have fulfilled their obligations according to Part I and II as well as Part III, if applicable, it is agreed, that on payment of the last month's hire instalment as per Clause 10 the Charterers have purchased the Vessel with everything belonging to her and the Vessel is fully paid for.

If the payment of the instalment due is delayed for less than 7 running days or for reason beyond the Charterers' control, the right of withdrawal under the terms of Clause 10(e) of Part II shall not be exercised However, any delay in payment of the instalment due shall entitle the Owners to an interest at the rate per annum as agreed in Box 22. If Box 22 has not been filled in the current market rate in the country where the Owners have their Principal Place of Business shall apply.

In the following paragraphs the Owners are referred to as the Sellers and the Charterers as the Buyers.

The Vessel shall be delivered by the Sellers and taken over by the Buyers on expiration of the Charter.

The Sellers guarantee that the Vessel, at the time of delivery, is free from all encumbrances and maritime liens or any debts whatsoever other than those arising from anything done or not done by the Buyers or any existing mortgage agreed not to be paid off by the time of delivery Should any claims, which have been incurred prior to the time of delivery be made against the Vessel, the Sellers hereby undertake to indemnify the Buyers against all consequences of such claims to the extent it can be proved that the Sellers are responsible 'or such claims Any taxes, notarial, consular and other charges and expenses connected with the purchase and registration under Buyers' flag, shall be for Buyers' account. Any taxes, consular and other charges and expenses connected with closing of the Sellers' register, shall be for Sellers' account.

In exchange for payment of the last month's hire instalment the Sellers shall furnish the Buyers with a Bill of Sale duly attested and legalized, together with a certificate setting out the registered encumbrances, if any. On delivery of the Vessel the Sellers shall provide for deletion of the Vessel from the Ship's Register and deliver a certificate of deletion to the Buyers.

The Sellers shall, at the time of delivery, hand to the Buyers all classification certificates (for hull, engines, anchors, chains etc), as well as all plans which may be in Sellers' possession.

The Wireless Installation and Nautical Instruments, unless on hire, shall be included in the sale without any extra payment.

The Vessel with everything belonging to her shall be at Sellers' risk and expense until she is delivered to the Buyers, subject to the conditions of this Contract and the Vessel with everything belonging to her shall be delivered and taken over as she is at the time of delivery, after which the Sellers shall have no responsibility for possible faults or deficiencies of any description.

The Buyers undertake to pay for the repatriation of the Captain, officers and other personnel if appointed by the Sellers to the port where the Vessel entered the Bareboat Charter as per Clause 2 (Part II) or to pay the equivalent cost for their journey to any other place.

PART V

PROVISIONS TO APPLY FOR VESSELS REGISTERED IN A BAREBOAT CHARTER REGISTRY
(Optional, only to apply it expressly agreed and stated in Box 40)

Definitions

For the purpose of this PART V, the following terms shall have the meanings hereby assigned to them:

"The Bareboat Charter Registry" shall mean the registry of the State whose flag the Vessel will fly and in which the Charterers are registered as the bareboat charterers during the period of the Bareboat Charter.

"The Underlying Registry" shall mean the registry of the State in which the Owners of the Vessel are registered as Owners and to which jurisdiction and control of the Vessel will revert upon termination of the Bareboat Charter Registration.

Mortgage

The Vessel chartered under this Charter is financed by a mortgage and the provisions of Clause 11 (b) (Part II) shall apply.

Termination of Charter by Default

If the Vessel chartered under this Charter is registered in a Bareboat Charter Registry as stated in Box 41, and if the Owners shall default in the payment of any amounts due under the mortgage(s) specified in Box 26, the Charterers shall, it so required by the mortgagee, direct the Owners to re-register the Vessel in the Underlying Registry as shown in Box 42.

In the event of the Vessel being deleted from the Bareboat Charter Registry as stated in Box 41, due to a default by the Owners in the payment of any amounts due under the mortgage(s), the Charterers shall have the right to terminate this Charter forthwith and without prejudice to any other claim they may have against the Owners under this Charter.

Appendix 17

NORGRAIN 89

Code Name: **Norgrain 89**
RECOMMENDED BY
THE BALTIC AND INTERNATIONAL MARITIME COUNCIL (BIMCO)
THE FEDERATION OF NATIONAL ASSOCIATIONS OF SHIP BROKERS AND
AGENTS (FONASBA)
AMENDED MAY 1989

NORTH AMERICAN GRAIN CHARTERPARTY 1973
ISSUED BY THE ASSOCIATION OF SHIP BROKERS AND AGENTS (U.S.A.) INC.

...................................19...........

Owners IT IS THIS DAY MUTUALLY AGREED, between...

Note: Delete as appropriate Owners }   Self/Non Self Trimming Bulk carrier
Disponent Owners }   of the .... SS   Tween Decker .... Call Sign ....
Time-chartered Owners }   M.V.   Tanker
Chartered Owners }

Description of Vessel Built .... at .... of .... tons of 2,240 lbs.

deadweight all told, or thereabouts, and with a grain cubic capacity available for cargo of .... cubic feet (including .... cubic feet in self-bleeding wing spaces)

....

Classification Classed .... in .... now ....

Note: Insert vessel's Itinerary.

....

....

Charterer and .... of .... Charterers

Loading Port(s) 1. That the said vessel, being tight, staunch strong and in every way fit for the voyage, shall with all convenient speed proceed to ....

.... and there load

Description of Cargo at .... safe loading berth(s) in Charterers' option.

always afloat, $\frac{\text{a full and complete*}}{\text{part*}}$ cargo in bulk of ....

....

....

at Charterers option .... tons of $\frac{2,240\ lbs.*}{1,000\ kilos*}$ ....% more or less, quantity at Owners option.

Notice and Loading Port Orders 2. Owners are to give Charterers (or their Agents) (telegraphic address * .... * telex number ....) 15 and 7 days notice of vessel's expected readiness to load date, and approximate quantity of cargo required with the 15 days' notice, such quantity to be based on a cargo of Heavy Grain, unless the cargo composition has been declared or indicated.

The Charterers are to be kept continuously advised by telegram/telex of any alteration in vessel's readiness to load date.

Master to apply to .... (telegraphic address * .... ") for first or sole loading port orders 144 hours before vessel's expected readiness to load date but not sooner than 144 hours before the laydays in Clause 4 and Charterers or their Agents are to give orders for first or sole loading port within 72 hours of receipt of Master's application, unless given earlier.

Orders for second port of loading, if used, to be given to the Master not later than ....

....

Master is to give Charterers (or their Agents) 72 and 12 hours notice of vessel's estimated time of arrival at first or sole loading port together with vessel's estimated readiness to load date.

Vessel Inspection 3. Vessel is to load under inspection of National Cargo Bureau, Inc in U.S.A. ports or of the Port Warden in Canadian ports. Vessel is also to load under inspection of a Grain Inspector licensed/ authorised by the Untied States Department of Agriculture pursuant to the U.S. Grain Standards Act and/or of a Grain Inspector employed by the Canada Department of Agriculture as required by the appropriate authorities.

If vessel loads at other than U.S. or Canadian ports, she is to load under inspection of such national and/or regulatory bodies as may be required.

Vessel is to comply with the rules of such authorities, and shall load cargo not exceeding what she can reasonably stow and carry over and above her Cabin, Tackle, Apparel, Provisions, Fuel, Furniture and Water. Cost of such inspections shall be borne by Owners.

Laydays/ Cancelling 4. Laytime for loading, if required by Charterers, not to commence before 0800 on the .... day of .... 19 ....

Should the vessel's notice of readiness not be tendered and accepted as per Clause 18 before 1200 on the .... day of .... 19 .... the Charterers have the option of cancelling this Charterpany any time thereafter, but not later than one hour after the tender of notice of readiness as per Clause 18.

Destination 5. On being so loaded, the vessel shall proceed to ....

....

as ordered by Charterers/Receivers*, and deliver the cargo, according to Bills of Lading at ....

safe discharging berths in Charterers' option, vessel being always afloat, on being* / having been* paid freight as per Clauses 8 and 9.

Discharging Port Orders Master to apply by radio to .... (telegraphic address * .... ") for first or sole discharging port orders 96 hours before vessel is due off/at* .... and they are to give first or sole discharging port orders by radio within 48 hours of receipt of Master's application unless given earlier. If Master's application is received on a Saturday, the time allowed shall be 52 hours instead of 48 hours.

Orders for second and/or third port(s) of discharge are to be given to the Master not later than vessel's arrival at first or subsequent port.

Master to radio Charterers/Receivers (or their Agents) 72 and 24 hours notice of vessel's estimated time of arrival at first or sole discharging port. Charterers/Receivers (or their Agents) are to be kept continuously advised by radio/telegram/telex of any alterations in such estimated time of arrival.

Bills of Lading 6. The Master is to sign Bills of Lading as presented on the North American Grain Bill of Lading form without prejudice to the terms, conditions and exceptions of this Charterparty. If the Master elects to delegate the signing of Bills of Lading to his Agents he shall given them authority to do so in writing, copy of which is to be furnished to Charterers if so required.

Bill of ports 7. Rotation of loading ports is to be in $\frac{\text{Owners'*}}{\text{Charterers' *}}$ option.

Rotation of discharging ports is to be in $\frac{\text{Owners'}}{\text{Charterers' *}}$ option, but if more than two (2) ports of discharge are used rotation is to be geographic .... to ....

Freight 8. Freight to be paid as follows:

....

....

....

per ton of 2,240 lbs./1,000 Kilos*
Charterers have the option of ordering the vessel to load at ....

in which case the rate of freight to be ....

....

per ton of 2.240 lbs./1,000 Kilos*

*Delete as appropriate

NORGRAIN 89 (continued)

Charterers/Receivers have the option of ordering the vessel to discharge at ....

....

in which case the rate of freight to be ....

....

per ton of 2.240 lbs./1,000 Kilos*

If more than one port of loading and/or discharging is used, the rate of freight shall be increased by ....

.... per ton of 2.240 lbs./1,000 Kilos* for each additional loading and/or discharging port on the entire cargo.

Freight Payment

9. *(a)* Freight shall be fully prepaid on surrender of signed Bills of Lading in .... in .... currency to

....

on Bill of Lading weight, discount less, not relumable, vessel and/or cargo lost or not lost. Freight shall be deemed earned as cargo is loaded on board.

Once the Bills of Lading have been signed, and Charterers call for surrender of Original Bills of Lading against freight payment above, it will be incumbent upon Owners or their Agents to comply immediately with such call for surrender during office hours, Mondays to Fridays inclusive.

(Other)

(b) ....

....

....

Cost of Loading and Discharging

10. *(a)** Cargo is to be loaded and spout trimmed (to Master's satisfaction in respect of seaworthiness) free of expense to the vessel.
Cargo is to be discharged free of expense to the vessel (to Master's satisfaction in respect of seaworthiness).

*(b)** Cargo is to be loaded and trimmed at Owners' expense.
Cargo is to be discharged free of expense to the vessel (to Master's satisfaction in respect of seaworthiness).

Stevedores at Loading Port (s) and Discharging Port(s)

11. Stevedores at loading Port(s) are to be appointed by $\frac{\text{Charterers*}}{\text{Owners*}}$ and paid by $\frac{\text{Charterers*}}{\text{Owners*}}$

If stevedores are appointed by Owners, they are to be approved by Charterers at loading port(s), and such approval is not to be unreasonably withheld.
Stevedores at discharging port(s) are to be appointed and paid for by Charterers/Receivers*.

In all cases, stevedores shall be deemed to be the servants of the Owners and shall work under the supervision of the Master.

Bulk Carrier and Wing Spaces

12. *(a)* The vessel is warranted to be a $\frac{\text{self-trimming bulk carrier.*}}{\text{non-self-trimmmg bulk carrier *}}$

(b) Cargo may be loaded into wing spaces if the cargo can bleed into centerholds. Wing spaces are to be spout trimmed; any further trimming in wing spaces and any additional expenses in discharging are to be for Owners' account, and additional time so used is not to count as laytime or time on demurrage.

Overtime

13. *(a)* **Expenses**

(i) All overtime expenses at loading and discharging ports shall be for account of the party ordering same.

(ii) If overtime is ordered by port authorities or the party controlling the loading and/or discharging terminal or facility all overtime expenses are to be equally shared between the

Owners and $\frac{\text{Charterers*}}{\text{Receivers*}}$

(iii) Overtime expenses for vessel's officers and crew shall always be for Owner's account.

(b) **Time Counting**

If overtime ordered by Owners be worked during periods excepted from laytime the actual time used shall count; if ordered by Charterers/Receivers, the actual time used shall not count; if ordered by port authorities or the party controlling the loading and/or discharging terminal or facility half the actual time used shall count.

Separations

14. Cost of cargo separations, including labor used for laying same, to be for Charterers' account unless required by Owners, in which case all resultant expenses shall be borne by the Owners. ordered by Charterers shall be made to Master's satisfaction (but not exceeding the requirements of the competent authorities).

Securing

15 *(a)* **For Owners' account**
Any securing required by Master, National Cargo Bureau or Port Warden for safe trim/stowage to be supplied by and paid for by Owners, and time so used not to count as laytime or time on demurrage
Bleeding of bags, if any, at discharge port(s) to be at Owners' expense, and time actually lost is not to count.

Delete para (a) or (b) as appropriate

(b) **For Charterers' account**
Any securing required by Master, National Cargo Bureau or Port Warden for safe trim/stowage to be supplied by and paid for by Charterers, and time so used to count as laytime or time on demurrage
Bleeding of bags, if any, at discharge port(s) to be at Charterers'/Receivers' expense.

Fumigation

16. If after loading has commenced, and at any time thereafter until completion of discharge, the cargo is required to be fumigated in vessel's holds, the Owners are to permit same to take place at Charterers' risk and expense, including necessary expenses for aceommodalitig and victualling vessel's personnel ashore.

The Charterers warrant that the fumigants used will not expose the vessel's personnel to any health hazards whatsoever, and will comply with current IMO regulations.

Time lost to the vessel is to count at the demurrage rate.

Opening/ Closing Hatches

17. At each loading and discharging port, cost of first opening and last closing of hatches and removal and replacing of beams, if any, shall be for Owners' account. Cost of all other opening and closing of hatches, removal and replacing of beams shall be for Charterers'/Receivers' account.

18. *(a)* **Notice of Readiness**
Notification of vessel's readiness to load and discharge at the first or sole loading and discharging port shall be delivered in writing at the office of Charterers/Receivers between 0900 and 1700 on all days except Sundays and holidays, and between 0900 and 1200 on Saturdays. Such notice of readiness shall be delivered when the vessel is in the loading or discharging berth if vacant, failing which from a lay berth or anchorage wiihin limits of the port, or otherwise as provided in Clause 18 (b) hereunder.

Time Counting

(b) **Waiting for Berth Outside Port Limits**
If the vessel is prevented from entering the limits of the loading/discharging port(s) because the first or sole loading/discharging berth or a lay berth or anchorage is not available within the port limits, or on the order of the Charterers/Receivers or any competent official body or authority, and the Master warrants that the vessel is physically ready in all respects to load or discharge, the Master may tender vessel's notice of readiness, by radio if desired, from the usual -anchorage outside the limits of the port, whether in free pratique or not. whether customs cleared or not. If after entering the limits of the loading port, vessel fails to pass inspections as per Clause 18 (e) any lime so lost shall not count as laytime or time on demurrage from the time vessel fails inspections until she is passed, but if this delay in obtaining said passes exceeds 24 running hours shex all time spent waiting oucside the limits of the port shall not count.

(c) **Commencement of Limits**
Following receipt of notice of readiness laytime will commence at 0800 on the next day not excepted from laytime. Time (not excepted from laytime) actually used before commencement of laytime shall count.

(d) **Subsequent Ports**
At sscend or subsequent port (0) sf ltading and/sr disharging, layisg sr time sn damurrage shall resume sounting from ressel's arrisel sithin the limite of the port ss previded in Clause 18 (b) if applicable.

(e) **Inspection**
Unless the conditions of Clause 18 (b) apply, at first or sole loading port Master's notice of readiness by pass of the National Cargo Bureau/Port Warden and Grain Inspector's certificate vessel's readiness in all compartments to be loaded, for the entire cargo covered by the Charterparty as per Clause 3. In the event that vessel loads in subsequent port (s) and is required to re-pass inspection in these port, any time lost threat in securing the required certificates shall not count as laytime or time on demurrage.

Laytime

19. *(a)* Vessel is to be loaded and discharged within .... working day of twenty-four (24) consecutive hours each (weather permitting). Sundays and Holidays excepted.

Delete para (a) or (b) as appropriate

(b) Vessel is to be loaded within .... working days of twenty-four (24) consecutive hours each (weather permitting). Sundays and Holidays excepted.

(c) Vessel is to be discharged at the average rate of .... tons of 2,240 lbs. */1,000 kilos. *per working day of twenty-four (24) consecutive hours are unavailable on Saturdays or available only at overtime and/or premium rates.

(d) Notwithstanding any custom of the port to the contrary, Saturdays shall not count as laytime at loading and discharging port or ports where stevedoring labor and/or grain handling facilities are unavailable on Saturdays or available only at overtime and/or premium rates.

In port where only part of Saturdays is affected by such conditions, as described above, laytime shall count until the expiration of the last straight time period.

Where six or more hours or work are performed at normal rates, Saturday shall count as a full lay day.

*Delete as approprate.

Appendix 17

NORGRAIN 89 (continued)

(e) In the event that the vessel is waiting for loading berth, no laytime is to be deducted during such period for reasons of weather unless the vessel occupying the loading or discharging berth is prevented from working grain case time so lost is not count.

Demurrage/ Despatch Money

20. Demurrage at loading and/or discharging ports is to be paid at the rate of .... per day or *pro rata* for part of a day and shall be paid by Charterers in respect of loading port(s) and by Charterers/Receivers* in respect of discharging port(s). Despatch money to be paid by Owners at half the demurrage rate for all laytime saved at loading and/or discharging ports.

Any time lost for which Charterers/Receivers are responsible, which is not excepted under this Charterparty, shall count as laytime, until same has expired, thence time on demurrage.

Shifting

21. *(a)* **Shifting expenses and time**

(i) Cost of shifting between loading berths and cost of shifting between discharging berths, including bunker fuel used, to be for Owners'*/Charterers'/Receivers'* account, time counting.

(ii) If vessel is required to shift from one loading or discharging berth to a lay berth or anchorage due to subsequent loading or discharging berth(s) not being available, all such shifting expenses, as defined above shall be for Owner'*/Charterers'/Receivers'* account time counting.

(iii) If the vessel shifts from the anchorage or waiting place outside the port limits either directly to the first loading or discharging berth or to a lay berth or anchorage within the port limits the cost of that shifting shall be for Owners' account and time so used shall not count even if vessel is on demurrage.

(iv) Cost of shifting from lay berth or anchorage within the port limits to first discharging berth to be Owners' account, time counting.

(b) **Shifting in and out of the same berth**

If vessel is required by Charterers/Receivers* to shift out loading berth or the discharging berth and back to the same berth, one berth shall be deemed to have been used, but shifting expenses from and back to the loading or discharging berth so incurred shall be for Charters'/Receivers'* account and laytime or time on demurrage shall count.

(c) Overtime expenses for vessel's officers and crew shall always be for Owners' account.

Gear and lights

22. If required, the master is to give free use of vessel's cargo gear, including runners, rope and slings as on power to operate the same.

Vessel's personnel is to operators the gear if permitted to do so by shore regulations, failing which shore operators are to be used.

Such shore operators are to be Owners' account at loading port(s) if the provisions of Clause 10 *(b)* apply, otherwise for Charterers' account at loading and Charters'*/Receivers'* account at discharging port(s).

Time lost on account of breakdowns of vessel's gear essential to the loading or discharging of this cargo is not count as laytime or time on demurrage, and if Clause 10 *(a)* applies any stevedore stanby time charges incurred thereby shall be for Owners' account.

If required, Master shall give free use of the vessel's lighting as on board for night work.

Seaworthy Trim

23. If ordered to be loaded or discharged at two or more ports, the vessel is to be left in seaworthy trim to Master's satisfaction (not exceeding the requirements of the Safety of Life at Sea Convention as applied in the country in which such ports are situated) for the passage between ports at Charterers' expenses at loading and at Charterers'/Receivers' expense at discharging ports, and time used for placing vessel in seaworthy trim shall count as laytime or time on demurrage.

Draft/ Lighterage

24. Owners warrant the vessel's deepest salt water draft shall not exceed .... feet .... inches on completion of loading and .... feet .... inches on arrival at first or sole discharging port.

Should the vessel be ordered to discharge at a place in which there is not sufficient water for her to get the first tide after arrival without lightening, and lie always afloat, laytime is to count as per Clause 18 at a safe anchorage for similar vessels bound for such a place and any lighterage expenses incurred to enable her to reach the place of discharge is to be at the expense and risk of the cargo, any custom of the port or place to the contrary notwithstanding, but time occupied in proceeding from the anchorage to the discharging berth is not to count as laytime or time on demurrage.

Unless loading and/or discharging ports are named in this Charteparty, the responsibility for providing safe port of loading and/or discharging lies with the chaterers/Receivers* provided Owners have complied with the maximum draft limitations in Lines 173/174.

Car Decks, etc.

25. It is understood that if this vessel is fitted with car decks, container fitting and/or any other special fitting not connected with the carriage of grain in bulk, any extra expenses incurred in loading and/ or discharging as a result of the presence of such car decks, container fitting and/or special fitting are to be Owners' account. Time so lost shall not count as laytime or time on demurrage.

Dues and/or Taxes

26. ....
....
....

Seaway Tolls

27. All St. Lawrence Seaway and/or Welland Canal tolls on vessel and/or cargo assessed by Canadian and United States Authorities are to be paid and borne by Owners.

Water Pollution

28. Any time lost on account of vessel's non-compliance with Government and /or State and /or Provincial regulations pertaining to water pollution shall not count as laytime on demurrage.

Agents

29. Owners*/Charters* are to appoint at loading port(s) and Owners*/Charters* are to appoint agents at discharging port(s).

In all instances, agency fees shall be for Owners' account but not exceed customary application fees.

Strikes, Stoppages, etc.

30. If the cargo cannot be loaded by reason of Riots, Civil Commotions or of a Strike or Lock-out of any class of workmen essential to the loading of the cargo, or by reason of obstructions or stoppages beyond the control of the Charters caused by Riots, Civil Commotions or a Strike or Lock-out on the Railways or in the Docks or other loading place, or if the cargo cannot be discharged by reason of Riots, Civil Commotions, or of a Strike or Lock-out of any class of workmen essential to the discharge, the time for loading or discharge, as the case may be shall not count during the continuance of such causes, provided that a Strike or Lock-out of Shippers' and/or Receivers' men shall not prevent demurrage accruing if by the use of reasonable diligence they could have obtained other suitable labor at rates current before the Strike or Lock-out. In case of any delay by reason of the before mentioned causes, no claim for damages or demurrage shall be made by the Charterers/Receivers of the cargo or Owners of the vessel. For the purpose, however, of setting despatch by rebate account, any time lost by the vessel through any of the above causes shall be counted as time used in loading, or discharging, as the case may be.

Ice

31. **Loading Port**

(a) If the Vessel cannot reach the loading port by reason of ice when she is ready to proceed from her last port, or at any time during the voyage, or on her arrival, or if frost sets in after her arrival, the Master – for fear of the Vessel being frozen in-is at liberty to leave without cargo; in such cases this Charterparty shall be null and void.

(b) If during loading the Master, for fear of Vessel being frozen in, deems it advisable to leave, he has the liberty to do so with what cargo he has on board and to proceed to any other port with option of completing cargo for Owners' own account to any port or ports including the port of discharge. Any part cargo thus loaded under this Charterparty to be forwarded to destination at Vessel's expense against payment of the agreed freight, provided that no extra expenses be thereby caused to the Consignees, freight being paid on quantity delivered (in proportion if lump sum), all other conditions as per Charterparty.

(c) In case of more than one loading port, and if one more of the ports are closed by ice, the Master or Owners to be at liberty either to load the part cargo at the open port and fill up elsewhere for the Owners' own account as under sub-clause *(b)* or to declare the Charterparty null and void unless the Charterers agree to load full cargo at the open port.

Voyage and Discharging Port

(d) Should ice prevent the Vessel from reaching the port of discharge, the Charterers/Receivers shall have the option of keeping the vessel waiting until the re-opening of navigation and paying demurrage or of ordering the vessel to a safe and immediately accessible port where she can safely discharge without risk of detention by ice. Such orders to be given within 48 hours after the Owners' or Master have given notice to the Charterers/Receivers of impossibility of reaching port of destination.

(e) If the during discharging the Master, for fear of Vessel being frozen in, deems it advisable to leave, he has liberty to do so with what cargo he has on board and to proceed to the nearest safe and accessible port. Such port to be nominated by Charterers/Receivers as soon as possible, but not later than 24 running hours, Sunday and holidays excluded, of receipt of Owners' request for nomination of a substitute discharging port, failing which the Master will himself choose such port.

(f) On delivery of the cargo at such port, all conditions of the Bill of Lading shall apply and the Owners shall receive the same freight as the Vessel had discharged at the original port of destination, expect that if the distance to the substitute port exceeds 100 nautical miles the freight on the cargo delivered at that port to be increased in proportion.

Extra Insurance

32. Any extra insurance on cargo incurred owing to vessel's age class, flag or ownership to be for Owner' account up to a maximum of .... and may be deducted from the freight, in Charterers' option. The Charterers shall furnish evidence of payment supporting such deduction.

P. & I. Bunker Clause

33. The vessel shall have the liberty as part of the contract voyage to any port or ports at which bunker oil is available for the purpose of bunkering at any stage of the voyage whatsoever and whether such ports are on or off the direct and/or customary route or routes between any of the ports of loading or discharge named in this Charterparty and may there take oil bunkers in any quantity in the discretion of Owners even to the full capacity of bunker tanks and any other compartment in which oil can carried whether such amount is or is not required for the chartered voyage.

Deviation

34. Any deviation in saving or attempting to save life or property at sea or any reasonable deviation shall not be deemed shall not be an infringement or breach of this Charterparty and Owners shall not be liable for any loss or damage resulting therefrom: provided however, that if the deviation is for the purpose of loading or unloading cargo or passengers shall, *primafacie*, be regarded as unreasonable.

Lien and Cesser Clause

35. The Owners shall have a lien on the cargo for freight, deadweight, demurrage, and average contribution due to them under this Charterparty.

Charterers' liability under this Charterparty is to cease on cargo being shipped except for payment of freight, deadfreight. and demurrage at loading, and except for all other matters provided for in this Charterparty where the Charterers' responsibility is specified.

Exceptions

36. Owners shall be bound before and at the beginning of the voyage to exercise due diligence to make the vessel seaworthy and to have her properly manned, equipped and supplied and neither the vessel nor the Master or Owners shall be or shall be held liable for any loss of or damage or delay to the cargo for causes excepted by the U.S. Carriage of Goods by Sea Act. 1936 or the Canadian Carriage of Goods by Water Act, 1970, or any statutory re-enactment thereof.

And neither the vessel, her Master or Owners, nor the Charterers or Receivers shall, unless otherwise in this Charterparty expressly provided, be responsible for loss of or damage or delay to or failure to supply, load, discharge or deliver the cargo arising or resulting from: - Act of God; act of war. act of public enemies, rates or assailing thieves; arrest or restraint of princes, rulers or people; seizure under legal process, provided bond is promptly furnished to release the vessel or cargo; floods; fires; blockades; riots; insurrections; Civil Commotions: earthquakes; explosions. No exception afforded the Charterers or Receivers under this clause shall relieve the Charterers or Receivers of or diminish their obligations for payment of any sums due to the Owners under provisions of this Charterparty.

*** Delete as appropriate**

Appendix 17

NORGRAIN 89 (continued)

U.S.A. Clause Paramount

37. If the vessel loads in the U.S A. the U.S.A. Clause Paramount shall be incorporated in all Bills of Lading and shall read as follows.

"This Bill of Lading, shall have effect subject to the provisions of the Carriage of Goods by Sea Act of the United States, approved April 16. 1936, or any statutory re-enactment thereof, which shall be deemed to be incorporated herein, and nothing herein contained shall be deemed a surrender by the carrier of any of its rights or immunities or an increase of any of its responsibilities or liabilities under said Act. If any term of this Bill of Lading be repugnant to said Act to any extent, such terms shall be void to that extent but no further".

Canadian Clause Paramount

38. If the vessel loads in Canada the Canadian Clause Paramount shall be incorporated in all Bills of Lading and shall read as follows.

"This Bill of Lading, so far as it relates to the carriage of goods by water, shall have effect, subject to the provisions of the Carriage of Goods by Water Act. 1970. Revised Statutes of Canada, Chapter C-15, enacted by the Parliament of the Dominion of Canada, or any statutory re-enactment thereof, which shall be deemed to be incorporated herein, and nothing herein contained shall be deemed a surrender by the carrier of any of its right or immunities or an increase of any of its responsibilities or liabilities under the said Act. If any term of this Bill of Lading be repugnant to said Act to any client, such term shall be void to that extent, but no further".

Both-to-Blame Collision Clause

39. If the liability for any collision in which the vessel is involved while performing this Charterparty falls to be determined in accordance with the laws of the United States of America, the following clause shall apply:

"If the vessel comes into collision with another vessel as a result of the negligence of the other vessel and any act, neglect or default of the master, manner, pilot or the servants of the Carrier in the navigation or in the management of the vessel, the owners of the goods earned hereunder will indemnify the Carrier against all loss or liability to the other or noncarrying vessel or her owners in so far as such loss or liability represents loss of or damage to or any claim whatsoever of the owners of the said goods, paid or payable by the other or non-carrying vessel or her owners to the owners of the said goods and set off. recouped or recovered by the other or non-carrying vessel or her owners as part of their claim against the carrying vessel or Carrier".

The forgoing provisions shall also apply where the Owners, operators or those in charge of any vessel or vessels or objects other than, or in addition to, the colliding vessels or objects are at fault in respect to a collision or contact".

The Charterers shall procure that all Bills of Lading issued under this Charterparty shall contain the same clause.

General Average/ New Jason

40. General Average shall be adjusted according to the York/Antwerp Rules 1974 and shall be settled in ....

Where the adjustment is made in accordance with the law and practice of the United States of America, the following clause shall apply.

"In the event of accident, danger, damage or disaster before or after commencement of the voyage, resulting from any cause whatsoever, whether due to negligence or not, for the consequences of which, the Carrier is not responsible, by Statute, contractor otherwise, the goods, shippers, consignees or owners of the goods shall contribute with the Carrier in general average to the payment of any sacrifices, losses expenses of a general average nature that may be made or incurred and shall pay salvage and special charges incurred in respect of the goods.

If a salving vessel is owned or operated by the Came salvage shall be paid for as fully as if the said salving vessel or vessels belonged to strangers. Such deposit as the Carrier or his agents may deem sufficient to cover the estimated contribution of the goods and any salvage and special charges thereon shall, if required, be made by the goods, shippers, consignees or owners of the goods to the Carrier before delivery."

The Charterers shall procure that all Bills of Lading issued under this Charterparty shall contain the same clause.

War risks

41 1. The Master shall not be required or bound otgn Bills of Lading for any blockaded port or for any port which the Master or Owners in his or their discretion consider dangerous or impossible to enter or reach

2 *(A)* If any port of loading or of discharge named in this Charterparty or to which the vessel may properly be ordered pursuant to the terms of the Bills of Lading be blockaded, or

(B) if owing to any war, hostilities, warlike operations, civil war, civil commotions, revolutions, or the operation of international law (a) entry to any such port of loading or of discharge or the loading or discharge of cargo at any such port be considered by the Master or Owners in his or their discretion dangerous or *(b)* it be considered by the Master or Owners in his or their discretion dangerous or impossible for the vessel to reach any such port of loading or of discharge - the Charterers shall have the right to order the cargo or such part of it as may be affected to be loaded or discharged at any other safe port of loading or of discharge within the range of loading or discharging ports respectively established under the provisions of the Charterparty (provided such other port is not blockaded or that entry thereto or loading or discharge of cargo thereat is not in the Master's or Owners' discretion dangerous or prohibited). If in respect of a port of discharge no orders be received from the Charterers within 48 hours after they or their agents have received from the Owners a request for the nomination of a substitute port, the Owners shall then be at liberty to discharge the cargo at any sate port which they or the Master may in their or his discretion decide on whether within the range of discharging ports established under the provisions of the Charterparty or not) and such discharge shall be deemed to be due fulfilment of the contract or contracts of affreightment so far as cargo so discharged is concerned. In the event of the cargo being loaded or discharged at any such other port within the respective range of loading or discharging ports established under the provisions of the Charterparty, the Charterparty shall be read in respect of the freight and all other conditions whatsoever as if the voyage performed were that originally designated. In the event, however, that the vessel discharges the cargo at a port outside the range of discharging ports established under the provisions of the Charterparty, freight shall be paid as for the voyage originally designated and all extra expenses involved in reaching the actual port of discharge and/or discharging the cargo thereat shall be paid by the Charterers or Cargo Owners In this latter event the Owners shall have a lien on the cargo for all such extra expenses.

3. The vessel shall have liberty to comply with any directions or recommendations as to departure, arrival, routes. ports of call, stoptages, destinations, /.ones, waters, delivery or many other wise whatsoever given by the government of the nation under whose flag the vessel sails or any other government or local authority including any de facto government or local authority or by any person or body acting or purporting to act as or with the authority of any such government or authority or by any committee or person having under the terms of the war risks insurance on the vessel the right to give any such directions or recommendations. If by reason of or in compliance with any such directions or recommendations, anything is done or is no in done such shall not be deemed a deviation.

If by reason of or in compliance with any such directions or recommendations the vessel does not proceed to the port or ports of discharge originally designated or to which she may have been ordered pursuant to the terms of the Bills of Lading, the vessel may proceed to any safe port of discharge which the Master or Owners in his or their discretion may decide on and there discharge the cargo. Such discharge shall be deemed to be due fulfilment of the contract or contracts of affrighment and the Owners shall be entitled to freight as if discharge has been effected at the port or ports originally designated or to which the vessel may have been ordered pursuant to the terms of the Bills of Lading All extra expenses involved in reaching and discharging the cargo at any such other port of discharge shall be paid by the Charterers and/or Cargo Owners and the Owners shall have a lien on the cargo for freight and all such expenses.

Address Commission

42. An address commission of .... % on gross freight, deadfreight and demurrage is due to Charterers at time freight and/or demurrage is paid. vessel lost or not lost. Charterers having the right to deduct such commission from payment of freight and/or demurrage.

Brokerage Commission

43. A brokerage commission of .... % on gross freight, deadfreight, and demurrage is payable by Owners to ....

....

at time of receiving freight payment and/or demurrage payments(s), vessel lost or not lost.

Assignment

44. Charterers have the privilege of transferring/assigning/reletting all or part of this Charterparty to others (guaranteeing to the Owners the due fulfilment of this Charterparty).

Arbitration

Delete para (a) or (b) as appropriate

45. *(a)* **New York.** All disputes arising out of this contract shall be arbitrated at New York in the following manner, and be subject to U.S. Law:
One Arbitrator is to be appointed by each of the parties hereto and a third by the two so chosen. Their decision or that of any two of them shall be final, and for the purpose of enforcing any award. this agreement may be made a rule of the court. The Arbitrators shall be commercial men, conversant with shipping matters. Such Arbitration is to be conducted in accordance with the rules of the Society of Maritime Arbitrators Inc.

For disputes where the total amount claimed by either party does not exceed U.S. $ .... ** the arbitration shall be conducted in accordance with the Shortened Arbitration Procedure of the Society of Maritime Arbitrators Inc.

(b) **London.** All disputes arising out of this contract shall be arbitrated at London and, unless the parties agree forthwith on a single Arbitrator, be referred to the final arbitrament of two Arbitrators carrying on business in London who shall be members of the Baltic Mercantile & Shipping Exchange and engaged in the Shipping and/or Grain Trades, one to be appointed by each of the parties, with power to such Arbitrators to appoint an Umpire. No award shall be questioned or invalidated on the ground that any of the Arbitrators is not qualified as above, unless objection to his action be taken before the award is made. Any dispute arising hereunder shall be governed by English Law.

For disputes where the total amount claimed by either party does not exceed U.S. $ .... ** the arbitration shall be conducted in accordance with the Small Claims Procedure of the London Maritime Arbitrators Association.

**Where no figure is supplied in the blank space this provision only shall be void but the other provisions of this clause shall have full force and remain in effect.

Appendix 18

OREVOY 1980

1. Shipbroker	THE BALTIC AND INTERNATIONAL MARITIME CONFERENCE STANDARD ORE CHARTER PARTY CODE NAME: "OREVOY"
	PART I
	2. Place and date of Charter Party
3. Owners/Disponent Owners/Time-Chartered Owners (indicate name, address & telex number)	4. Charterers (indicate name, address & telex number)
5. Vessel's name and flag	6. Rate in tons per hour (load.) (Cl. 1.4.)
7. Vessel's particulars, if required (Cl. 1)	8. Present position and prior commitments, if known (Cl. 2.2.)
9. Laydays date (Cl. 2.1.)	10. Expected readiness to load (Cl. 2.2.)
11. Cancelling date (also state if other period of declaration of cancelling agreed) (Cl. 2.3.)	12. Substitution (state "no" if not agreed) (Cl. 4)
13. Cargo (5 per cent more or less in Owners' option unless other margin agreed) in tons of 1000 kilos (if full and complete cargo not agreed indicate "part cargo") (Cl. 5.1.)	
14. Advance notices (load. and disch.) (State number of running days' notice to be given and to whom) (Cl. 6)	
15. Loading port(s)/berth(s) (Cl. 7.1.)	16. Discharging port(s)/berth(s) (Cl. 7.2.)
17. Reduced voyage speed (state "no" if not agreed) (Cl. 7.2.)	18. Notice time in running hours (load. and disch.) (only to be filled in if agreed) (Cl. 8.2.1.)
19. Laytime (if separate laytime for load. and disch. is agreed, till in a) and b); If total laytime for load. and disch., fill in c) only) (Cl. 8.2.5. a 8.2.6.)	20. Laytime exceptions (loading) (Cl. 8.3.1.)
a) Laytime for loading	
b) Laytime for discharging	21. Laytime exceptions (discharging) (Cl. 8.3.1.)
c) Total laytime for loading and discharging	
22. Demurrage rate (loading) (Cl. 8.5.2.)	23. Demurrage rate (discharging) (Cl. 8.5.2.)
24. Despatch money (load. &/or disch.) (Optional; if agreed indicate rate of despatch money) (Cl. 8.5.3.)	25. Freight tax (state whether for Owners' or Charterers' account) (Cl. 11.3.)
26. Agents at loading port(s) (Cl. 12)	27. Agents at discharging port(s) (Cl. 12)
28. Freight rate per metric ton (state whether fully or partly prepaid) (Cl. 13)	29. Freight payment (currency and when/where payable; also state beneficiary and bank account) (Cl. 13)
30. General average shall be adjusted/settled at (Cl. 20)	31. Law and Arbitration (state 23.1., 232. or 23.3. of Cl. 23, as agreed; if 23.3. agreed state place of arbitration) (if not tilled in 23.1. shall apply) (Cl. 23)
32. Brokerage commission and to whom payable (Cl. 24)	
	33. Numbers of additional clauses covering special provisions, if agreed

It is mutually agreed that this Contract shall be performed subject to the conditions contained in the Charter consisting of PART I including additional clauses, if any agreed and stated in Box 33 and PART II. In the event of a conflict of conditions, the provisions of PART I shall prevail over those of PART II to the extent of such conflict but no further.

Signature (Owners)	Signature (Charterers)

Appendix 18

OREVOY 1980 (continued)

PART II
"OREVOY" Charter Party

1. **Vessel**

   The Owners shall

   1.1. before and at the beginning of the loaded voyage exercise due diligence to make the Vessel seaworthy and in every way fit for the voyage, with a full complement of Master, officers and crew for a vessel of her type, tonnage and flag;

   1.2. ensure that the Vessel and her Master and crew will comply with all safety and health regulations and other statutory rules or regulations and internationally recognized requirements necessary to secure safe and unhindered loading of the cargo, performance of the voyage and discharge of the cargo.

   The Vessel shall

   1.3. be classed Lloyd's 100 A1 or equivalent unless otherwise agreed in Box 7, the Owners exercising due diligence to maintain that class during the currency of this Charter Party;

   1.4. be suitable for mechanical loading of the cargo and capable of receiving the cargo at the rate (if any) specified in Box 6 and be suitable for grab discharge, failing which Clause 8.3.3. shall apply and the Owners shall reimburse the Charterers any actual extra discharge costs;

   1.5. be equipped to meet the technical requirements specified in Box 7.

2. **Laydays Data, Expected Time of Arrival (E.T.A.) and Cancelling**

   2.1. Laydays shall not commence before 00.00 hours on the date stated in Box 9. However, notice of readiness may be given before that date and notice time, if provided for in Box 18, shall run forthwith.

   2.2. Present position of Vessel as per Box 8.

   Commitments prior to commencement of this Charter as per Box 8. Expected readiness to load as per Box 10.

   2.3. The Charterers shall have the option of cancelling the Charter Party if the Vessel be not ready to load on or before twelve midnight (24.00 hours) on the cancelling date stated in Box 11.

   If it appears that the Vessel will be delayed beyond the cancelling date stated in Box 11 the Owners shall, as soon as they are in a position to state with reasonable certainty the day on which the Vessel should be ready, give notice thereof to the Charterers asking whether they will exercise their option of cancelling the Charter Party. The option must then be declared within five (5) running days (unless otherwise agreed in Box 11) of the receipt by the Charterers of such notice, but not earlier than twenty (20) running days before the revised date of load readiness. If the Charterers do not then exercise their option of cancelling, the seventh (7th) day after the readiness date stated in the Owners' notice shall be regarded as a new cancelling date. This provision shall operate only once, and should the Vessel not be ready to load on the new cancelling date the Charterers shall have the option of cancelling the Charter Party. The Charterers shall in any event declare whether they exercise any option of cancelling under sub-clause 2.3. no later than the time of the Vessel's readiness to load.

3. **Subletting, Assigning**

   The Charterers shall have the liberty of subletting or assigning this Charter Party to any individual or company, but the Charterers shall always remain responsible for the due fulfilment of all the terms and conditions of this Charter Party and shall warrant that any such sublet or assignment will not result in the Vessel being restricted in her future trading.

4. **Substitution**

   The Owners shall have liberty to substitute a Vessel, provided that such substitute Vessel's main particulars and position shall be subject to the Charterers' prior approval, which is not to be unreasonably withheld, but the Owners under this Charter Party shall remain responsible to the Charterers for the due fulfilment of this Charter Party. This Clause shall not apply if "No" inserted in Box 12.

5. **Cargo**

   5.1. The Charterers warrant that unless otherwise specified in Part I, the cargo referred to in Box 13 is non-hazardous and non-dangerous for carriage according to applicable safety regulations including IMCO Code(s).

   5.2. The Charterers shall have the right to ship parcels of different qualities and/or for different receivers in separate holds within the Vessel's natural segregation and suitable for her trim provided that such parcels can be loaded, carried and discharged in accordance with the Vessel's seaworthiness. Other means of separation of different parcels may be specified in Part I.

   5.3. Unless otherwise agreed in Part I, all quantities shall be expressed in tons of 1,000 kilograms.

6. **Advance Notices**

   The Owners or the Master shall give notices of expected readiness to load/discharge as specified in Box 14 to the parties named therein and shall keep those parties advised of any alteration in expected readiness.

7. **Port of Loading, Voyage, Port of Discharge**

   7.1. After completion of prior commitments as may be stated in Box 8, the Vessel shall proceed to the loading port(s)/berth(s) as stated in Box 15.

7.2. The Vessel shall carry the cargo with all possible despatch to the port(s)/berth(s) of discharge stated in Box 16. However, unless "No" is inserted in Box 17, the Owners may order the Vessel to proceed at reduced speed solely to conserve fuel.

If the Charterers have the right to order the Vessel to discharge at one or more ports out of several ports named or within a specific range, the Charterers shall declare the actual port(s) of discharge to be inserted in the Bills of Lading prior to the arrival of the Vessel at the port of loading.

7.3. Only when the loading/discharging port(s)/berth(s) are not specifically mentioned herein, the Charterers warrant the safety of port(s)/ berth(s) nominated and that the Vessel will be loaded and discharged always afloat.

7.4. The Vessel shall be left in seaworthy trim for shifting between berths and ports.

7.5. Unless otherwise agreed, loading and/or discharging at two or more ports shall be effected in geographical rotation.

8. **Notices of Readiness, Laytime, Demurrage/Despatch Money**

   8.1. *Notice of Readiness*

   8.1.1. At each port of loading and discharging notice of readiness shall be given to the Charterers or their Agents when the Vessel is in all respects ready to load/discharge at the loading/discharging berth.

   8.1.2. If a loading/discharging berth is not designated or if such designated berth is not available upon the Vessel's arrival at or off the port, notice of readiness may be given upon arrival at the waiting place at or off the port.

   However, if the Vessel is at that time prevented from proceeding to the loading/discharging berth due to her inefficiency, weather, tidal conditions, strikes of tugs or pilots or mandatory regulations, notice of readiness may be given only when such hindrance(s) has (have) ceased.

   8.13. Notice of readiness may be given on any day at any time.

   8.2. *Laytime*

   8.2.1. The laytime shall commence when notice of readiness has been given and after expiration of notice time, if any, provided for in Box 18.

   Should the Vessel arrive at the (first) loading port and be ready to load before the date stated in Box 9, the Charterers shall have the right to start loading. The Charterers shall also have the right to load/discharge before the expiration of notice time. In either event, during such periods only time actually used shall count as laytime or as time on demurrage.

   8.2.2. The notice time shall run continuously.

   8.2.3. The notice time, if any, shall only apply at first or sole loading and discharging port, respectively.

   8.2.4. If total time for loading and discharging has been agreed in Box 19 notice time, if any, at port of discharge shall be applied whether the Vessel be on demurrage or not on sailing from the (last) loading port.

   8.2.5. *Separate laytime.* - The cargo shall be loaded within the number of hours/days of 24 consecutive hours or at the average loading rate per day of 24 consecutive hours as stated in Box 19a).

   The cargo shall be discharged within the number of hours/days of 24 consecutive hours or at the average discharging rate per day of 24 consecutive hours as stated in Box 19b).

   8.2.6. *Total laytime.* - The cargo shall be loaded and discharged within the number of hours/days of 24 consecutive hours stated in Box 19c).

   8.2.7. In the case of loading and/or discharging at more than one berth, laytime shall run continuously as if loading/discharging had been effected at one berth only but without prejudice to sub-clause 8.3.

   8.3. *Suspension of Laytime*

   8.3.1. Unless the Vessel is on demurrage, laytime shall not count

   (i) during periods excepted as per Boxes 20 and 21, unless used, in which case only time actually used shall count;

   (ii) for the duration of bad weather or sea conditions which actually prevent the Vessel's loading, discharging or the shifting between loading/discharging berths of the Vessel;

   (iii) if so provided for in Clause 14.

   8.3.2. Time shall not count as laytime or as time on demurrage whilst Vessel actually moving from waiting place whether at or off the port or from a lightening place off the port, until the Vessel is securely moored at the designated loading/discharging berth.

   8.3.3. Time lost due to inefficiency or any other cause attributable to the Vessel, her Master, her crew or the Owners shall not count as notice time or as laytime or as time on demurrage to the extent that loading or discharging or the matters covered by sub-clause 8.4.1. are thereby affected.

   8.3.4. If pursuant to Clause 9.13. the Vessel has to vacate the loading/ discharging berth, notice time or laytime or time on demurrage shall not count from that time until she be in all respects ready to load/discharge and notification has been given to the Charterers accordingly.

   8.3.5. If due to the matters referred to in sub-clauses 8.3.3. or 8.3.4., the Vessel loses her turn, time shall count again only as from 24 hours after notification of the Vessel's new readiness has been given to the Charterers or when loading/discharging resumes whichever may be the sooner.

   8.4. *Termination of Laytime*

   8.4.1. Laytime/Demurrage shall stop counting on completion of:

   (a) loading/discharging at the relevant port, (b) cargo documentation and/or draft survey for determination of cargo weight, (c) repairs to stevedore damage under Clause 10.2., whichever may be the later.

   8.4.2. If required, the Vessel shall leave the berth as soon as possible within her control on completion of loading/discharging, falling which the Charterers shall be entitled to proved damages provided that if she then has to wait for reasons (b) and/or (c) above, there must be a place available at which she can safely wait, and any extra expenses shall be for the Charterers' account.

Appendix 18

OREVOY 1980 (continued)

PART II

"OREVOY" Charter Party

8.5. _Demurrage/Despatch Money_

8.5.1. Demurrage accrued under this Charter Party shall be considered as constituting liquidated damages for exceeding the laytime provided for herein. However, if the Vessel has been on demurrage for 15 days or more and no cargo has been loaded, the Owners shall have the option of cancelling this Charter Party. No claim which the Owners may otherwise have against the Charterers shall be prejudiced by the Owners exercising their option of cancelling.

8.5.2. Demurrage shall be due and payable by the Charterers day by day at the rate specified in Boxes 22 and 23 and in the manner provided for in Box 29.

8.5.3. Despatch money, if agreed upon in Box 24, shall be paid promptly by the Owners to the Charterers at half the demurrage rate or as otherwise agreed upon in Box 24 for laytime saved in loading and/or discharging.

9. Loading and Discharging

9.1. The Vessel shall be loaded and discharged as and where ordered by the Charterers.

9.2. If the Charterers have not nominated a suitable loading or discharging berth on the Vessel's arrival off the port, or if such berth should not be available, the Vessel is to wait at a suitable place at or off the port.

The Charterers shall have the right to designate a safe waiting place, otherwise the Master shall choose a waiting place using due diligence to minimize extra shifting costs provided for in sub-clause 9.4.

9.3. The Charterers shall have the right to load and/or discharge at two berths at each port or place subject to sub-clause 9.4.

9.4. _Shifting._ - Costs of moving the Vessel, including bunkers, in excess of those which would have been incurred if the Charterers had nominated a free loading or discharging berth on arrival, provided the Vessel arrives on or after the date stated in Box 9, and/or if all cargo had been loaded or discharged during one operation at the first berth only other than a lightening place off the port, shall be for the Charterers' account unless caused by the Vessel's default. Other costs on board the Vessel including wages and officers' and crew's overtime charges to be for the Owners' account.

9.5. The Owners or the Master shall in due time prior to commencement of loading submit to the Charterers (or their nominees) at the loading port a loading plan which shall be based on a reasonable number of shiftings between hatches and also meet applicable rules and regulations, including IMCO Code(s). The Charterers shall inform the Owners/Master of any special composition of cargo required in sufficient time to permit the Owners/Master to work out and submit such loading plan.

9.6. Prior to loading, the Vessel's holds shall be adequately cleaned for loading the contracted cargo.

9.7. The Charterers shall, always within the capacity of the loading installations, load and trim the cargo as per the loading plan, free of any risk, liability and expense to the Vessel. Any extra trimming and/or levelling required by the Master or Owners shall be performed at the Owners' expense and any time lost thereby shall not count as laytime/demurrage. Discharging, including shovel cleaning, shall be effected by the Charterers free of any risk, liability and expense to the Vessel.

9.8. The Vessel shall move along any one berth, as reasonably required by the Charterers, solely for the purpose of making any hatch or hatches available to the loading/discharging appliances at that berth, and costs on board the Vessel including bunkers, wages and officers' and crew's overtime charges shall be for the Owners' account. However, the costs of any necessary outside services shall be for the Charterers' account. Laytime or time on demurrage shall not be interrupted thereby.

9.9. The Vessel shall work day and night and during any time as may be excepted as per Box 20 and Box 21, as required by the Charterers.

9.10. The Vessel shall, at her own risk and expense, open and close hatches prior to and after loading/discharging and also during loading/discharging as may be required by the Charterers to protect the cargo, provided local shore regulations permit. If same, however, is not permitted by local shore labour regulations, shore labour is to be employed by the Charterers at their risk, liability and expense. The Vessel shall furnish and give free use of sufficient light for deck and holds, as on board.

9.11. The Charterers shall have the right to order the Vessel to leave without having loaded a full cargo, always provided that the Vessel be in seaworthy condition and that the Charterers pay deadweight according to Clause 13.7.

9.12. Overtime for loading and discharging to be for the account of the party ordering the same. If overtime be ordered by Port Authorities or any other Governmental Agencies, the Charterers to pay any extra expenses incurred. Officers' and crew's overtime charges always to be paid by the Owners.

9.13. In the event of loading/discharging being impossible due to inefficiency or any other cause attributable to the Vessel, her Master, her crew or the Owners and such impossibility continuing for more than three consecutive hours, the Charterers shall have the right to order the Vessel to vacate the berth and shifting from and back to berth shall be at the Owners' expense and time.

10. Stevedore Damage

10.1. The Charterers shall be responsible for damage (beyond ordinary wear and tear) to any part of the Vessel caused by Stevedores at both ends. Such damage, as soon as apparent, shall be notified immediately by the Master to the Charterers or their port agents and to their Stevedores. The Owners/Master shall endeavour to obtain the Stevedores' written acknowledgment of liability and to settle stevedore damage claims direct with the Stevedores.

10.2. The Charterers have the right to perform any repairs of stevedore damage at any moment prior to or before the completion of the voyage, but must repair stevedore damage affecting the Vessel's seaworthiness before the Vessel sails from the port where such damage was caused.

11. Dues, Taxes and Charges, Extra Insurance

11.1. _On the Vessel._ - The Owners shall pay all dues, duties, taxes and other charges customarily levied on the Vessel, howsoever the amount thereof may be assessed.

11.2. _On the cargo._ - The Charterers shall pay all dues, duties, taxes and charges levied on the cargo at the port of loading/discharging, howsoever the amount thereof may be assessed.

11.3. _On the freight._ - Taxes levied on the freight shall be paid by the Owners or the Charterers as agreed in Box 25.

11.4. _Extra Insurance._ - Any extra insurance on cargo actually paid by the Charterers owing to Vessel's age, class, flag or ownership shall be for the Owners' account and may be deducted from the freight. The Charterers shall furnish evidence of payment supporting any such deduction. Unless a maximum amount has been agreed in Part I, such extra insurance shall not exceed the lowest extra premium which would be charged for the Vessel and voyage in the London insurance market.

12. Agents

At the port(s) of loading the Vessel shall be consigned to the Agents as stated in Box 26 and at the port(s) of discharge to the Agents as stipulated in Box 27, the Owners always paying the customary fees.

13. Freight

The freight at the rate stated in Box 28 shall be calculated on intaken quantity.

13.1. _Prepaid._ - If according to Boxes 28 or 29 freight is to be paid on shipment, it shall be deemed earned and non-returnable Vessel and/or cargo lost or not lost.

Bills of Lading showing "Freight prepaid" or the like shall not be released until the freight has been duly paid.

13.2. _After shipment._ - If according to Box 29 freight shall be payable within a number of days after shipment, the freight shall be deemed earned as per sub-clause 13.1.

In such case Bills of Lading shall not be endorsed "Freight prepaid" or the like, unless the freight has been paid.

13.3. _Partly on Delivery._ - If according to Boxes 28 or 29 a percentage of the freight shall be payable as per sub-clauses 13.1. or 13.2. the balance shall be paid as per sub-clause 13.4. However, in such case the total freight shall be deemed earned as per sub-clause 13.1. and the Charterers shall not have the option referred to in sub-clause 13.4.1.

13.4. _On Delivery._ - If according to Boxes 28 or 29 freight is payable at destination or on right and true delivery of the cargo, it shall not be deemed earned until the cargo is thus delivered.

13.4.1. _On Delivered Weight._ - When the freight is payable on delivery of cargo the Charterers shall have the option of paying freight on delivered weight, provided such option be declared in writing before breaking bulk and the weight be ascertained by official weighing machine, otherwise by joint draught survey. The Charterers shall pay all costs incurred in connection with weighing or draught survey. The Owners shall be at liberty to appoint check clerks at their own expense.

13.5. _Deductions._ - The freight shall be paid in cash without discount in the manner described in Box 29. The Charterers shall only be entitled to deduct from the freight any freight advances made as per sub-clause 13.6., despatch money and extra insurance, provided properly documented, as per Clause 11.4.

13.6. _Freight Advances._ - The Owners shall put the Agents at the loading port(s) in funds to cover the Vessel's ordinary disbursements for Owners' account, prior to the Vessel's sailing from the port(s) of loading. Otherwise the amount shall be advanced by Charterers and be endorsed upon Bills of Lading as advance freight, with the addition of 3 per cent, to cover interest, commission and the cost of insurance.

13.7. _Deadfreight._ - If the Charterers fail to supply a cargo as specified in Box 13, deadfreight shall be payable but the Charterers shall not be bound to supply cargo in excess of any quantity stated by the Owners as the Vessel's capacity made available to the Charterers. The laytime shall be calculated on that quantity.

The Owners/Master shall be entitled to clause Bills of Lading for any deadfreight due.

If the Shippers/Suppliers state in writing that no more cargo will be shipped, the Owners shall not need to have any such statement confirmed by the Charterers.

14. Strikes and Other Hindrances

In the event of any of the causes referred to in Clause 21.2. either preventing or delaying or, being already in existence, threatening to prevent or delay the loading of the cargo intended for the Vessel, or its discharging, the following provisions shall apply:

14.1. _Loading Port._ - When the Vessel is ready to proceed from her last port or at any time during the voyage to the port or ports of loading or after her arrival there, the Owners may ask the Charterers to declare that they agree to count the laytime as if there were to be no such hindrance. Unless the Charterers have given such declaration in writing (by telegram or telex if necessary) on the second business day after receipt of the request, the Owners shall have the option of cancelling this Charter Party. If part cargo has already been loaded the Vessel must carry it to the port of discharge (freight payable on loaded quantity only) having liberty to complete with other cargo on the way for the Owners' own account, but the Owners are entitled to keep the Vessel waiting at the loading port

Appendix 18

OREVOY1980 (continued)

PART II

"OREVOY" Charter Party

without time counting. In case of more than one loading port and if the causes referred to above do not prevent the loading in all ports, the Charterers are entitled to order the Vessel to proceed to the second or subsequent port and there to load a full cargo; in such event, the Owners are not entitled to cancel the Charter Party as hereabove stipulated.

14.2. *Discharging Port.* - On or after the Vessel's arrival at or off the port of discharge, the Vessel shall wait until any such hindrance is at an end, the Charterers paying half demurrage after expiration of the laytime (unless the Vessel is already on demurrage in which event full demurrage remains payable) full demurrage being payable from the moment when the hindrance is at an end. The Charterers shall have the option at any time of ordering the Vessel to another safe port within 600 nautical miles' distance where she can safely discharge without being detained by any cause enumerated above. Shifting time shall count as laytime or as full demurrage time as the case may be.

The Charterers shall reimburse the Owners additional port charges including pilotage and canal dues, if any, incurred thereby; however, the Owners shall bear the costs of bunkers consumed. All conditions of this Charter Party and/or of the Bills of Lading issued hereunder shall apply to the delivery of the cargo at the substituted port and the Owners shall receive the same freight as if the cargo had been discharged at the original destination.

15. Ice

Loading Port

15.1. If the Vessel cannot reach the loading port by reason of ice when she is ready to proceed from her last port, or at any time during the voyage, or on her arrival, or if frost sets in after her arrival, the Master - for fear of the Vessel being frozen in - is at liberty to leave without cargo; in such cases this Charter Party shall become null and void.

15.2. If during the loading the Master, for fear of the Vessel being frozen in, deems it advisable to leave, he has liberty to do so with what cargo he has on board and to proceed to any other port with option of completing with cargo for the Owners' own account to any port or ports including the port of discharge. Any part cargo thus loaded under this Charter Party is to be forwarded to destination at the Vessel's expense against payment of the agreed freight, provided that no extra expenses be thereby caused to the Charterers, freight being paid on the quantity delivered (in proportion if lump sum), all other conditions as per Charter Party.

15.3. In the case of more than one loading port, and if one or more of the ports are closed by ice, the Master or Owners are to be at liberty either to load the part cargo at the open port and fill up elsewhere for the Owners' own account as under sub-clause 15.2. or to declare the Charter Party null and void, unless the Charterers agree to load full cargo at the open port.

Voyage and Discharging Port

15.4. Should ice prevent the Vessel from reaching the port of discharge, the Charterers shall have the option of keeping the Vessel waiting until the re-opening of navigation and paying demurrage, or of ordering the Vessel to a safe and immediately accessible port where she can safely discharge without risk of detention by ice. Such orders are to be given within 48 hours after the Owners or Master have given notice to the Charterers of the impossibility of reaching the port of destination.

15.5. If during discharging the Master, for fear of the Vessel being frozen in, deems it advisable to leave, he has liberty to do so with what cargo he has on board and to proceed to the nearest safe and accessible port. Such port to be nominated by the Charterers as soon as possible, but not later than 24 running hours, Sundays and holidays excluded, of receipt of the Owners' request for nomination of a substitute discharging port, failing which the Master will himself choose such port.

15.6. On delivery of the cargo at such port, all conditions of the Bill of Lading shall apply and the Owners shall receive the same freight as if the Vessel had discharged at the original port of destination except that if the distance to the substitute port exceeds 100 nautical miles, the freight on the cargo delivered at that port is to be increased in proportion.

16. War Risks ("Voywar 1950")

16.1. In these Clauses "war risks" shall include any blockade or any action which is announced as a blockade by any Government or by any belligerent or by any organized body, sabotage, piracy, and any actual or threatened war, hostilities, warlike operations, civil war, civil commotion, or revolution.

16.2. If at any time before the Vessel commences loading, it appears that performance of the contract will subject the Vessel or her Master and crew or her cargo to war risks at any stage of the adventure, the Owners shall be entitled by letter or telegram despatched to the Charterers, to cancel this Charter Party.

16 3. The Master shall not be required to load cargo or to continue loading or to proceed on or to sign Bill(s) of Lading for any adventure on which or any port at which it appears that the Vessel, her Master and crew or her cargo will be subjected to war risks. In the event of the exercise by the Master of his right under this Clause after part or full cargo has been loaded, the Master shall be at liberty either to discharge such cargo at the loading port or to proceed therewith. In the latter case the Vessel shall have liberty to carry other cargo for Owners' benefit and accordingly to proceed to and load or discharge such other cargo at any other port or ports whatsoever, backwards or forwards, although in a contrary direction to or out of or beyond the ordinary route, in the event of the Master electing to proceed with part cargo under this Clause freight shall in any case be payable on the quantity delivered.

16.4. If at the time the Master elects to proceed with part or full cargo under Clause 16.3. or after the Vessel has left the loading port, or the last of the loading ports if more than one, it appears that further performance of the Charter Party will subject the Vessel, her Master and crew or her cargo, to war risks, the cargo shall be discharged, or if the discharge has been commenced shall be completed, at any safe port in vicinity of the port of discharge as may be ordered by the Charterers. If no such orders shall be received from the Charterers within 48 hours after the Owners have despatched a request by telegram or telex to the Charterers for the nomination of a substitute discharging port, the Owners shall be at liberty to discharge the cargo at any safe port which they may, in their discretion, decide on and such discharge shall be deemed to be due fulfilment of the Charter Party. In the event of cargo being discharged at any such other port, the Owners shall be entitled to freight as if the discharge had been effected at the port or ports named in the Bill(s) of Lading, or to which the Vessel may have been ordered pursuant thereto.

16.5. (a) The Vessel shall have liberty to comply with any directions or recommendations as to loading, departure, arrival, routes, ports of call, stoppages, destination, zones, waters, discharges, delivery or in any other wise whatsoever (including any direction or recommendation not to go to the port of destination or to delay proceeding thereto or to proceed to some other port) given by any Government or by any belligerent or by any organized body engaged in civil war, hostilities or warlike operations or by any person or body acting or purporting to act as or with the authority of any Government or belligerent or of any such organized body or by any committee or person having under the terms of the war risks insurance on the Vessel, the right to give any such directions or recommendations. If, by reason of or in compliance with any such direction or recommendation, anything is done or is not done, such shall not be deemed a deviation.
(b) If, by reason of or in compliance with any such directions or recommendations, the Vessel does not proceed to the port or ports named in the Bill(s) of Lading or to which she may have been ordered pursuant thereto, the Vessel may proceed to any port as directed or recommended or to any safe port which the Owners in their discretion may decide on and there discharge the cargo. Such discharge shall be deemed to be due fulfilment of the Charter Party and the Owners shall be entitled to freight as if discharge had been effected at the port or ports named in the Bill(s) of Lading or to which the Vessel may have been ordered pursuant thereto.

16.6. All extra expenses (including insurance costs) involved in discharging cargo at the loading port or in reaching or discharging the cargo at any port as provided in Clauses 16.4. and 16.5.(b) hereof shall be paid by the Charterers and/or cargo owners, and the Owners shall have a lien on the cargo for all moneys due under these Clauses.

17. Lien

The Owners shall have a lien on the cargo for freight, deadweight, demurrage and damages for detention. The Charterers shall remain responsible for deadfreight and demurrage (including damages for detention), incurred at port of loading. The Charterers shall also remain responsible for freight and demurrage (including damages for detention) incurred at port of discharge, but only to such extent as the Owners have been unable to obtain payment thereof by exercising the lien on the cargo.

18. Liberty

The Vessel shall have liberty to sail with or without pilots, to tow or go to the assistance of vessels in distress, to call at any port or place for oil fuel supplies, and to deviate for the purpose of saving life or property, or for any other reasonable purpose whatsoever.

19. Both-to-Blame Collision Clause

If the Vessel comes into collision with another vessel as a result of the negligence of the other vessel and any act, neglect or default of the Master, mariner, pilot or the servants of the Owners in the navigation or in the management of the Vessel, the owners of the cargo carried hereunder will indemnify Owners against all loss or liability to the other or non-carrying vessel or her Owners in so far as such loss or liability represents loss of, or damage to, or any claim whatsoever of the owners of said cargo, paid or payable by the other or non-carrying vessel or her Owners to the owners of said cargo and set-off, recouped or recovered by the other or non-carrying vessel or her Owners as part of their claim against the carrying vessel or Owners.

The foregoing provisions shall also apply where the owners, operators or those in charge of any vessel or vessels or objects other than, or in addition to, the colliding vessels or objects are at fault in respect of a collision or contact.

20. General Average and New Jason Clause

General Average shall be adjusted and settled at the place indicated in Box 30 according to the York/Antwerp Rules, 1974, or any modification thereof, but if, notwithstanding the provisions specified in Box 30, the adjustment is made in accordance with the law and practice of the United States of America, the following clause shall apply:

"In the event of accident, danger, damage or disaster before or after the commencement of the voyage, resulting from any cause whatsoever, whether due to negligence or not, for which, or for the consequence of which, Owners are not responsible, by statute, contract or otherwise, the goods, shippers, consignees or owners of the goods shall contribute with Owners in general average to the payment of any sacrifices, losses or expenses of a general average nature that may be made or incurred and shall pay salvage and special charges incurred in respect of the goods, if a salving Vessel is owned or operated by Owners, salvage shall be paid for as fully as if the said salving Vessel or vessels belonged to strangers. Such deposit as Owners, or their agents, may deem sufficient to cover the estimated contribution of the goods and any salvage and special charges thereon shall, if required, be made by the goods, shippers, consignees or owners of the goods to Owners before delivery".

Appendix 18

OREVOY 1980 (continued)

OREVOY 1980 (continued)

PART II

"OREVOY" Charter Party

21. Responsibilities and Immunities

21.1.1. The Hague Rules contained in the International Convention for the Unification of certain rules relating to Bills of Lading, dated Brussels the 25th August 1924 as enacted in the country of shipment shall apply to this Contract and to any Bill of Lading issued here under.

When no such enactment is in force in the country of shipment, the corresponding legislation of the country of destination shall apply, but in respect of shipments to which no such enactments are compulsorily applicable, the terms of the said Convention shall apply.

21.1.2. In trades where the International Brussels Convention 1924 as amended by the Protocol signed at Brussels on February 23rd, 1968 - The Hague-Visby Rules - apply compulsorily, the provisions of the respective legislation shall apply.

21.1.3. The Owners shall in no case be responsible for loss of or damage to cargo howsoever arising prior to loading into and after discharge from the Vessel or while the goods are in the charge of another owner nor in respect of deck cargo and live animals. This sub-clause shall not detract from the Owners' obligations under Clause 4.

21.2. Save to the extent otherwise in this Charter Party expressly provided, neither party shall be responsible for any loss or damage or delay or failure in performance hereunder resulting from Act of God, war, civil commotion, quarantine, strikes, lockouts, arrest or restraint of princes, rulers and peoples or any other event whatsoever which cannot be avoided or guarded against.

22. Bills of Lading

22.1. Bills of Lading are to be signed as per the "Orevoybill" Bill of Lading without prejudice to this Charter Party, and the Charterers hereby indemnify the Owners against all liabilities that may arise from the signing of Bills of Lading as presented to the extent that the terms of such Bills of Lading impose more onerous liabilities upon the Owners than those assumed by the Owners under the terms of this Charter Party.

Neither the Owners nor their Servants shall be required to sign or endorse Bills of Lading showing freight prepaid unless and until the freight due to the Owners has actually been paid.

22.2. The Master may be required to sign separate Bills of Lading for cargo in different holds or for parcels properly separated upon shipment by the Charterers or their Agents, the Owners not being answerable for separate delivery, nor for the cost of cargo short-delivered (if any) provided all the cargo taken on board is delivered.

23. Law and Arbitration

23.1. Unless otherwise agreed in Box 31, this Charter Party shall be governed by English Law and any dispute arising out of this Charter Party or any Bill of Lading issued thereunder shall be referred to arbitration in London, one arbitrator being appointed by each party, in accordance with the Arbitration Acts 1950 and 1979 or any statutory modification or re-enactment thereof for the time being in force. On the receipt by one party of the notification in writing of the appointment of the other party's arbitrator, that party shall appoint their arbitrator within fourteen days failing which the decision of the single arbitrator appointed shall apply. If two arbitrators properly appointed shall not agree they shall appoint an umpire whose decision shall be final.

23.2. If agreed and stated in Box 31, this Charter Party shall be governed by U.S. Law and all disputes arising out of this Charter Party or any Bill of Lading issued thereunder shall be arbitrated at New York in the following manner:

One arbitrator is to be appointed by each of the parties hereto and a third by the two so chosen. Their decision or that of any two of them shall be final, and for the purpose of enforcing any award, (his agreement may be made a rule of the court. The arbitrators shall be commercial men. Such arbitration is to be conducted in accordance with the rules of the Society of Maritime Arbitrators, Inc.

For disputes where the total amount claimed by either party does not exceed U.S. $ 3,500.00, or an amount as mutually agreed, the arbitration may be conducted in accordance with the Simplified Arbitration Procedure of the Society of Maritime Arbitrators Inc. if so desired by both parties.

23.3. If agreed and stated in Box 31, any disputes arising out of this Charter Party or any Bill of Lading issued thereunder shall be referred to arbitration at the place or before the arbitration tribunal indicated in Box 31, subject to the law and procedures applicable there.

24. Brokerage

24.1. The brokerage as stated in Box 32 on freight and deadweight shall be paid by the Owners and is deemed to be earned by the Brokers upon shipment of cargo.

24.2. In case of cancellation pursuant to Clause 2.3., at least one third of the brokerage on the estimated amount of freight shall be paid by the Owners as indemnity to the Brokers.

Appendix 19

AFRICANPHOS1950

PHOSPHATE CHARTER-PARTY

(AFRICANPHOS 1950)

(Layout 1987)

Paris, ...

1. Owners (Clause 1)	2. Charterers (Clause 1)	
3. Vessel's name (Clause 1)	4. CRT (Clause 1)	5. NRT (Clause 1)
	6. DWAT (Clause 1)	7. Flag (Clause 1)
8. Present position (Clause 1)	9. Laydays (Clause 11)	10. Cancelling date (Clause 11)
11. Port of loading (Clause 1)	12. Loading rate (Clause 8)	13. Loading costs (Clause 7)
	14. Demurrage rate (load.) (Clause 13)	
15. Port of discharge (Clause 1)	16. Discharging rate (Clause 20)	
	17. Demurrage rate (disch.) (Clause 21)	
18. Cargo (minimum/maximum quantity, exact quantity in Master's option) (Clause 2)		
19. Freight/payment/payee (Clause 27)		
20. Brokerage (Clause 35)		
21. Advance notices to Shippers (Clause 2)	22. Sailing telegram and ETA notice (disch.) (Clause 37)	
23. Agents at discharging port(s) (Clause 16)		

1. It is agreed between the parties mentioned in box 1 as Owners of the motor vessel named in box 3 of the GRT/NRT indicated in box 4 & 5 and having a deadweight capacity stated in box 6 and the party mentioned as Charterers in box 2 that the said vessel, being tight staunch and strong and in every way fitted for the voyage shall proceed to the port stated in box 11 and there load a cargo of phosphate/fertilizers in bulk, not exceeding what she can reasonably stow and carry over and above her tackle, apparel, provisions, bunkers and equipment as stated in box 18. The vessel so loaded shall proceed with all possible despatch to the port indicated in box 15 and there deliver her cargo.

THE OWNERS   THE CHARTERERS

Appendix 19

AFRICANPHOS 1950 (continued)

2º <u>Notice</u>. - Before leaving last discharging port and at latest three days before arrival at loading port, the Captain shall telegraph to agents at loadport stated in BOX 21/CLAUSE 4 stating vessels's probable date of arrival there, falling which Shippers are to be allowed 24 hours extra for loading.

<u>IMPORTANT</u> : Further to clause 2, it is in the interest of Owners and Shippers (acting as ship's agents) that the Master and/or agents should radio to Shippers approximately 24 hours before arrival of vessel at loading port confirming the date and approximate time at which she will arrive, stating if she needs bunkers and. If possible, the quantity required and the name of the suppliers.

It is compulsory that such notice, together with all information regarding eventual remittance of funds or transfers, or openings of bank credits, must specify the vessel's name, otherwise Shippers shall decline all responsibility in case of incomplete information.

3° <u>Completion clause</u>. - The vessel shall not load any goods other than those stipulated by the present Charterparty under penalty of damages.

4° <u>Agency at loading port</u>. - The vessel shall be consigned for her phosphate/fertilizers cargo and Customs business to the Shippers stated in BOX 21 :

CASABLANCA	SAFI	LAAYOUNE
Office Chérifien des Phosphates	Office Chérifien des Phosphates	Phosphates de Boucraa S.A.
Service des Embarquements	Service des Embarquements	
Bolte Postale 119	Bolte Postale 26	
Tel. address : PHOSPHAT	Tel. address : PHOSPHAT	Tel. address : PHOSBOUCRAA
Telex nr 25987	Telex nr 71708	Telex nr 25685

Owners to pay in cash the customary agency fee, Shippers having the right to choose at their expense the shipbroker who will Shippers' agents. Owners shall still pay Charterers the customary agency fee:

5° <u>Expenses at loading port</u>.- Vessel to pay all customary dues and port expenses, all tolls ("peage" dues) at the rates ruling on the day of signing Bill of Lading, as well as other charges customarily paid by the vessel. Owners shall pay in cash all their disbursements including amounts due by them under clauses 4, 7 and 13. A sufficient amount for ship's disbursements only, not exceeding one third of the freight, may be advanced to the Captain if required by him. Owners paying a commission of 2% on the amount of such advances. The Captain to give a receipt on the Bills of Lading for the total amount of advances, including the 2% commission. Charterers shall not be held responsible for the employment of these advances, which will be deducted on the settlement of freight and will not be refunded in case of vessel's loss. The Shippers decline all responsibility towards Owners if, in order to avoid delaying the vessel's departure, they shall be called upon, on justification of the expenses, to advance to the Captain amounts over and above one third of the freight.

6° <u>Loading turn</u>.- The vessel will be loaded in turn not exceeding 48 hours, Sundays and legal or local holidays included, counting from 7 am or 1 pm after the vessel is in free pratique and Captain having given written notice to Shippers of readiness to load between usual office hours.

7° <u>Cost of loading</u>.- The cargo to be loaded into the vessel's holds by Shippers, levelling or any other special trimming required by the Captain, to be at Owners' risk and expense.

8° <u>Daily rate of loading</u>. - The rates for loading to be :

up to	9.999 metric tons	3.000 m.t. (1)
between	10.000 and 14.999 m.t.	3.600 m.t.
"	15.000 and 19.999 m.t.	4.500 m.t.
"	20.000 and 24.999 m.t.	6.000 m.t.
"	25.000 and 29.999 m.t.	7.500 m.t.
"	30.000 and 39.999 m.t.	9.000 m.t.
above	40.000 metric tons	10.000 m.t.

(1) with a minimum of 36 consecutive hours.

The vessel will be loaded in the customary manner alongside the wharf reserved to Shippers at the berth indicated by them and according to their orders. They shall have the right to load by all the hatches of the holds which are to receive cargo without interruption by night as well as by day.

9° <u>Time counting at loading port</u>. - Laytime to commence on expiry of turn according to clause 6 or, if there is no turn, at 1 pm if the vessel complies with the prescribed conditions before noon, and at 7 am on the following day if she complies with the said conditions after noon, the Captain or his representative having advised Shippers in writing that he is ready to load and that the vessel, being in free pratique, has occupied the berth indicated by the Shippers. Legal and local holidays, each being considered as a day of 24 hours, and the time between 1 pm on Saturday and 7 am on Monday shall not count as laytime, but if the loading proceeds during these periods or before laytime commences, only half such time employed shall be deducted from the time saved for the calculation of despatch-money. If necessary, vessel's holds shall be

AFRICANPHOS1950 (continued)

cleaned at vessel's expense before loading commences. All time occupied in shifting berths at Shippers' request shall count as lay time. Time allowed will be calculated based on the B/L weight expressed in metric tons. Days to be of 24 consecutive hours, weather permitting, (portions prorata) force majeure excepted. The Captain is to facilitate the rapid loading of his vessel by all means on board. Vessel shall leave the loading berth as soon as loading is completed, if the Captain is required to do so failing which Owners are to indemnify Shippers for time so lost at the demurrage rate stipulated in clause 13. Any delays which may be attributed to the vessel or her crew or special trimming are not to count as lay time.

10° Strike and force majeure clause at loading port.- Should loading be rendered impossible in consequence of a strike, lock-out or any cause of force majeure beyond the Shippers' control, latter to give written notice to Owners (eventually by telegram) latest on receipt of the telegraphic notice stipulated in clause 2. If vessel has already telegraphed this preliminary notice. Shippers shall notify her of the case of force majeure as soon as this is known to them. At any time before vessel's arrival at loading port of before loading commences. Owners may notify Shippers of their intention to cancel the present charter-party. This cancelling is to become effective if within 18 running hours following the receipt of this notification. Shippers have not declared that they maintain the charter-party. In case the charter-party should be maintained, the time shall count as stipulated by the said charter notwithstanding the invocation of the case of force majeure.

At any time during the interruption of the loading owing to force majeure. Shippers to have the option of cancelling this charter by giving 18 running hours notice to the Captain or Owners. If the vessel has started loading, the Captain to have the option of salling with the quantity loaded 18 running hours after the interruption of the loading through force majeure, unless, before expiration of this delay, Shippers maintain the charter-party, the time counting notwithstanding the case of force majeure invoked. Should the vessel sail with a part cargo, she is to have the option to complete for her own benefit, according to the terms of clause 3, and the freight to be settled on quantity delivered according to clause 27.

11° Laydays and cancelling dates.- Laydays not to count before the date indicated in BOX 9 unless with Charterers' consent, latter having the option of cancelling the charter if the vessel has not arrived and is not ready to load before midnight on the date indicated in BOX 10.

12° Draft at loading port.- If vessel's draft makes it necessary to complete loading at another berth, or in the roads. Captain to obtain the necessary lighters at Owners' expense. The risk and cost of transport from the wharf to another berth or to the roads and transhipment expenses are to be borne by the vessel, and time spent in loading at such other berth or in the roads and in shifting, not to count as laytime.

Shippers guarantee that vessels can load, and sail from their usual loading berth, with a draught of :

at CASABLANCA	at SAFI	at JORF LASFAR	at LAAYOUNE
Berths N°1 & 2 : 30' and N°3 : 36'	30'	45'	15'

13° Demurrage and despatch-money at loading port.- Demurrage, if any, to be paid to Owners by Shippers at the rate indicated in BOX 14 per gross register ton per day (portions prorata). For all working time saved Owners to pay in cash to Shippers despatch-money at half of the demurrage rate per day (portions prorata). It is understood that despatch-money will only be calculated on time saved after expiration of the actual turn, if any (see clause 9). Any delays which may be attributed to the vessel or her crew shall not count as laytime.

14° Putting in at port (s).- If after loading her phosphate/fertilizers the vessel calls at one or more ports, the Captain shall immediately inform Charterers by telegram stating the reason and the maximum duration of the call, even if this call is made for bunkering purposes.

15° Signing of loading documents.- In case of dispute on the interpretation of the above clauses, Captain to sign papers or official documents as presented to him by Shippers, in as many copies as required by them in respect of all or part of the cargo on board, endorsing his objections on such documents.

16° Agency and expenses at discharging port.- Vessel to be addressed for Customs business to agents indicated in BOX 23 on usual terms and to pay all customary dues and port charges.

17° Particular average.- All damage to vessel or cargo shall be immediately notified to the Receivers or their agents by the Captain in writing; he shall also allow Receivers of their agents access to all papers or official documents which might enable them to protect their rights with their underwriters.

18° Discharging turn.- Vessel to deliver her cargo in turn not exceeding 36 running hours, Sundays and legal or local holidays included, such turn counting after the vessel is in free pratique and has given Receivers or their agents written notice of readiness during usual office hours for cargo of phosphate/fertilizers.

19° Cost of discharge.- Owners to employ Receiver's stevedores for discharging free for expense to the vessel. If any cargo is loaded in the "deep tanks" or in places inaccessible to grabs, any extra discharging expenses resulting therefrom to be for Owners' account. Vessel to be redelivered to Owners shovel clean; sweeping, if required by the Master, to be for Owners' account.

20° Daily rate of discharging. - For the purpose of calculating laytime, the cargo is to be discharged at the average rate indicated in BOX 16 per 21 consecutive hours, weather permitting, (portions prorata). The vessel is to deliver her cargo alongside any wharf, quay or jetty, afloat or safe aground, or in any dock, or into lighters (if this method of discharging is usual), as ordered by Receivers or their agents on vessel's arrival. Receivers to have the right of working by day and by night without interruption, by all hatches of holds containing cargo. Vessel to be suitable for grab discharge.

21° Time counting at discharging port. - Laytime to commence on expiry of turn according to clause 18, or if there is no turn, at 2 pm if the vessel complies with the prescribed condition before noon and at 8 am the following day if she complies with the said condition after noon, the Captain or his representative having advised the Receivers in writing during usual office hours that he is ready to discharge and that the vessel being in free pratique has occupied the berth

Appendix 19

AFRICANPHOS 1950 (continued)

indicated by Receivers or their agents. Legal and Local holidays, each being considered as a day of 24 hours, and the 143
time between 4 pm on Friday/day preceding a holiday and 8 am on Monday/day following a holiday shall not count as 144
laytime, but if discharging proceeds during These periods or before laytime commences, only half such time employed 145
shall be deducted from the time saved for the calculation of despatch-money. Discharging time will be calculated on the 146
delivered weight or on B/L weight less 18, as the case may be. Delays which may be attributed to the vessel or her crew 147
are not to count as laytime. 148
149
22° <u>Strike and force majeure clause at discharging port</u>.- Time shall not count during which discharging is 150
hindered, delayed or stopped by reason of strikes, lock-outs, disturbances, requisitions, intervention of constituted 151
authorities, quarantine, accidents, fire, floods, ice or other cases of force majeure. The same will apply to all delays caused 152
by the vessel or her crew or by any other cause beyond the control of the Receivers. 153
154
23° <u>Demurrage and despatch-money at discharging port</u>.- Demurrage, if any, to be paid to Owners by Receivers 155
at the rate indicated in BOX 17 per day (portions prorata). For all working time saved Owners to pay in cash to Receivers 156
despatch-money at half demurrage rate per day (portions prorata). It is understood that despatch-money will only be 157
calculated on time saved after expiration of the actual turn, if any (see clause 21). Any delays which may be attributed to 158
the vessel or her crew shall not count as laytime. 159
160
24° <u>Freight</u>.- The freight is due on right and true delivery of the entire cargo at the rate stated in BOX 19 per 161
ton of 1,000 kilos and shall be paid by Receivers/Charterers on receipt of freight account made up by Owners or their 162
agents in accordance with the conditions of charter-party. The freight to be paid on total B/L weight less 1% (one per 163
cent). Provided they notify Master before discharging commences. Receivers shall have the right to weigh cargo or to 164
gauge the barges receiving it. If this option be exercised, the Master may employ at his expense a tallyman nominated by 165
him to supervise and check the weighing and gauging of the barges during the discharging, and payment of freight to be 166
effected on the delivered weight. 167
168
25° <u>Charterers' responsibility</u>.- Charterers' responsibility under this charter-party shall cease when cargo is 169
loaded, Owners or their agents having a lien on the cargo for the freight, dead freight and/or demurrage. 170
171
26° <u>Negligence clause</u>.- The act of God, decrees of Princes and Rulers, acts of enemies and pirates and 171
perils of the sea are excepted. Also excepted are fire, barratries of the Master or crew, collisions, strandings, accidents of 172
navigation, or latent defects in hull or machinery, even when occasioned by the negligence or error in judgment of pilots. 173
Captain or crew or other persons employed by the Owners or for whom he is responsible, not resulting, however, from 174
lack of due diligence of the Owners or manager. The Captain to have the liberty to sail with or without pilots, to call at any 175
port for bunkering, to tow, to be towed and to assist other vessels in distress. 176
177
27° <u>General average</u>.- All claims for general average to be settled in\ LONDON according to the YORK/ 178
ANTWERP Rules 1974, as amended 1990. 179
180
28° <u>Extra insurance</u>.- Any extra insurance premium on the cargo (and/or freight in the case of freight advances), 180
borne by Charterers by reason of the age, nationality or class of the vessel, shall be paid by Owners and the amount 181
thereof deducted from the freight. 182
183
29° <u>Arbitration</u>.- Any disputes concerning the present charter to be settled by arbitration in LONDON, in the 183
ordinary manner, and to be governed and construed in accordance with English Law both as regards sub-stance and 184
procedure. 185
186
30° <u>Penalty</u>.- The penalty for non-performance of the present contract to be proved damages not exceeding 187
the amount of freight. 188
189
31° <u>Brokerage</u>.- A brokerage of on the gross amount of freight and eventual dead-freight and demurrage is 189
payable by the Owners to such commission being due ship lost or not lost. 190
191
32° <u>Overtime</u>, - Overtime to be for party ordering same; however. Officer's and crew's overtime always to be 191
for Owners' account. 192
193
33° <u>Soiling telegram</u>.- On sailing from loading port. Master to cable to agents at discharging port (BOX 23) 193
stating ; date and time of sailing. Bill of Loading quantity and E.T.A. at discharging port. 194
195
34° <u>Protective clauses</u>. - This charter-party is to be subject to the conditions of the "NEW JASON CLAUSE", 196
the "NEW BOTH TO BLAME COLLISION CLAUSE", the "VOYWAR 1950 CLAUSE" and the "P. & I. "CLUB BUNKERING 197
CLAUSE" which ore deemed to be fully incorporated herein and/or in oil Bills of Lading issued under this charter-party. 198
35. Owners to accept responsibility to meet limitations concerning discharging port. 199

Appendix 20

GENCON

1. Shipbroker	RECOMMENDED **THE BALTIC AND INTERNATIONAL MARITIME COUNCIL** **UNIFORM GENERAL CHARTER (AS REVISED 1922,1976 and 1994)** (To be used for trades for which no specially approved form is in force) **CODE NAME: "GENCON"** Part I
	2. Place and date
3. Owners/Place of business (Cl. 1)	4. Charterers/Place of business (Cl. 1)
5. Vessel's name (Cl. 1)	6. GT/NT(Cl. 1)
7. DWT all told on summer load line in metric tons (abt.) (Cl. 1)	8. Present position (Cl. 1)
9. Expected ready to load (abt.) (Cl. 1)	
10. Loading port or place (Cl. 1)	11 Discharging port or place (Cl. 1)
12. Cargo (also state quantity and margin in Owners' option, if agreed; if full and complete cargo not agreed state "part cargo" (Cl. 1)	
13. Freight rate (also state whether freight prepaid or payable on delivery) (Cl. 4)	14. Freight payment (state currency and method of payment; also beneficiary and bank account) (Cl. 4)
15. State if vessel's cargo handling gear shall not be used (Cl. 5)	16. Laytime (if separate laytime for load, and disch. is agreed, fill in a) and b). If total laytime for load, and disch., fill in c) only) (Cl. 6)
17. Shippers/Place of business (Cl. 6)	(a) Laytime for loading
18. Agents (loading) (Cl. 6)	(b) Laytime for discharging
19. Agents (discharging) (Cl. 6)	(c) Total laytime for loading and discharging
20. Demurrage rate and manner payable (loading and discharging) (Cl. 7)	21. Cancelling date (Cl. 9)
	22. General Average to be adjusted at (Cl. 12)
23. Freight Tax (state if for the Owners' account (Cl .13 (c))	24. Brokerage commission and to whom payable (Cl. 15)
25. Law and Arbitration (state 19 (a), 19 (b) or 19 (c) of Cl. 19; if 19 (c) agreed also state Place of Arbitration) (if not filled in 19 (a) shall apply) (Cl. 19)	
(a) State maximum amount for small claims/shortened arbitration (Cl. 19)	26. Additional clauses covering special provisions, if agreed

It is mutually agreed that this Contract shall be performed subject to the conditions contained in this Charter Party which shall include Part I as well as Part II. In the event of a conflict of conditions, the provisions of Part I shall prevail over those of Part II to the extent of such conflict.

Signature (Owners)	Signature (Charterers)

Appendix 20

GENCON (continued)

1. It is agreed between the party mentioned in Box 3 as the Owners of the Vessel named in Box 5, of the GT/NT indicated in Box 6 and carrying about the number of metric tons of deadweight capacity all told on summer loadline stated in Box 7, now in position as stated in Box 8 and expected ready to load under this Charter Party about the date indicated in Box 9, and the party mentioned as the Charterers in Box 4 that:

The said Vessel shall, as soon as her prior commitments have been completed, proceed to the loading port(a) or place(s) stated in Box 10 or so near thereto as she may safely get and lie always afloat, and there load a full and complete cargo (if shipment of deck cargo agreed same to be at the Charterers' risk and responsibility) as stated in Box 12, which the Charterers bind themselves to ship, and being so loaded the Vessel shall proceed to the discharging port(s) or place(s) stated in Box 11 as ordered on signing Bills of Lading, or so near thereto as she may safely get and lie always afloat, and there deliver the cargo.

2. **Owners' Responsibility Clause**

The Owners are to be responsible for loss of or damage to the goods or for delay in delivery of the goods only in case the loss, damage or delay has been caused by personal want of due diligence on the part of the Owners or their Manager to make the Vessel in all respects seaworthy and to secure that she is properly manned, equipped and supplied, or by the personal act or default of the Owners or their Manager.

And the Owners are not responsible for loss, damage or delay arising from any other cause whatsoever, even from the neglect or default of the Master or crew or some other person employed by the Owners on board or ashore for whose acts they would, but for this Clause, be responsible, or from unseaworthiness of the Vessel on loading or commencement of the voyage or at any time whatsoever.

3. **Deviation Clause**

The Vessel has liberty to call at any port or ports in any order, for any purpose, to sail without pilots, to tow and/or assist Vessels in all situations, and also to deviate for the purpose of saving life and/or property.

4. **Payment of Freight**

(a) The freight at the rate stated in Box 13 shall be paid in cash calculated on the intaken quantity of cargo.

(b) *Prepaid.* If according to Box 13 freight is to be paid on shipment, it shall be deemed earned and non-returnable, Vessel and/or cargo lost or not lost.

Neither the Owners nor their agents shall be required to sign or endorse bills of lading showing freight prepaid unless the freight due to the Owners has actually been paid.

(c) *On delivery.* If according to Box 13 freight, or part thereof, is payable at destination it shall not be deemed earned until the cargo is thus delivered. Notwithstanding the provisions under (a), if freight or part thereof is payable on delivery of the cargo the Charterers shall have the option of paying the freight on delivered weight/quantity provided such option is declared before breaking bulk and the weight/quantity can be ascertained by official weighing machine, joint draft survey or tally.

Cash for Vessel's ordinary disbursements at the port of loading to be advanced by the Charterers, if required, at highest current rate of exchange, subject to two (2) per cent to cover insurance and other expenses.

5. **Loading/Discharging**

(a) Costs/Risks

The cargo shall be brought into the holds, loaded, stowed and/or trimmed, tallied, lashed and/or secured and taken from the holds and discharged by the Charterers, free of any risk, liability and expense whatsoever to the Owners. The Charterers shall provide and lay all dunnage material as required for the proper stowage and protection of the cargo on board, the Owners allowing the use of all dunnage available on board. The Charterers shall be responsible for and pay the cost of removing their dunnage after discharge of the cargo under this Charter Party and time to count until dunnage has been removed.

(b) Cargo Handling Gear

Unless the Vessel Is gearless or unless it has been agreed between the parties that the Vessel's gear shall not be used and stated as such in Box 15, the Owners shall throughout the duration of loading/discharging give free use of the Vessel's cargo handling gear and of sufficient motive power to operate all such cargo handling gear. All such equipment to be in good working order. Unless caused by negligence of the stevedores, time lost by breakdown of the Vessel's cargo handling gear or motive power - pro rata the total number of cranes/winches required at that time for the loading/discharging of cargo under this Charter Party - shall not count as laytime or time on demurrage. On request the Owners shall provide free of charge cranemen/winchmen from the crew to operate the Vessel's cargo handling gear, unless local regulations prohibit this, in which latter event shore labourers shall be for the account of the Charterers. Cranemen/winchmen shall be under the Charterers' risk and responsibility and as stevedores to be deemed as their servants but shall always work under the supervision of the Master.

(c) Stevedore Damage

The Charterers shall be responsible for damage (beyond ordinary wear and tear) to any part of the Vessel caused by Stevedores. Such damage shall be notified as soon as reasonably possible by the Master to the Charterers or their agents and to their Stevedores, failing which the Charterers shall not be held responsible. The Master shall endeavour to obtain the Stevedores' written acknowledgement of liability.

The Charterers are obliged to repair any stevedore damage prior to completion of the voyage, but must repair stevedore damage affecting the Vessel's seaworthiness or class before the Vessel sails from the port where such damage was caused or found. All additional expenses Incurred shall be for the account of the Charterers and any time lost shall be for the account of and shall be paid to the Owners by the Charterers at the demurrage rate.

6. **Laytime**

* *(a) Separate laytime for loading and discharging*

The cargo shall be loaded within the number of running days/hours as indicated in Box 16, weather permitting, Sundays and holidays excepted, unless used, in which event time used shall count.

The cargo shall be discharged within the number of running days/hours as indicated in Box 16, weather permitting, Sundays and holidays excepted, unless used, in which event time used shall count.

* *(b) Total laytime for loading and discharging*

The cargo shall be loaded and discharged within the number of total running days/ hours as indicated, in Box 16, weather permitting, Sundays and holidays excepted, unless used, in which event time used shall count.

(c) Commencement of laytime (loading and discharging)

Laytime for loading and discharging shall commence at 13.00 hours, if notice of readiness is given up to and including 12.00 hours, and at 06.00 hours next working day if notice given during office hours after 12.00 hours. Notice of readiness at loading port to be given to the Shippers named in Box 17 or if not named, to the Charterers or their agents named in Box 18. Notice of readiness at the discharging port to be given to the Receivers or. If not known, to the Charterers or their agents named in Box 19.

If the loading/discharging berth is not available on the Vessel's arrival at or off the port of loading/discharging, the Vessel shall be entitled to give notice of readiness within ordinary office hours on arrival there, whether in free pratique or not, whether customs cleared or not. Laytime or time on demurrage shall then count as if she were In berth and in all respects ready for loading/discharging provided that the Master warrants that she is in fact ready In all respects. Time used in moving from the place of waiting to the loading/discharging berth shall not count as laytime.

If, after inspection, the Vessel Is found not to be ready in all respects to load/discharge time lost after the discovery thereof until the Vessel is again ready to load/discharge shall not count as laytime.

Time used before commencement of laytime shall count.

* *Indicate alternative (a) or (b) as agreed, in Box 16.*

7. **Demurrage**

Demurrage at the loading and discharging port is payable by the Charterers at the rate stated in Box 20 in the manner stated in Box 20 per day or pro rata for any part of a day. Demurrage shall fall due day by day and shall be payable upon receipt of the Owners' invoice.

In the event the demurrage is not paid in accordance with the above, the Owners shall give the Charterers 96 running hours written notice to rectify the failure. If the demurrage is not paid at the expiration of this time limit and if the vessel is in or at the loading port, the Owners are entitled at any time to terminate the Charter Party and claim damages for any losses caused thereby.

8. **Lien Clause**

The Owners shall have a lien on the cargo and on all sub-freights payable in respect of the cargo, for freight, deadweight, demurrage, claims for damages and for all other amounts due under this Charter Party including costs of recovering same.

9. **Cancelling Clause**

(a) Should the Vessel not be ready to load (whether in berth or not) on the cancelling date indicated in Box 21, the Charterers shall have the option of cancelling this Charter Party.

(b) Should the Owners anticipate that, despite the exercise of due diligence, the Vessel will not be ready to load by the cancelling date, they shall notify the Charterers thereof without delay stating the expected date of the Vessel's readiness to load and asking whether the Charterers will exercise their option of cancelling the Charter Party, or agree to a new cancelling date.

Such option must be declared by the Charterers within 48 running hours after the receipt of the Owners' notice. If the Charterers do not exercise their option of cancelling, then this Charter Party shall be deemed to be amended such that the seventh day after the new readiness date stated in the Owners' notification to the Charterers shall be the new cancelling date.

The provisions of sub-clause (b) of this Clause shall operate only once, and In case of the Vessel's further delay, the Charterers shall have the option of cancelling the Charter Party as per sub-clause (a) of this Clause.

10. **Bills of Lading**

Bills of Lading shall be presented and signed by the Master as per the "Cangenbill" Bill of Lading form, Edition 1994, without prejudice to this Charter Party, or by the Owners' agents provided written authority has been given by Owners to the agents, a copy of which is to be furnished to the Charterers. The Charterers shall indemnify the Owners against all consequences or liabilities that may arise from the signing of bills of lading as presented to the extent that the terms or contents of such bills of lading impose or result In the imposition of more onerous liabilities upon the Owners than those assumed by the Owners under this Charter Party.

11. **Both-to-Blame Collision Clause**

If the Vessel comes into collision with another vessel as a result of the negligence of the other vessel and any act, neglect or default of the Master. Mariner, Pilot or the servants of the Owners In the navigation or in the management of the Vessel, the owners of the cargo carried hereunder will indemnify the Owners against all loss or liability to the other or non-carrying vessel or her owners in so far as such loss or liability represents loss of, or damage to, or any claim whatsoever of the owners of said cargo, paid or payable by the other or non-carrying vessel or her owners to the owners of said cargo and set-off, recouped or recovered by the other or non-carrying vessel or her owners as part of their claim against the carrying Vessel or the Owners. The foregoing provisions shall also apply where the owners, operators or those in charge of any vessel or vessels or objects other than, or in addition to, the colliding vessels or objects are at fault in respect of a collision or contact.

12. **General Average and New Jason Clause**

General Average shall be adjusted In London unless otherwise agreed in Box 22 according to York-Antwerp Rules 1994 and any subsequent modification thereof. Proprietors of cargo to pay the cargo's share in the general expenses even if same have been necessitated through neglect or default of the Owners' servants (see Clause 2).

If General Average is to be adjusted in accordance with the law and practice of the United States of America, the following Clause shall apply: "In the event of accident, danger, damage or disaster before or after the commencement of the voyage, resulting from any cause whatsoever, whether due to negligence or not, for which, or for the consequence of which, the Owners are not responsible, by statute, contract or otherwise, the cargo shippers, consignees or the owners of the cargo shall contribute with the Owners In General Average to the payment of any sacrifices, losses or expenses of a General Average nature that may be made or incurred and shall pay salvage and special charges incurred in respect of the cargo. If a salving vessel is owned or operated by the Owners, salvage shall be paid for as fully as if the said salving vessel or vessels belonged to strangers. Such deposit as the Owners, or their agents, may deem sufficient to cover the estimated contribution of the goods and any salvage and special charges thereon shall, if required, be made by the cargo, shippers, consignees or owners of the goods to the Owners before delivery".

13. **Taxes and Dues Clause**

(a) *On Vessel* -The Owners shall pay all dues, charges and taxes customarily levied on the Vessel, howsoever the amount thereof may be assessed.

(b) *On cargo* -The Charterers shall pay all dues, charges, duties and taxes customarily levied on the cargo, howsoever the amount thereof may be assessed.

(c) *On freight* -Unless otherwise agreed In Box 23, taxes levied on the freight shall be for the Charterers' account.

Appendix 20

GENCON (continued)

PART II

"Gencon" Charter (As Revised 1922, 1976 and 1994)

14. Agency

In every case the Owners shall appoint their own Agent both at the port of loading and the port of discharge.

15. Brokerage

A brokerage commission at the rate stated In Box 24 on the freight, dead-freight and demurrage earned is due to the party mentioned In Box 24.

In case of non-execution 1/3 of the brokerage on the estimated amount of freight to be paid by the party responsible for such non-execution to the Brokers as indemnity for the tatter's expenses and work. In case of more voyages the amount of indemnity to be agreed.

16. General Strike Clause

(a) If there is a strike or lock-out affecting or preventing the actual loading of the cargo, or any part of it, when the Vessel is ready to proceed from her last port or at any time during the voyage to the port or ports of loading or after her arrival there, the Master or the Owners may ask the Charterers to declare, that they agree to reckon the laydays as if there were no strike or lock-out. Unless the Charterers have given such declaration in writing (by telegram, if necessary) within 24 hours, the Owners shall have the option of cancelling this Charter Party. If part cargo has already been loaded, the Owners must proceed with same, (freight payable on loaded quantity only) having liberty to complete with other cargo on the way for their own account.

(b) If there is a strike or lock-out affecting or preventing the actual discharging of the cargo on or after the Vessel's arrival at or off port of discharge and same has not been settled within 46 hours, the Charterers shall have the option of keeping the Vessel waiting until such strike or lock-out is at an end against paying half demurrage after expiration of the time provided for discharging until the strike or lock-out terminates and thereafter full demurrage shall be payable until the completion of discharging, or of ordering the Vessel to a safe port where she can safely discharge without risk of being detained by strike or lock-out. Such orders to be given within 48 hours after the Master or the Owners have given notice to the Charterers of the strike or lock-out affecting the discharge. On delivery of the cargo at such port, all conditions of this Charter Party and of the Bill of Lading shall apply and the Vessel shall receive the same freight as if she had discharged at the original port of destination, except that if the distance to the substituted port exceeds 100 nautical miles, the freight on the cargo delivered at the substituted port to be increased in proportion.

(c) Except for the obligations described above, neither the Charterers nor the Owners shall be responsible for the consequences of any strikes or lock-outs preventing or affecting the actual loading or discharging of the cargo.

17. War Risks ("Voywar 1993")

(1) For the purpose of this Clause, the words:

(a) The "Owners" shall include the shipowners, bareboat charterers, disponent owners, managers or other operators who are charged with the management of the Vessel, and the Master; and

(b) "War Risks" shall Include any war (whether actual or threatened), act of war, civil war, hostilities, revolution, rebellion, civil commotion, warlike operations, the laying of mines (whether actual or reported), acts of piracy, acts of terrorists, acts of hostility or malicious damage, blockades (whether imposed against all Vessels or imposed selectively against Vessels of certain flags or ownership, or against certain cargoes or crews or otherwise howsoever), by any person, body, terrorist or political group, or the Government of any state whatsoever, which, in the reasonable Judgement of the Master and/or the Owners, may be dangerous or are likely to be or to become dangerous to the Vessel, her cargo, crew or other persons on board the Vessel.

(2) If at any time before the Vessel commences loading, it appears that, in the reasonable judgement of the Master and/or the Owners, performance of the Contract of Carriage, or any part of it, may expose, or is likely to expose, the Vessel, her cargo, crew or other persons on board the Vessel to War Risks, the Owners may give notice to the Charterers cancelling this Contract of Carriage, or may refuse to perform such part of it as may expose, or may be likely to expose, the Vessel, her cargo, crew or other persons on board the Vessel to War Risks; provided always that if this Contract of Carriage provides that loading or discharging is to take place within a range of ports, and at the port or ports nominated by the Charterers the Vessel, her cargo, crew, or other persons onboard the Vessel may be exposed, or may be likely to be exposed, to War Risks, the Owners shall first require the Charterers to nominate any other safe port which lies within the range for loading or discharging, and may only cancel this Contract of Carriage It the Charterers shall not have nominated such safe port or ports within 48 hours of receipt of notice of such requirement.

(3) The Owners shall not be required to continue to load cargo for any voyage, or to sign Bills of Lading for any port or place, or to proceed or continue on any voyage, or on any part thereof, or to proceed through any canal or waterway, or to proceed to or remain at any port or place whatsoever, where it appears, either after the loading of the cargo commences, or at any stage of the voyage thereafter before the discharge of the cargo is completed, that. In the reasonable judgement of the Master and/or the Owners, the Vessel, her cargo (or any part thereof), crew or other persons on board the Vessel (or any one or more of them) may be, or are likely to be, exposed to War Risks, if it should so appear, the Owners may by notice request the Charterers to nominate a safe port for the discharge of the cargo or any part thereof, and if within 48 hours of the receipt of such notice, the Charterers shall not have nominated such a port, the Owners may discharge the cargo at any safe port of their choice (including the port of loading) in complete fulfilment of the Contract of Carriage. The Owners shall be entitled to recover from the Charterers the extra expenses of such discharge and, if the discharge takes place at any port other than the loading port to receive the full freight as though the cargo had been carried to the discharging port and if the extra distance exceeds 100 miles, to additional freight which shall be the same percentage of the freight contracted for as the percentage which the extra distance represents to the distance of the normal and customary route, the Owners having a lien on the cargo for such expenses and freight.

(4) If at any stage of the voyage after the loading of the cargo commences, it appears that, in the reasonable judgement of the Master and/or the Owners, the Vessel, her cargo, crew or other persons on board the Vessel may be, or are likely to be, exposed to War Risks on any part of the route (including any canal or waterway) which is normally and customarily used in a voyage of the nature contracted for, and there is another longer route to the discharging port, the Owners shall give notice to the Charterers that this route will be taken, in this event the Owners shall be entitled, if the total extra distance exceeds 100 miles, to additional freight which shall be the same percentage of the freight contracted for as the percentage which the extra distance represents to the distance of the normal and customary route.

(5) The Vessel shall have liberty:-

(a) to comply with all orders, directions, recommendations or advice as to departure, arrival, routes, sailing in convoy, ports of call, stoppages, destinations, discharge of cargo, delivery or in any way whatsoever which are given by the Government of the Nation under whose flag the Vessel sails, or other Government to whose laws the Owners are subject, or any other Government which so requires, or any body or group acting with the power to compel compliance with their orders or directions;

(b) to comply with the orders, directions or recommendations of any war risks underwriters who have the authority to give the same under the terms of the war risks insurance;

(c) to comply with the terms of any resolution of the Security Council of the United Nations, any directives of the European Community, the effective orders of any other Supranational body which has the right to issue and give the same, and with national laws aimed at enforcing the same to which the Owners are subject, and to obey the orders and directions of those who are charged with their enforcement;

(d) to discharge at any other port any cargo or part thereof which may render the Vessel liable to confiscation as a contraband carrier;

(e) to call at any other port to change the crew or any part thereof or other persons on board the Vessel when there is reason to believe that they may be subject to internment, imprisonment or other sanctions;

(f) where cargo has not been loaded or has been discharged by the Owners under any provisions of this Clause, to load other cargo for the Owners' own benefit and carry it to any other port or ports whatsoever, whether backwards or forwards or in a contrary direction to the ordinary or customary route.

(6) If in compliance with any of the provisions of sub-clauses (2) to (5) of this Clause anything is done or not done, such shall not be deemed to be a deviation, but shall be considered as due fulfilment of the Contract of Carriage.

18. General Ice Clause

Port of loading

(a) In the event of the loading port being inaccessible by reason of ice when the Vessel is ready to proceed from her last port or at any time during the voyage or on the Vessel's arrival or in case frost sets In after the Vessel's arrival, the Master for fear of being frozen in is at liberty to leave without cargo, and this Charter Party shall be null and void.

(b) If during loading the Master, for fear of the Vessel being frozen In, deems it advisable to leave, he has liberty to do so with what cargo he has on board and to proceed to any other port or ports with option of completing cargo for the Owners' benefit for any port or ports including port of discharge. Any part cargo thus loaded under this Charter Party to be forwarded to destination at the Vessel's expense but against payment of freight, provided that no extra expenses be thereby caused to the Charterers, freight being paid on quantity delivered (in proportion if lumpsum), all other conditions as per this Charter Party.

(c) In case of more than one loading port, and if one or more of the ports are closed by ice, the Master or the Owners to be at liberty either to load the part cargo at the open port and fill up elsewhere for their own account as under section (b) or to declare the Charter Party null and void unless the Charterers agree to load full cargo at the open port.

Port of discharge

(a) Should ice prevent the Vessel from reaching port of discharge the Charterers shall have the option of keeping the Vessel waiting until there opening of navigation and paying demurrage or of ordering the Vessel to a safe and immediately accessible port where she can safely discharge without risk of detention by ice. Such orders to be given within 48 hours after the Master or the Owners have given notice to the Charterers of the Impossibility of reaching port of destination.

(b) If during discharging the Master for fear of the Vessel being frozen in deems it advisable to leave, he has liberty to do so with what cargo he has on board and to proceed to the nearest accessible port where she can safely discharge.

(c) On delivery of the cargo at such port, all conditions of the Bill of Lading shall apply and the Vessel shall receive the same freight as if she had discharged at the original port of destination, except that if the distance of the substituted port exceeds 100 nautical miles, the freight on the cargo delivered at the substituted port to be increased in proportion.

19. Law and Arbitration

* (a) This Charter Party shall be governed by and construed in accordance with English law and any dispute arising out of this Charter Party shall be referred to arbitration in London in accordance with the Arbitration Acts 1950 and 1979 or any statutory modification or re-enactment thereof for the time being in force. Unless the parties agree upon a sole arbitrator, one arbitrator shall be appointed by each party and the arbitrators so appointed shall appoint a third arbitrator, the decision of the three-man tribunal thus constituted or any two of them, shall be final. On the receipt by one party of the nomination in writing of the other party's arbitrator, that party shall appoint their arbitrator within fourteen days, failing which the decision of the single arbitrator appointed shall be final.

For disputes where the total amount claimed by either party does not exceed the amount stated in Box 25** the arbitration shall be conducted in accordance with the Small Claims Procedure of the London Maritime Arbitrators Association.

* (b) This Charter Party shall be governed by and construed In accordance with Title 9 of the United States Code and the Maritime Law of the United States and should any dispute arise out of this Charter Party, the matter in dispute shall be referred to three persons at New York, one to be appointed by each of the parties hereto, and the third by the two so chosen; their decision or that of any two of them shall be final, and for purpose of enforcing any award, this agreement may be made a rule of the Court. The proceedings shall be conducted in accordance with the rules of the Society of Maritime Arbitrators, Inc..

For disputes where the total amount claimed by either party does not exceed the amount stated in Box 25** the arbitration shall be conducted In accordance with the Shortened Arbitration Procedure of the Society of Maritime Arbitrators, Inc..

* (c) Any dispute arising out of this Charter Party shall be referred to arbitration at the place indicated In Box 25, subject to the procedures applicable there. The laws of the place indicated in Box 25 shall govern this Charter Party.

(d) If Box 25 in Part I is not filled in, sub-clause (a) of this Clause shall apply.

* *(a), (b) and (c) are alternatives; indicate alternative agreed in Box 25.*

** *Where no figure is supplied in Box 25 in Part I, this provision only shall be void but the other provisions of this Clause shall have full force and remain in effect.*

Appendix 21

FONASBA

FONASBA

The Federation of National Associations of Ship Brokers and Agents

INTERNATIONAL BROKERS COMMISSION CONTRACT
Recommended by BIMCO

THIS AGREEMENTS is made the   day of   200

between: ....

Shipowner/Timechartered Owner/Disponent Owner   ....

(hereinafter referred to as the "Owner") and :   ....

Shipbroker/Chartering Broker of :
(hereinafter referred to as the "Broker")   ....

WHEREAS:

The Broker has fixed the Owner's vessel on the terms and conditions contained in the Charter Party.
dated: .... annexed hereto.

NOW IT IS HEREBY AGREED AS FOLLOWS:

1.   The Owner shall pay commission to or otherwise remunerate the Broker:

❖   (a)   In accordance with the relevant provisions of the Charter Party.

❖   (b)   As follows..

2.   Any dispute arising out of this Contract shall be referred to
     Arbitration at .... and shall be subject to the law
     and procedures applicable there.

For and on behalf of   **For and on behalf of**

....
     (Owner)   **(Broker)**

❖   **(Delete as appropriate)**

STATEMENT OF FACTS – BIMCO

STANDARD STATEMENT OF FACTS (SHORT FORM)
RECOMMENDED BY
THE BALTIC AND INTERNATIONAL MARITIME CONFERENCE (BIMCO)
AND THE FEDERATION OF NATIONAL ASSOCIATIONS
OF SHIP BROKERS AND AGENTS (FONASBA)

1. Agents TUTORSHIP AGENCY COMPANY	
2. Vessel's name M.V. OSPREY	**3. Port** ANYPORT
4. Owners Disponent Owners ST. HELENS SHIPPING	**5. Vessel berthed** 0600 THURSDAY. 9 FEBRUARY
	6. Loading commenced 0700 10 FEB / **7. Loading completed** 1515 15 FEB
8. Cargo 22,000 METRIC TONS	**9. Discharging commenced** — / **10. Discharging completed** —
	11. Cargo documents on board — / **12. Vessel sailed** 0600 16 FEB
13. Charter Party —	**14. Working hours: meal hours of the port** 0700 – 1700 HOURS MONDAY TO FRIDAY
15. Bill of Lading weight/quantity — / **16. Outturn weight/quantity** —	
17. Vessel arrived on roads —	**18.** HOLDS PASSED BY INSPECTOR 1230 9FEB
19. Notice of readiness tendered 0900 THURS 9 FEBRUARY	**20.** NOR ACCEPTED 1230 THURS 9 FEB
21. Next tide available —	**22.**

DETAILS OF DAILY WORKING

Date	Day	Hours worked From	to	Hours stopped From	to	No. of gangs	Quantity load. disch.	Remarks
10 FEB	FRIDAY	0700	1700				5000 T	
11 FEB	SATURDAY	0700	1200				4000 T	
13 FEB	MONDAY	0800	1700				6000 T	
14 FEB	TUESDAY			0700	1130			RAIN
14 FEB	TUESDAY	1130	1700				2500 T	
15 FEB	WEDNESDAY	0700	1515				4500 T	

General remarks
SAILING DELAYED AFTER LOADING DUE TO REPAIRS TO VESSELS AUXILIARY ENGINE.

Place and date ANYPORT 15 FEBRUARY	**Name and signature (Master)** XXXX.
Name and signature (Agents) TUTORSHIP AGENCY COMPANY	**Name and signature (for the Charterers/Shippers Receivers)** CARGO SHIPPERS INC.

* See Explanatory Notes overleaf for filling in the boxes

Published by The Baltic and International Maritime Conference (BIMCO), Copenhagen

Printed and sold by Fr. G. Knudtzon Ltd., 55, Toldbodgade, Copenhagen, by authority of BIMCO

Appendix 22

STATEMENT OF FACTS – BIMCO (continued)

1. Agents	STANDARD STATEMENT OF FACTS (SHORT FORM)
	RECOMMENDED BY
	THE BALTIC AND INTERNATIONAL MARITIME CONFERENCE (BIMCO)
	ANDTHE FEDERATION OF NATIONAL ASSOCIATIONS
	OF SHIP BROKERS AND AGENTS (FONSABA)

2. Vessel's name	3. Port	
4. Owners/Disponent Owners	5. Vessel berthed	
	6. Loading commenced	7. Loading completed
8. Cargo	9. Discharging commenced	10. Discharging completed
	11. Cargo documents on board	12. Vessel sailed
13. Charter Party*	14. Working hours/meal hours of the port*	
15. Bill of Lading weight/quantity	16. Outturn weight/quantity	
17. Vessel arrived on roads	18.	
19. Notice of readiness tendered	20.	
21. Next tide available	22.	

DETAILS OF DAILY WORKING*

Date	Day	Hours worked		Hours stopped		No. of gangs	Quantity load./disch.	Remarks*
		From	to	From	to			

General remarks*

Place and date	Name and signature (Master)*
Name and signature (Agents)*	Name and signature (for the Charterers/Shippers/Receivers)*

* See Explanatory Notes overleaf for filling in the boxes

STATEMENT OF FACTS – BIMCO (continued)

INSTRUCTIONS FOR FILLING IN THE BOXES

General
It is recommended to fill in the boxes with a short text. When it is a matter of figures to be inserted as is the case in most of the boxes, this should be done as follows:

> 6. Loading commenced
> 1975-03-15-0800

the figures being mentioned in the following order: year-month-date-time.

Boxes Calling for Special Attention

Charter Party*:
Insert name and date of charter, for instance, "Gencon" dated 1975-03-01.

Working hours/meal hours of the port*:
Indicate normal working hours/meal hours of the port and not the actual hours worked on board the vessel which may be longer or shorter than the hours normally worked in the port. Such day-by-day figures should be indicated in the box provided for under "Details of daily working".

Some empty boxes are made available in which other relevant information applying to the particular port or vessel could be inserted, such as, time of granting free pratique, if applicable, etc.

Details of daily working*:
Insert day-by-day figures and indicate in the vertical column marked "Remarks*" all relevant details as to reasons for stoppages such as bad weather, strikes, breakdown of winches/cranes, shortage of cargo, etc.

General Remarks*:
This box should be used for insertion of such general observations which are not covered in any of the boxes provided for in the first main group of boxes, for instance, reasons for berthing delay or other general observations.

Signatures*:
It is of importance that the boxes provided for signatures are duly signed by the parties concerned.

Appendix 23

TIME SHEET – BIMCO

1. Agents	STANDARD TIME SHEET (SHORT FORM) RECOMMENDED BY THE BALTIC AND INTERNATIONAL MARITIME CONFERENCE (BIMCO) AND THE FEDERATION OF NATIONAL ASSOCIATIONS OF SHIP BROKERS AND AGENTS (FONSABA)	
2. Vessel's name	3. Port	
4. Owners/Disponent Owners	5. Vessel berthed	
	6. Loading commenced	7. Loading completed
8. Cargo	9. Discharging commenced	10. Discharging completed
	11. Cargo documents on board	12. Vessel sailed
13. Charter Party*	14. Working hours/meal hours of the port*	
15. Bill of Lading weight/quantity · 16. Outturn weight/quantity		
17. Vessel arrived on roads	18. Time to count from	
19. Notice of readiness tendered	20. Rate of demurrage	21. Rate of despatch money
22. Next tide available	23.	
24. Laytime allowed for loading · 25. Laytime allowed for discharging	26.	

LAYTIME COMPUTATION*

Date	Day	Time worked		Laytime used			Time saved on demurrage			Remarks*
		From	to	days	hours	minutes	days	hours	minutes	

General remarks*

Place and date	Signature*
Signature*	Signature*

* See Explanatory Notes overleaf for filling in the boxes

Appendix 23

TIME SHEET – BIMCO (continued)

INSTRUCTIONS FOR FILLING IN THE BOXES

General
It is recommended to fill in the boxes with a short text. When it is a matter of figures to be inserted as is the case in most of the boxes, this should be done as follows:

6. Loading commenced
1975-03-15-0800

the figures being mentioned in the following order: year–month–date–time.

Boxes Calling for Special Attention

Charter Party*:
Insert name and date of charter, for instance, "Gencon" dated 1975-03-01.

Working hours/meal hours of the port*:
Indicate normal working hours/meal hours of the port and not the actual hours worked on board the vessel which may be longer or shorter than the hours normally worked in the port. Such day-by-day figures should be indicated in the box provided for under "Laytime Computation".

Some empty boxes are made available in which other relevant information applying to the particular port or vessel could be inserted, such as, time of granting free pratique, if applicable, etc.

Laytime Computation*:
Insert day-by-day figures and indicate in the vertical column marked "Remarks*" all relevant details as to reasons for stoppages such as bad weather, strikes, breakdown of winches/cranes, shortage of cargo, etc.

General Remarks*:
This box should be used for insertion of such general observations which are not covered in any of the boxes provided for in the first main group of boxes, for instance, reasons for berthing delay or other general observations.

Signatures*:
It is of importance that the boxes provided for signatures are duly signed by the parties concerned.

Appendix 24

DECIMAL PARTS OF A DAY

Hours		Minutes					
1	.041666	1	.000694	25	.017361	49	.034027
2	.083333	2	.001388	26	.018055	50	.034722
3	.125	3	.002083	27	.018749	51	.035416
4	.166666	4	.002777	28	.019444	52	.036111
5	.208333	5	.003472	29	.020138	53	.036805
6	.25	6	.004166	30	.020833	54	.037499
7	.291666	7	.004861	31	.021527	55	.038194
8	.333333	8	.005555	32	.022222	56	.038888
9	.375	9	.006249	33	.022916	57	.039583
10	.416666	10	.006944	34	.023611	58	.040277
11	.458333	11	.007638	35	.024305	59	.040972
12	.5	12	.008333	36	.024999	60	.041666
13	.541666	13	.009027	37	.025694		
14	.583333	14	.009722	38	.026388		
15	.625	15	.010416	39	.027083		
16	.666666	16	.011111	40	.027777		
17	.708333	17	.011805	41	.028472		
18	.75	18	.012499	42	.029166		
19	.791666	19	.013194	43	.029861		
20	.833333	20	.013888	44	.030555		
21	.875	21	.014583	45	.031249		
22	.916666	22	.015277	46	.031944		
23	.958333	23	.015972	47	.032638		
24	1.0	24	.016666	48	.033333		

Examples:

1. **4 days 17 hours 37 minutes, expressed as a decimal:**

   4 days – 4.000000
   17 hours – .708333 +
   37mins. – .025694
   4.734027

2. **What is 4.468444 in days, hours and minutes?**

   4.468444 –
   4.000000   4 days

   .468444
   .458333   11 hours

   .011111   16 mins.
                   4 days, 11 hours, 16 minutes

NOTICE OF READINESS

To Messrs _____

Notice of Readiness

Please note that the ship _____
nationality: _____ call sign: _____
has arrived at _____ on _____ at _____
hours, and is in every respect ready to commence loading/discharging a cargo of
_____, in accordance with the terms and conditions of the
Charter-Party/Booking Note dated _____.

Time is to count as per the terms and conditions of above-mentioned Charter-Party/
Booking Note.

Please confirm receipt of this Notice of Readiness by signing and returning the copy
attached.

Place: _____ Date:_____hours.

_____
Master/Agent

_____
Charterer/Shipper/Receiver

Appendix 26

VOYLAYRULES 93

VOYAGE CHARTERPARTY LAYTIME INTERPRETATION RULES 1993

Code Name: VOYLAYRULES 93

issued jointly by BIMCO, CMI, FONASBA and INTERCARGO.

PREAMBLE

The interpretations of words and phrases used in a charterparty, as set out below, and the corresponding initials if customarily used, shall apply when expressly incorporated in the charterparty, wholly or partly, save only to the extent that they are inconsistent with any express provision of it.

When the word "charterparty" is used, it shall be understood to extend to any form of contract of carriage or affreightment including contracts evidenced by bills of lading.

LIST OF RULES

1. "PORT"
2. "BERTH"
3. "REACHABLE ON HER ARRIVAL" or "ALWAYS ACCESSIBLE"
4. "LAYTIME"
5. "PER HATCH PER DAY"
6. "PER WORKING HATCH PER DAY" (WHD) or "PER WORKABLE HATCH PER DAY (WHD)
7. "DAY"
8. "CLEAR DAYS"
9. "HOLIDAY"
10. "WORKING DAY" (WD)
11. "RUNNING DAYS" or "CONSECUTIVE DAYS"
12. "WEATHER WORKING DAY" (WWD) or "WEATHER WORKING DAY OF 24 HOURS" or "WEATHER WORKING DAY OF 24 CONSECUTIVE HOURS"
13. "WEATHER PERMITTING" (WP)
14. EXCEPTED" or "EXCLUDED"
15. "UNLESS SOONER COMMENCED"
16. "UNLESS USED" (UU)
17. "TO AVERAGE LAYTIME"
18. "REVERSIBLE LAYTIME"
19. "NOTICE OF READINESS" (NOR)
20. "IN WRITING"
21. "TIME LOST WAITING FOR BERTH TO COUNT AS LOADING OR DISCHARGING TIME" or "AS LAYTIME"
22. "WHETHER IN BERTH OR NOT" (WIBON) or "BERTH OR NO BERTH"
23. "VESSEL BEING IN FREE PRATIQUE" and/or "HAVING BEEN ENTERED AT THE CUSTOM HOUSE"
24. "DEMURRAGE"
25. "DESPATCH MONEY" or "DESPATCH"
26. "DESPATCH ON (ALL) WORKING TIME SAVED" (WTS) or "ON (ALL) LAYTIME SAVED"
27. "DESPATCH ON ALL TIME SAVED" (ATS)
28. "STRIKE"

RULES

1. "PORT" shall mean an area, within which vessels load or discharge cargo whether at berths, anchorages, buoys, or the like, and shall also include the usual places where vessels wait for their turn or are ordered or obliged to wait for their turn no matter the distance from that area. If the word "PORT" is not used, but the port is (or is to be) identified by its name, this definition shall still apply.

2. "BERTH" shall mean the specific place within a port where the vessel is to load or discharge. If the word "BERTH" is not used, but the specific place is (or is to be) identified by its name, this definition shall still apply.

3. "REACHABLE ON HER ARRIVAL" or "ALWAYS ACCESSIBLE" shall mean that the charterer undertakes that an available loading or discharging berth be provided to the vessel on her arrival at the port which she can reach safely without delay in the absence of an abnormal occurrence.

4. "LAYTIME" shall mean the period of time agreed between the parties during which the owner will make and keep the vessel available for loading or discharging without payment additional to the freight.

5. "PER HATCH PER DAY" shall mean that the laytime is to be calculated by dividing (A), the quantity of cargo, by (B), the result of multiplying the agreed daily rate per hatch by the number of the vessel's hatches. Thus:

$$\text{Laytime} = \frac{\text{Quantity of cargo}}{\text{Daily Rate X Number of Hatches}} = \text{Days}$$

Each pair of parallel twin hatches shall count as one hatch. Nevertheless, a hatch that is capable of being worked by two gangs simultaneously shall be counted as two hatches.

6. "PER WORKING HATCH PER DAY" (WHD) or "PER WORKABLE HATCH PER DAY" (WHD) shall mean that the laytime is to be calculated by dividing (A), the

VOYLAYRULES 93 (continued)

quantity of cargo in the hold with the largest quantity, by (B), the result of multiplying the agreed daily rate per working or workable hatch by the number of hatches serving that hold. Thus:

$$\text{Laytime} = \frac{\text{Largest Quantity in one Hold}}{\text{Daily Rate per Hatch} \times \text{Number of Hatches serving that Hold.}} = \text{Days}$$

Each pair of parallel twin hatches shall count as one hatch. Nevertheless, a hatch that is capable of being worked by two gangs simultaneously shall be counted as two hatches.

7. "DAY" shall mean a period of twenty-four consecutive hours running from 0000 hours to 2400 hours. Any part of a day shall be counted pro rata.

8. "CLEAR DAYS" shall mean consecutive days commencing at 0000 hours on the day following that on which a notice is given and ending at 2400 hours on the last of the number of days stipulated.

9. "HOLIDAY" shall mean a day other than the normal weekly day(s) of rest, or part thereof, when by local law or practice the relevant work during what would otherwise be ordinary working hours is not normally carried out.

10. "WORKING DAYS" (WD) shall mean days not expressly excluded from laytime.

11. "RUNNING DAYS" or "CONSECUTIVE DAYS" shall mean days which follow one immediately after the other.

12. "WEATHER WORKING DAY" (WWD) or "WEATHER WORKING DAY OF 24 HOURS" or "WEATHER WORKING DAY OF 24 CONSECUTIVE HOURS" shall mean a working day of 24 consecutive hours except for any time when weather prevents the loading or discharging of the vessel or would have prevented it, had work been in progress.

13. "WEATHER PERMITTING" (WP) shall mean that any time when weather prevents the loading or discharging of the vessel shall not count as laytime.

14. "EXCEPTED" or "EXCLUDED" shall mean that the days specified do not count as laytime even if loading or discharging is carried out on them.

15. "UNLESS SOONER COMMENCED" shall mean that if laytime has not commenced but loading or discharging is carried out, time used shall count against laytime.

16. "UNLESS USED" (UU) shall mean that if laytime has commenced but loading or discharging is carried out during periods excepted from it, such time shall count.

17. "TO AVERAGE LAYTIME" shall mean that separate calculations are to be made for loading and discharging and that any time saved in one operation is to be set off against any excess time used in the other.

18. "REVERSIBLE LAYTIME" shall mean an option given to the charterer to add together the time allowed for loading and discharging. Where the option is exercised the effect is the same as a total time being specified to cover both operations.

19. "NOTICE OF READINESS" (NOR) shall mean the notice to charterer, shipper, receiver or other person as required by the charterparty that the vessel has arrived at the port or berth, as the case may be, and is ready to load or discharge.

20. "IN WRITING" shall mean any visibly expressed form of reproducing words; the medium of transmission shall include electronic communications such as radio communications and telecommunications.

21. "TIME LOST WAITING FOR BERTH TO COUNT AS LOADING OR DISCHARGING TIME" or "AS LAYTIME" shall mean that if no loading or discharging berth is available and the vessel is unable to tender notice of readiness at the waiting-place then any time lost to the vessel shall count as if laytime were running, or as time on demurrage if laytime has expired. Such time shall cease to count once the berth becomes available. When the vessel reaches a place where she is able to tender notice of readiness laytime or time on demurrage shall resume after such tender and, in respect of laytime, on expiry of any notice time provided in the charterparty.

22. "WHETHER IN BERTH OR NOT" (WIBON) or "BERTH OR NO BERTH" shall mean that if no loading or discharging berth is available on her arrival the vessel, on reaching any usual waiting-place at or off the port, shall be entitled to tender notice of readiness from it and laytime shall commence in accordance with the charterparty. Laytime or time on demurrage shall cease to count once the berth becomes available and shall resume when the vessel is ready to load or discharge at the berth.

23. "VESSEL BEING IN FREE PRATIQUE" and/or "HAVING BEEN ENTERED AT THE CUSTOM HOUSE" shall mean that the completion of these formalities shall not be a condition precedent to tendering notice of readiness, but any time lost by reason of delay in the vessel's completion of either of these formalities shall not count as laytime or time on demurrage.

24. "DEMURRAGE" shall mean an agreed amount payable to the owner in respect of delay to the vessel beyond the laytime, for which the owner is not responsible. Demurrage shall not be subject to laytime exceptions.

25. "DESPATCH MONEY" or "DESPATCH" shall mean an agreed amount payable by the owner if the vessel completes loading or discharging before the laytime has expired.

26. "DESPATCH ON (ALL) WORKING TIME SAVED" (WTS) or "ON (ALL) LAYTIME SAVED" shall mean that despatch money shall be payable for the time from the completion of loading or discharging to the expiry of the laytime excluding any periods excepted from the laytime.

27. "DESPATCH ON ALL TIME SAVED" (ATS) shall mean that despatch money shall be payable for the time from the completion of loading or discharging to the expiry of the laytime including periods excepted from the laytime.

28. "STRIKE" shall mean a concerted industrial action by workmen causing a complete stoppage of their work which directly interferes with the working of the vessel. Refusal to work overtime, go-slow or working to rule and comparable actions not causing a complete stoppage shall not be considered a strike. A strike shall be understood to exclude its consequences when it has ended, such as congestion in the port or effects upon the means of transportation bringing or taking the cargo to or from the port.

Appendix 27

THE VOYAGE ESTIMATE FORM

Vessel: CURLEW	Speed:L		Miles:L		Daily Bunker Consumption			
	Speed:B		Miles:B		At Sea		In Port	
Cargo Details					Fuel oil	Diesel	Idle	Working
					L			
					B			
VOYAGE LEGS					Miles	Days	F.O.	D.O.
Canal Transit								
Port Time	Load		Disch					
Totals								

CARGO CALCULATIONS		DRAFT & DEADWEIGHT CALCULATIONS
Zone Load		
DWT		
Less		
	Bunkers	
	Constants	
DWCC		

VOYAGE EXPENSES

BUNKERS

Type	Port	Quantity	Price	Cost	Totals
Fuel Oil					
Diesel Oil					
Bunker Costs					

OTHER COSTS

Loading port disbursements	
Discharging port disbursements	
Bunkering port disbursements	
Canal transit expenses	
Insurance premiums	
Stevedoring expenses	
Other expenses	
TOTAL VOYAGE EXPENSES	

VOYAGE COMPARISONS

Cargo	Rate	Gross Freight	Commission	Nett Freight

Gross Voy. Surplus	Gross daily	Running Costs	Nett daily	10c rate	T/C rate

TYPICAL ESTIMATING PROBLEM

mv 'CURLEW'
Gearless panamax bulkcarrier
- 64,650 mt sdwt on 13.02 metres ssw
- 7 Holds/7 Hatches
- 3,029,000 cubic feet grain capacity in main holds
- 225 metres loa
- 13.21 metres beam
- 14 knots on 40 tonnes f/o + 2 tonnes d/o - daily laden at sea
- 14 knots on 36 tonnes f/o + 2 tonnes d/0 - daily ballast at sea
- 2 tonnes d/o daily idle or working in port
- Daily running costs US$ 4,500
- Canal Transit Consumption: 10 tonnes f/o + 10 tonnes d/o

Fixture:
- 60,000 tonnes coal in bulk - 10% more or less owner's option
- Loading 1 sb Newcastle (NSW) 20/30 April
- Discharging 1 sb Rotterdam
- 20,000 mt shex load
- 20,000 mt shinc discharge
- fiot
- Freight US$ 16.00 per mt
- Coal grade stows maximum 45 cubic feet per tonne
- Freight Insurance Charterer's Account
- Total Commission/Brokerage: 5%

Voyage Data:
Port Disbursement:

Newcastle: US $50,000
Rotterdam: US $60,000
Suez Canal: US $120,000 (including $110,000 tolls)

Distances:
Osaka/Newcastle: 4323 nmiles
Newcastle/Cape Town: 6545 nm
Newcastle/Rotterdam: 12765 nm
Cape Town/Rotterdam: 6220 nm
Newcastle/Suez Canal: 8177 nm
Suez Canal/Rotterdam: 3287 nm

Appendix 29

SUGGESTED ANSWER FOR ONE ALTERNATIVE

Vessel:	Speed:L	14	Miles:L	336	Daily Bunker Consumption			
CURLEW	Speed:B	14	Miles:B	336	At Sea		In Port	
Cargo Details					Fuel oil	Diesel	Idle	Working
60,000 +/- 10% MOLOO bulk coal, SF 45(max)					40 L	2	2	2
Newcastle-Rotterdam, 20,000 SHEX/SHINC, $16 FIOT					36 B	2		
VOYAGE LEGS					Miles	Days	F.O.	D.O.
Osaka/Newcastle (Ballast)					4323	13	468	26
Newcastle/Cape Town (Loaded)					6545	20	800	40
Cape Town/Rotterdam (Loaded)					6220	19	760	38
Adverse weather allowance						2	80	4
Bunkering Ports - Cape Town						0.5	--	1
Canal Transit								
Port Time	Load	5	Disch	4		9	--	18
Totals					17088	63.5	2108	127

CARGO CALCULATIONS				DRAFT & DEADWEIGHT CALCULATIONS	
Zone Load	Summer + 0 Draft				
DWT			64,650		
Less					
	Bunkers	1100			
	Constants	500			
DWCC			63,050		

VOYAGE EXPENSES

BUNKERS

Type	Port	Quantity	Price	Cost	Totals
Fuel Oil	Osaka	1,468	520	763,360	
	Cape Town	640	500	320,000	
Diesel Oil	Osaka	127	820	104,140	
Bunker Costs					1,187,500

OTHER COSTS

Loading port disbursements	50,000	
Discharging port disbursements	60,000	
Bunkering port disbursements	2,500	
Canal transit expenses		
Insurance premiums		
Stevedoring expenses		
Other expenses		112,500
TOTAL VOYAGE EXPENSES		1,300,000

VOYAGE COMPARISONS

Cargo	Rate		Gross Freight	Commission		Nett Freight	
63,050	30.00		1,891,500	5% = 94,575		1,796,925	
63,050	30.10		1,897,805	5% = 94,890		1,802,915	
Gross Voy. Surplus		Gross daily	Running Costs	Nett daily		10c rate	T/C rate
496,925		7,826	4,500	3,326			8,238
502,915		7,920	4,500	3,420		$106	

BILL OF LADING

CODE NAME: "CONGENBILL". EDITION 1994

Shipper

BILL OF LADING

B/L No.

TO BE USED WITH CHARTER-PARTIES

Reference No.

Consignee

Notify address

Vessel	Port of loading

Port of discharge

Shipper's description of goods — Gross weight

(of which _____ on deck at Shipper's risk; the Carrier not being responsible for loss or damage howsoever arising)

Freight payable as per
CHARTER-PARTY dated ....

FREIGHT ADVANCE.
Received on account of freight:

....

Time used for loading .... days....................................
hours.

SHIPPED at the port of Loading in apparent good order and condition on board the Vessel for carriage to the Port of Discharge or so near thereto as she may safely get the goods specified above.

Weight, measure, quality, quantity, condition, contents and value unknown.

IN WITNESS whereof the Master or Agent of the said Vessel has signed the number of Bills of Lading indicated below all of this tenor and date, any one of which being accomplished the others shall be void.

FOR CONDITIONS OF CARRIAGE SEE OVERLEAF

Freight payable at	Place and date of Issue
Number of original Bs/L	Signature

Appendix 30

BILL OF LADING (continued)

BILL OF LADING
TO BE USED WITH CHARTER-PARTIES
CODE NAME: "CONGENBILL"
EDITION 1994
ADOPTED BY
THE BALTIC AND INTERNATIONAL MARITIME COUNCIL (BIMCO)

Conditions of Carriage

(1) All terms and conditions, liberties and exceptions of the Charter Party, dated as overleaf, including the Law and Arbitration Clause, are herewith incorporated.

(2) **General Paramount Clause.**

    (a) The Hague Rules contained in the International Convention for the Unification of certain rules relating to Bills of Lading, dated Brussels the 25th August 1924 as enacted in the country of shipment, shall apply to this Bill of Lading. When no such enactment is in force in the country of shipment, the corresponding legislation of the country of destination shall apply, but in respect of shipments to which no such enactments are compulsorily applicable, the terms of the said Convention shall apply.

    (b) *Trades where Hague-Visby Rules apply.*
    In trades where the International Brussels Convention 1924 as amended by the Protocol signed at Brussels on February 23rd 1968 - the Hague-Visby Rules – apply compulsorily, the provisions of the respective legislation shall apply to this Bill of Lading.

    (c) The Carrier shall in no case be responsible for loss of or damage to the cargo, howsoever arising prior to loading into and after discharge from the Vessel or while the cargo is in the charge of another Carrier, nor in respect of deck cargo or live animals.

(3) **General Average.**
General Average shall be adjusted, stated and settled according to York-Antwerp Rules 1994, or any subsequent modification thereof, in London unless another place is agreed in the Charter Party.
Cargo's contribution to General Average shall be paid to the Carrier even when such average is the result of a fault, neglect or error of the Master, Pilot or Crew.
The Charterers, Shippers and Consignees expressly renounce the Belgian Commercial Code, Part II, Art. 148.

(4) **New Jason Clause.**
In the event of accident, danger, damage or disaster before or after the commencement of the voyage, resulting from any cause whatsoever, whether due to negligence or not, for which, or for the consequence of which, the Carrier is not responsible, by statute, contract or otherwise, the cargo, shippers, consignees or the owners of the cargo shall contribute with the Carrier in General Average to the payment of any sacrifices, losses or expenses of a General Average nature that may be made or incurred and shall pay salvage and special charges incurred in respect of the cargo. If a salving vessel is owned or operated by the Carrier, salvage shall be paid for as fully as if the said salving vessel or vessels belonged to strangers. Such deposit as the Carrier, or his agents, may deem sufficient to cover the estimated contribution of the goods and any salvage and special charges thereon shall, if required, be made by the cargo, shippers, consignees or owners of the goods to the Carrier before delivery.

(5) **Both-to-Blame Collision Clause.**
If the Vessel comes into collision with another vessel as a result of the negligence of the other vessel and any act, neglect or default of the Master, Mariner, Pilot or the servants of the Carrier in the navigation or in the management of the Vessel, the owners of the cargo carried hereunder will indemnify the Carrier against all loss or liability to the other or non-carrying vessel or her owners in so far as such loss or liability represents loss of, or damage to, or any claim whatsoever of the owners of said cargo, paid or payable by the other or non-carrying vessel or her owners to the owners of said cargo and set-off, recouped or recovered by the other or non-carrying vessel or her owners as part of their claim against the carrying Vessel or the Carrier.
The foregoing provisions shall also apply where the owners, operators or those in charge of any vessel or vessels or objects other than, or in addition to, the colliding vessels or objects are at fault in respect of a collision or contact.

For particulars of cargo, freight,
destination, etc., see overleaf.

Appendix 31

LETTER TO THE PORT AGENT

Date ....   Messrs ....

Port ....

Dear Sirs,

This will serve as my authorisation to sign by and on my behalf the Bill(s) of Lading which the Shipper may present to you for cargo loaded on board m.v. ....under my command. This signature may only be given after ensuring that the following itemsare properly inserted and are correct:-

Name of the carrier; name of the vessel; name of the shipper and of the consignee; loading port; discharging port (or when 'for orders') the position where discharging port orders can be obtained); description of cargo, quantity, number, weight, marks, and superficial recognisable condition; terms of freight payment; place and date signed; number of signed, original bills of lading.

Please note that you do not have authority to sign any bill of lading which does not specifically incorporate the terms, conditions and exceptions of the charterparty dated .... and/or The Hague/Visby Rules (or legislation of similar effect).

On no account should" freight prepaid" bills be issued without the express authority of my owners, to whom you should refer on this or on any other matter concerning the signing and issuing of the bills.

As to the condition of the goods, the statements therein have to correspond with the signed mate's or tally clerk's receipts, and where no such receipt is issued, to my personal remarks, which I will bring to your attention in writing if the goods received cannot be truthfully described as being in "APPARENT GOOD ORDER AND CONDITION". You are not entitled to sign a bill of lading other than in "APPARENT GOOD ORDER AND CONDITION" or with my personal remarks. The cargo weight should be qualified by "WEIGHT UNKNOWN".

Receipt Confirmation:
Date & Place: ....
Signature & Stamp: ....

Yours faithfully,
Master, m.v., "........................."

c.c. Owners

Appendix 32

LETTER OF INDEMNITY

To ....
The owners of m.v. "...................."
Dear Sirs,
m.v. "...................."
Goods ....
No ....
Description ....
Marks ....

The above goods are shipped on the above vessel by Messrs...but the relevant bills of lading have not yet arrived.

We hereby request you to deliver such goods to...without production of the bills of lading.

In consideration of your complying with our request we hereby agree as follows:

1. To indemnify you, your servants and agents and to hold all of you harmless in respect of any liability, loss or damage or whatsoever nature which you may sustain by reason of delivering goods to...in accordance with our request.

2. In the event of any proceedings being commenced against you or any of your servants or agents in connection with the delivery of the goods as aforesaid to provide you or them from time to time with sufficient funds to defend the same.

3. If the ship or any other ship or property belonging to you should be arrested or detained or if the arrest or detention thereof should be threatened to provide such bail or other security as may be required to prevent such arrest or detention or to secure the release of such ship or property and to indemnify you in respect of any loss, damage or expenses caused by such arrest or detention whether or not the same may be justified.

4. As soon as all original bills of lading for the above goods shall have arrived and/or come into our possession, to produce and deliver the same to you whereupon our liability hereunder shall cease.

LETTER OF INDEMNITY (continued)

5. The liability of each and every person under this indemnity shall be joint and several and shall not be conditional upon your proceeding first against any person, whether or not such person is party to or liable under this indemnity.

6. This indemnity shall be construed in accordance with English law and each and every person liable under this indemnity shall at your request submit to the jurisdiction of the high court of justice of England.

Yours faithfully,

Signed ....

Duly authorised and on behalf of
.... Name and address
.... of person or
.... company to whom
.... goods delivered

We join in the above guarantee

....
....
....

For the .... Bank
Manager

Appendix 33

CONLINE BILL OF LADING

Shipper

LINER BILL OF LADING

Reference No.

Consignee

Notify address

Pre-carriage by*	Place of receipt by pre-carrier*
Vessel	Port of loading
Port of discharge	Place of delivery by on-carrier*
Make and Nos.	Number and kind of packages; description of goods	Gross weight Measurement

Particulars furnished by the Merchant

Freight details, charges etc.

SHIPPED on board in apparent good order and condition, weight, measure, marks, numbers, quality, contents and value unknown, for carriage to the Port of Discharge or so near thereunto as the Vessel may safely get and lie always afloat, to be delivered in the like good order and condition at the aforesaid Port unto" Consignees or their Assigns, they paying freight as indicated to the left plus other charges incurred in accordance with the provisions contained in this Bill of Lading. In accepting, this Bill of Lading the Merchant expressly accepts and agrees to all its stipulations on both pages, whether written, printed, stamped or otherwise incorporated, as fully as if they were all signed by the Merchant.

One original Bill of Lading must be surrendered duly endorsed in exchange for the goods or delivery order.

IN W I T N E S S whereof the Master of the said Vessel has signed the number of original Bills of Lading stated below, all of this tenor and date, one of which being accomplished, the others to stand void.

Daily demurrage rate (additional Clause A)

* Applicable only when document used as a Through Bill of Lading

| Freight payable at | Place and date of issue |
| Number of original Bs/L | Signature |

Appendix 33

CONLINE BILL OF LADING (continued)

LINER BILL OF LADING

(Liner terms approved by The Baltic and International Maritime Conference)

Code Name: "CONLINEBILL"
Amended January 1st, 1950, August 1st, 1952 January 1st, 1973 July 1st, 1974 August 1st, 1976 January 1st, 1978.

1. **Definition.**
Wherever the term "Merchant" is used in this Bill of Lading, it shall be deemed to include the Shipper, (the Receiver, the Consignee, the Holder of the Bill of Lading and the Owner of the cargo.

2. **General Paramount Clause.**
The Hague Rules contained in the International Convention for the Unification of certain rules relating to Bills of lading, dated Brussels the 25th August 1924 as enacted in the country of shipment shall apply to this contract. When no such enactment is in force in the country of shipment, the corresponding legislation of the country of destination shall apply, but in respect of shipments to which no such enactments are compulsorily applicable, the terms of the said Convention shall apply.

:

In trades where the international Brussels Convention 1924 as amended by the Protocol signed at Brussels on February 23rd 1968. The Hague-Visby Rules apply compulsorily, the provisions of the respective legislation shall be considered incorporated in this Bill of Lading. The Carrier takes all reservations possible under such applicable legislation relating to (the period before loading and alter discharging and while the goods are in the charge of another Carrier and to deck cargo and live animals.

3. **Jurisdiction.**
Any dispute arising under this Bill of Lading shall be decided in the country where the carrier has his principal place of business, and the law of such country shall apply except as provided elsewhere herein.

4. **Period of Responsibility.**
The Carrier or his Agent shall not be liable for loss of or damage to the goods during the period before loading and after discharge from the vessel, howsoever such loss or damage arises.

5. **The Scope of Voyage.**
As the vessel is engaged in liner service (the intended voyage shall not be limited to the direct route but shall be deemed to include any proceeding or returning to or stopping or slowing down at or off any ports or places for any reasonable purpose connected with the service including maintenance of vessel and crew.

6. **Substitution of Vessel, Transhipment and Forwarding.**
Whether expressly arranged beforehand or otherwise, the Carrier shall be at liberty to carry the goods to their port of destination by the said or other vessel or vessels either belonging to the Carrier or others, or by other means of transport, proceeding either directly or indirectly to such port and to carry the goods or part of them beyond their port of destination, and to tranship, land and store the goods either on shore or afloat and reship and forward the same at Carrier's expense but at Merchant's risk. When the ultimate destination at which the Carrier may have engaged to deliver the goods is other than the vessel's port of discharge, the Carrier acts as Forwarding Agent only.
The responsibility of the Carrier shall be limited to the part of the transport performed by him on vessels under his management and no claim will be acknowledged by the Carrier for damage or loss arising during any other part of the transport evert though the freight for the whole transport has been collected by him.

7. **Lighterage.**
Any lightering in or off ports of loading or ports of discharge to be for the account of the Merchant.

8. **Loading, Discharging and Delivery**
of the cargo shall be arranged by the Carrier's Agent unless otherwise agreed.
Landing, storing and delivery shall be for the Merchant's account.
Loading and discharging may commence without previous notice.
The Merchant or his Assign shall tender the goods when the vessel is ready to load and as fast as the vessel can receive and - but only if required by the Carrier - also outside ordinary working hours notwithstanding any custom of the port. Otherwise the Carrier shall be relieved of any obligation to load such cargo and the vessel may leave the port without further notice and deadweight is to be paid.
The Merchant or his Assign shall take delivery of the goods and continue to receive the goods as fast as the vessel can deliver and - but only if required by the Carrier - also outside ordinary working hours notwithstanding any custom of the port. Otherwise the Carrier shall be at liberty to discharge the goods and any discharge to be deemed a true fulfilment of the contract, or alternatively to act under Clause 16.
The Merchant shall bear all overtime charges in connection with tendering and taking delivery of the goods as above.
If the goods are not applied for within a reasonable time, the Carrier may sell the same privately or by auction.
The Merchant shall accept his reasonable proportion of unidentified loose cargo,

9. **Live Animals and Deck Cargo**
shall be carried subject to the Hague Rules as referred to in Clause 2 hereof with the exception that notwithstanding anything contained in Clause 19 the Carrier shall not be liable for any loss or damage resulting from any act. neglect or default of his servants in the management of such animals and deck cargo.

10. **Options.**
The port of discharge for optional cargo must be declared to the vessel's Agents at the first of the optional ports not later Wan 48 hours before the vessel's arrival there. In the absence of such declaration the Carrier may elect to discharge at the first or any other optional port and the contract of carriage shall then be considered as having been fulfilled. Any option can be exercised for the total quantity under this Bill of Lading only.

11. **Freight and Charges.**
(a) Prepayable freight, whether actually paid or not, shall be considered as fully earned upon loading and non-returnable in any event. The Carrier's claim for any charges under this contract shall be con sidered definitely payable in like manner as soon as the charges have been incurred.
Interest at 5 per cent., shall run from the date when freight and charges are due.
(b) The Merchant shall be liable for expenses of fumigation and of gathering and sorting loose cargo and of weighing onboard and expenses incurred in repairing damage to and replacing of packing due to excepted causes and for all expenses caused by extra handling of the cargo for any of the aforementioned reasons.
(c) Any dues, duties, taxes and charges which under any denomination may be levied on any basis such as amount of freight, weight of cargo or tonnage of the vessel shall be paid by the Merchant.
(d) The Merchant shall be liable for all fines and/or losses which the Carrier, vessel or cargo may incur through non-observance of Custom House and/or import or export regulations.
(e) The Carrier is entitled in case of incorrect declaration of contents, weights, measurements or value of the goods to claim double the amount of freight which would have been due if such declaration had been correctly given. For the purpose of ascertaining the actual facts, the Carrier reserves the right to obtain from the Merchant the original invoice and to have the contents inspected and the weight, measurement or value verified.

12. **Lien.**
The Carrier shall have a lien for any amount due under this contract and costs of recovering same and shall be entitled to sell the goods privately or by auction to cover any claims.

13. **Delay.**
The Carrier shall not be responsible for any loss sustained by the Merchant through delay of the goods unless caused by the Carrier's personal gross negligence.

14. **General Average and Salvage.**
General Average to be adjusted at any port or place at Carrier's option and to be settled according to the York-Antwerp Rules 1974. In the event of accident, danger, damage or disaster before or after commencement of the voyage resulting from any cause whatsoever, whether due to negligence of not, for which or for the consequence of which the Carrier is not responsible by statute, contract or otherwise, the Merchant shall contribute with the. Carrier in General Average to the payment of any sacrifice, losses or expenses of a General Average nature that may be made or incurred, and shall pay salvage and special charges incurred in respect of the goods. If a salving vessel is owned or operated by the Carrier, salvage shall be paid for as fully as if the salving vessel or vessels belonged to strangers.

15. **Both-to-Blame Collision Clause.** (This clause to remain in effect even if unenforceable in the Courts of the United States of America).
If the vessel comes into collision with another vessel as a result of the negligence of the other vessel and any act, negligence or default of the Master, Mariner, Pilot or the servants of the Carrier in the navigation or in the management of the vessel, the Merchant will indemnify the Carrier against all loss or liability to the other or non-carrying vessel of her Owner in so far as such loss or liability represents loss of or damage to or any claim whatsoever of the owner of the said goods paid or payable by the other or non carrying vessel or her Owner to the owner of said cargo and set-off, or recouped or recovered by the other or non-carrying vessel or her Owner as part of his claim against the carrying vessel or Carrier. The foregoing provisions shall also apply where the Owner, operator or those in charge of any vessel or vessels or objects other than, or in addition to, the colliding vessels or objects are at fault in respect of a collision or contact.

16. **Government directions, War, Epidemics, Ice, Strikes, etc.**
(a) The Master and the Carrier shall have liberty to comply with any order or directions or recommendations in connection with the transport under this contract given by any Government or Authority, or anybody acting or purporting to act on behalf of such Government or Authority, or having under the terms of the insurance on the vessel the right to give such orders or directions or recommendations.
(b) Should it appear that the performance of the transport would expose the vessel or any goods onboard to risk of seizure or damage or delay, resulting from war, warlike operations, blockade, riots, civil commotions or piracy, or any person onboard to the risk of loss of life or freedom, or that any such risk has increased, the Master may discharge the cargo at port of loading or any other safe and convenient port.
(c) Should it appear that epidemics, quarantine, ice - labour troubles, labour obstructions, strikes, lockouts, any of which onboard or on shore - difficulties in loading or discharging would prevent the vessel from leaving the port of loading or reaching or entering the port of discharge or there discharging in the usual manner and leaving again, all of which safely and without delay, the Master may discharge the cargo at port of loading or any other safe and convenient port.
(d) The discharge under the provisions of this clause of any cargo for which a Bill of Lading has been issued shall be deemed due fulfilment of the contract. If in connection with the exercise of any liberty under-this clause any extra expenses are incurred, they shall be paid by the Merchant in addition to the freight, together with return freight if any and a reasonable compensation for any extra services rendered to the goods.
(e) If any situation referred to in this clause may be anticipated, or if for any such reason the vessel cannot safely and without delay reach or enter the loading port or must undergo repairs, the Carrier may cancel the contract before the Bill of Ladino is issued.
(f) The Merchant shall be informed if possible

17. **Identity of Carrier.**
The Contract evidenced by this Bill of Lading Is between the Merchant and the Owner of the vessel named herein (or substitute) and it is therefore agreed that said Shipowner only shall be liable for any damage or loss due to any breach or non-performance of any obligation arising out of the contract of carriage, whether or not relating to the vessel's seaworthiness. If, despite the foregoing, it is adjudged that any other is the Carrier and/or bailee of the goods shipped hereunder, all limitations of and exonerations from, liability provided for by law or by this Bill of Lading shall be available to such other.
It is further understood and agreed that as the Line, Company or Agents who has executed this Bill of Lading for and on behalf of the Master is not a principal in the transaction, said Line, Company or Agents shall not be under any liability arising out of the contract of carnage, nor as Carrier nor bailee of the goods.

18. **Exemptions and Immunities of all servants and agents of the Carrier.**
It is hereby expressly agreed that no servant or agent of the Carrier (including every independent contractor from time to time employed by the Carrier) shall in any circumstances whatsoever be under any liability whatsoever to the Merchant for any loss damage or delay arising or resulting directly or indirectly from any act, neglect or default on his part while acting in the course of or in connection with his employment and,, but without prejudice to the generality of the foregoing provisions in this clause every exemption, limitation, condition and liberty herein contained and every right, exemption from liability, defence and immunity of whatsoever nature applicable to the Carrier or to which the Carrier is entitled hereunder shall also be available and shall extend to protect every such servant or agent of the Carrier acting as aforesaid and for the purpose of all the foregoing provisions of this clause the Carrier is or shall be deemed to be acting as agent or trustee on behalf of and for the benefit of all persons who are or might be his servants or agents from time to time (including independent contractors as aforesaid) and all such persons shall to this extent be or be deemed to be parties to the contract evidenced by this Bill of Lading. The Carrier shall be entitled to be paid by the Merchant on demand any sum recovered or recoverable by the Merchant or any other from such servant or agent of the Carriage for any such loss, damage or delay or otherwise.

19. **Optional Stowage. Unitization.**
(a) Goods maybe stowed by the Carrier as received, or, at Carriers option, by means of containers, of similar articles of transport used to consolidate goods.
(b) Containers, trailers and transportable tanks, whether stowed by the Carrier or received by him in a stowed condition from the Merchant, may be carried on or under deck without notice to the Merchant.
(c) The Carrier's liability for cargo stowed as aforesaid shall be governed by the Hague Rules as defined above notwithstanding the fact that the goods are being carried on deck and the goods shall contribute to general average and shall receive compensation in general average.

ADDITIONAL CLAUSES
(To be added if required in the contemplated trade).

A. Demurrage.
The Carrier shall be paid demurrage at the daily rate per ton of the vessel's gross register tonnage as indicated on Page 2 if the vessel is not loaded or discharged with the dispatch set out in Clause 8, any delay in waiting for berth at or off port to count. Provided that if the delay is due to causes beyond the control of the Merchant, 24 hours shall be deducted from the time on demurrage. Each Merchant shall be liable towards the Carrier for a proportionate part of the total demurrage due, based upon the total freight on the goods to be loaded or discharged at the port in question. No Merchant shall be liable in demurrage for any delay arisen only in connection with goods belonging to other Merchants.
The demurrage in respect of each parcel shall not exceed its freight.
(This Clause shall only apply if the Demurrage Box on Page 2 is tilled in).

B. U.S. Trade. Period of Responsibility.
In case the Contract evidenced by this Bill of Lading is subject to the U.S. Carriage of Goods by Sea Act, then the provisions stated in said Act shall govem before loading and after discharge and throughout the entire time the goods are in the Carrier's custody.

Appendix 34

INTER CLUB NEW YORK PRODUCE EXCHANGE AGREEMENT

Inter-Club New York
Produce Exchange Agreement 1996

Although the New York Produce Exchange Form (NYPE) Charterparty has been in widespread use for many years, the cargo responsibility provisions do not readily enable Owners and Charterers to apportion responsibility for cargo claims. More than 25 years ago the International Group Clubs reached an agreement on a relatively simple formula for the apportionment of cargo claims which they would recommend to their Members. The NYPE Inter-Club Agreement seems to have become an industry standard in the sense that NYPE charterparties now routinely regulate the settlement of cargo claims between Owners and Charterers in accordance with the Agreement's formulae.

The Agreement was updated in 1984 to deal with one particular shortcoming relating to the time limit for the making of claims. Otherwise, there have been no significant changes.

Whilst the Agreement has worked very well, it has in certain areas become outdated and subject to certain legal anomalies, particularly with regard to its application to containerized cargo. In view of these deficiencies, a small Sub-Committee representing the International Group of P&I Clubs was given the task of producing a redrafted Agreement to reflect modern practices and to encourage its continued use.

The Inter-Club Agreement 1996 does not deviate from the fundamental nature of its predecessor and retains a mechanical approach to the apportionment of liability, which has been so successful in avoiding protracted and costly litigation.

Whilst the fundamental nature of the Agreement remains unchanged, the Agreement has been arranged in a more logically structured way to make it simpler, easier to read and therefore more user friendly. A number of redundant or unnecessary provisions have been removed.

The following new features should be noted:

■ The definition of cargo claim(s) has been broadened and now includes related customs dues or fines, interest and certain costs.

■ Claims arising under Through Transport or Combined Transport Bills of Lading are included but only when it is established that the cause of the loss or damage occurs between and including loading and discharge of the chartered vessel. Claims arising under other types of contracts of carriage, such as waybills and voyage charterparties are also included.

■ The new time bar provision also caters for the possibility that the Hamburg Rules will apply.

American Steamship Owners Mutual
Protection & Indemnity Association, Inc.
Assuranceforeningen Gard
Assuranceforeningen Skuld
The Britannia Steam Ship Insurance
Association Ltd.
The Japan Ship Owners' Mutual Protection
and Indemnity Association
Liverpool and London Steamship Protection
and Indemnity Association Ltd.
The London Steam-Ship Owners' Mutual
Insurance Association Ltd.
Newcastle Protection and Indemnity
Association
The North of England Protecting and
Indemnity Association Ltd.
The Shipowners' Mutual Protection and
Indemnity Association (Luxembourg)
Skuld Mutual Protection and Indemnity
Association (Bermuda) Ltd.
The Standard Steamship Owners' Protection
and Indemnity Association Ltd.
The Standard Steamship Owners' Protection
& Indemnity Association (Bermuda) Ltd.
The Steamship Mutual Underwriting
Association (Bermuda) Ltd.
Sveriges Angfartygs Assurans Forening
(The Swedish Club)
The United Kingdom Mutual Steam Ship
Assurance Association (Bermuda) Ltd.
The West of England Ship Owners Mutual
Insurance Association (Luxembourg)

EXCHANGE AGREEMENT (continued)

Inter-Club New York
Produce Exchange Agreement 1996

This Agreement is made on the 1st day of September 1996 between the P&I Clubs being members of the InternationalGroup of P&I Associations listed below (hereafter referred to as "the Clubs").

This Agreement replaces the Inter Club Agreement 1984 in respect of all charterparties specified in clause (1) hereof

and shall continue in force until varied or terminated. Any variation to be effective must be approved in writing by all the Clubs but it is open to any Club to withdraw from the Agreement on giving to all the other Clubs not less than three months' written notice therof, such withdrawal to take effect at the expiration of that period. After the expiry of such notice the Agreement shall nevertheless continue as between all the Clubs, other than the Club giving such notice who shall remain bound by and be entitled to the benefit of this Agreement in respect of all Cargo Claims arising out of charterparties commenced prior to the expiration of such notice.

The Clubs will recommend to their Members without qualification that their Members adopt this Agreement for the purpose of apportioning liability for claims in respect of cargo which arise under, out of or in connection with all charterparties on the New York Produce Exchange Form 1946 or 1933 or Asbatime Form 1981 (or any subsequent amendment of such Forms), whether or not this Agreement has been incorporated into such charterparties.

Scope of application

(1) This Agreement applies to any charterparty which is entered into after the date hereof on the New York Produce Exchange Form 1946 or 1933 or Asbatime Form 1981 (or any subsequent amendment of such Forms).

(2) The terms of this Agreement shall apply notwithstanding anything to the contrary in any other provisions of the charterparty; in particular the provisions of clause (6) (time bar) shall apply notwithstanding any provision of the charterparty or rule of law to the contrary.

(3) For the purposes of this Agreement, Cargo Claim(s) means claims for loss, damage, shortage (including slackage, ullage or pilferage), overcarriage of or delay to cargo including customs dues or fines in respect of such loss, damage, shortage, overcarriage or delay and include

(a) any legal costs claimed by the original person making any such claim;

(b) any interest claimed by the original person making any such claim;

(c) all legal, Club correspondents' and experts' costs reasonably incurred in the defence of or in the settlement of the claim made by the original person, but shall not include any costs of whatsoever nature incurred in making a claim under this Agreement or in seeking an indemnity under the charterparty.

(4) Apportionment under this Agreement shall only be applied to Cargo Claims where:

(a) the claim was made under a contract of carriage, whatever its form,

(i) which was authorised under the charter-party; or

(ii) which would have been authorised under the charterparty but for the inclusion in that contract of carriage of Through Transport or Combined Transport provisions, provided that

(iii) in the case of contracts of carriage containing Through Transport or Combined Transport provisions (whether falling within

Appendix 34

EXCHANGE AGREEMENT (continued)

(i) or (ii) above) the loss, damage, shortage, overcarriage or delay occurred after commencement of the loading of the cargo onto the chartered vessel and prior to completion of its discharge from that vessel (the burden of proof being on the Chartered to establish that the loss, damage, shortage, overcarriage or delay did or did not so occur); and

(iv) the contract of carriage (or that part of the transit that comprised carriage on the chartered vessel) incorporated terms no less favourable to the carrier than the Hague or Hague Visby Rules, or, when compulsorily applicable by operation of law to the contract of carriage, the Hamburg Rules or any national law giving effect thereto, and

(b) the cargo responsibility clauses in the charterparty have not been materially amended. A material amendment is one which makes the liability as between Owners and Charterers, for Cargo Claims clear. In particular, it is agreed solely for the purposes of this Agreement.

(i) that the addition of the words "and responsibility" in clause 8 of the New York Produce Exchange Form 1946 or 1933 or clause 8 of the Asbatime Form 1981, or any similar amendment of the charterparty making the Master responsible for cargo handling, is not a material amendment; and

(ii) that if the words "cargo claims" are added to the second sentence of clause 26 of the New York Produce Exchange Form 1946 or 1933 or clause 25 of the Asbatime Form 1981, apportionment under this Agreement shall not be applied under any circumstances even if the charterparty is made subject to the terms of this Agreement; and

(c) the claim has been properly settled or compromised and paid.

(5) This Agreement applies regardless of legal forum or place of arbitration specified in the charterparty and regardless of any incorporation of the Hague, Hague Visby Rules of Hamburg Rules therein.

Time Bar

(6) Recovery under this Agreement by an Owner or Charterer shall be deemed to be waived and absolutely barred unless written notification of the Cargo Claim has been given to the other party to the charterparty within 24 months of the date of delivery of the cargo or the date that cargo should have been delivered, save that, where the Hamburg Rules or any national legislation giving effect thereto are compulsorily applicable by operation of law to the contract of carriage or to that part of the transit that comprised carriage on the chartered vessel, the period shall be 36 months. Such notification shall if possible include details of the contract of carriage, the nature of the claim and the amount claimed.

The apportionment

(7) The amount of any Cargo Claim to be apportioned under this Agreement shall be the amount in fact borne by the party to the charterparty seeking apportionment, regardless of whether that claim may be or has been apportioned by application of this Agreement to another charterparty.

(8) Cargo Claims shall be apportioned as follows:

(a) Claims in fact arising out of unseaworthiness and/or error or fault in navigation or management of the vessel

100% – Owners

save where the Owner provides that the unseaworthiness was caused by the loading, stowage, lashing, discharge or other handling of the cargo, in which case the claim shall be apportioned under sub-clause (b).

(b) Claims in fact arising out of the loading, stowage, lashing, discharge, storage or other handling of cargo:

100% – Charterers

unless the words "and responsibility" are added in clause 8 or there is a similar amendment making the Master ▶

EXCHANGE AGREEMENT (continued)

◄ responsible for cargo handling in which case:

50% Charterers – 50% Owners

save where the Charterer proves that the failure properly to load, stow, lash, discharge or handle the cargo was caused by the unseaworthiness of the vessel in which case:

100% – Owners

(c) Subject to (a) and (b) above, claims for shortage or overcariage:

50% Charterers – 50% Owners

unless there is clear and irrefutable evidence that the claim arose out of pilferage or act of neglect by one or the other (including their servants or sub-contractors) in which case that party shall then bear 100% of the claim.

(d) All other cargo claims whatsoever (including claims for delay to cargo):

50% – Charterers
50% – Owners

unless there is clear and irrefutable evidence that the claim arose out of the act or neglect of the one or the other (including their servants or sub-contractors) in which case that party shall then bear 100% of the claim.

Governing Law
(9) This Agreement shall be subject to English Law and Jurisdiction, unless it is incorporated into the charterparty (or the settlement of claims in respect of cargo under the charterparty is made subject to this Agreement), in which case it shall be subject to the law and jurisdiction provisions governing the charterparty. ■

Appendix 35

MAJOR MOVEMENTS OF IRON ORE

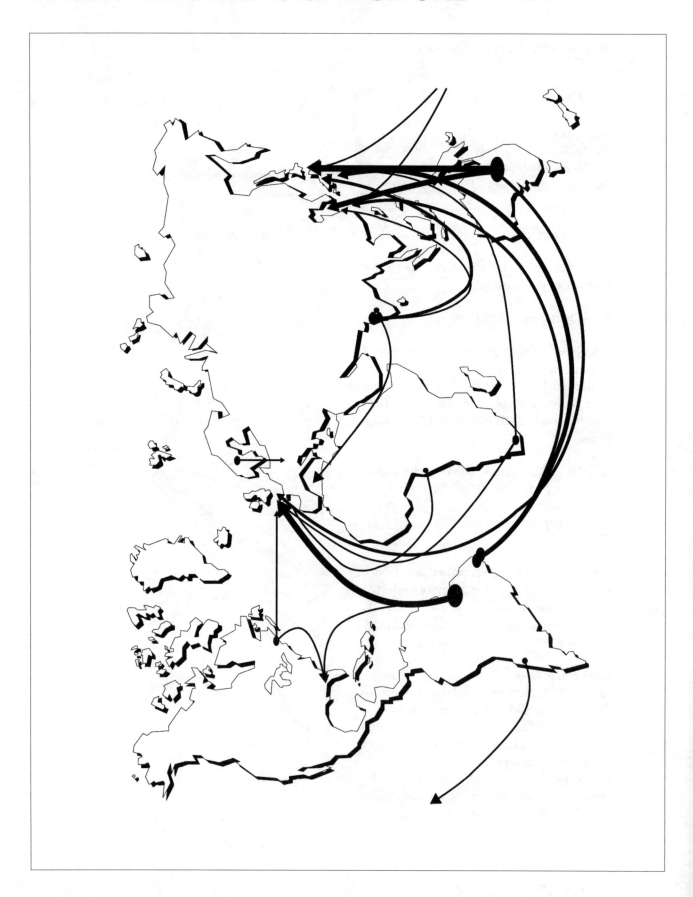

MAJOR MOVEMENTS OF COAL

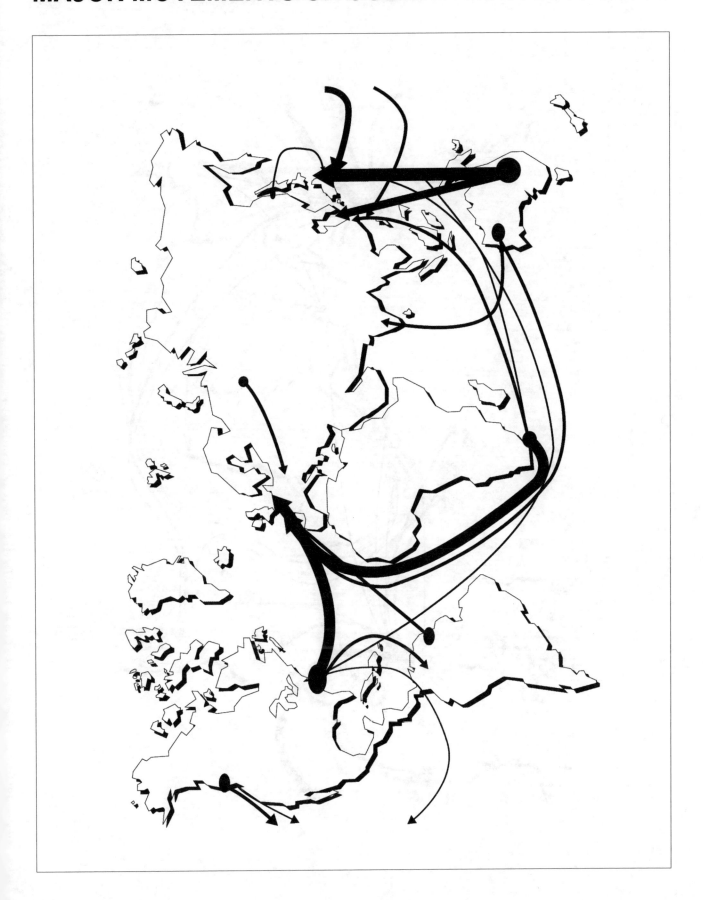

Appendix 37

MAJOR MOVEMENTS OF GRAIN

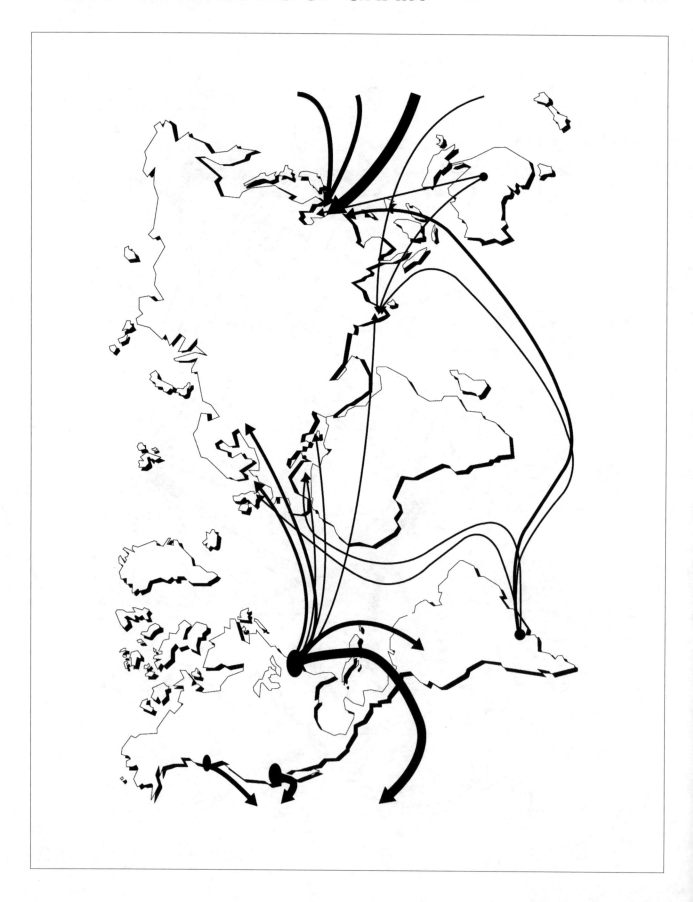

MAJOR MOVEMENTS OF BAUXITE AND ALUMINA

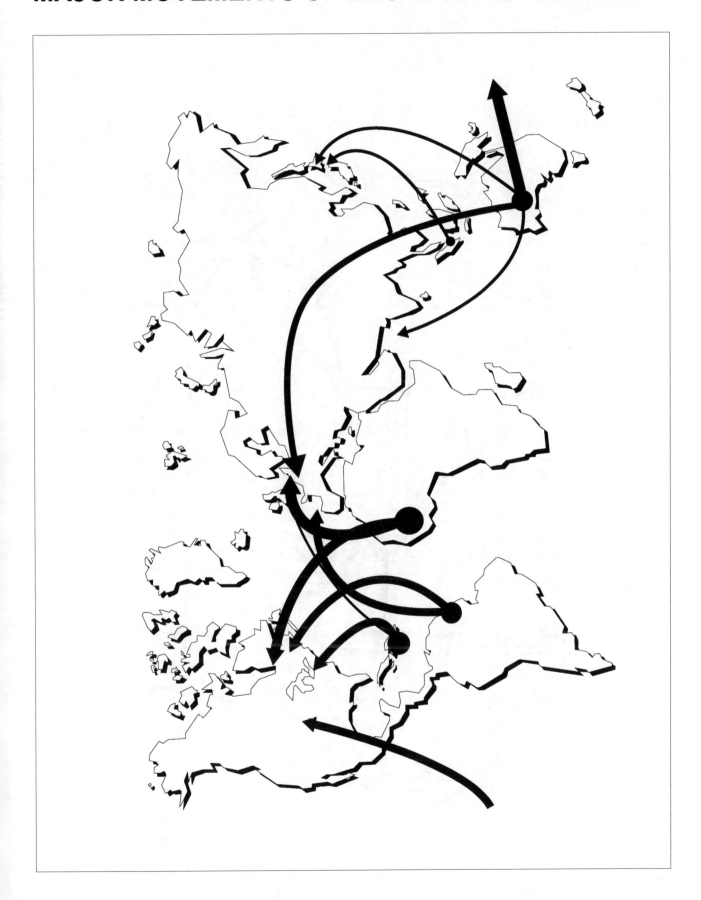

Appendix 39

MAJOR MOVEMENTS OF ROCK PHOSPHATE

PARTICULAR ARBITRATION CLAUSE

BIMCO/LMAA Arbitration Clause

After consultation with the LMAA, BIMCO have adopted and are recommending the following amended arbitration clause, which the LMAA recommends for future use in place of the present LMAA Clause.

"(a) This Contract shall be governed by and construed in accordance with English law and any dispute arising out of or in connection with this Contract shall be referred to arbitration in London in accordance with the Arbitration Act 1996 or any statutory modification or re-enactment thereof save to the extent necessary to give effect to the provisions of this Clause.

The arbitration shall be conducted in accordance with the London Maritime Arbitrators Association (LMAA) Terms current at the time when the arbitration proceedings are commenced.

The reference shall be to three arbitrators. A party wishing to refer a dispute to arbitration shall appoint its arbitrator and send notice of such appointment in writing to the other party requiring the other party to appoint its own arbitrator within 14 calendar days of that notice and stating that it will appoint its arbitrator as sole arbitrator unless the other party appoints its own arbitrator and give notice that it has done so within the 14 days specified. If the other party does not appoint its own arbitrator and give notice that it has done so within the 14 days specified, the party referring a dispute to arbitration may, without the requirement of any further prior notice to the other party, appoint its arbitrator as sole arbitrator and shall advise the other party accordingly. The award of a sole arbitrator shall be binding on both parties as if he had been appointed by agreement.

Nothing herein shall prevent the parties agreeing in writing to vary these provisions to provide for the appointment of a sole arbitrator.

In cases where neither the claim nor any counterclaim exceeds the sum of US$50,000 (or such other sum as the parties may agree) the arbitration shall be conducted in accordance with the LMAA Small Claims Procedure current at the time when the arbitration proceedings are commenced.

Appendix 40

PARTICULAR ARBITRATION CLAUSE (continued)

(b) Notwithstanding (a) above, the parties may agree at any time to refer to mediation any difference and/or dispute arising out of or in connection with this Contract.

In the case of a dispute in respect of which arbitration has been commenced under (a), above, the following shall apply:-

(i)   Either party may at any time and from time to time elect to refer the dispute or part of the dispute to mediation by service on the other party of a written notice (the "Mediation Notice") calling on the other party to agree to mediation.

(ii) The other party shall thereupon within 14 calendar days of receipt of the Mediation Notice confirm that they agree to mediation, in which case the parties shall thereafter agree a mediator within a further 14 calendar days, failing which on the application of either party a mediator will be appointed promptly by the Arbitration Tribunal ("the Tribunal") or such person as the Tribunal may designate for that purpose. The mediation shall be conducted in such place and in accordance with such procedure and on such terms as the parties may agree or, in the event of disagreement, as may be set by the mediator.

(iii) If the other party does not agree to mediate, that fact may be brought to the attention of the Tribunal and may be taken into account by the Tribunal when allocating the costs of the arbitration as between the parties.

(iv) The mediation shall not affect the right of either party to seek such relief or take such steps as it considers necessary to protect its interest.

(v)   Either party may advise the Tribunal that they have agreed to mediation. The arbitration procedure shall continue during the conduct of the mediation but the Tribunal may take the mediation timetable into account when setting the timetable for steps in the arbitration.

(vi) Unless otherwise agreed or specified in the mediation terms, each party shall bear its own costs incurred in the mediation and the parties shall share equally the mediator's costs and expenses.

Appendix 40

PARTICULAR ARBITRATION CLAUSE (continued)

(vii)   The mediation process shall he without prejudice and confidential and no information or documents disclosed during it shall he revealed to the Tribunal except to the extent that they are disclosable under the law and procedure governing the arbitration."

(Note: The parties should be aware that the mediation process may not necessarily interrupt time limits)

Appendix 41

TIME CHARTER INTERPRETATION CODE 2000

FONASBA

The Federation of National Associations of Ship Brokers and Agents

TIME CHARTER INTERPRETATION CODE 2000

Disclaimer

Where any of this code conflicts with any of the terms of the relevant time charter, those of the latter shall prevail to that extent, but no further:

Introduction:

AIMS AND OBJECTS

In commercial practice many aims and objectives for standardisation are often frustrated by the laws in different jurisdictions and where the legal understanding and interpretation may differ the one from the other.

The main jurisdictions applicable to maritime disputes are:

    a)   The Common Law countries – mainly England and the USA.

    b)   The Civil Law countries such as France, Germany, Italy, etc.

The endeavour is not going to be the alter-ego of the Laytime Definitions for Voyage Charters; nor is this an attempt to create new charter party clauses, but merely a Code of how to interpret existing charter party clauses as well as to assist disputing parties where charter parties are silent or non-determining.

There is a vast difference between definition and interpretation, but in some ways and sometimes they may compliment one another. For example, nobody in shipping needs

TIME CHARTER INTERPRETATION CODE 2000 (cont)

a definition of what speed and consumption are or mean, but how should one deal with a speed claim, if any?

The chief objective of the Code is to try to eliminate many often occurring and avoidable maritime charter parties disputes in the field of time charter.

1. Speed and Consumption

The following is to apply to any dry cargo time charter not containing a performance clause, and to any combination carrier when engaged in dry cargo trading:

The speed and consumption warrantees of the time charter are to apply for its duration and whether the vessel is fully, partly loaded or in ballast, and shall be computed from pilot station to pilot station on all sea passages while the vessel is on hire, **excluding:**

a)   Any day on which winds of Beaufort Wind Scale 4 or above are encountered for more than six (6) consecutive hours;

b)   Any time during which speed is deliberately reduced for reasons of safety, or on charterers' orders to steam at economical or reduced speed, or when the vessel is navigating within confined waters, or when assisting vessels in distress;

c)   Any complete sea passage of less than 24 hours duration from pilot station to pilot station;

d)   Periods in which time is lost on charterers' instructions or due to causes expressly excepted under terms of the time charter;

e)   Periods when the vessels' speed is reduced by reason of hull fouling caused by charterers' trading orders.

When specific figures have been agreed to for the vessel in ballasted condition these shall be taken into consideration as shall agreed specifics for reduced or economical speed and consumption, when computations are made.

The mileage made good during qualifying periods shall be divided by the warranted speed and compared to the time actually spent.

Any excess is to be treated as off-hire. If the word 'about' precedes the speed and consumption, same will be understood to mean ½ knot less in the speed and 5% more in the consumption, not be cumulative.

Appendix 41

TIME CHARTER INTERPRETATION CODE 2000 (cont)

As to consumption, the recorded qualifying periods, as above shall be multiplied by the warranted consumption on the qualifying days and compared to the actual consumption. In case of any excess, the charterers are be to compensated by the owners for such excess during the time charter, or those at delivery whichever applicable.

Such amount may be deducted from hire.

The immediate financial consequences of a speed deficiency shall be set-off with any saving caused by under-consumption.

The computations shall be made sea passage by sea passage. The vessel's speed and consumption shall be reviewed at the end of each twelve months, or other lesser period as appropriate.

If in respect of any such review period it is found that the vessel's speed has fallen below the warranted speed, hire shall be reduced by an amount equivalent to the loss in time involved at the rate of hire. And if in respect of any review period it is found that the vessel's consumption has exceeded the warranted consumption, the additional costs shall be borne by the owners.

The foregoing is without prejudice to any other claim(s) that a party may have on the other.

2. Withdrawal for late/non payment of hire

Except where otherwise specifically permitted in the provisions of the charter party, the charterers shall have no right to make arbitrary deductions from hire which shall remain payable punctually and regularly as stipulated therein. Nothing in the charter party shall, however, prejudice the charterers' right to make any equitable set-off against a hire payment due provided that the calculation is reasonable, made bona fide, and that it is in respect of a claim arising directly out of their deprivation of the use of the vessel in whole or in part.

Except as provided herein, the owners shall have a right of permanent withdrawal of their vessel when payment of hire has not been received by their bankers by the due date by reason of oversight, negligence, errors or omissions of charterers or their bankers. In such cases prior to effecting a withdrawal of the vessel, the owners shall put the charterers on preliminary notice of their failure to pay hire on the due date, following which the charterers shall be given two clear banking days to remedy the default. Where the breach has been cured the payment shall be deemed to have been made punctually.

TIME CHARTER INTERPRETATION CODE 2000 (cont)

In respect to a payment of hire made in due time, but insufficient in amount, the owners shall be permitted a reasonable time to verify the correctness of a deduction. If, thereafter, there is found to be disagreement on the amount of the deduction, then the amount in dispute shall be placed in escrow by the charterers and the matter referred to immediate arbitration in accordance with the terms of the charter party's arbitration clause. In that event there shall be no right of withdrawal.

Except as provided heretofore, withdrawal of the vessel may be made by the owners, which shall be without prejudice to any other claim they may otherwise have on the charterers.

3. Off-hire

Any period of time qualifying as off-hire under terms of the charter party shall be allowed to the charterers for any time lost in excess of three consecutive hours for each occurrence.

In addition to matters referred to as off-hire in the charter party, shall be included time lost to the charterers caused by interference by a legal, port of governmental authority, resulting in the charterers being deprived of their unfettered use of the vessel at any given time during the currency of the charter party, or in the vessel being prevented from leaving the jurisdiction contrary to charterers' requirements.

4. Deviation

All periods of off-hire due to deviation shall run from the commencement of the loss of time to charterers, deviation or putting back, and shall continue until the vessel is again in a fully efficient state to resume her service from a position not less favourable to the charterers than that at which the loss of time, deviation or putting back occurred.

5. Legitimacy of the Last Voyage

In the absence of any specific provision in the time charter relating to redelivery and orders for the final voyage, the following shall apply:

Charterers undertake to arrange the vessel's trading so as to permit redelivery within the period and permissible redelivery area as contained in the charter party. As soon as the charterers have arranged the final voyage they shall immediately so inform the owners giving a realistic estimated itinerary up to redelivery time. The owners shall

Appendix 41

TIME CHARTER INTERPRETATION CODE 2000 (cunt)

notify the charterers within two working days thereafter as to whether they agree or disagree with charterers' estimate. Should they disagree and consider the vessel will overlap the maximum period, they shall nonetheless allow the voyage to be undertaken at the time charter rate of the charter party without prejudice to their ultimate right to compensation for additional hire at the market rate should an overlap subsequently have proven to have occurred, and should the market rate be higher than the charter party rate of hire.

MOCK EXAMINATION

Do not turn to the next page until you have followed the suggestions below.

Overleaf is a sample examination paper. In your own interest do not look at it yet but instead, do the same revision of the course as you would do for any examination.

On completing your revision, put away your notes, have pen and paper ready and set aside three hours when you will not be interrupted. In other words create as near as possible examination room conditions.

It is recommended that you hand write this mock examination. You will have to write the actual examination and many students find that it is difficult to write legibly for three hours without practice. If your writing is illegible you will lose marks. Examiners cannot mark what they cannot read.

Carry out the instructions on the question paper and send your answers to your tutor for marking (Note your start and finish times on the front of your answer paper).

THE INSTITUTE OF CHARTERED SHIPBROKERS

MOCK EXAM

Time allowed – Three hours

Answer any FIVE questions – All questions carry equal marks

1. Using a vessel of your choice draft a comprehensive firm offer on a voyage basis for a prospective cargo.
   Draw up a calculation to show the owner of said vessel the time charter equivalent for the voyage.

2. Charterers have asked that you, as a broker, request your owners to sign bills of lading prior to the completion of loading of the cargo. Draft a message to your owner with your advice.

3. Sketch a general arrangement plan of a vessel of your choice Describe the principal trade routes for said vessel.

4. With reference to the calculation of laytime explain the significance of the following terms and discuss any problems that may arise in each case.
   NOR
   Interruptions
   Demurrage and Despatch
   Reversible

5. Analyse the role of the broker in fixing a charter party contract and discuss the concept of warranty of authority including examples of breaches.

6. Select **TWO** of the following cargoes:
   Grain
   Timber
   Iron ore
   Containers
   Set out the main trade routes and any peculiarities and/or hazards in the carriage of these cargoes.

7. You are acting for a principal who has only one vessel and is quite new to the market. You are negotiating this vessel on a long term timecharter agreement. Draft a message explaining the main points of the proposed charter party, including any advice on clauses that must be included and those that he might want to amend.

8. The year 2004 was phenomenal for the dry bulk market, as far as earnings were concerned, and owners' expectations have risen accordingly. Write a report for your principal detailing the main factors affecting the current dry bulk market and your forecast for the next 18 months.

   Your answer may include real or imaginary data.